CW00644211

INDONESIAN HERITAGE

Ancient
History

SPONSORS

This encyclopedia project was initiated and guided by the **Yayasan Dana Bakti**

with the support of the **Shangri-la Hotel**, *Jakarta.*

It was also made possible thanks to the generous and enlightened support of the following companies:

PT. Makindo
Sinar Mas Group
Bakrie Group
Bank Artha Graha
Satelindo
Telekomindo
Telekomunikasi Indonesia
Indobuildco
Indosat
Inti
Pasifik Satelit Nusantara
Plaza Indonesia Realty
Siemens Indonesia
WES Intratama Consortium
Wahana Tigamas Buana/AT&T
Konsorsium Pramindo Ikat
Artha Telekomindo
Amalgam Indocorpora
Elektrindo Nusantara
PT. Ratelindo
Komselindo

Reprinted 1999
Published by Archipelago Press,
an imprint of Editions Didier Millet Pte Ltd,
593, Havelock Road, #02-01/02
Isetan Office Building, Singapore 169641
E-mail: edm@pacific.net.sg
Tel: 65-735 7990 Fax: 65-735 8981

Jakarta Office:
Buku Antar Bangsa
Menara Batavia 11th Floor Kav. 126
Jl. K. H. Mas Mansyur
Jakarta 10220 Indonesia
E-mail: bab@dnet.net.id
Tel: 62-21-574 9147 Fax: 62-21-574 9148

Printed by APP Printing Pte Ltd, Indonesia

ISBN 981-3018-26-7
ISBN 981-3018-58-5 (multi-volume set)

INDONESIAN HERITAGE

Ancient History

VOLUME EDITOR

John Miksic *Southeast Asian Studies Programme, National University of Singapore*

VOLUME EDITORIAL TEAM

Senior Editor
Sian Jay

Editor
Goh Geok Yian

Designer
Joseph G. Reganit

AUTHORS

I Wayan Ardika - *Department of Archaeology, Udayana University*
Bernard Arps - *Department of Language and Culture, Rijksuniversiteit, Leiden*
Bambang Soemadio - *(almarhum) University of Indonesia*
Peter Bellwood - *Department of Prehistory and Anthropology, Australian National University*
J. G. de Casparis - *Rijksuniversiteit, Leiden (retired)*
Henri Chambert-Loir - *Ecole Française d'Extrême–Orient*
Jan Christie - *Centre for South–East Asian Studies, University of Hull*
Jacques Dumarçay - *Ecole Française d'Extrême–Orient*
Edi Sedyawati -*Ministry of Education and Culture, Indonesia*
Endang Sri Hardiati - *National Research Centre for Archaeology, Jakarta*
Dominique Grimaud-Hervé - *Ecole Française d'Extrême–Orient*
Harry Widianto - *Centre for Archaeology, Yogyakarta*
Hasan M. Ambary - *National Research Centre for Archaeology, Jakarta*
Denys Lombard - *Ecole Française d'Extrême–Orient*
Pierre-Yves Manguin - *Ecole Française d'Extrême–Orient*
Manu Jayaatmaja - *Faculty of Letters, Gadjah Mada University*
Mundardjito - *Department of Archaeology, University of Indonesia*
S. O. Robson - *Department of Asian Languages and Studies, Monash University*
Anne-Marie Sémah - *ORSTOM, New Caledonia*
Françoise Sémah - *ORSTOM, New Caledonia*
H.T. Simanjuntak - *National Research Centre for Archaeology, Jakarta*
R. Soekmono - *Department of Archaeology, University of Indonesia*
Ph. Subroto - *Department of Archaeology, Gadjah Mada University*
Timbul Haryono - *Department of Archaeology, Gadjah Mada University*
Wahyono M. - *National Museum, Jakarta*

ARCHIPELAGO PRESS

Contents

LIFE IN EARLY CLASSIC INDONESIA

MIDDLE CLASSIC PERIOD

LATE CLASSIC PERIOD: 14TH TO 16TH CENTURIES

EARLY ISLAMIC PERIOD: 1300–1600

HERITAGE OF INDONESIAN LITERATURE

LEGEND

- Capital
- Towns
- Mountains
- Archaeological sites (Major)
- Archaeological sites (Minor)
- Temples
- Megaliths
- Inscriptions
- Bronze drums

Note: This legend applies to all the maps in this volume.

Introduction

INDONESIA: Digging Up Our Ancient Past

Stone monster head, Early Classic Period, Central Java.

The bones of some of the earliest humans lie deep in the earth of Indonesia. For over a million years, Indonesia has been the scene of human activity. Although ancient fossils have also been found in remote parts of Africa and China, Indonesia possesses the longest continuous record of human occupation in the world, from the formation of early humans through the early agricultural phase, through the development of technology for working bronze and iron, into the age of classical art, into the Islamic era, the colonial phase, and finally independence after World War II. Although no single archaeological site contains evidence from all the phases of Indonesian history, similar sites from all phases can be found lying close to one another. If such a site existed, it would contain many layers.

Layers of Ancient Civilisations

Imagine for a moment that you are an archaeologist excavating such a hypothetical site on one of the islands in western Indonesia, such as Java, Bali, or Sumatra. (Of course the results would be very different in eastern Indonesia, which was further from the main densely–populated centres of early history.) In the uppermost layer of soil, just beneath the grass roots, you would find a mixture of glass, metal, charcoal, bone, and pottery: the detritus of early industrial life from the 19th and 20th centuries. As you dug deeper, you would find that the bones and plant remains would soon disappear. The hot and wet Indonesian climate has harsh effects on organic remains, ensuring that they quickly return to the soil from which they originally grew. Even iron after two or three centuries is usually reduced to an ill–defined lump of rust. One particularly troublesome result of this climate's effect on the study of the past is that no written documents except those specially engraved on such hard materials as stone, bronze, silver, or gold, would be found.

At the top of this early modern layer, some artifacts such as coins and pottery would bear traces of European presence. Probing this layer more deeply, European artifacts would become increasingly rare until they eventually ceased to appear. We would now be at the level corresponding to approximately the year 1600 AD.

Although European artifacts would no longer be found, digging deeper we would continue to find much evidence of active urban life, a diversity of industrial activity, and international trade. Sherds of pottery would be the most common artifacts. They would show that many forms of pottery were made by Indonesian crafts–workers, and that many more types were imported from China. Chinese and locally–minted coins were widely used in daily life. Evidence of many kinds of metalworking by specialised smiths would also be found. You might also discover clay spindle whorls, indications of the importance of textile spinning and weaving in the local economy and society. Like the books and papers of this time, however, the elaborately woven cloths themselves have long ago rotted away.

Although we would have to be extremely lucky to find a fragment of an inscribed stone. The most probable type of inscription we could find at this depth would be an early Islamic tombstone. By 1600 Islam had become the religion of the majority of Indonesians. Traces of early Islam might also include coins with Arabic script issued by one of the Indonesian kingdoms.

As you continued your excavation, the next layer of soil would represent the transitional period to Islam from earlier Buddhist, Hindu, and indigenous religious traditions. Islamic artifacts would continue to be found down to the level representing the year 1300 AD, but in most of this stratum the majority of evidence would show that the site's inhabitants had been devotees of non–Islamic deities which would also be unfamiliar to most modern Buddhists or Hindus. During the late Classic period, Indonesians had turned to the worship of gods associated with a cult of immortality and fertility. Although

Stone lion, Borobudur.

their names were adopted from India, their statues and attributes had evolved locally in such as way that they became unrecognisable to non–Indonesians

Statues would be rare in this layer in any case. In the late Classic period, many Indonesians believed that statues were not needed for enlightenment. Only when we reached the level of the 14th century would statues of stone begin to become more common. We might find inscriptions on stone or bronze; in order to read them we would have to learn a script based on an alphabet imported from India a thousand years previously which then evolved many local variants in different parts of Indonesia. These documents would mainly concern donations made by nobility to religious establishments. From them we could draw some conclusions regarding the structure of the kingdom and the range of occupations, but only in exceptional cases would we be able to read any records of actual events. We would never obtain a description of such aspects of life as the appearance of the houses of the common people or what they wore; documents focus on the religious concerns of the royalty. Except for accounts from Chinese and Arab visitors, only our archaeological research can teach us about the conditions in which most Indonesians lived.

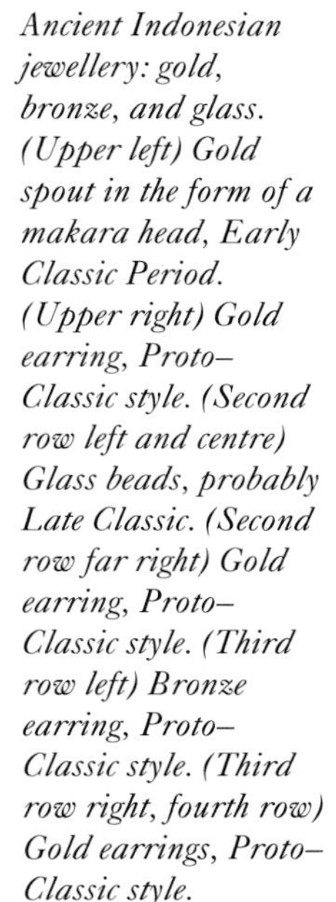

Ancient Indonesian jewellery: gold, bronze, and glass. (Upper left) Gold spout in the form of a makara head, Early Classic Period. (Upper right) Gold earring, Proto–Classic style. (Second row left and centre) Glass beads, probably Late Classic. (Second row far right) Gold earring, Proto–Classic style. (Third row left) Bronze earring, Proto–Classic style. (Third row right, fourth row) Gold earrings, Proto–Classic style.

Chinese coins would continue to appear right down to 1300 AD. There would be a period without Chinese pottery, however. Instead Indonesian pottery would be accompanied by glazed ceramics from Thailand and Vietnam. This layer would correspond to the 15th century, when China went through an isolationist period, and other Southeast Asian ceramic producers actively pursued Indonesian markets.

(Left) Nineteenth century European artist's rendering of Candi Jabung, a brick Buddhist shrine of the 14th century in East Java.

The vast majority of artifacts found would bear the imprint of the local culture characteristic of whichever area of Indonesia we were excavating in. Most pottery was locally made. In Sumatra it would be decorated with carving and stamped designs. In Java it might be painted red and polished until it gleamed. Despite this local character of the artifact assemblage, most sites in Indonesia, even as far east as Maluku, as far west as Sumatra, might provide you with one or two artifacts bearing the cultural imprint of Java. Beginning in the late 13th century, Java rose to become the dominant political force in the Archipelago. Java was probably more densely populated than other parts of Indonesia, and the idea of unifying the vast area from Sumatra and the Malay Peninsula to the edge of the western Pacific already seemed like a logical and viable objective. This goal was in fact achieved by the kingdom of Majapahit during the 14th century. Although the kingdom was unable to create a lasting framework for centralised administration, the image of the archipelago as a cultural and political unit persisted for the next 600 years, through periods of fragmentation and colonial rule, until Majapahit's embryonic concept of a unified nusantara was reincarnated in 1945.

If we found any remains of buildings, they would be made of brick or stone. We could be almost completely certain that they were once temples. Other than temples, only one other type of structure was built of stone or brick in pre–modern Indonesia: bathing places. Some elaborate examples were built in Java, Sumatra and Bali as communal areas where people obtained water for househould use as well as for bathing; they may have had some religious functions as well. Even the palaces of kings must have been made entirely of wood; no archaeologist has ever discovered the site of an ancient Indonesian palace!

Only in a few sites in east Java have archaeologists found remains of dwelling areas. We do not yet know who lived in these houses. The best guess is that the habitation sites which we have found so far, with brick or stone floors and drains for water, wells, and such appurtenances as piggy banks, belonged to an urban semi–elite, analogous to what today might be termed the "middle class". City life in Java and Sumatra seems to have begun in the 13th or early 14th century. Archaeologically, city life can be recognised by such features as housing made of semi–permanent materials, with evidence of some mass–produced household items. Earlier than this, we find no evidence for such a lifestyle in Indonesia.

Let us now dig deeper, beneath the 14th century layer. The next stratum, representing the 13th century, would not appear much

*(Below) Detail from ceremonial wooden backrest (*pepadon*), Lampung, possibly 17th century.*

different from the 14th century above it. It would contain similar artifacts: fragments of temples, evidence of much trade with China, Javanese expansionism, and vigorous local cultures. At the bottom of this layer, representing the early 13th century, we would see a sudden change. Chinese coins would practically vanish, although Chinese porcelain would continue to appear. If we were digging on Java, we would not see any ruins of any temples, but on Sumatra we would hope to discover traces of large Buddhist sanctuaries. On Java, we would find more and better examples of religious statuary, Buddhist and Hindu, than in later times, either carved from stone or made from beautifully–cast bronze. On some of these bronzes or on stone slabs we would also find inscriptions carved in ornate letters. No evidence of middle–class urban housing from this period has yet emerged. It may have been built of perishable materials: wood and thatch.

(Above) Gold kala face, approximately ten centimetres wide, Early Classic style.

The 11th and 12th centuries marked a different kind of civilisation in Indonesia. As we dig through the level deposited between 1200 AD and 1000 AD, we would see signs that a variety of small kingdoms co–existed. This was not a time of poverty; in addition to the statuary, inscriptions, and Sumatran temples, we have manuscripts of many works of literature which were written during this period. Many sites provide evidence that maritime trade was also flourishing during this period. Thus the age of political disunity was not accompanied by economic or cultural stagnation; instead this was a period of great artistic, intellectual, commercial, and religious activity.

At a depth corresponding to around 1000 AD (in Sumatra) or 900 AD (in Java) we will again discover artistic and epigraphic evidence of greater political unity. In Sumatra remains of temples will be rare, but statues mainly of Buddhist deities will show that Sumatra formed part of an artistic style identified with the international Buddhist network of travel and trade covering an enormous triangular area with one corner in north western India, another in Japan, and the third in Bali.

In Java, we would be most likely to find fragments of religious monuments and statues made from local volcanic rock called andesite. These might be either Buddhist or Hindu. Their styles would be related to those of various regions of south Asia, from Sri Lanka to Bengal, but with a quality of carving and design which is at least equal to the finest examples from the homeland of those two religions. Other evidence of contact with the mainland of Asia would be limited: inscriptions in scripts related to those of India but already showing much local development; the use of local languages with much admixture from Sanskrit; and perhaps in the very topmost part of the layer some Chinese ceramics. Otherwise the data would be consistent with the interpretation that a highly artistic culture with strong affinities to the peoples of the Polynesian area of the Pacific had become enamoured of the artistic possibilities offered by the myths and symbols of south Asia, much as the peoples of east Asia were also doing with Buddhism at the same time, or in the same way as Europe had adopted myths and symbols of Christanity a thousand years earlier.

(Right) Three figures, two of whom are rsi *holding palm leaf books. Candi Morangan, Central Java, 9th century.*

(Below) Door guardian approximately three metres high, probably from a royal temple or palace. Singasari, East Java, 13th century.

We would also be confronted with the unfortunate problem that most of our archaeological information is only relevant to the activities of a small elite segment of society. We still need to refine our techniques and perform many more excavations before we can draw conclusions regarding the lives of the bulk of Indonesia's population, the masses who in fact were responsible for most of the achievements reflected in the archaeological record.

In this layer, we have no evidence of urbanisation. This situation, in which evidence of skillful sculpture and monumental art are plentiful, but no habitation remains are found, is not unknown. It is also characteristic of the phase of early Egyptian civilisation when the largest pyramids were built. "Civilisation without cities" is a recognised phenomenon in the ancient world. Economically, coinage was already in use at this period, locally made of gold and silver. This medium of exchange was used down to the level of the local market place, according to inscriptions, but cannot have been very easy to operate. Even a small silver coin was worth a lot in terms of goods or services. Some scholars think these coins were mainly used for ritual purposes, but other data implies that they were also used in daily exchanges between common people.

This layer, corresponding to the Early Classic phase (600 AD to 900 AD), is a rather deep one. It was a time of great artistic achievements and probably much social activity, but we are much less informed about the latter than the former.

If we continued to probe even deeper in the pit, we would reach the depth corresponding to about 600 AD, in most parts of Indonesia we would lose most evidence of contact with the world beyond Southeast Asia. Statues of Buddhist and Hindu deities would vanish, as would written inscriptions. Only a few types of artifacts would provide evidence that Indonesians were already trading with the more distant parts of the world. We might however find a few sherds of pottery or glass and stone beads from south Asia, as evidence that trade with that part of the world began several hundred years before the artistic and literary aspects of that civilisation were incorporated into the Indonesian repertoire.

(Above) Terracotta image of female musician, Trowulan, East Java, 14th–15th century.

Most of our data from the protohistoric and late prehistoric era would consist of ceremonial objects such as large bronze items in a style which we might recognise as being found also as far north as Vietnam; this style is called Dong Son, after a Vietnamese site. For the first time, we might find some burials; the practice of burying the dead, sometimes with rich burial offerings, was typical of much of Indonesia until the Early Classic period. These offerings might consist of beautifully worked and polished stones in the form of adzes, or gold foil decorations made from pure gold nuggets beaten into the shape of a human face.

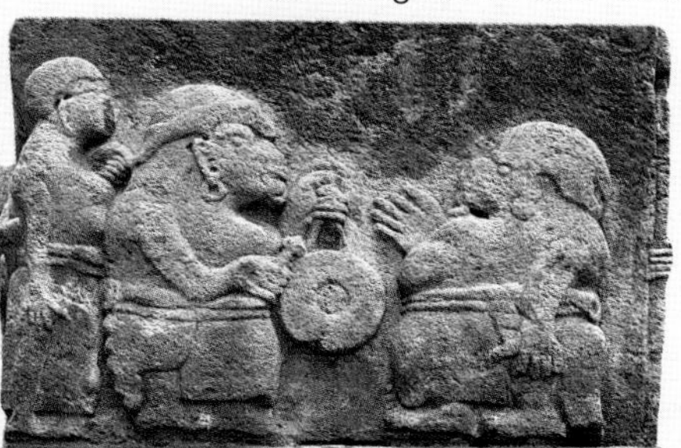

(Left) Relief showing the panakawan characters (led by Semar, oafish servant and supernaturally powerful demi-god), Candi Sukuh, Mount Lawu, 15th century.

Continuing our hypothetical excavation below the protohistoric, we enter the time of prehistory. The top of this layer would be different, depending on which part of Indonesia we were digging in. In the eastern part of the Archipelago, we might discover large burial sites with urns and ceramic offerings; in the western area, we might find graves lined with slabs of stone painted with scenes from local mythology. Yet deeper down, we would see litttle more with the naked eye than some stone tools, or possibly some worked bone harpoon points. If we used more elaborate scientific techniques, however, such as froth flotation or phytolith analysis (the study of small particles of silica from the stems of grasses), we might be able to discover something of the ways in which Indonesians were using plants. These would represent traces of early farmers who bred wild fruits, seeds, roots, and animals to domesticate sources of food now found in many parts of the world. Because the Indonesian climate is hot and wet, we would not find many preserved specimens of organic material; the evidence for this is indirect. Not much research of this type has yet been conducted in Indonesia, but the potential for such studies is great.

For the period between 2,500 and 10,000 years ago, we would find the same sorts of artifacts. At the 10,000–year old boundary, we would see evidence of a different climate. During most of the past one million years, Indonesia was drier and cooler than today. It also had much more dry land; the sea level was lower, and Java, Borneo and Sumatra were all part of the mainland Asia.

Data for the period over 10,000 years ago is sparse. Only in parts of central and east Java has much evidence been found of earlier human activity. Beyond 40,000 years ago, we would find bones of pre–modern humans, and in a very few cases their artifacts. We could pursue this research a long way down; if the soil of our imaginary site contained layers from all of prehistory, here would be the million–year–old fossilised bones of some of mankind's earlier ancestors.

(Below) Bhrkuti, esoteric Buddhist deity from Candi Jago, East Java, late 13th century.

Accomplishments and Challenges

In the pages of the book before you, this story is told in the opposite order, starting from the earliest times and proceeding until the coming of the Europeans. It has not been possible to present all the data available in the few pages of this book. The authors have endeavoured to select the most important and reliable information available, but in many cases they have noted that until further discoveries are made, certain basic questions cannot be answered. Nevertheless, the general outlines of the story of human affairs in this Archipelago are much clearer than they were just a few years ago. We hope that readers with little or no previous knowledge of Indonesia will finish this book with a new appreciation for the accomplishments of the segment of mankind who have made this Archipelago their home.

J. M.

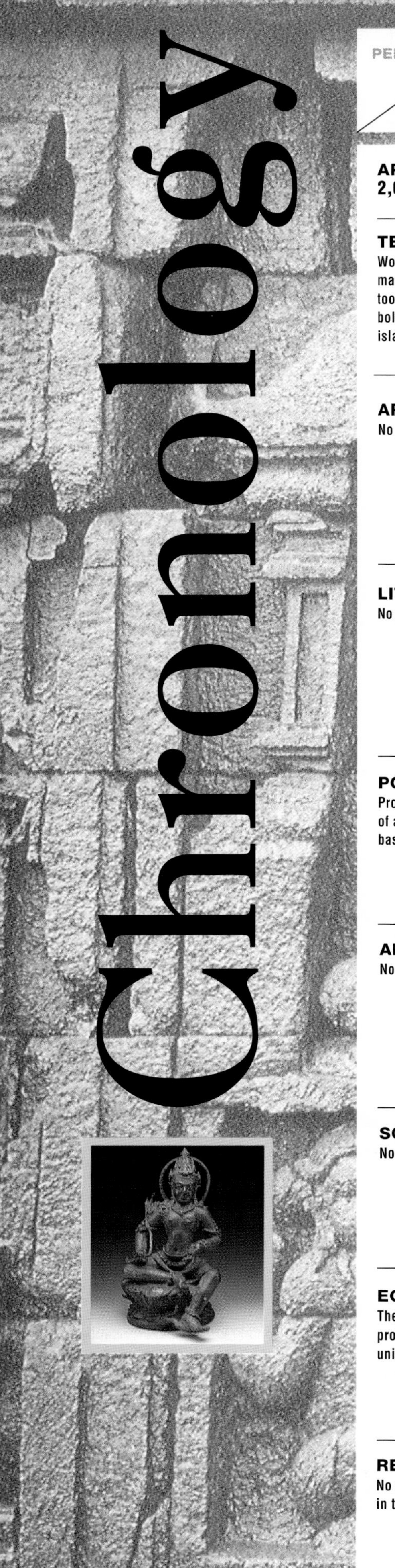

Chronology

PERIOD / SUBJECT	EARLY PREHISTORY	 LATE PREHISTORY	 PROTOHISTORY
APPROXIMATE DATES	2,000,000 – 10,000 BC	10,000 BC – 200 AD	200 AD – 600 AD
TECHNOLOGY	Wood was probably the most important material but no examples survive. Stone tools include large flakes, hammers, and bolas. Large gaps in data exist, many islands remain to be explored.	Sumatraliths; bone tools; Toalian points, Dong Son drums, iron; gold used in native unalloyed form. Agriculture domestication of main crops (rice, taro, yam, banana, coconut, sugarcane) and animals (dog, buffalo, chicken, duck, goat, pig). Irrigation systems, terracing.	Increasing use of iron for agricultural tools. Alloying of gold. Increasingly sophisticated pottery production. Lost wax casting of bronze.
ARCHITECTURE	No preserved examples.	Slab graves: Pasemah, Gunung Kidul, Bondowoso. Terraced megalithic sites: Leeuwilang, Matesih, Pasirangin. Probably the saddle-shaped roofs characteristic of modern Sumatra and Sulawesi evolved during this time.	Terraced megalithic sites continue. Possibly some early permanent architecture in stone or brick is constructed during this period.
LITERATURE	No preserved examples.	No preserved examples.	Oldest preserved Indonesian writing: royal edicts from east Kalimantan and West Java. Introduction of Sanskrit language and Pallava script from India.
POLITICS	Probably no units larger than bands of about 30 or 40 individuals. Leadership based largely on seniority.	Probable evolution of leadership positions based on prowess of individuals.	Earliest known kingdom in Indonesia: Tarumanagara in West Java. Kings have ritual importance but little real power outside the environs of their courts. Standing armies do not exist. Polities are held together by charisma.
ART	No preserved examples.	Paintings on caves and slab graves: Pasemah, Maros (South Sulawesi). Stone sculptures: Pasemah. Large ceremonial bronze axes, Java. Stone bracelets and beads.	Earliest classic sculpture: bronze Buddha images from Sulawesi and East Java. Early Visnu images from West Java.
SOCIAL CONDITIONS	No differentiation of social groups.	By the end of the period, there is evidence for some kind of status differentiation, based on the existence of some burials which are much wealthier than others. Some of these status differences may have been inherited.	Consolidation of permanent division of society into nobility and commoners. The boundaries between these categories however remain permeable.
ECONOMICS	The entire band of 30 to 40 people probably formed the basic subsistence unit.	By the end of the period, long distance trade with India had begun. The main motivation for this trade was probably the urge to acquire rare objects as status symbols.	Trade with China begins. Tributary system of relations with China is established. Wealth from trade becomes an important tool of aspiring rulers.
RELIGION	No data; possible evolution of belief in the power of ancestors.	Increasing elaborate cult of the dead. The large bronze drums probably served some kind of religious function, possibly connected with fertility and rain-making	Hinduism and Buddhism gain footholds along the trade routes. In many areas Preclassic religious tradition continue.

EARLY CLASSIC	MIDDLE CLASSIC	LATE CLASSIC	EARLY ISLAMIC
600 AD – 900 AD	**900 AD – 1250 AD**	**1250 AD – 1500 AD**	**1500 AD – 1600 AD**
Advances in ship-building. Organisational technical skills for the construction of large stone monuments. Stone brick edifices erected. Some pottery made using the potter's wheel. Granulation and filigree in gold-working.	Larger irrigation and flood-control systems are built in Java. Specialised iron-working sites arise in the Outer Islands to supply iron-poor Java.	Mass production methods instituted for metal and pottery working. Paper-making. The kris becomes an important weapon and symbol.	Early use of firearms. Probably imported from the Near East.
Indonesia's greatest ancient monuments, Borobudur and Prambanan are built in Central Java, along with hundreds of smaller shrines. Brick structures are erected in south Sumatra. All other architecture continue to be built of perishable material.	Brick temples of Sumatra: Padang Lawas; Muara Takus and Muara Jambi.	Construction of temples of brick and stone reappears in Java. The styles of construction differ significantly from those of the earlier period. Important structures are built over much of East Java. The terraced temples built on mountain slopes become popular late in the period.	Major forms of preserved monuments are mosques, tomb complexes, and palaces. Structures such as split and linteled gateways and multi-tiered roofs are carried over from pre-Islamic times. Palace gardens from a slightly later period in Cirebon and Yogyakarta provide some impression of this important form.
The Indian epics, Mahabharata and Ramayana, are translated into Old Javanese. Buddhist scriptures in Sanskrit are widely disseminated. The oldest surviving Buddhist texts written in Indonesia, the Sang Hyang Kamahayanikan is composed.	The golden age of Kadiri court literature. The *kakawin* genre is developed to a peak. Mpu Sedah and Mpu Panuluh comprise their version of the Bharatayuddha. Ornamental Kadiri script is created. Other great works such as the Smaradahana are also written.	The Desawarnana is composed by Prapanca, describing the kingdom of Majapahit in 1365. Other important works from this period include the Korawasrama and Nawaruci, which glorify Bima and his search for the elixir of immortality.	The oldest preserved Islamic literature in Indonesia dates from the 16th century. It consists mainly of philosophical speculation on the nature of the relationship between God and man. While mystical in orientation, most of the early literature is not heterodox, in that it preserves the concept of dualism.
Two extended families, the Buddhist Sailendra and the Hindu Sanjaya, contend for power in Java and Sumatra. The rivalry in Java is resolved by intermarriage. The Sailendra continue to rule in Sriwijaya.	Anak Wungsu rules Bali. The central Javanese kingdom vanishes. New centres appear in East Java. The most vital is Kadiri. In Sumatra, Sriwijaya is replaced by Malayu and other smaller kingdoms.	The kingdom of Singasari reunifies much of east Java, and then continues to expand until it has extended suzerainty over the most important kingdom in Sumatra, Malayu. Singasari is succeeded by Majapahit, which becomes the largest kingdom in ancient Indonesian history.	New kingdoms such as Demak, Banten, and Cirebon arise on Java's north coast. Majapahit fades into oblivion by about 1527. The kingdom of Mataram in hinterland central Java soon re-asserts that region's predominance. In Sulawesi, Goa flourishes due to its key position on the spice routes.
Javanese sculptors create the medium of the extended narrative relief at Borobudur. Exquisite statuary of bronze, silver, and gold are cast. Monumental stone sculptures are erected in Central Java and South Sumatra.	Kadiri sculpture deviates from the earlier central Java style: more rigid, funereal in appearance. Indirect evidence suggests that the statues were believed to depict vessels for the souls of departed rulers, who were sometimes thought to be reincarnated gods.	Bronze sculpture practically dies out early in the Majapahit era. Stone sculpture declines as well, apparently the result of the introduction of new religious beliefs. A kind of middle-class art medium, the terracotta figurine, appears in Majapahit's capital.	Islamic prohibitions against portraying living beings are incorporated gradually. Camouflaged beings such as tortoises, Hanuman and Garuda are still visible in early sites such as Sendang Duwur, Demak, and Mantingan. Important motifs include winged gateways, hermit's pavilions and Mount Meru.
Rulers begin to identify themselves as having special relations with deities. They do not yet claim to be gods. The gap between nobility and commoners grows wider. Occupational specialisation becomes increasingly significant.	Bureaucracy becomes more highly developed. Status of intellectuals rises. Military organisation becomes more institutionalised. Government becomes more involved in water control and inland transport.	Many people earn their living by selling their services for wages. The ports along the north coast of Java and the east coast of Sumatra become highly prosperous. Coastal populations become heterogenous mixtures of people from many parts of Indonesia and neighbouring countries.	Urbanisation becomes highly developed. By the end of the 16th century Indonesia is at least as urbanised as Europe. Trade flourishes, and occupational specialisation intensifies. In most areas labour is scarce and expensive. Land is still plentiful, so that dissatisfied rural dwellers could move away.
Locally minted gold and silver coins appear. Periodic markets become widespread. Sriwijaya and Mataram jostle for control over international maritime trade in Southeast Asia.	Chinese immigrants begin to establish settlements in Indonesia. Many new ports begin to develop. Chinese coins become an important currency in some areas. Taxation becomes more complex.	China becomes more isolationist after 1368, but trade links with India and other parts of Southeast Asia expand in compensation. Chinese coinage becomes the main medium of exchange.	Coinage is in widespread use. Economic relationships are a major determinant of social structure. Patron-client relationships based on creditor-debtor ties are a fundamental feature of most Indonesian societies which impresses early European observers.
Devotional Hinduism, with Siva and Visnu, the most popular deities, and Mahayana Buddhism dominate the courts and increasingly permeate the lives of villagers.	Kadiri rulers identify themselves both with Visnu and a personal deity of their own choice. Buddhism of an increasingly esoteric character spreads in Sumatra.	The Sivasiddhanta philosophy of Hinduism makes a strong impact in Java and Bali. In this belief, statues are unnecessary for enlightenment. Islam begins to make converts in north Sumatra and along the north coast of Java.	Islam spreads gradually and largely peacefully. By 1500 Islam becomes dominant in coastal ports. During the 16th century it begins to penetrate the agricultural hinterlands and in the process new variants appear incorporating pre-Islamic beliefs in the potential unity of man and God.

Thomas S. Raffles

J.L.A. Brandes

Th. van Erp

N.J. Krom

R. Ng. Poerbatjaraka

S. Suleiman, R. Soekmono, A.J. Bernet Kempers

Dr. & Mrs. J.P. Vogel, P.V. van Stein Callenfels

R.P. Soejono, Basuki, H.R. van Heekeren

W.F. Stutterheim

F.D.K. Bosch

P. A. Hoesein Djajadiningrat

Noble antiquarians ca 1930

(Left) Princes fr Bali and Centra Java who playe important role in supporting archaeological w and the revival of traditional Javanese art in early 20th centu

Faces of Indonesian Archaeology. *Thomas Stamford Raffles showed great interest in Indonesian archaeology during the brief period of British rule from 1811–16, but an Archaeological Service was not established until the early 20th century. The people depicted here are some of the prominent archaeologists who have contributed much to our knowledge of ancient Indonesia.*

Candi Lara Jonggrang, from Raffles' History of Java. *The National Research Centre for Archaeology traces its ancestry to an association founded in the late 1800s to excavate this site. Directors of the Centre have included R. Soekmono, Satyawati Suleiman, R.P. Soejono, and Hasan Muarif Ambary. Since 1975 monuments has been under the care of the Directorate for Conservation and Restoration, headed first by Uka Tjandrasasmita and succeeded by I Gusti Ngurah Anom.*

LAND, PEOPLE AND HISTORY

The study of Indonesia's ancient history is important not only for its own sake, but also because it has general lessons to teach mankind. The time spanned by the record of human activity in Indonesia is unparallelled; it covers the entire range of human existence, beginning over one million years ago through the intermediate periods from the introduction of agriculture and village life to the age of sophisticated maritime trade, which by the 12th century affected the lives of most Indonesians. Another source of Indonesia's distinctiveness stems from the country's unique geographical setting. It is the world's largest archipelago, whose cultures have evolved along parallel but separate tracks in an adaptive relationship with the resources available in each geographic unit of each island. This chapter outlines the natural setting in which Indonesia's cultures have developed. The image presented here displays many gaps, which are certain to be augmented by future research.

Traditional Indonesian societies believed that it was important to remember the past. Ancient inscriptions record events and date them according to an elaborate calendrical system. Indonesian literary genres portray and manipulate the past in various ways to provide lessons for later generations. Indonesian societies were not typified by a single form of historical consciousness. Some emphasised the repetitive nature of events. Others assumed that history is a linear progression toward a specific conclusion.

In a nation with a written history spanning over 1,500 years, it is inevitable that important changes in historical consciousness have occurred. Written records are rare at best in Indonesia, and some regions lack them completely. No doubt many more documents once existed, but when circumstances changed and old moral frameworks were replaced by new ones, old writings were considered irrelevant and allowed to vanish. This did not mean that manuscripts were actively destroyed; in the Indonesian climate, any manuscript not laboriously recopied every few generations decays and disappears. Warfare and other disasters such as fires have ensured that only a few precious documents have survived as witnesses to Indonesia's past.

Archaeological research in Indonesia was actively pursued during the 1920s. In the 1930s the worldwide economic downturn hindered progress in this field. In the 1940s World War II and the Indonesian revolution had an even more disastrous effect. Now Indonesian archaeologists are doing much to make up for lost time.

Indonesian Geography and Cultural Diversity

Indonesia, situated between latitudes 6 degrees north and 11 degrees south, and longitudes 95 and 140 degrees east, is the largest island complex in the world. In its immense area, stretching from the Asian continent to Australia, and from the Pacific to the Indian Oceans, it contains a wide variety of natural and human communities.

Rural versus Urban. While most Indonesians still live in rural conditions symbolised by the west Sumatran house (upper right), urban lifestyles represented by movie posters (above) are increasingly popular.

Geographical Units

Indonesia's land area, approximately 1,904,000 square kilometres, is divided into four geographical units. The first comprises the Greater Sunda islands, consisting of Sumatra, Java, Bali, Kalimantan and Sulawesi, together with various smaller surrounding islands. All these except Sulawesi lie on the Sunda Shelf, a sub-oceanic extension of the Asian continent. The second unit is made up of the Lesser Sundas consisting of the islands to the southeast, stretching from Lombok to Timor. They include Sumbawa, Sumba, Komodo, Flores, Alor, Savu and Lembata. The Maluku (Moluccas) islands make up the third area. They comprise Halmahera, Ternate and Tidore, as well as Seram and Ambon, and numerous smaller islands. This region is often referred to as the Spice Islands. Irian Jaya, the western part of New Guinea comprises the fourth area, and together with the Aru islands of Maluku and the Australian continent, lies on the Sahul Shelf.

Environmental Conditions

Indonesia's islands all fall within the equatorial climatic zone, with an equable temperature. However, due to its situation between the monsoonal Asian regions and the landmass of Australia, which is two-thirds desert, Indonesia is influenced by both monsoon and trade winds. Geologically, Indonesia is also very complex. Volcanic and non-volcanic formations are intertwined, and topographic features produce marked local differences in soils and rain-fall, which varies between 712 and 4,156 millimetres per year depending on the region. Heavy rainfall

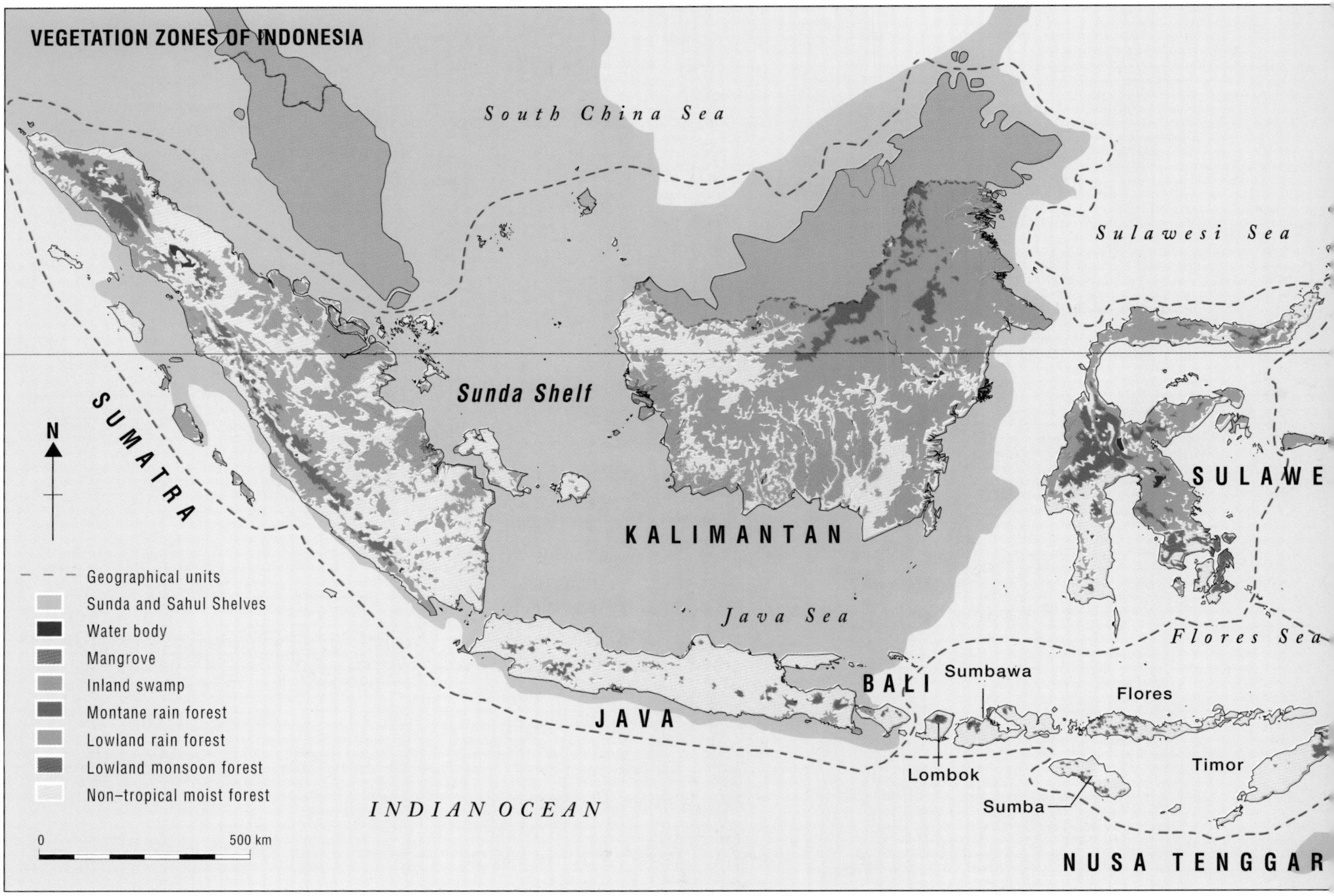

VEGETATION ZONES OF INDONESIA

South China Sea
Sulawesi Sea
Sunda Shelf
SUMATRA
KALIMANTAN
SULAWE
Java Sea
Flores Sea
JAVA
BALI
Sumbawa
Flores
Lombok
Timor
Sumba
INDIAN OCEAN
NUSA TENGGAR
N

- - - Geographical units
Sunda and Sahul Shelves
Water body
Mangrove
Inland swamp
Montane rain forest
Lowland rain forest
Lowland monsoon forest
Non-tropical moist forest

0 500 km

frequently causes rivers to swell and flood the surrounding lowlands. Indonesia belongs to the most seismically-active area in the world, registering about 500 earthquakes per year. For humans living exposed to these vicissitudes, there is compensation for the disastrous eruptions and floods in the form of soil fertility which is frequently replenished. Not surprisingly, the most dangerous volcanic areas and river courses are usually very populous.

Ecological Diversity

Conditions vary greatly from island to island, and often within an island. Overcultivated and overpopulated islands like Java and Bali are juxtaposed to Sumatra and Kalimantan with their enormous jungles that were until recently almost virgin. Smaller islands with arid areas requiring special irrigation measures contrast with Sulawesi with its seasonally heavy rainfall. Differences in flora and fauna are likewise notable. In 1860 Alfred Russel Wallace was struck by the fact that the wildlife of the western part of Indonesia is predominantly Asian, whereas the eastern islands are dominated by typically Australian species of plants and animals. This observation gave rise to the famous 'Wallace Line'. His theory has since been modified by the addition of a transitional zone between the Asian and Australian zones, but in general the differences between the two natural realms are still significant.

Comparison of the Sizes of Indonesia and Europe.

Equator 0°

KU

da Sea

IRIAN JAYA

Arafura Sea

or Sea

Sahul Shelf

«« Village Life
For much of Indonesia's population, social life still revolves around the cycle of sowing, transplanting, and harvesting rice.

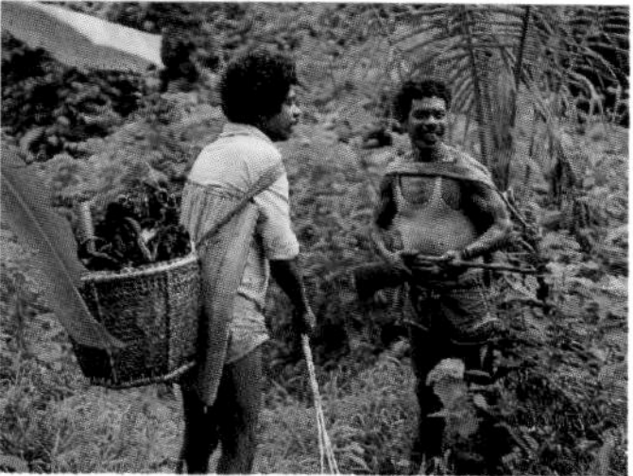

Aru Islanders carry on an ancient tradition of collecting produce for international markets.

Cultural Diversity

Many Indonesians would agree that Indonesia's ecological diversity is responsible for the cultural diversity of its population. However, it is difficult to formulate universal rules relating forms of culture to forms of natural habitat. Historically the seas surrounding the various islands often were the means of communication between ethnic groups, but these same seas sometimes were avoided by others, such as the Balinese. Groups with very different forms of social and technological organisation may exist in close proximity; in Bali the people of Trunyan living within the volcanic crater of Mount Batur persist in maintaining a lifestyle which was replaced in most of Bali many centuries ago. The Tengger and Badui peoples of highland Java are other groups who have chosen to retain patterns of life which the vast majority of the surrounding populations modified long ago. Although such groups tend to be found in isolated mountain areas, their cultural conservatism is due at least as much to conscious decisions as to environmental factors. Different soils, availability of natural materials, and communication routes have obviously been responsible for other patterns of diversity. Thus in alluvial plains agricultural settlements developed in early times, whereas in less heavily populated areas lifestyles based on hunting and gathering wild resources have lingered until the present.

High and Low Places. One basic element found in the symbolic systems of most Indonesian groups has been the idea of complementary opposition between mountains and seas. (Top) Transporting rambutan by sea represents the importance of the seas in Indonesian life, and the sea as a unifying factor. Volcanoes, such as Rinjani in Lombok (below), are associated with fertility and supernatural power.

Unity in Diversity

It was only through the experience of Dutch colonialism that the Indonesians gradually became conscious of the basic similarities that united them, this awareness culminating in the 1945–50 revolution and the creation of the Republic of Indonesia with its national motto, Bhinneka Tunggal Ika. This is usually translated as 'Unity in Diversity'. Indonesia's multi-layered cultural configuration is not entirely a result of the impersonal operation of history and environmental determinism. Rather Indonesia's complex cultural make-up can be said to be due both to natural conditions and to conscious human decisions.

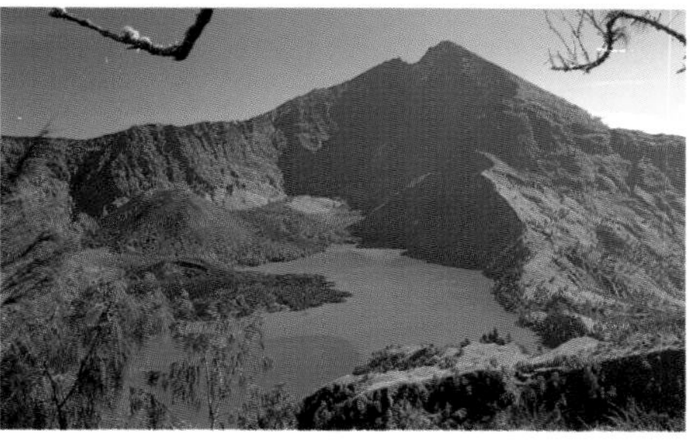

Periods of Indonesian Prehistory

Historians are not merely interested in recording the past. A simple list of dates, names, and events would hold no interest and would be of no functional value. The main goal of scholars who study the past is to search for patterns of behaviour and to draw conclusions regarding the cause and effect relationships which recur at different times and in different places.

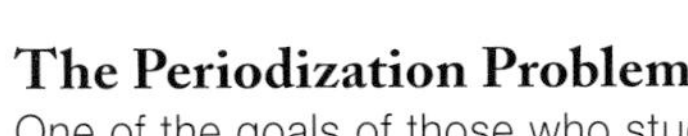

The Periodization Problem

One of the goals of those who study the past is to identify time periods marked by a few strong cultural traits. In Europe the Dark Ages, the Mediaeval Period, the Renaissance, and the Enlightenment, have been identified as historic periods. The prehistoric period is divided into ages named after types of technology: Palaeolithic (Old Stone Age), Mesolithic (Middle), Neolithic (New Stone Age), Bronze Age and Iron Age.

In Indonesia there are traditional genres of writing which deal with the past. These include categories such as *hikayat*, *babad,* and *tambo*, all of which constitute treasuries of traditional perceptions of the past held by different groups in the archipelago. These genres do not divide the past into time periods; instead they stress continuity and the cyclical nature of historical events.

During the 19th century, Western researchers began to investigate Indonesia's history using approaches based on the assumption that the different stages characteristic of the European sequence of development could be universally applied. They began collecting historical sources spared by the Indonesian climate. Initially the sources exploited were literary and epigraphic. Only later was this followed by archaeological research on the many *candi*. Prehistoric research only began in the 1920s.

Painting from interior of slab grave, Sumatra. The burials of members of the elite from the late prehistoric period indicate an increasing development of status differences among Indonesian societies.

Developing a Chronology

Periodization of Indonesian prehistory would enable us to observe and understand historical developments as processes rather than random collections of dated events. Researchers initially copied the system employed in Europe, based on technology. Cultural change was assumed to be due to migration. In the early 1920s the first prehistoric research in Indonesia was limited by lack of qualified personnel. Pioneers in this field, P.V. van Stein Callenfels, A.N.J. Th. a Th. van der Hoop, and H.R. van Heekeren, for example, used the periodization of Palaeolithic, Mesolithic, Neolithic, Bronze, and Iron Ages (sometimes combining bronze and iron into one early Metal Age).

In Indonesia a special phase was introduced, termed Megalithic. In Europe, such remains were also present, but no separate period was defined on their basis. This was partly due to the fact that they were not as widely distributed in Europe as in Indonesia. The distribution of megalithic remains in Indonesia signifies a special cultural pattern, which was at first thought to have constituted a unique chronological phase of development.

To clarify many issues in Indonesian prehistory, it was necessary to wait until after World War II, when progress was made in several areas, including both theory and also techniques such as radiocarbon and other forms of absolute dating. The status of the 'Megalithic' phase has been re–evaluated. It is now recognised that a 'living' megalithic tradition still exists in many parts of Indonesia as a legacy of the prehistoric era. This raises the question of whether a division based solely on technology can properly represent the dynamics of cultural evolution. Many

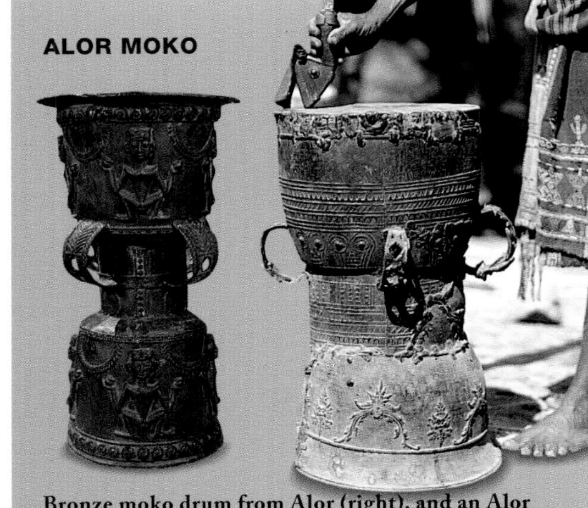

Bronze moko drum from Alor (right), and an Alor style moko (left) that may have been made as a copy in Java. Such drums can be traced directly to the bronze work of late prehistoric Bali, 2,000 years ago. They were in use in eastern Indonesia until Dutch colonial officers confiscated most of them in order to implement policies of cultural change.

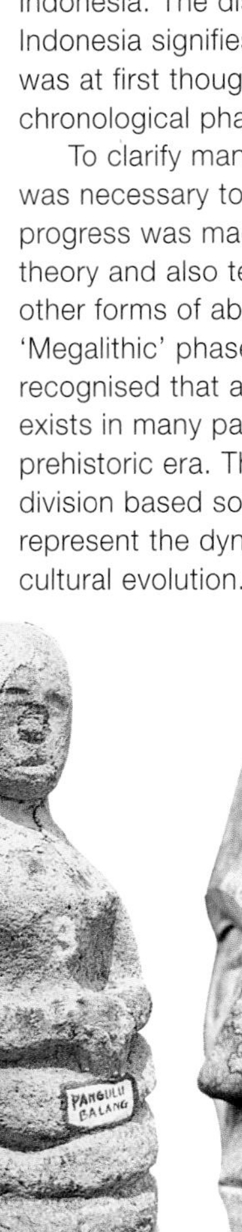

»Batak pangulubalang statue from Sumatra (left) and Toraja tau–tau from Sulawesi. These statues are so similar to the sculpture of the Pacific islands that they are usually termed 'Polynesian–style'. The practice of placing such statues, made of wood or stone, near villages for protection was still found in almost all parts of Indonesia in the 19th century. They are an example of continuity of style and function which makes periodization of Indonesia's past difficult.

discoveries are known of 'Neolithic' elements which persisted into the period of metal-using society. It is also suspected that Mesolithic-style artefacts persisted and continued to form parts of assemblages which would be termed Neolithic on stylistic grounds.

It is clear that the older periodization of Indonesia's prehistory is not acceptable. The European periods were defined on the basis of links between the material used for tools and other cultural subsystems: political and economic structures, for example. Archaeologists have now discovered that the correlation between technology and wider spheres of culture in European prehistory does not appear to be accurate for Indonesia.

The Indonesian Model

A new system of periodization for Indonesian prehistory had to be created. R.P. Soejono, Indonesia's most famous prehistorian, has suggested a three-stage periodization to take account of these possibilities: a Hunting–Gathering period, succeeded by an Agricultural Period, and finally a Craftsmanship Period. This system can be further developed by identifying sub-divisions within each period.

This model was based on traditional models, and needs further testing in the field. It is necessary to obtain comparisons with other models, and more absolute dates. The goal of this model is to place greater stress on the often complex relationship between the environment, humans, and culture rather than one variable, technology. However this model is still close to the old one, and more time is needed before its usefulness can be discerned.

Prehistoric Indonesian societies during the transition to the historic period were in the Agricultural Period or the following Agriculture and Metal-Using Period. Research shows that society had become complexly organised by this time, with an institutionalised stratification and leadership system. The leaders and their assistants were responsible for society's preservation and welfare. In this system leadership was based on trust rather than inherited authority. Those who demonstrated their abilty to lead received respect, and honours after death, as shown by burial offerings found in the Agricultural Period and in the Craftsmanship Period. Ritual sites with groups of megaliths, and slab graves with painted walls indicate more than primitive efforts to display this respect. During this time social units were forming which developed into the kingdoms of the Archaic age.

INDONESIAN PREHISTORIC PERIODIZATION

Hunting–Gathering Stage. The societies that developed at this stage inhabited lowland areas. Their principal artefact forms were chopping tools, flakes, and bone tools. People lived in small bands of four to five families (consisting of about 20–30 people). They migrated seasonally from one resource zone to another. At a certain time of year they possibly met other bands for ceremonial activities. Tools were few and simple, enabling people to move frequently.

Epi–Palaeolithic and Hunting period. During this period groups mainly inhabited caves. They produced blades and stone tools. Some groups became more specialised in hunting certain prey, and gradually developed more varied tool kits to fit particular activities. A wide variety of plants and aquatic foods such as fish, shellfish, and aquatic birds and mammals become more important in the diet. Some groups became semi-sedentary. Bone tools were also used.

Agricultural Stage: This period saw the development of a Neolithic tradition. People started living in permanent villages with populations of 300 to 400 people. Some sections of the population were still inhabiting caves. Technology was changing and stone tools were being produced using new techniques such as grinding and polishing. The main kinds of artefacts included axes, adzes and ground bracelets, and also blades. Pottery storage vessels were made to store food and seeds for replanting. Beads were also created for decoration. People probably practised cults of the ancestors and natural forces, and learned how to domesticate crops and animals. Some groups appointed leaders, the beginning of a political system.

Craftsmanship Stage. Metalworking began. Iron and bronze may have been introduced almost simultaneously. These new materials eventually became symbols of status, as social hierarchies became differentiated. Long distance trade in metals including both ore and finished products developed. Gold was used for jewellery and burial offerings. Sacred monuments using large stones set on terraces began to be constructed.

(After Soejono)

Blades (left) made by striking a flake from a pre-shaped stone core, and stone chopping tool (right).

Fine polished adzes made of chalcedony.

«Chalcedony bracelets made by drilling and polishing.

Pottery vessel from Melolo, east Sumba. Neolithic or very early Metal Age.

«Axe from Roti (left), and gold ear ornaments from Java (below).

Archaeological Techniques

Archaeological techniques range from the very simple to the newest and most expensive, which can be performed in only a few laboratories around the world. In order to evaluate the state of our knowledge of ancient Indonesia, the reliability and comprehensiveness of our inferences must be judged in the light of the techniques of recovery and analysis employed.

CERAMICS
Earthenware sherds from Kota Cina, north Sumatra, 11th century, made by paddle and anvil, and (below) Javanese burnished red ware, 14th century. Pottery is one of the archaeologist's favourite artefacts. It is sensitive to changing time and place. Javanese and Malay traditional pottery for example are quite distinct. It is also almost impervious to decay.

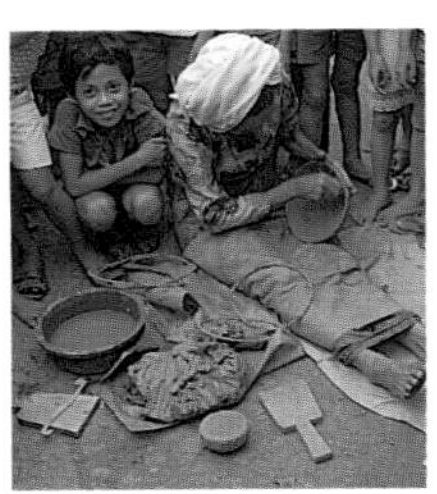

Ethno–archaeology. Studies of modern crafts made with traditional techniques are valuable guides to behaviour of peoples of the past. This Minangkabau potter from Galogandang, west Sumatra, is using the paddle and anvil technique by which much prehistoric Indonesian pottery was also made. Ethno–archaeology has shown that most ancient potters were probably women.

From the Soil

Archaeology's oldest and most readily understandable research principle is founded on the concept of stratigraphy. Soil forms in layers which can be distinguished from one another by simple visual means, for example colour, texture, and material. These layers, or strata, if undisturbed will form a sequence which corresponds to the passage of time. Deeper layers are older. Human activity tends to upset this neat pattern. People have dug holes for burial and for building foundations, and tilled the soil for agriculture for thousands of years. These disturbances make the interpretation of the stratigraphic sequence more difficult. Some sites are, of course, more disturbed than others, and differences can also occur even between different parts of the same site. The drawing of a stratigraphic profile is one of the most important tasks of the archaeologist. Once a site has been excavated, this eliminates the possibility that another archaeologist can ever study it except through the records made by the original excavators. Although artefacts and soil samples may be restudied, the soil profile can only be recorded by the first observer. Careful observers will note both strata and features, which are usually small, localised pockets of soil containing a record of some special activity such as a hearth, or post moulds, for example.

Soil itself is an important source of information for the archaeologist. It contains ecofacts, a term coined to correspond to the more common artefacts. An ecofact is any object or feature consisting of natural material which preserves the record of interaction between humans and their environment. The most common ecofacts are plant remains. Pollen grains can be preserved under certain conditions for thousands of years, and allow us to reconstruct ancient environments, and the beginning of human interference with the natural world by forest clearing and introduction of new species. Pollen research, or palynology, has also been applied to historic sites such as Borobudur to try to determine the conditions which existed around the monument. Soil can also provide valuable clues to the effects of human activity. Patterns of erosion and deposition can tell us much about past land use in an area. Analysis of soil phosphate can indicate the presence of past populations even in the absence of artefacts.

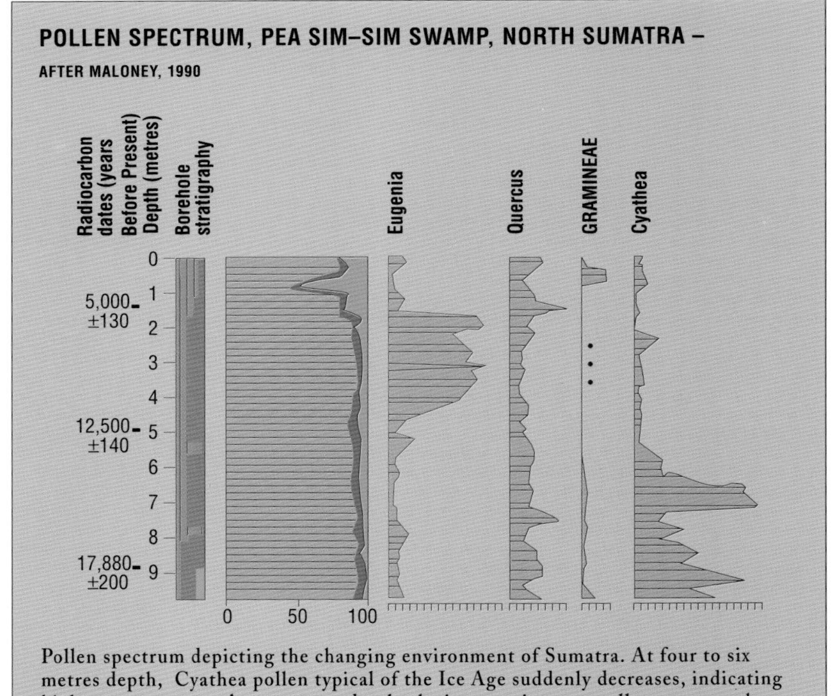

Pollen spectrum depicting the changing environment of Sumatra. At four to six metres depth, Cyathea pollen typical of the Ice Age suddenly decreases, indicating higher temperature. At one metre depth, the increase in grass pollen suggests that humans were clearing large areas of forest for agriculture about 5,000 years ago.

In the Laboratory

The first concern of an archaeologist is to be able to locate artefacts in space. The second is to locate them in time. There are two kinds of time in archaeology: relative and absolute. Relative dating simply means that one object is older than another. Stratigraphy is one means whereby objects can be relatively dated, but this normally only works for objects from the same site. Another standard method is called seriation, in which artefacts are arranged in sequence according to stylistic differences. This approach is particularly useful for dating complex works of art such as statues or temples. It is difficult to date many of the temples of central Java with precision. The seriation method, however, can at least give a relative chronological sequence for the temples according to the development of their mouldings and finials.

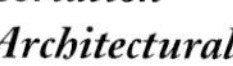

Absolute dating can give the approximate age of an object in years. The first such technique to be invented was radiocarbon analysis, which was developed in the late 1940s. Because of the variable nature of radioactivity of carbon isotopes, on which this method depends, there is always a margin for error. Radiocarbon (carbon 14 or C14) dates are usually written with a plus or minus figure, for example 5000 +/– 75. This indicates that the true date has a 67 per cent chance of being between 4,925 and 5,075 years ago, or a 90 per cent chance of falling within the range of 4,850 to 5,150 years. These are broad margins, but for prehistoric sites they are not very significant. Where more recent sites are concerned, especially those of the last 1,000 years, absolute dating is not very useful because of this imprecision. Radiocarbon dating can only be applied to material such as wood or bone which was once alive. It cannot be used for direct dating of inorganic objects such as pottery and metalwork. A technique called thermoluminescence has been tested to date earthenware pottery, but this is also imprecise, and it cannot be used for porcelain. The carbon 14 method can only be used for sites up to about 50,000 years old. Archaeologists working on older sites can make use of other techniques using the radioactive decay of other elements such a potassium–argon.

Finding Sites

Archaeological reconnaissance or exploration of sites, as opposed to excavation, is becoming increasingly important. Remote sensing enables archaeologists to study large areas very efficiently. Many archaeological problems can only be solved with a knowledge of the distribution of sites. Another practical consideration which has led to an increased emphasis on remote sensing is the fact that excavation is becoming increasingly expensive. The largest city of ancient Indonesia, which is now known as the site of Trowulan, in east Java, covers an area estimated at between 50 and 100 square kilometres. Survey of this huge area is yielding information about the density of population and range of occupations practised in this important site. Excavation of such a huge area would be impractical.

Studying Objects

In some cases it is possible to answer questions of origin, technology, and function, just by looking at artefacts. For most of the objects left behind by past generations, however, we have no information with which to answer these questions. Chemical analysis has long been practised in an attempt to trace artefacts to their sources. Such approaches are now being applied to such materials as metal, pottery and glass. Petrography, neutron activation, flame spectroscopy, and X–ray diffraction are only a few of the techniques used to analyse materials. Ancient patterns of trade and communication are now becoming known as such analyses are performed. It is difficult to determine where metal objects came from; in many cases the metal used came from more than one origin and may have been recycled locally. We can, however, study the techniques used to work metal. Electron microscopy has been particularly useful in detecting miniscule marks which enable us to trace the stages of production of metal artefacts.

85 cm

Seriation — Architectural Finials
These decorations from classical Javanese temples display slight variations which enable archaeologists to work out a sequence of development for ancient Javanese architecture.
(1) *Arjuna, Dieng* – ca. *700*
(2) *Ngawen II – gate,* ca. *770*
(3) *Borobudur* – ca. *800*

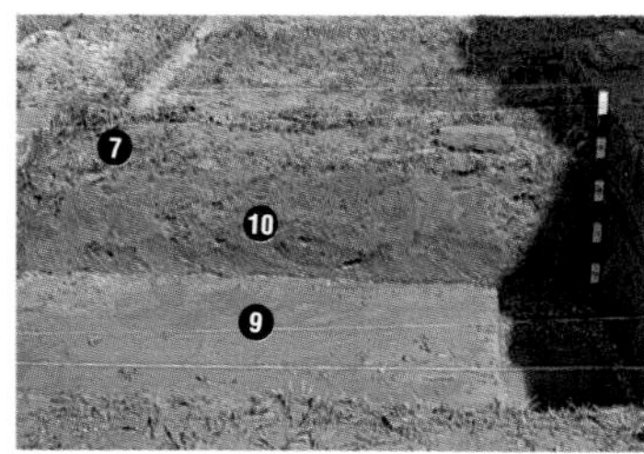

ECOFACTS

(Left) Construction level of Puntadewa showing round marks of ancient scaffolding (3)
(Centre) Excavation site between Sembadra and Puntadewa, Dieng.
(Right) Soil profile showing where an ancient wall may have stood (areas (7) (9) (10)).

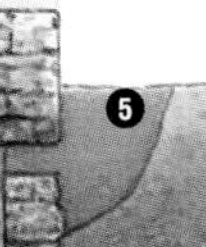

Stratigraphic Diagram, Dieng Plateau
(1) *Candi Puntadewa*
(2) *White gravel beneath Puntadewa*
(3) *Soil fill of the foot of Puntadewa*
(4) *Unexcavated area*
(5) *Disturbed soil around the foot of Puntadewa*
(6) *Disturbed soil where an ancient wall may have stood.*
(7) *Modern drain*
(8) *Soil fill of a wall built around 850 AD*
(9) *White gravel*
(10) *Brown soil that accumulated in the temple courtyard of Candi Sembadra.*
(11) *Soil occupying the place of the now–vanished foot of Sembadra.*
(12) *Brown soil on which the foot of the temple was built*
(13) *Candi Sembadra*

Development of Indonesian Scripts

Apart from the use of Arabic script for religious texts after the 11th century and of Latin script in more recent times, all Indonesian scripts can be traced back to Indian prototypes. The prototype of nearly all Indonesian scripts was the script used especially by the Pallava kings of South India from the 4th to the 9th century AD. Our knowledge of earlier developments is based on inscriptions in stone or metal from western Indonesia and Malaysia.

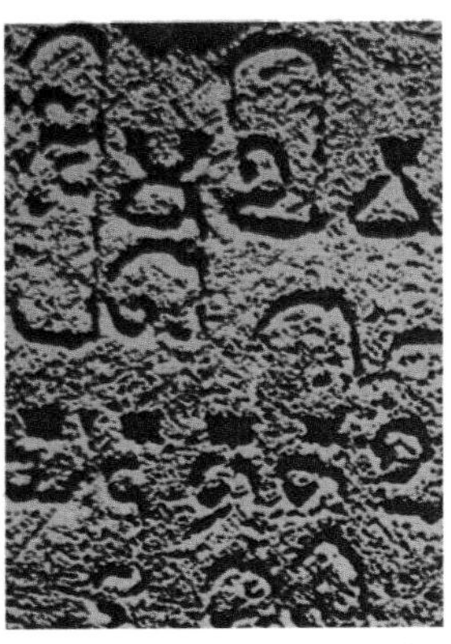

Pallava script Kutai inscription, east Kalimantan. The oldest surviving documents from Indonesia, written in about 400 AD, make use of this kind of script designed especially for carving on stone. Probably other kinds of script were used in everyday writing.

Muslim tombstone found in Aceh province but imported from northwest India.

The Evidence

There are some 3,000 inscriptions known from ancient Indonesia. They are written in various languages: Sanskrit, Old Malay, Old Javanese, Old Balinese, Arabic, and Tamil. Many are badly worn. It is somewhat easier to decipher Sanskrit inscriptions because they are written in poetic form according to Indian rules, helping us to guess what is missing or debatable. The most numerous type in Java deals with the founding of *sima*, areas where the ruler transferred some tax–collecting rights to religious institutions. Some inscriptions exist only in the form of copies, written several centuries later than the originals. The contents of the later versions sometimes suggest that the documents were not simply copied, but were also changed. The inscriptions follow a more or less standard format: complex date, name of officials involved, usually, but not always, starting with the king; then the location of, and reasons for setting up the *sima*.

Earliest Scripts

Between the 4th and 8th centuries AD several Sanskrit inscriptions were written in 'Pallava' script similar to that used in South India, Sri Lanka and mainland Southeast Asia. This script is intermediate between a syllabic and an alphabetic script. There are no dated inscriptions before the end of the 7th century and earlier inscriptions can only be approximately dated by comparison with dated inscriptions elsewhere in southern Asia.

This script was designed to be carved on stone. The oldest script is that used in seven inscrip–tions found in east Kalimantan at Kutai. It is found on monuments and resembles that used in Andhra Pradesh at the end of the 4th century. Certain features of the Kutai script are clearly archaic and suggest a date not later than the beginning of the 5th century. The script of King Purnavarman of west Java, which is similar but lacks most of the typical archaic features of the Kutai inscriptions, may be dated at least half a century later to the latter half of the 5th century. One of these inscriptions which originated from the kingdom of Taruma has an additional inscription in so–called shell–script which some scholars have interpreted as the king's personal signature.

A later stage of 'Pallava' script is used in early Old Malay inscriptions in South Sumatra and on the island of Bangka, dating to the end of the 7th century. The script is less ornamental and more regularised in that all letters are of equal height. The script of the Sanskrit inscription of Canggal in central Java, dated 732 AD, is more ornamental than the Sriwijaya inscriptions, but essentially similar. By this stage the development of scripts in Indonesia had already diverged from the evolution of Indian scripts.

Early Kawi Script

The Dinoyo inscription from east Java, dated 760 AD, is the oldest example of Kawi, or Old Javanese script. Although related to later 'Pallava' it has several unique features. It is slightly cursive and has lost its monumental character, and gives the impression of being based on a writing system designed for palm leaves using a stylus, as in manuscripts. It is a clear and functional script. It remained in vogue with only minor, mainly stylistic, changes till the end of the 15th century. Unlike the Pallava script, which is found all over South and Southeast Asia in almost the same form, early Kawi

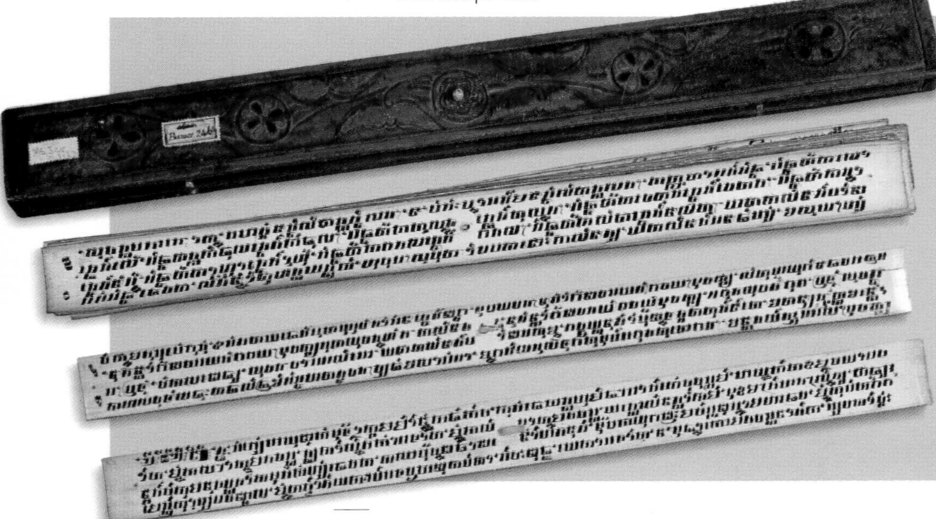

OLD JAVANESE SCRIPT (KAWI)

This palm leaf manuscript from the border between central and west Java was presented to the Bodleian Library in England in 1627. At that time it was already described as being antique. The quadratic script, a distinctive variant of Old Javanese, or Kawi, may date from the 14th century. The spelling suggests that it might have been written in west Java.

The text consists of what is called a *tutur*, a prose discourse on Hindu–Buddhist teachings. In this example it is presented in the form of a lesson by a teacher, or *guru*, to his pupils. Part of this text consists of an explanation of Sanskrit terms and verses. Several such religious treatises were kept as heirlooms in Java up until the 19th century.

Copper–plate inscription of Krtawijaya dated 1369 Saka (1447 AD) from Waringin Pitu. The calligraphy of this example is typical of that used in the Majapahit era. This style of writing is closer to the script which was used more frequently for writing on palm leaves than the ornamental script used on stone.

KADIRI SCRIPT
Ornamental Kadiri quadrate script of the 12th century on bronze mirror handles. On the curved part of the handle (right), a mirror was once attached, but it is now lost. It is decorated with squarish and swollen Kadiri script, named after an East Javanese kingdom of the 11th and 12th centuries, which is quite difficult to decipher. Many mirrors have been found with Kadiri inscriptions. These inscriptions normally consist of a single word which evokes the beauty of a woman or an expression of love.

PHASES OF INDONESIAN SCRIPTS

	Pallava	EK	SK	LK I	LK II	KADIRI
ma						
sa						
ta						NAGARI
ya						
ka						

EK – Early Kawi, **SK** – Standard Kawi, **LK I**– Late Kawi I, **LK II** – Late Kawi II

is typically Javanese and shows the beginning of proto–regional forms. Although early Kawi is well adapted to expressing Indonesian languages, the origin of the symbols used in Old Javanese is unknown, being different from that used in India or mainland South–east Asia. There are a considerable number of examples of 'Archaic phase Kawi', dating from 750–850 AD. This was followed by a 'Standard' phase, approximately from 850–925 AD. These were mostly written during the reigns of two kings: Kayuwangi, 856–882 AD, and Balitung, 899–910 AD. Over one third of all inscriptions from Java are in this script.

Early Nagari

With few exceptions this script was used for writing Sanskrit. There are five examples, all but one from south central Java, dating from the late 8th to early 9th centuries. This script may have had a north Indian origin, perhaps associated with the Buddhist monastery at Nalanda. It is sometimes called Pre–Nagari because the oldest known examples in India only date from the 11th and 12th centuries. It is also possible that the script evolved in Indonesian Bud–dhist monasteries before being used in inscriptions. A complicated inscription from Sanur, Bali consists of three parts: one in early Nagari script and Sanskrit language; another in Nagari script, Old Balinese language; and the third in Early Kawi script, and Old Balinese language. Its probable date is 914 AD.

Later Kawi Script

This form of writing can be roughly dated to 925–1250, but the beginning and end of the period are not clearly marked. In the East Javanese and Balinese inscriptions from the 10th to the 15th centuries there was an increasing tendency to add decorative elements to the basic letter forms. Thus initial verticals were written with an elegant double bend and lend a slender appearance to the letters. In the 12th century (Kadiri period), letters were sometimes shaped into complicated patterns.

In the Majapahit period (14th and 15th centuries), several different styles of writing emerged. In addition to scripts with numerous flourishes there was also a tendency to revert to a simpler monumental style. The oldest extant palm leaf manuscripts also date back to this period. They represent a different style adapted to writing on palm leaves with a stylus. Fourteenth century inscriptions from west Sumatra associated with King Adityavarman, however, present quite a different style, probably due to the region's independent development over several centuries.

Arabic Script

Arabic–Persian script was mainly used for religious texts and inscriptions on tombstones. The earliest example is an 11th century inscription at Leran, east Java, written in 'Kufic' script. The tombstone of King Maliku–'s–Saleh in north Sumatra (1297) is written in ordinary Arabic script, as is that of Malik Ibrahim, east Java, dated 1429.

«« Indonesian scripts show considerable stylistic change during their 1,000 year history.

Sri Manggala sima stone, erected in 874 AD, written in Kawi script. The stone was found near Prambanan.

Macan Ali (Ali's tiger): an example of Javanese use of Arabic letters to form a design. This motif was used as the emblem of Cirebon, one of the first Islamic kingdoms established in Java, in the mid–15th century.

Indonesian Calendrical Systems

The first calendrical system in Indonesia is attested in the 5th century AD inscription of King Purnavarman, west Java, which gives a date consisting of the regnal year and Indian months. However, since the first year of the king's reign is unknown, we cannot 'translate' this date into an absolute date. Absolute dates in a known era are first attested to the 7th century. In many Indonesian inscriptions, numerical signs are replaced by words suggesting a particular number (thus 'sage' equals seven because there were traditionally seven sages).

Candrasengkala, Kasepuhan Palace, Cirebon. The symbol, "the bull on the red gate", indicates the Saka year 1367, or 1445 AD.

Continuous and Cyclic Time

Time is now perceived in Western tradition as a continuum without beginning or end. However, the classical view of India and Indonesia was quite different, for time was conceived as moving in cycles of four aeons (*yuga*) from the perfection of a golden age to less perfect periods, until in the present Kaliyuga (beginning 3,102 BC) deterioration is nearing a state of complete disaster when the entire cosmos will have to be annihilated. After an immeasurably long period of chaos the god Brahma will create a new cosmos which will gradually deteriorate from an ideal state, the process repeating itself *ad infinitum*. If one accepts such a world view, one may see this process of decay reflected in historical periods. The downward trend is not however irreversible, since strong kings who set good examples and maintain the law may slow down or temporarily halt the decline. The action of time is however essentially one of decay, not progress.

Tralaya tombstone Although this is a Muslim memorial, it bears a date in Javanese numerals and Saka era.

Short Cycles

Apart from these cosmic cycles, Indonesians were also acquainted with yearly and monthly cycles. Shorter cycles of five days or even fewer have long been used in Java, Bali, Sumatra, and elsewhere. The five–day week was popular for regulating market days. All the names of the five– and six–day weeks as attested by Old Javanese inscriptions from the 8th century AD were Austronesian, whereas those of the seven–day week were Sanskrit, replaced by Arabic after Islam's expansion. For Sunday, however, the term Minggu (from the Portuguese Domingo) is more commonly used than the Arabic name Ahad. The use of weeks of different length gives rise to a year of 210 days (5x6x7), after which the same combinations of week–days are repeated. The 30 weeks (*wuku*) of 7 days have Austronesian names.

The Saka Era

From the 7th to the end of the 14th century nearly all inscriptions used the Saka ('Scythian') era, traditionally initiated by a ruler in western India in 78 AD. Unlike the Christian (solar) era, based on a year of 365.24 days divided into 12 months of 28 to 31 days, or the Muslim (lunar) era beginning in 622 AD divided into 12 months averaging 29.5 days, the Saka year is luni–solar. Like the Muslim year, it consists of 12 lunar months, but about once every three years another month is added to compensate for the deviation from the solar year. The beginning of the year may fall anywhere between 25th February and 25th March. The Saka months bear Sanskrit names. They begin at the new moon and are divided into two 15–day halves: the bright half from the new moon to full moon, and the dark half ending at the next new moon. Indonesian inscriptions normally mention the Saka year, the month, the number of the day, the half of the month, and the day of the six,

Pawukon or almanac, (Bodleian Library, Oxford), used for divination. The illustration depicts the seventh wuku, or week in the traditional Javanese calender, Warigalit. Asmara, the god of love, faces the week's tree and bird. The matrix on the left lists prescriptions and prohibitions connected with the week, and individual days.

BATAK DIVINATORY CALENDAR

Batak divinatory calendar, or *parhalaan*. The chart of 13 lines and 30 squares mark auspicious or inauspicious days.

five, and seven–day week (in that order).

These details are more than sufficient to determine a date, but by the 10th century inscriptions add further details such as the name of the constellation within which the moon appears (one of 27 *naksatras*, 'moon–houses'), and a gradually increasing quantity of other astronomical data, meant to show that the document was dated at an auspicious moment.

The Muslim Era

Before 1500 the Muslim era was only occasionally used, on tombstones. As the Muslim year is nearly 11 days shorter than the solar year, the difference between Muslim and Christian years is gradually decreasing, now totalling 571 years. Almost all of the Muslim tombstones at Tralaya in the great Javanese capital at Majapahit, though inscribed in Arabic, are dated in the Saka era with Old Javanese numerals.

An interesting variant of the Muslim era is used in Java. In Saka 1555 (1633 AD) Sultan Agung of Mataram decided that the length of the year should be harmonized with the Muslim year, but the numbering of years should continue as before. Thus the difference between the Javanese and Christian year is reduced by about three years each century and has now become 68.

Indonesians have always been time–conscious: all documents were securely dated. Historical texts rarely omit dates for important events. Many temples, mosques, even statues bear dates. So do the chronicles of Java, Sulawesi, Sumatra, and Malaysia. The concept of time plays an important part in Indonesian culture, reflected in the use of several tables for calculating the correct date for important decisions such as marriage and travel.

Bamboo parhalaan used by the Batak, Sumatra. It is inscribed with a divinatory calendar.

Zodiac Systems

The Indonesians also had a concept analogous to that of the Western zodiac. This set of 12 symbols was sometimes used to decorate bronze vessels for containing holy water in east Java; similar vessels are still used by Balinese priests. In a typical example, the designs are divided into two registers, an upper and a lower, horizontally encircling the body of the vessel. The upper register usually depicts deities in the *wayang* style; the lower row depicts signs of constellations, many of which are similar to western symbols. They include the crab (Cancer), water vessel (Aquarius), fish (Pisces), ram (Aries), bull (Taurus), scales (Libra), scorpion (Scorpio), goat (Capricorn), archer (Sagittarius), lion (Leo), and human twins (Gemini).

Evidence From Inscriptions

The following is an example of a typical date found on a Javanese inscription: 'The Saka year of 843, the month of Asuji, the 15th day of the bright half of the month, *haryang* (a day in the Javanese six day week), *umanis* (a day in the Javanese five day week), Wednesday, while the lunar mansion Uttarabhadrapada stood under the deity Ahirabudhna during the conjunction of Dhruva'. The date is thus stated in very precise terms.

Inscriptions from Java contain the names of at least 40 stars. This indicates that the ancient Javanese probably had a very good knowledge of astronomy which they undoubtedly used for navigational purposes as well as time–keeping and divination.

Bronze zodiac beaker (National Museum, Jakarta) used for storing holy water, Majapahit kingdom, Java (14th century). The upper band depicts figures rendered in the wayang style, while the lower band shows various zodiacal symbols.

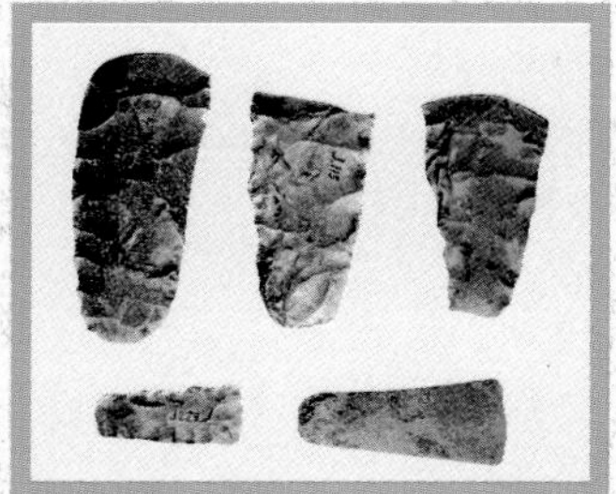

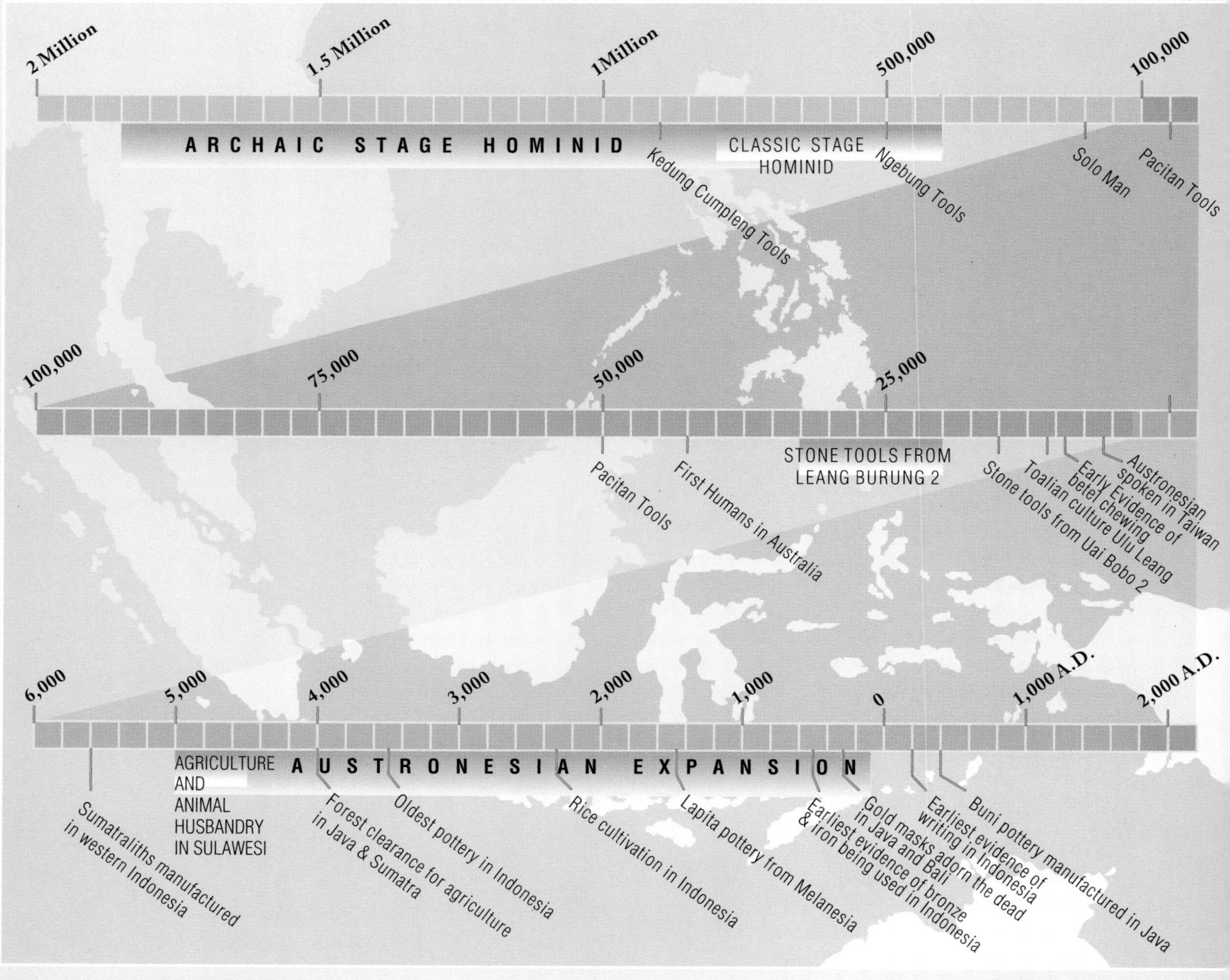

2 Million
1.5 Million
1Million
500,000
100,000

ARCHAIC STAGE HOMINID
CLASSIC STAGE HOMINID

Kedung Cumpleng Tools
Ngebung Tools
Solo Man
Pacitan Tools

100,000
75,000
50,000
25,000

STONE TOOLS FROM LEANG BURUNG 2

Pacitan Tools
First Humans in Australia
Stone tools from Uai Bobo 2
Toalian culture Ulu Leang
Early Evidence of betel chewing
Austronesian spoken in Taiwan

6,000
5,000
4,000
3,000
2,000
1,000
0
1,000 A.D.
2,000 A.D.

AGRICULTURE AND ANIMAL HUSBANDRY IN SULAWESI
AUSTRONESIAN EXPANSION

Sumatraliths manufactured in western Indonesia
Forest clearance for agriculture in Java & Sumatra
Oldest pottery in Indonesia
Rice cultivation in Indonesia
Lapita pottery from Melanesia
Earliest evidence of bronze & iron being used in Indonesia
Gold masks adorn the dead in Java and Bali
Earliest evidence of writing in Indonesia
Buni pottery manufactured in Java

PROBLEMS OF PREHISTORIC DATA.

Indonesian prehistory consists of a series of isolated dates separated by long periods for which no evidence exists. Thus it is not yet possible to discuss Indonesian prehistory in terms of sequences of either human or cultural evolution. Without evidence of the intermediate stages we cannot tell how or why one phase developed into the next one.

The geographical distribution of evidence is also uneven. For the last 10,000 years BC we know almost next to nothing about Sumatra and Java, which must have been important centres of technical and social innovation. For early man, for example, one of the main controversies involves the question of whether Africa alone is responsible for the development of Homo sapiens. Sites where ancient human fossils are found in direct association with tools are still extremely rare. Compared to other areas of the world our knowledge of Indonesia's Old Stone Age is extremely poor. When modern humans appear, they may have come as migrants from the west, but it is also possible that modern people owe at least part of their ancestry to the pre-human forms whose fossils have been found in Java. Javanese hominids were not static, but followed an evolutionary path toward anatomically modern humans parallel to the course of development found in Africa. Similar difficulties afflict the study of early Indonesian agriculture. Some tantalisingly early dates from New Guinea suggest that tubers, and other root crops were already being cultivated 10,000 years ago. However, we have no data on the subject of the domestication of important food crops in Indonesia.

(From left) Stone tools from the Pacitanian industry, central Java.
Cist grave, Pasemah, Sumatra.
Guardian statue, near a group of Pasemah slab graves.
Sculpted head decorating the top of a stone sarcophagus, Tomok, north Sumatra. This site represents a continuation into recent centuries of the prehistoric burial tradition.

PREHISTORY

The island of Java has one of the longest sequences of proven human habitation in the world. Research conducted at an increasing rate during the past 20 years has revealed much new and important information about the earliest inhabitants of Southeast Asia and their artefacts.

The rise and fall of the sea levels during the last million years, due to glacial retreat and advance, and the alternation of wet and dry periods had important implications for human evolution in Java. Potential sites of the ancient sea coasts and river valleys of the submerged continent lying under the Java and South China Seas are lost to archaeologists. All that remains are the hominid fossils of Java, and their tools.

The position of the early Southeast Asian hominids in the process of modern human evolution is still in question. Many recent studies suggest that all modern humans descend from African forebears. However, the relationship between the African and Asian early humans is unclear. The Javanese fossils demonstrate a long period of evolution which parallels that of African forms. It seems at least possible if not likely that the early African and Asian hominids were part of a single gene pool. Thus the Javanese would also have participated in the general process by which modern humans evolved.

We do not know when Indonesians began to domesticate food sources, or to work metals. Many common modern plants were almost certainly first domesticated in Indonesia. Animals such as the chicken, duck, dog, and pig were also raised by early Indonesian farmers. By late prehistoric times Indonesians were working bronze into large ceremonial objects. The earlier stages of technological evolution remain to be discovered.

New data compiled after 1970 demonstrate that Indonesians had already begun to evolve complex social organisations before contacts were made with centres of culture outside the region. Older theories claimed that Indonesia's early civilisations owed their existence to immigration or direct inspiration from India. New data on late prehistoric Indonesia show that local developments were the key to the formation of the Indonesian kingdoms which existed at the beginning of history. Our picture of prehistoric Indonesia is still in a state of rapid development. Only for Java and Bali is there even the semblance of an adequate framework for characterising the prehistoric sequence of development. For other regions and islands, the state of knowledge ranges from sparse data to a complete vacuum.

Buni pottery burial offering from Java (ca. 1st–5th century AD).

Sumatraliths left by toolmakers in Sumatra (mid–late Holocene).

Fossilised jaw of Hanoman 1 from Java (named after a Hindu god).

Stone head from Pasemah Plateau in Sumatra (500 BC–100 AD).

Pleistocene and Holocene Environmental Changes

Geologists refer to the last two million years as the Quaternary. The Quaternary is divided into the Pleistocene (2 million –10,000 years ago) and Holocene (10,000 years ago to the present). During this era several worldwide climatic changes called glacials and inter–glacials occurred. During the glacial periods sea levels dropped, sometimes to 100 metres below today's levels.

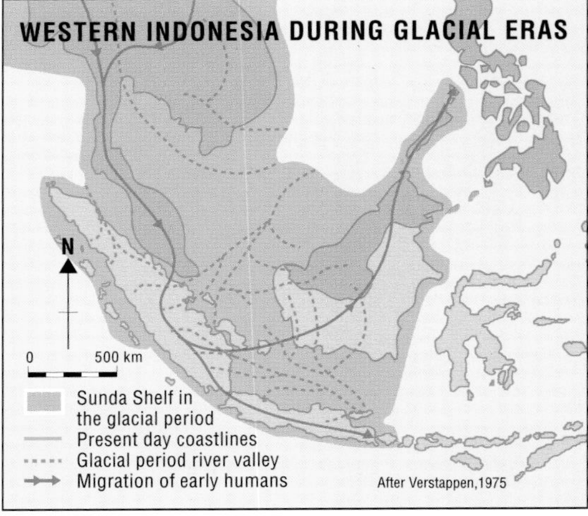

Sea Level Changes

A system called oxygen isotope analysis of deep sea sediments has enabled scientists to map variations in sea levels which had major repercussions on the physical geography of the archipelago. Large areas of the shallow South China Sea and Java Sea, (Sunda Shelf), became periodically dry land. In fact large river valleys can still be observed on submarine maps of the Sunda shelf (see map, above right). These land bridges did not extend east of Wallace's line — the natural zoogeographical barrier which separates the western part of Indonesia under Asian influence from the eastern part under Australian influence. Climate (precipitation and seasonal patterns) underwent drastic changes throughout the Quaternary, as did the natural environment (palaeogeography and vegetation).

Death and Rebirth. Anak Krakatau, a new volcano, rises from the sea where in 1883 Mt. Rakata, popularly known as Krakatoa, exploded in a mighty blast. Volcanic activity in Indonesia has increased during the last two million years, and may have had a significant effect on the world's climate.

Land Bridges and Migrations

When the seas retreated they created land bridges between mainland Southeast Asia and the western part of Indonesia. These bridges allowed animals to reach as far south in the archipelago as the island of Java. By successive steps during the Quaternary era, the mammal fauna of Java was successively enriched by new species. The oldest fossil fauna, circa 1.8 million years old, yields only proboscidians (related to modern elephants), hippopotamus, and cervids (members of the deer family). Then other herbivorous mammals and several carnivores arrived. *Homo erectus* (man) probably reached Java more than one million years ago.

The fauna had to adapt to these peculiar geographic and ecological conditions. During interglacial periods, the sea level rose and the islands of the archipelago became isolated both from the mainland as well as from each other. The fauna also developed specific characteristics, exemplifying an evolutionary phenomenon called endemism. In the most extreme cases, pigmy forms could appear. Such forms are found most commonly in eastern Indonesia, especially among animals like the proboscidians (pigmy *Stegodon* or elephant) of Flores and Timor.

Reconstructing Prehistoric Vegetation Patterns

A useful method for reconstructing the vegetation of the past is the study of pollen grains that have become fossilised in ancient sediments. The microscopic pollen grains of each species of plant have a specific morphology which allows us to identify the plants from a particular time and region. Such studies give a good picture of the older vegetation pattern and its changes during the Quaternary. These studies also provide us with a clear picture of the climate pattern.

Humid conditions prevailed during the inter–glacials. Tropical rain forest covered the area, with

GEOLOGY AND HUMAN EVOLUTION

The last two million years are known to geologists as the Quaternary era. Most of human prehistory falls into the geological period known as the Pleistocene, except for the last 10,000 years which are called the Holocene or Recent.

ISOTOPIC CHRONOLOGY OF GLACIALS AND INTERGLACIALS

18 0 (to PDB) .2 .1 0

NOW — ONE MILLION YEARS AGO — 2 MILLION YEARS AGO

The graph shows the changing ratio of two isotopes of oxygen in shellfish from deep sea sediments. The curve reflects the changing temperature of sea water. The peaks represent warmer climate, while the troughs represent cold periods. The graph shows that the earth's climate is becoming more and more variable.

10,000 — 250,000 — 500,000 — 1,000,000

HOLOCENE — UPPER PLEISTOCENE — MIDDLE PLEISTOCENE — LOWER PLEISTOCENE

Schima and *Altingia* (shrubs), *Podocarpus* (firs) and *Quercus* (oaks).

During the glacial periods, Indonesia's mean air temperature is believed to have dropped a few degrees Celsius, while sea temperatures, as inferred from recent studies, would have been only two degrees lower than today. This cooling, however, was enough to cause a downward shift of vegetation zones on mountains: trees like *Podocarpus imbricatus*, which presently grow only higher than 2,000 metres above sea level could be found at lower altitudes. But the main change during these glacials related to the precipitation pattern: the dry season was longer and more severe, and the tropical rain forest shrank, replaced in many areas by a more open monsoon-like forest with an abundance of *Leguminosae*, and *Mimosaceae*. Grasslands developed during those drier periods and several studies even give evidence of the existence of *Gramineae* (grass)-dominated savanna-like environments in Kalimantan and Java. The vegetation had a mosaic-like character at such times, as rain forest galleries persisted along the rivers and also on the upper parts of the mountain slopes where the climate was constantly wet.

Palaeoenvironmental evolution was not only affected by climatic changes. Geological phenomena like volcanic eruptions also deeply changed the landscape. These eruptions periodically disturbed the vegetation and led to the colonisation of the moun-tain slopes by pioneer plants. At the same time, tectonic uplift — which has given Java its present shape — also caused great changes in the landscape. As the sea receded, large mangrove and swamp forests were created on the lowlands of Java, only to vanish as they were filled in by the products of volcanic eruptions and erosion.

The First Humans and their Environment

Pithecanthropus (the scientific name given to Javanese fossil hominids) were the first humans to cross the equatorial area. As the sea levels rose and fell he became — periodically — an islander. Human evolution on Java lasted approximately one million years. These early humans had to adapt to a frequently changing environment, which is likely to have deeply influenced their subsistence and culture. How did they use the natural resources offered by the rain forest? Did they develop a unique culture in such an unusual environment? Current studies are attempting to correlate palaeoenvironmental reconstructions with other aspects of prehistoric life, including the use of stone tools; vegetal resources like bamboo; and the significance in terms of diet of wear features on the fossil teeth such as striations and enamel chips.

EVOLUTION OF THE LANDSCAPE IN THE AMBARAWA BASIN, JAVA DURING THE LAST 4,000 YEARS BP (BEFORE PRESENT)

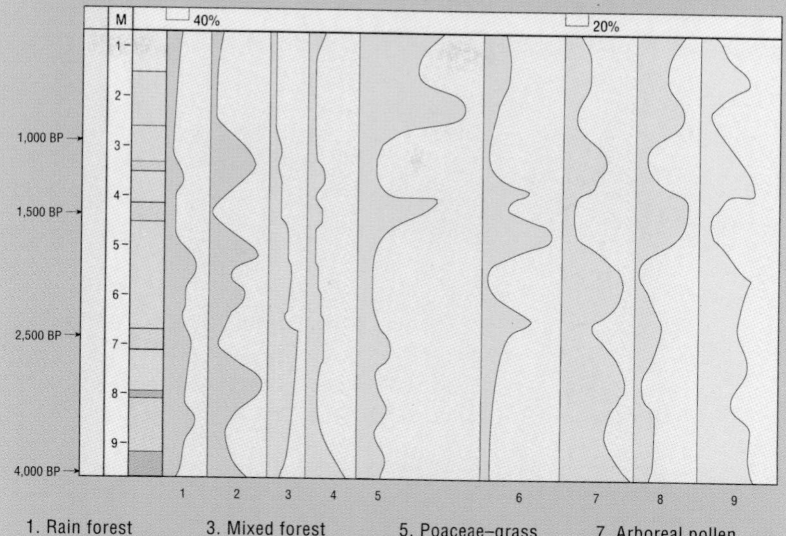

The pollen record of a Holocene core from the Ambarawa swamp, central Java, gives evidence of several recession periods of the swamp forest. The base of the core (carbon 14 dating gives 4,000 years BP) reflects a severe dry season (See Open Forest Curve). During the second event (1,500 years BP) the trees almost disappear. This event probably reflects the first clearing activity in the area. The last event, which postdates the 13th century, is likely to represent human colonisation of the Ambarawa plain and the beginning of intensive agriculture (rice fields). *Pollen Grains (below left to right) Casuarina (Cemara* or filao tree) pollen grain, *Podocarpus imbricatus* pollen grain, *Poaceae* (grass) pollen grain.

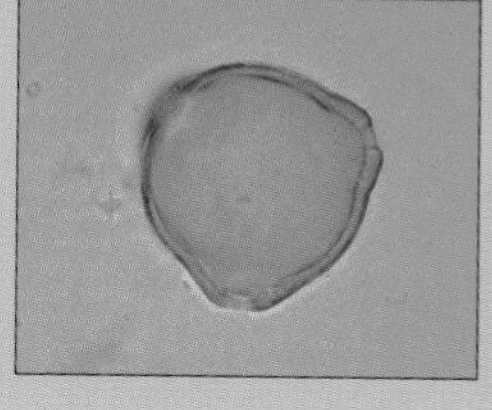

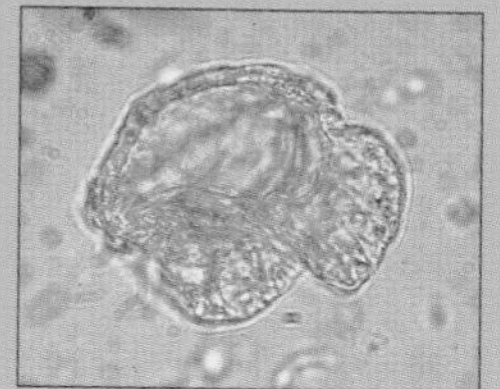

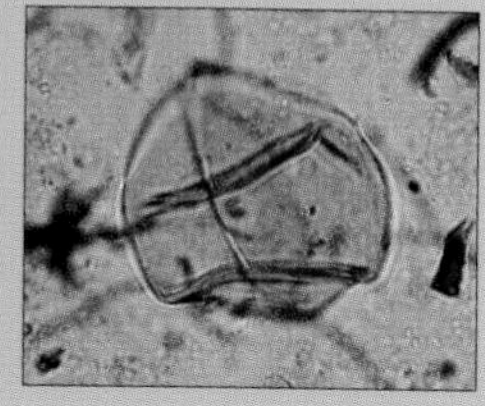

The Upper Pleistocene and Holocene Environmental Changes

The Pleistocene-Holocene transition corresponds to the most recent major climatic change from glacial to the interglacial conditions which persist today. Pollen analysis has been widely used for research into this era and gives excellent results for such a period of changing climate; the study of pollen preserved in lake and swamp deposits, together with good chronological control of carbon 14 dating, enables scientists to put together a detailed picture of paleo-environmental evolution. The precise quantification of vegetation zone shifts between higher and lower elevations indicates the magnitude of the decrease and increase in tem-peratures in Indonesia during the glacial event. The influence of man upon his environment during the later periods of prehistory is also reflected in the pollen diagrams.

Mangrove, South Sumatra. Such vegetation would have covered large areas of the near submerged Sunda Shelf in colder periods.

The Javanese Pleistocene Hominids

The fossil hominids of Java are popularly known as Pithecanthropus, meaning 'ape–man', a name coined by Eugene Dubois to designate the species represented by a fossil skull and femur he excavated at Trinil in 1891. Now anthropologists agree that all the human fossils discovered in Java belong to the species Homo erectus.

CRANIAL EVOLUTION IN JAVANESE HOMO ERECTUS: THE PHENOMENON OF OCCIPITAL ROUNDING

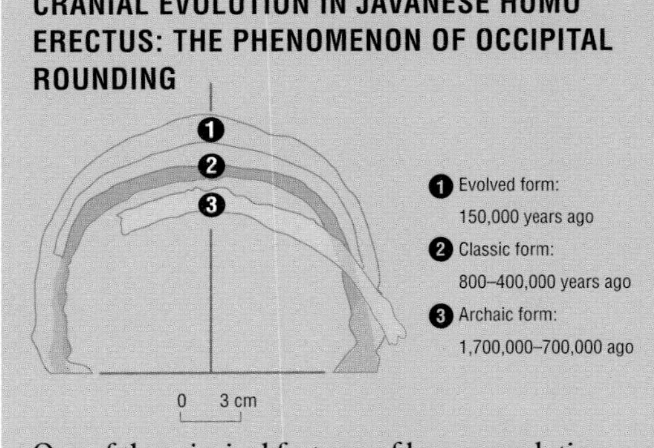

One of the principal features of human evolution has been a continuous tendency for the skull to become higher and narrower. Javanese fossils exhibit this trend, indicating that they were developing in the same direction as their African cousins.

SANGIRAN 17: CRANIAL FEATURES

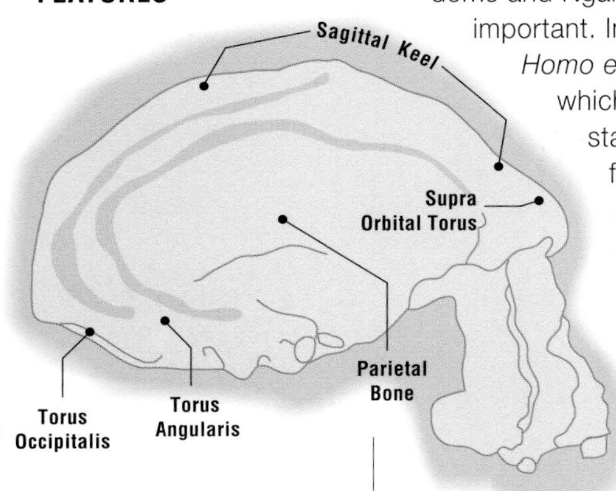

Homo Erectus in Java

Homo erectus (upright man) underwent evolutionary change throughout his million–year history. Other hominid–bearing sites in addition to Trinil have been excavated in central and eastern Java. The Sangiran dome and Ngandong alluvial terraces are the most important. In Java, we can discern three stages in *Homo erectus* history: an archaic stage (from which no complete skulls exist), a classic stage, and an evolved form. Similar fossils are found in several parts of Asia but are most numerous in the Javanese fossil–bearing sites. The oldest remains have been discovered in the Pucangan layers of the Sangiran dome, which date back to 1.7 to 0.7 million years. Classic *Homo erectus* is represented by the Trinil fossils and by the remains found at Sangiran in the Kabuh layers, dating from 0.8 million to 0.4 million years ago. The youngest specimens (representing evolved *Homo erectus*), perhaps 150,000 years old, often called Solo Man, have been found at three sites: Ngandong, Sambungmacan and Ngawi.

The Skull

The best preserved and most easily identified human bones are the upper parts of the skull, or cranial vaults. The shape of the skull tells us a great deal about the human being it belonged to and about its evolutionary stage. The most archaic cranial vaults are broad and flat, indicating a weakly developed brain. The thick cranial bones (up to 12 millimetres against an average of nine millimetres on other fossils) bear many robust super–structures such as a sagittal keel (thickening along the sagittal suture, the point where two skull plates join), a *torus angularis* (at the posterior part of the temporal lines, where the temporal muscle is inserted into the skull), and a *torus occipitalis* (point of attachment of posterior neck muscles). The sagittal thickening of the most archaic specimen, Sangiran 31, has been interpreted by several scholars as a true sagittal crest (a pronounced ridge), characteristic of the African *Australopithecus*. There is not yet enough evidence to conclude that *Australopithecus*–like forms existed in Java during the lower Pleistocene.

The face of Java Man, Sangiran 17, Musée National d' Histoire Naturelle, Paris. The best preserved ancient Javanese skull.

Classic *Homo erectus* fossils have long, flat cranial vaults. One of them (Sangiran 17) preserves a robust prognathic face where the lower part of the face juts forward — a 'primitive' characteristic — and a conspicuous ridge over the eyebrows, called a supra–orbital torus. A transverse sulcus (depression) precedes a flattened frontal bone. Other cranial superstructures such as the sagittal keel or the *torus angularis,* which are present on all Asiatic *Homo erectus* forms, are still found in this group. The more evolved Ngandong, Sambungmacan and Ngawi skulls are still long, but have increased in elevation and width. The frontal bone is more curved, and the biparietal vault is wider. The characteristics observed on these three groups of *Homo erectus* which show the most evolution over time are the widening and elevation of the vault, and the progressive curving of the bones. The cranial superstructures persist throughout *Homo erectus*' existence.

The Brain

Casts of the interior of the skull provide information about the brain's volume and stage of evolution. The Archaic and Classic forms give cranial capacities between 840 and 1,000 cubic centimetres. The more modern Solo Man forms show an increase of almost 50 per cent (1,030 to 1,250 cubic centimetres). Important features concerning the evolution of the brain can be studied by comparing casts of Archaic and Classic forms with Solo Man fossils.

Over time the shape of the brain becomes more rounded with an expansion and downward move of the frontal and occipital lobes, changes linked to a general evolutionary phenomenon called occipital rounding. The anterior part of the frontal lobe becomes wider and shorter on the Solo Man fossils, and the lobe itself expands. The study of the width of the precentral and post–central convolutions provides evidence that the development of the frontal

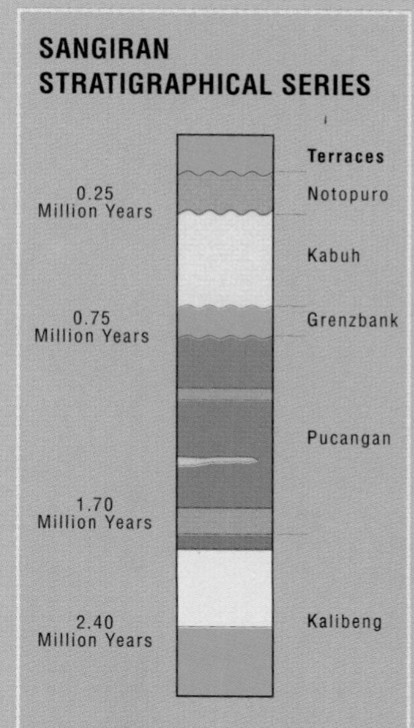

THE STRATIGRAPHY OF THE SANGIRAN DOME
The Sangiran dome, in the Solo depression, is the richest hominid–bearing site in Java, and possesses the most complete stratigraphic sequence. The Sangiran series begins with Late Pliocene lagoonal deposits (Upper Kalibeng), followed by volcanic breccia. During the Early Pleistocene the Pucangan black clays were deposited in a swampy environment. The most archaic *Pithecanthropus* fossils are found in these layers. A pebbly fossiliferous layer called *Grenzbank* marks the apex of this unit, deposited about 800,000 years ago, and forms the base of the volcanic–sedimentary fluviatile Kabuh layers, deposited at the beginning of the Middle Pleistocene era. Many fossils are found in this layer. The top of the geological series comprises the Notopuro volcanic breccia and lahars, which are about 200,000 years old. The Sangiran stratigraphic section ends with gravel terraces whose deposition predated the folding of the dome, due to a diapiric process. Erosion caused by the Cemoro river then cut through these layers, displaying the whole Plio–Pleistocene geological history of that area.

area — where movement is controlled — could have predated the development of the parietal area or sensory cortical zone (see top right of previous page).

The Mandible and the Teeth

More or less complete human mandibles (jawbones) are known for only the two oldest *Homo erectus* groups in Java. One of them, *Meganthropus palaeojavanicus* discovered by Ralph von Koenigswald, still poses a taxonomic problem. This human mandible is extraordinarily huge and robust, which could mean that it should be placed in a genus more archaic than *Homo*.

The Javanese fossil mandibles are long and thick, and show strong muscular insertions. They have no chin, and a retro molar space exists between the third molar and the ascending branch. The incisors are shovel–shaped, and the height of the thick canine teeth is comparable with that of modern humans.

The Post–Cranial Skeleton

Bones from other parts of the bodies of *Homo erectus* are mainly fragments of long bones from the legs: femora (thighbones), tibiae (shinbones), and a fragment of acetabulum (hip socket). The femoral features are similar to those of modern humans, but they are thicker and present robust muscular insertion scars. The shape and the position of the femoral head suggests that *Homo Erectus* had already acquired perfect bipedal locomotion. The length of the bones indicates the stature of fully–grown adults to be about 1.70 metres.

The Phyletic Position

Even if we could ascribe the archaic and classic Javanese *Homo erectus* fossils to the *Homo erectus* species with any certainty, Solo Man's position within the phylum would still be questionable. They present typical *Homo erectus* characteristics including the thickness of the bones or the cranial super–structures. At the same time the fossils already show features that are very like *Homo sapiens* — the increased cranial capacity and the expansion of the parietal and frontal parts of the brain, which led to a general widening and elevation of the vault. If Solo Man can be considered an evolved form originating from older *Pithecanthropus* populations, it is still debatable whether Solo Man is actually an archaic *Homo sapiens* or an evolved form of *Homo erectus*.

SOLO MAN IN HIS NATURAL HABITAT.
This hypothetical view depicts evolved *Homo erectus* in the Notopuro era, when volcanic eruptions were beginning to fill in the ancient lagoon which once covered east central Java. This rich environment provided many resources which ancient humans could exploit, including various types of cattle and elephant now extinct.

Indonesia's Oldest Tools

We have little information about the nature and chronology of the lithic or stone tool assemblages of the Pleistocene era, and what we do have is often controversial. Some scholars have argued that Javanese "Pithecanthropus", isolated in a peculiar environment, did not use stone tools like his continental cousins, but such a theory seems implausible.

»»Animal horns are found next to stone tools at the Ngebung site, Sangiran. This is the oldest site known in Indonesia where we have some contextual evidence to suggest how the tools were used. The tools are about 500,000 years old, and comparable to African tools of the same age.

Until the discovery of the Ngebung site, all the fossils of premodern men and their supposed tools were discovered in alluvial deposits. They had been transported by water from their original locations. The Solo river and its tributaries have carved a shallow, broad valley through the fossil-bearing layers, thus exposing them but also disturbing them.

Java

The basic handicap confronting those who search for stone tools in Pleistocene fossil-bearing strata of Java is of a geological nature. Before they became fossilised, early human remains were transported by water from their original habitat. The search for cultural remains therefore should not be concentrated near the fossils, but rather in the geological formations further upstream. In other words, it is necessary to discover 'fossil' hills and riverbanks in order to find evidence for the tool-using behaviour of early man in Java.

Pacitan

During the 1930s Ralph von Koenigswald made an intensive survey of the upper Solo River in the southern mountains of Java. There, in the Baksoko Valley, he found a Palaeolithic-looking assemblage which has become known as the Pacitanian industry. These tools can be found in several alluvial terraces of the river, up to 30 metres above the present bed. The outcrops themselves are highly weathered, and the tools are most often found in the riverbed, mixed together with an abundant Neolithic industry.

The Pacitanian tools comprise many choppers and chopping tools, usually made of silicified tuff, fossil wood, or limestone. Hand axes are present but scarce. The age of this assemblage is unknown. When it was first discovered, scholars connected it with the *Homo erectus* found further north in the Solo depression, but recent studies attribute the Pacitanian tools to more recent times (Upper Pleistocene, about 50,000 years ago). No absolute dating is yet available for this site.

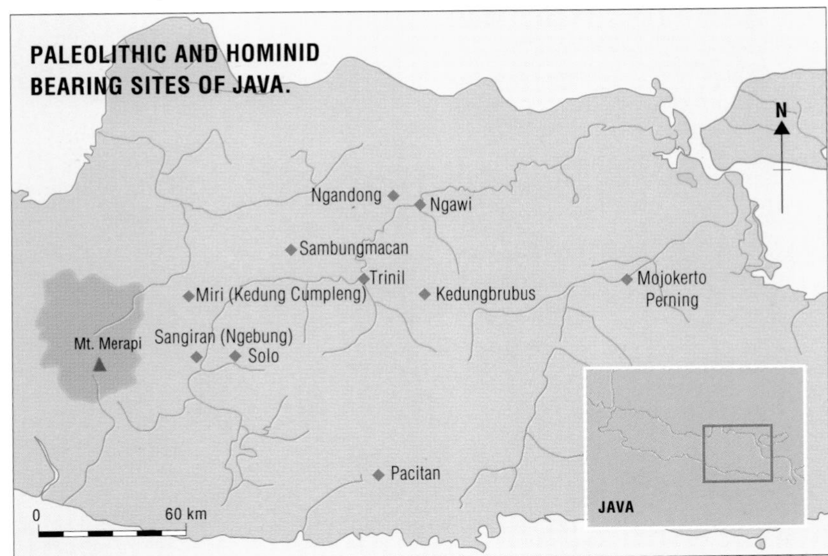

The Sangiran Flakes

Since 1934, small jasper and chalcedony cores, flakes, and retouched tools have been found in alluvial layers capping the Middle Pleistocene Kabuh layers of the Sangiran dome. The 'Sangiran flake industry' very quickly became famous and was thought to represent *Pithecanthropus* tools. Its age however remains somewhat controversial.

In recent years excavations within the Middle Pleistocene Kabuh layers at Sangiran have yielded more Sangiran flakes, providing evidence that at least part of this industry was created by *Homo erectus*. The small size of the items may be due to two reasons. Some of the tools could have been carried by streams from further inland, and consequently only the smaller pieces would have been transported this far. The other hypothesis, which is more plausible, is that *Homo erectus*, searching for hard siliceous stones to make his tools, preferred chalcedony and jasper, from the southern mountains of Java, but could find only small pebbles of these materials around Sangiran.

Ngandong

Excavations conducted at Ngandong, where a dozen evolved *Homo erectus* skulls of Solo Man have been discovered, yielded only a few flakes possibly made by man. Stone and bone tools, some shaped like harpoon points, found in the same area, are known as the 'Ngandong industry'. These obviously originated from layers younger than Solo Man.

Sambungmacan and Kedung Cumpleng

The first confirmed *Homo erectus* stone tools were discovered at Sambungmacan. After a *Homo erectus* skull was found there in 1973, further research in the basal conglomeratic layer of the site uncovered two artefacts of andesite: a chopper on a big flake and a retouched flake. Kedung Cumpleng at Miri is a deltaic conglomerate which was deposited in the Solo lagoon about 900,000 years ago. Pebbles deposited here originated from the Kedung Hills to the north. In 1988 excavators discovered several limestone artefacts. These subsequently proved to be the oldest man-made objects in Java to date.

The Ngebung Site at Sangiran

All artefacts mentioned above were found in coarse sediments washed downstream from areas formerly inhabited by prehistoric man: in valleys such as Pacitan, or in conglomeratic layers deposited by streams at such sites as Sambungmacan and Miri. Unfortunately these sites do not provide an archaeological context, that is, the tools were not found in the place where they were made, used and discarded. They give no information about the life-styles of the people who made them. If they had been found in a campsite or quarry, their distribution around the site could tell us much about how people organised their activities.

At Ngebung, within Middle Pleistocene Kabuh layers (*circa* 500,000 years old), recent excavations brought to light the existence of an older riverbank fossilised by younger fluviate deposits. This river bank had been occupied by *Homo erectus* who left behind numerous objects, including pebbles, broken bones and stone artefacts: rough polyhedric tools, bolas (stone balls), and flake tools (choppers, chopping tools, and cleavers), all of andesite with the exception of one quartz pebble from the southern mountains used as a hammerstone. The high proportion of rough polyhedral tools compared to 'sophisticated' tools in the assemblage is linked to the available raw material. The Sangiran area yields coarse-grained andesite pebbles which are difficult to trim but are easy to use as stone balls. Hard fine-grained andesite used for making choppers is rare, and large pebbles of other siliceous rocks like quartz are extremely rare. Ngebung provides the first evidence of the existence, among the Javanese *Homo erectus*, of a lithic tradition which is comparable to other lithic cultures at that time.

Other Lower Paleolithic Sites

Other sites scattered throughout Indonesia have also yielded artefacts believed to date from the Lower Palaeolithic era. However, most of these sites have not yet been properly dated.

In South Sumatra, north of Bengkulu, on the Mungrup river, and also in the Kikim riverbed, choppers, chopping-tools and flakes have been found. In the Walanae depression within an area near Cabenge, Sulawesi, Palaeolithic implements were discovered on river terraces 40 metres above the present river beds. However, their association with the Pleistocene faunal remains is still a topic of much discussion. At other sites, such as Nulbaki, Timor, and Mata Menge, Flores, tools are associated with remains of *stegodon,* an extinct elephant.

Conclusion

Further research is necessary to determine the chronology of the cultural sequence. Implements associated with *Homo erectus* are still extremely rare and it is very difficult to describe cultural evolution in the Lower and Middle Pleistocene.

The most complete Lower Palaeolithic-looking assemblages are the remains at Pacitan. The search for Palaeolithic sites of occupation in the southern mountains of Java should be allocated a high priority in the endeavour to determine the precise age of the Pacitan deposits.

❶ *A retouched Sangiran flake, Musée National d' Histoire Naturelle, Paris.*
❷ *Ngebung : a stone ball.*
❸ *Ngebung : chopper on a big flake, Musée National d' Histoire Naturelle, Paris.*

ARTEFACTS OF THE STONE AGE IN JAVA

It was long believed that the stone tool technology of Java, from the earliest period until the age of metals, was characterised entirely by the use of large, crude tools made from large cobblestones. These tools are normally called core tools, because they are made by striking off flakes which are discarded, leaving behind the centre of the original cobblestone which is then utilised. The artefacts below consist of core tools: a chopper or cleaver, a chopping tool, and a hand axe. The latter resembles tools from Africa, the Middle East, and Europe, which belong to the early Stone Age or Palaeolithic. Recent discoveries of flake tools such as those on the far right of the top row prove that Javanese *Homo erectus* also advanced to the stage of making and using finer tools. The excavations at Ngebung (right) provide the oldest such evidence. The late Stone Age or Neolithic of Indonesia has long been recognised as having produced stone tools shaped like axes and adzes of high quality (four examples at lower right), using the technique of grinding and polishing stone rather than flaking or chipping.

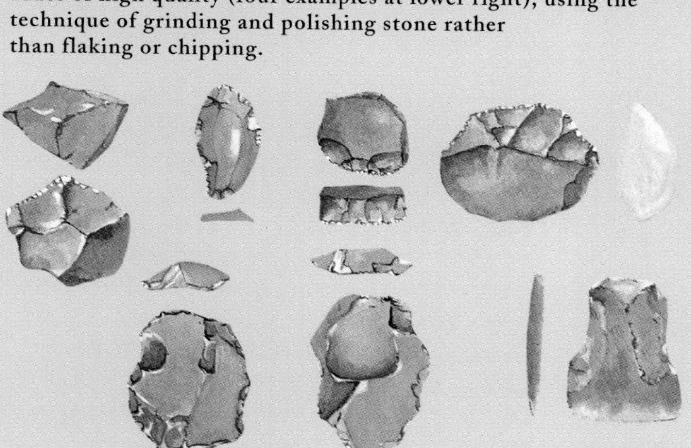

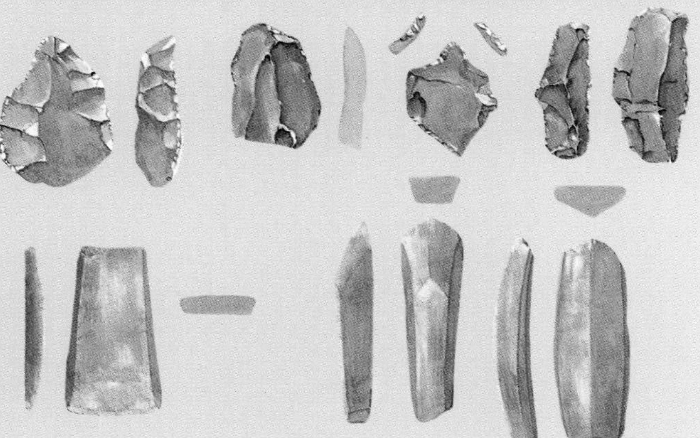

The Hunting and Gathering Stage in Eastern Indonesia

Eastern Indonesia is separated from the western part of the archipelago by what is termed the Wallace Line. Eastern Indonesia was never linked to the mainland of Asia even during the periods of lowest sea level during the Pleistocene era. Evolution, both natural and cultural, has followed a slightly different path from that which characterises western Indonesia.

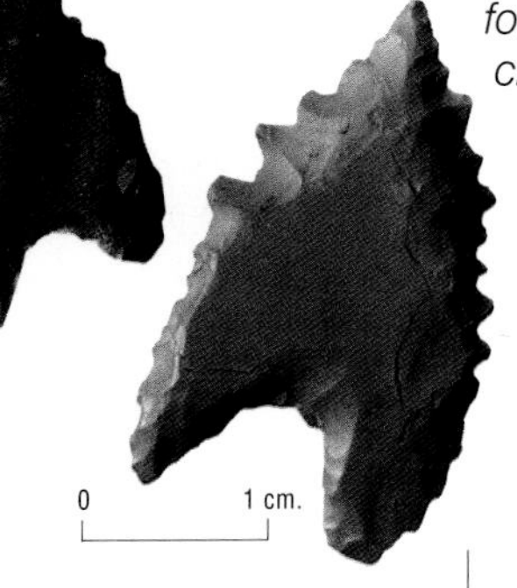

Maros points from the Toalian industry of South Sulawesi, from the site of Leang Burung 1 and dated to around 5,000–4,000 years ago.

Cave paintings of hand stencils, Leang Petta Kere, South Sulawesi. All these stencils are of left hands, and several of them have missing fingers, recalling the practice of finger amputation as a sign of mourning still carried out in New Guinea.

Geography

The Wallace Line runs along the eastern edge of the Sunda Shelf, down the Makassar Strait between Borneo and Sulawesi. The territory east of this line, beginning with Sulawesi and Lombok and extending to Timor and Maluku, has been separated from all continental land masses for millions of years. Islands in this zone, termed Wallacea, exhibit plant and animal forms transitional between those of Asia and Australia. Large mammals never found their way across this zone until about 40,000 years ago, when the first humans landed in Australia. Culturally and biologically they were similar to the pre-Austronesian Upper Pleistocene inhabitants of Indonesia. The prehistoric populations of Wallacea were sparse, but their cultural development was not retarded by their isolation or relative lack of variation in resources. By late prehistoric times, several societies in this vast region of much water and little land had evolved distinctive customs and art styles, including sophisticated stone tools, colourful cave paintings, and highly decorative bronze artefacts.

Late Pleistocene and Early Holocene Sites

Stone tools found at Cabenge in South Sulawesi were once thought to be as old as the Middle Pleistocene era, and thus among the oldest artefacts in Indonesia, partly because very old animal fossil bones were found in the same area. It is now agreed that the tools, cores and thick flakes, are not as old

as the bones. Their true age is not known. Other tools which may be very old have been found in Sumbawa and Flores but in these cases too no dates can yet be determined. Many Sulawesian sites lie in caves and rock shelters in limestone hills. The oldest absolute dates from eastern Indonesia come from sites in South Sulawesi.

These early dates were obtained from shells dated with the carbon 14 method. Shells can give misleading carbon 14 results as they absorb ancient carbon dissolved in water; however, the dates in this case (29,000 to 17,000 years ago) seem reliable. The site where they were found, Leang Burung (Bird Cave) 2, yielded shells of freshwater species, probably remains of human meals, and stone blades and flakes, some with a gloss on the sharp edges caused by the accumulation of silica. Such gloss is usually an indication that the tools were used to cut grass or bamboo, possibly for plaiting mats or baskets, or producing nets for hunting and fishing.

In Timor, a cave site, Uai Bobo 2, yielded a carbon 14 date of over 13,000 years for stone tools, mainly flakes. The inhabitants hunted local fauna including a now-extinct giant rat, and made use of a plant from the Areca family, probably the betel nut, more than 7,000 years ago. This is possibly the oldest evidence for the existence of betel chewing. A shell midden on the edge of Lake Tondano, north Sulawesi, contained remains dated to the time before the spread of the Austronesians, 8,500 years ago.

The best known prehistoric industry of eastern Indonesia is the Toalian, named after the ethnonym of the people who inhabited the areas of the cave sites where these artefacts were found in the early 20th century. The Toalian appears about 8,000 years ago. The main new tool forms typical of the Toalian are microliths in the form of flakes and blades with fine flaking along one edge which is thicker than the others; this is sometimes termed 'backing'. Sites such as Ulu Leang have yielded artefacts called Maros Points, resembling arrowheads of Amerindians but with serrated edges, probably used for hunting. Other typical artefacts include pointed bone tools.

Paintings appear on some cave walls containing Toalian artefacts. We are not sure of the precise age of the paintings, but they may be several thousand years old. They are executed with red haematite, samples of which are also found. Cave paintings are also found in other parts of eastern Indonesia though some probably date from more recent times. Subjects include hand stencils and wild boar.

Early Agriculture

By 4,500 to 5,000 years ago agriculture, both plant domestication and animal husbandry, had appeared in eastern Indonesia. Rice may have been planted in South Sulawesi as early as this; charred rice grains from Ulu Leang may date as early as 6,000 years ago, although there is some uncertainty over this date because the carbon 14 results from the site are not in perfect sequence. Pigs, goats, and pottery had appeared over a wide area from Sulawesi to Timor 4,500 years ago.

Early Pottery

The oldest pottery in eastern Indonesia is smooth-surfaced, and sometimes coloured with a red slip. Around 3,000 years ago a new pottery style appeared, decorated by incising, carving, stamping, and punching. This pottery, sometimes termed Sahuynh-Kalanay, is similar to a type of pottery called Lapita found in the western Pacific. The general similarity between Lapita and other pottery found at such places as Ulu Leang 2 and Kalumpang, Sulawesi, and Timor, gives a clue to the place from which the first human explorers entered the Pacific. Research now under way in north Maluku is likely to add further evidence on this subject.

Late Prehistory

By late prehistoric times eastern Indonesians had developed sophisticated metal-working techniques. Bronze, the ingredients for which would have to have been imported, was used to make items such as ceremonial axes. Other sophisticated bronze objects found in eastern Indonesia may well date from pre-historic times too. Their styles show no relationship to those which developed during the classical period in western Indonesia, but this is not conclusive evidence for their age, since eastern Indonesian art was not influenced by Indic or Chinese designs until the early modern period.

The practice of burying the dead with grave offerings evolved in several parts of east Indonesia. Excavations at the site of Melolo, east Sumba, revealed the existence of a large prehistoric burial ground. The site contains hundreds of secondary burials in which some bones of the dead were put into urns 25 to 50 centimetres in diameter, along with such items as beads and other jewellery of shell and stone, and earthenware pottery including distinctive high-necked flasks (see right). A burial site with similar artefacts, but with bronze and iron and without urns, has been found at Gunung Piring, south Lombok.

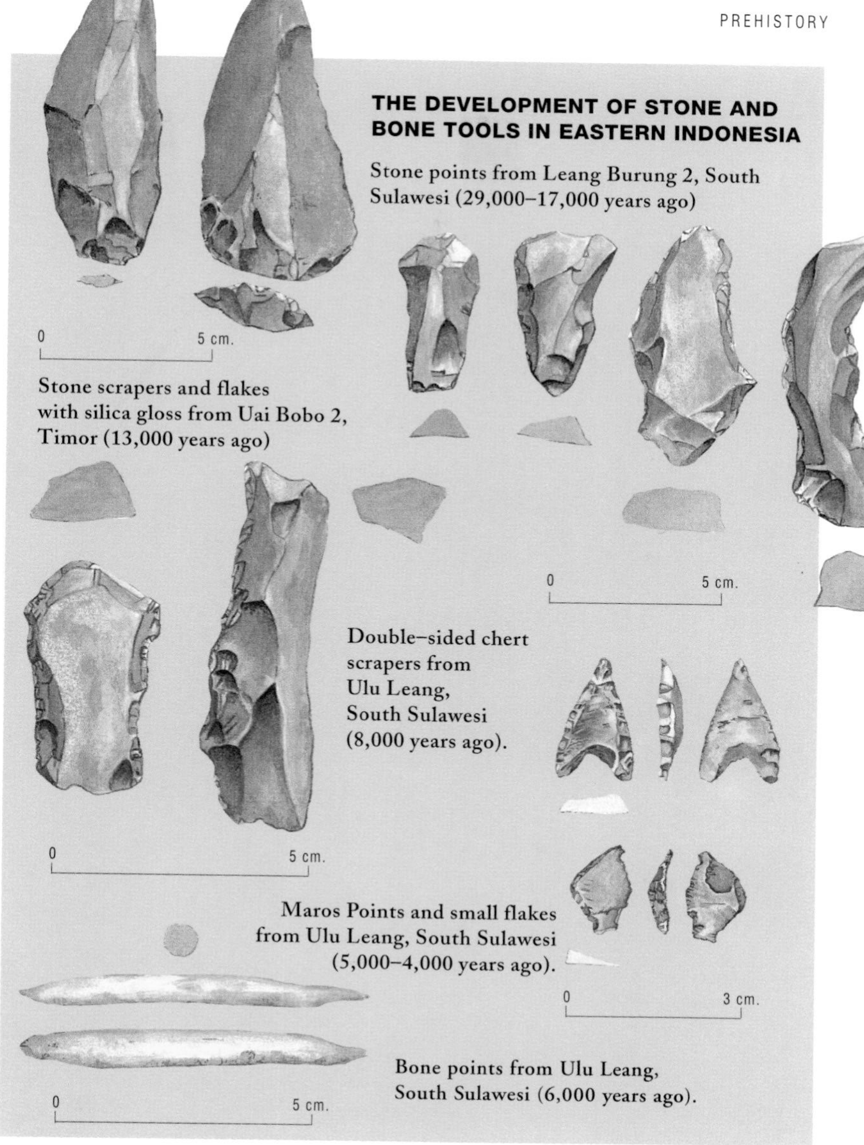

Drinking vessel from Melolo, east Sumba (National Museum, Jakarta).

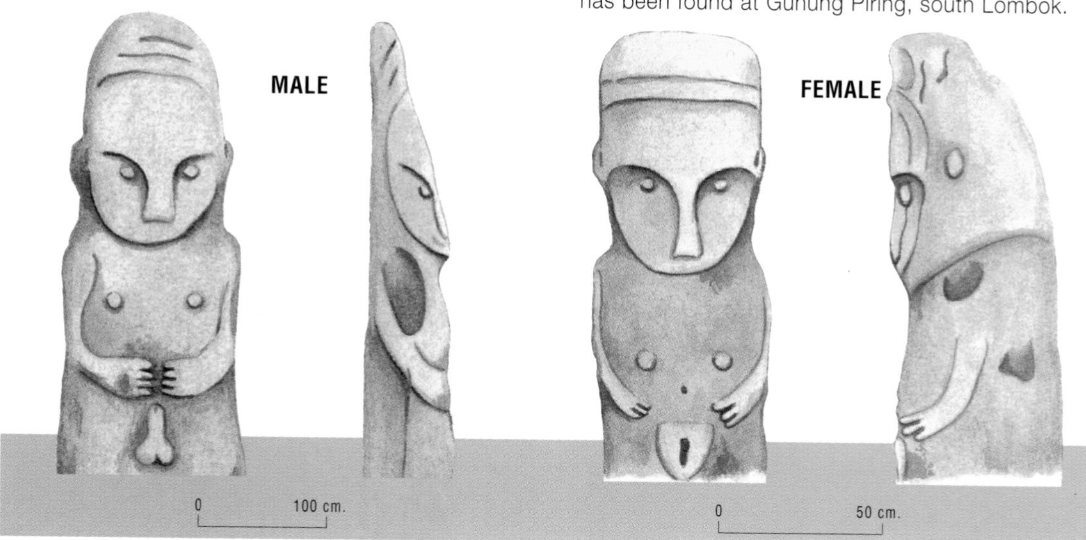

Megalithic figures from the Bada Valley, central Sulawesi. Although they may date from prehistoric times, it is not yet possible to prove that they are of great antiquity.

Austronesian Languages and Population Movements

For several thousand years, Austronesian was the most widespread language family in the world. Its history reflects one of the most phenomenal records of colonisation and dispersal in history. Austronesian languages are now spoken in Taiwan, parts of Vietnam, Malaysia, the Philippines, and Indonesia; outside Southeast Asia, they reach as far as Madagascar and Hawaii, Easter Island and New Zealand.

Austronesian Languages

Linguistic and archaeological records suggest that the speakers of Austronesian languages, who spread through Indonesia about 4,000–2,500 years ago, were also the first agriculturalists in much of the archipelago. This population probably intermarried with the preceding hunter–gatherers, absorbing or replacing their cultures and languages. Early stages of Austronesian languages can be reconstructed by searching present–day languages for shared features which can then be linked in sub–groups. Languages within a sub–group share a common origin, and can be ranked hierarchically in terms of their order of separation from the remainder of languages in the family.

A single outrigger craft, perhaps similar to the type used by prehistoric Austronesian explorers.

A Language Tree

The roots of Austronesian probably go back to southern coastal China, but the history of Austronesian as a separate language family begins in Taiwan, after agricultural settlers arrived there between 5,000 and 6,000 years ago. Linguist Robert Blust postulates a family tree of the highest–order Austronesian sub–groups, starting from Proto–Austronesian beginning in Taiwan, then encompassing the Philippines, Borneo, and Sulawesi, finally spreading in two branches, one moving west to Java, Sumatra and the Malay Peninsula, the other east via Halmahera into Oceania. (A proto–language is a reconstructed ancestor of all the languages in a family or sub–group.) The languages of all these regions as far as Madagascar and Easter Island are classified as Malayo–Polynesian, as opposed to the Formosan sub–groups which form the other major division in the Austronesian family.

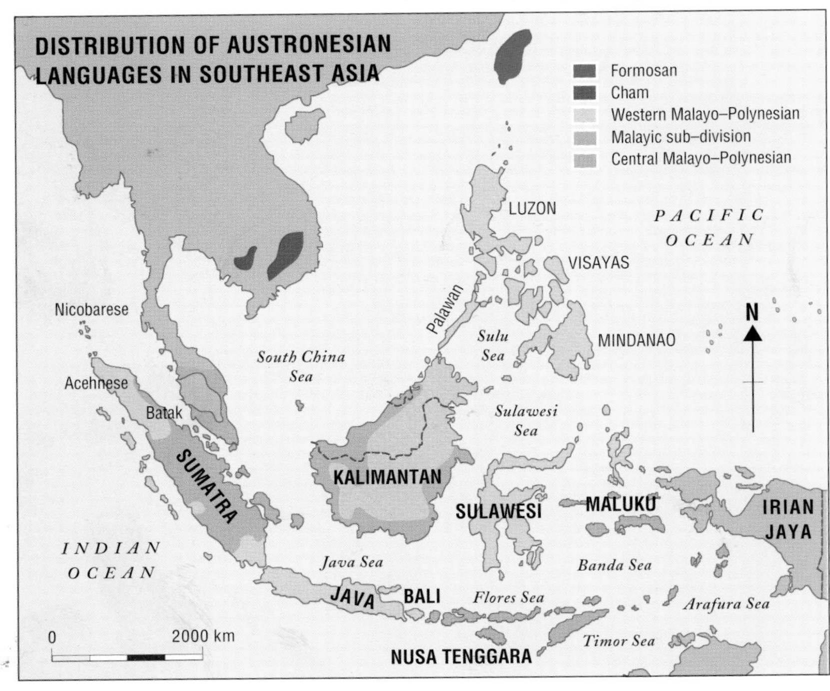

SAMPLE OF COGNATE WORDS WITH STABLE MEANINGS FOUND THROUGHOUT THE AUSTRONESIAN WORLD

	PAN = Proto –Austronesian	Rukai (Taiwan)	Javanese	Fijian
two	*DuSa	dosa	lo-ro	rua
four	*Sepat	sepate	pat	vā
five	*limaH	lima	limo	limā
six	*?enem	eneme	enem	ono
eye	*maCa	maca	moto	mata
ear	*Caliŋa	caliŋa	(Kupiŋ)	daliŋa
headlouse	*kuCuH	koco	kutu	kutu
road	*Zalan	ka-dalan-ane	dalan	sala
pandanus	*paŋuDaN	paŋodale	pandan	vadra
sugarcane	*tebuS	cubusu	tebu	dovu
stone	*batu	(lenege)	watu	vatu
canoe	*awaŋ	avaŋe	(prau)	waga

*Lexical reconstruction

Courtesy Malcolm Ross

Proto–Austronesian vocabulary, representing languages spoken in Taiwan about 5,000 years ago, indicates an economy well suited to marginal tropical latitudes with rice, millet, sugar cane, domesticated dogs and pigs, and canoes. As a result of the further colonising movements through the Philippines into Borneo, Sulawesi, and Maluku, the Malayo–Polynesian sub–group eventually separated into Central–Eastern and Western language divisions. The vocabulary of Proto–Malayo–Polynesian, which may have been located somewhere in the Philippines, is of great interest because it contains a number of tropical plant names which were absent in earlier Proto–Austronesian. These include taro, bread–fruit, banana, yam, sago, and coconut; their presences reflect a shift away from rice toward greater dependence on tubers and fruits as the farmers moved into the equatorial environment.

Linguistic Diversity

The divergence of the Central–Eastern sub–group began in Maluku or Nusa Tenggara. This sub–group contains all the Austronesian languages of the Pacific Islands, except some in western Micronesia. The record of the expansion of the Western Malayo–Polynesian languages into Java, Sumatra, and the Malay Peninsula may be masked by the spread of the Malayic and Javanese languages in the past 1,500 years. Bernd Nothofer believes that the oldest Austronesian settlement of this region is represented by the languages in the islands off west Sumatra and in the northern Sumatran highlands. Most major

TERMS FOR EVERYDAY OBJECTS REFERRING TO RECONSTRUCTED CATEGORIES OF MATERIAL CULTURE IN EARLY AUSTRONESIAN SOCIETIES

Class of material culture	Reconstruction	Terms
House and contents	NWE	house/family dwelling
	WE	ridgepole, rafter, thatch, house–post, storage rack above hearth, notched log ladder, hearth, public building
Tools utensils, weapons	NWE	bow, shoot an arrow, rope/cord
	WE	putty, caulking substance, comb, conch shell trumpet, cooking pot, nail, pillow/wooden headrest, digging stick, bamboo trail–spikes, torch, hew/plane
Arts and crafts	NWE	needle
	NW	loom (early Western Malayo–Polynesian only?)
	WE	plait/weave, draw, whet/sharpen, sew
Adornment	NW	tattoo
Refreshment	NW	drunk (adjective)
	WE	time for betel quid, betel nut
Hunting and Fishing	NW	hunt, go hunting
	WE	bait, bamboo basket trap for fish, kind of fishnet, fishhook, fish drive, drag–net, derris root fish poison, bird lime, snare.
The canoe	NW	canoe/boat
	WE	canoe, canoe paddle, outrigger, rollers for beaching a canoe, sail, canoe bailer, to paddle, rudder/steer,
Domesticated animals	NWE	raft, cross–seat in a boat, punting pole.
	WE	domesticated pig, dog
Garden and fields	NWE	cock/rooster
	NW	rice (E cognates not beyond west New Guinea). pestle, garden/cultivated field, sugarcane,
	WE	husked rice, mortar, cooked rice, winnow, rice straw, millet to weed, Alocasia sp. (an aroid), breadfruit, ginger, citrus fruit, banana, yam, sago, taro, fallow land, to plant, melon
Food preparation	NWE	to smoke meat or fish
	WE	salt
N(north) = Formosan: W(west) = Western-Malayo-Polynesian: E(east) = Eastern Malayo-Polynesian		

Source : After Blust, 1976

Western Malayo–Polynesian languages, including those of the Malayic sub–group, and Acehnese, Chamic, Javanese and Balinese have been separating from each other since the first millennium BC or later. A great deal of the expansion of Malay as a lingua franca around the coasts of Borneo and eastern Indonesia occurred in historic times.

In eastern Indonesia, linguistic diversity is greater than in the western regions, perhaps reflecting looser political integration. Another cause of diversity, especially close to New Guinea, has been a process of mutual influence between languages in the Austronesian and Papuan families; these processes have been particularly important in Melanesia leading to such rapid lexical diversification that some linguists have claimed western Melanesia, to be the homeland of Proto–Austronesian. This opinion is not supported by comparative phonological or grammatical research. The linguistic picture of the origin and dispersal of Austronesian has some points of overlap with the archaeological record. Stages in the history of unwritten languages cannot be dated, but the archaeological record makes it clear that the major phase of Austronesian colonisation, from Taiwan through the Philippines and Indonesia, and into western Oceania, took place between 3,000 and 1,500 BC. The major period of colonisation within Indonesia probably took place between 2,000 and as late as 500 BC, since some westerly regions might already have been settled by Austroasiatic speaking agriculturalists from the Malay Peninsula prior to the period of Austronesian dispersal. In addition, some parts of western Melanesia were settled by agriculturalists prior to Austronesian dispersal. Austronesian languages made little headway here, especially in New Guinea where they only occur in coastal pockets among the Papuan language families.

A POSSIBLE GENEALOGY OF THE AUSTRONESIAN LANGUAGES

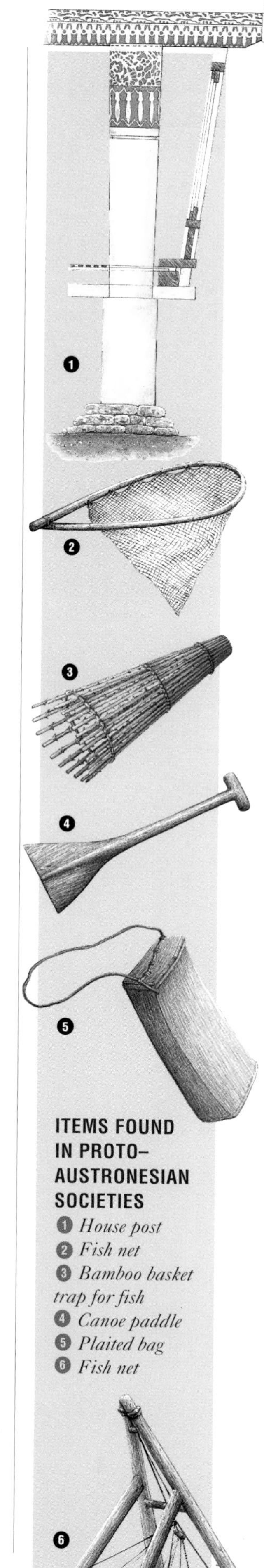

ITEMS FOUND IN PROTO–AUSTRONESIAN SOCIETIES

1. *House post*
2. *Fish net*
3. *Bamboo basket trap for fish*
4. *Canoe paddle*
5. *Plaited bag*
6. *Fish net*

Early Cultivation and Domestication

Agriculture seems to have been introduced to Indonesia by people already acquainted with rice, millet, and other sub-tropical crops like yams, taro, and sugarcane. They also kept pigs, chickens, and dogs. Many tropical fruits and tubers native to Indonesia were brought into cultivation as agriculturalists moved south and eastward toward a region of separate agricultural origin in New Guinea.

» Prototypical woodworking tool: bent-knee shaped adze handle made from wood, a type used in prehistoric times in South China, Island Southeast Asia and Oceania. This example was discovered preserved in a swampy site at Hemudu, southeastern China, near the mouth of the Yangzi River.

Original Settlers

The origins of the Austronesian languages and the first agriculturalists to enter Indonesia, around 4,500 years ago, can be traced to the island of Taiwan and southern China. Societies with rice cultivation and a highly developed Neolithic technology existed in coastal regions south of the Yangzi about 7,000 years ago, when the climate was slightly warmer. Important elements of artefact design and subsistence economy found in southeastern China during the Neolithic also characterised later cultures of island Southeast Asia. These elements of similarity include the coating of pottery with a red slip, use of a cord-wrapped or carved wooden paddle to decorate pottery, bent-knee shaped adze handles, untanged or stepped stone adzes, and art motifs that emphasise spirals and circles. The past 4,500 years have seen much interaction between different populations throughout the whole region from China to Melanesia, and also continuous biological and cultural exchange.

Expansion of Agriculturalists

The southward expansion of agriculture into equatorial Indonesia is not clearly traceable because of the hot and humid environmental conditions which are inimical to the preservation of organic remains. However, there does exist linguistic information about Proto-Austronesian and Proto-Malayo-Polynesian agriculture. Plain or red-slipped pottery, which seems to be associated with the early expansion of agricultural communities, dispersed from Taiwan into the Philippines, northern Borneo, eastern Java, and eastern Indonesia between 4,500 and 3,000 years ago. Bones of domestic pigs and dogs are often found with this pottery. Presumably the chicken had been introduced by this time as well. Rice grains in pottery from Borneo have been dated to about 4,500 years ago. Evidence for forest clearance in pollen records in the Javanese and Sumatran highlands also supports the widespread presence of agriculturalists by indicating intermittent forest clearance at least 4,000 years ago.

At the same time as the Austronesians colonised Indonesia, the Papuan-speaking people of New Guinea were independently developing a form of agriculture that focused on fruits and tubers. The two systems met and mixed in eastern Indonesia, creating a blend of economies, with typical Melanesian plants such as sago and canarium nuts being heavily exploited in Maluku and Irian Jaya. It is believed that taro may also have been domesticated independently in New Guinea. Rice seems to have been dropped from cultivation in this region and it was never grown in the Pacific islands.

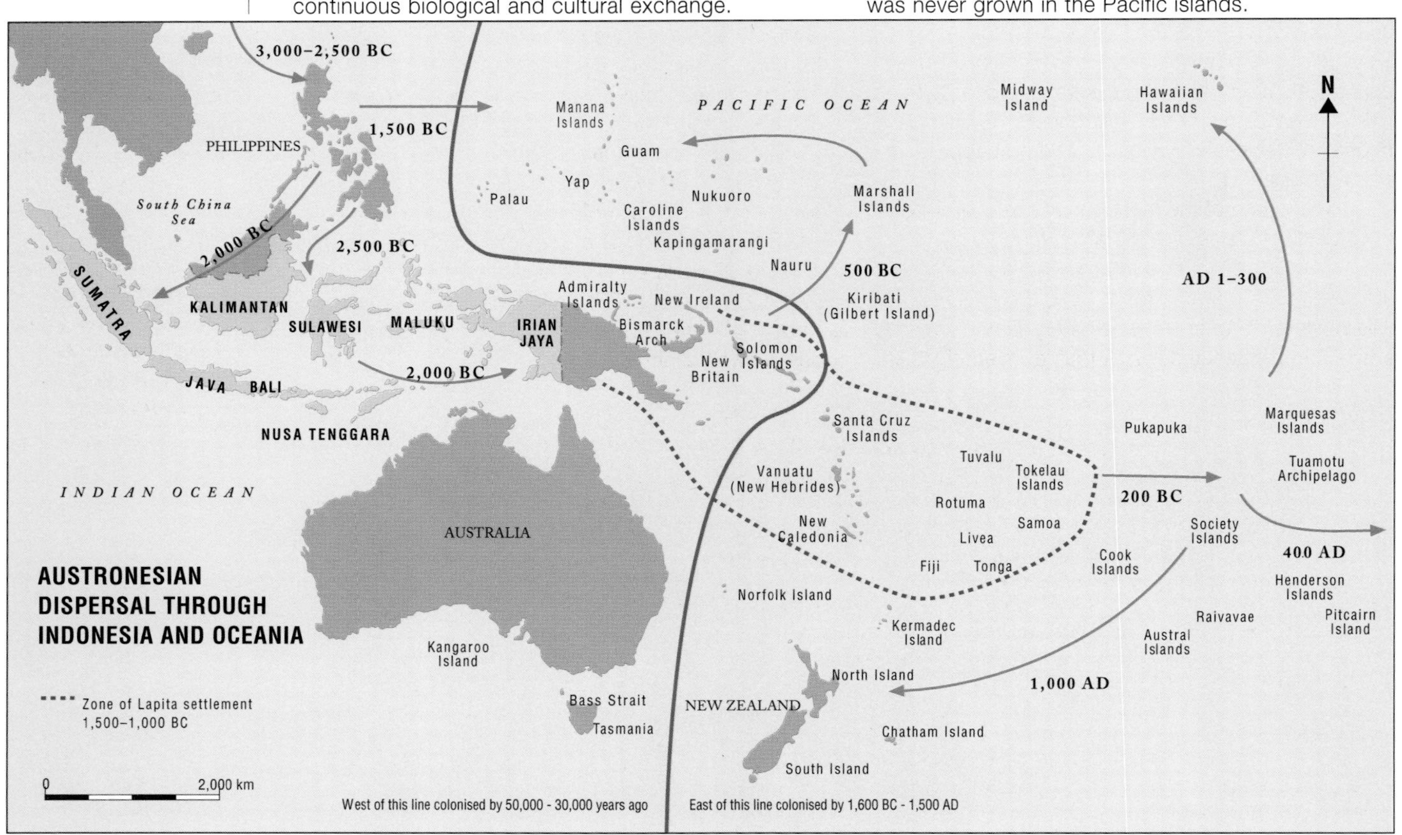

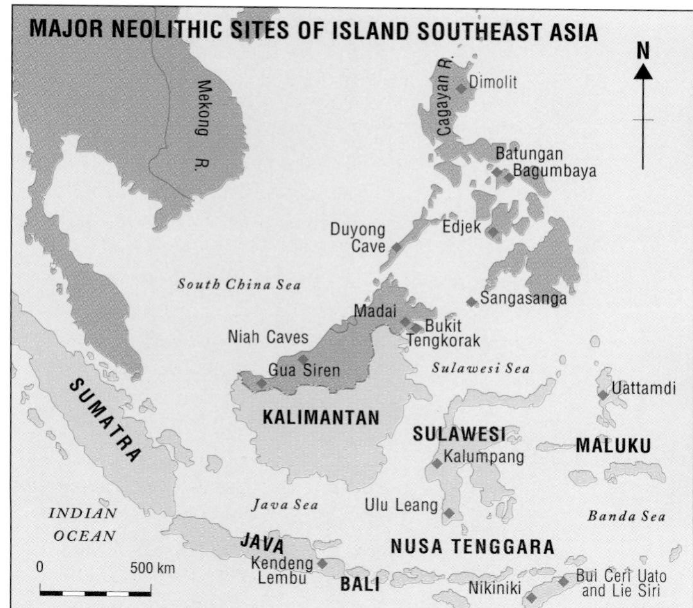

Evidence from Melanesia–Lapita Culture

Starting about 3,500 years ago Austronesian farmers colonised part of Melanesia. The area that was affected by this colonisation, known as the Lapita culture, is far better understood than contemporary Indonesia owing to the great volume of research which has been carried out in Melanesia. The Lapita story involved the colonisation of a 5,000 kilometre wide area stretching from the Admiralty Islands to Samoa, during the mid–and late second millennium BC. Western Melanesia, particularly New Guinea, the Bismarck Archipelago, and the Solomons, had already been settled by Melanesians during the late Pleistocene, whereas the islands from Santa Cruz and Vanuatu to Tonga and Samoa in western Polynesia were now settled for the first time. There can be little doubt that the makers of Lapita pottery were the ancestors of the Austronesian–speaking people of Melanesia, Polynesia, and probably much of Micronesia.

Perhaps one of the most remarkable features of Lapita assemblages are intricately decorated dentate–stamped or incised pottery. Also found are stone adzes, a range of tools, body ornaments, and fishhooks made of shell, remains of stilt–houses, and a far–flung exchange network that involved obsidian obtained from sources in the Admiralty Islands and New Britain. The immediate origins of these Lapita colonists lay somewhere in the eastern part of island Southeast Asia, most probably among populations who had already abandoned the cultivation of rice under equatorial conditions and had developed instead an economy based on tubers, fruit, marine resources and the domestication of pigs, dogs and fowl, together with a reliance on inter–island travel by canoe.

Archaeologically, however, there are as yet no specific regions or assemblages which can be isolated as definite ancestors for Lapita. This is undoubtedly due to lack of research, although contemporary assemblages which show close relations with Lapita have been excavated in parts of the Philippines (especially in northern Luzon), western Micronesia, and Kayoa in Maluku Utara (Uattamdi).

Unfortunately, the Neolithic in western Indonesia still remains somewhat poorly known, and there are almost no data at all from Sumatra or Java. This situation is probably due to the enormous degree of lowland alluviation and site burial resulting from the clearance of forest. This period is a most important target for future research, and exciting discoveries surely await exposure.

Southeast Asian–Melanesian Relations. Dentate–stamped Lapita pottery from Massau Islands, western Melanesia, ca. *1, 500 BC (above) compared with incised Neolithic pottery from Bukit Tengkorak in Sabah,* ca. *1, 000 BC (left).*

Many important crops were almost certainly developed in Indonesia, but data on the process of their domestication is still negligible. The coconut for example is one of a number of fruit trees which spread from Indonesia to much of tropical Asia in prehistoric times.

BAMBOO AND TARO

One of the major problems confronting the study of prehistoric tropical agriculture is the problem of preservation. Bamboo played many roles in Southeast Asia which in other parts of the world were occupied by stone or clay, which are much more likely to survive in archaeological sites. Even cooking containers, such as the bamboo tubes used for cooking rice (above right) were often made of bamboo.

The domestication of grains such as rice is easy to study because grains have silica–rich husks which can survive especially if they are carbonised. It is possible however that root crops such as taro preceded rice as an important domesticated food source. Taro is still grown in many parts of Indonesia, sometimes on the dikes between rice fields (below right). Taro has no hard parts which are preserved in archaeological sites, and therefore evidence of its prehistoric cultivation is almost impossible to obtain. Since it is propagated vegetatively, there is not even any pollen to betray its existence.

Ceremonial Bronzes of the Pre-Classic Era

In Indonesia the first evidence for the use of both bronze and iron appears around 500 BC, there apparently being no separate and earlier Bronze Age. Most of the earliest bronze objects were ceremonial in nature. They include highly stylised axe-like forms in various local styles, and kettledrums. Some drums were made in the tradition called Dong Son which spread from north Vietnam; others represented local variations.

Detail of frog on Dong Son drum from Salayar Island, South Sulawesi, 92 cm high and 126 cm typanum diameter. Some of its designs suggest an origin in western Indonesia, although there is as yet no evidence that drums of this shape were ever cast in Indonesia.

Dong Son Drums

The best known bronze artefacts from Indonesia are undoubtedly the large drums, called Dong Son drums, which were probably imported after about 200 BC from manufacturing centres of the Dong Son culture in northern Vietnam (although many later drums could have been cast elsewhere).

Such drums have been found all along the Sunda island chain from Sumatra, through Java, into Nusa Tenggara and as far east as the Kai Islands near Irian Jaya. To date, however, only one has been reported from Kalimantan, and none in Sulawesi, northern Maluku, nor the Philippines. This restriction of the distribution of Dong Son drums to the Sunda Islands is interesting since it could suggest a relationship with the contemporary initiation of trade with India.

The Dong Son drums were made using the lost wax method. A wax model in the shape of the drum was made around a hollow clay core, and then standardised geometric, human, animal and bird friezes for the tympana and upper sides were impressed into the wax using incised stone moulds. This process resulted in the creation of designs in low relief on the bronze surface. The more detailed designs, such as the houses with people and drums inside shown on the tympanum of the Makalamau drum from Sangeang Island near Sumbawa, appear to have been carved individually into the wax. They thus appear as incised rather than relief decorations on the bronze drums. Some of the Indonesian drums have four frogs cast in relief on their tympana, although frogs seem to be rather rare on the drums found in mainland Southeast Asia. This circumstance might reflect local taste and preference. The oldest drums are regarded as the most naturalistic in their decoration, although none of these occur in Indonesia. In many of the later drums some of the standardised decoration became highly schematised.

The typology for these drums was formulated in the earlier 20th century, and four classes of drums are generally recognised, named Heger I–IV after the scholar responsible. Of these, only the Heger type I is widespread. The distinctive attributes of this type include the broad upper surface, short body, handles decorated to resemble plaited rattan, and the star

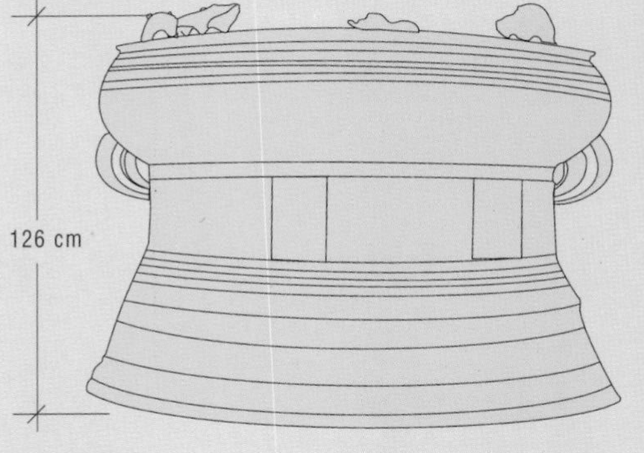

This drum displays the typical waisted shape and squat proportions identified with the Dong Son style of Vietnam.

»»A bronze ceremonial axe from Landau, Roti, decorated with human figures. Design elements combine motifs similar to some anthromorphic designs of early art of the southwest Pacific with geometric motifs also found in mainland Asian bronzes.

Bronze socketed axe from Leang Buidane, Talaud Islands, ca. *500–1000 AD.*

motif which occupies the centre of the typanum. The drums may have evolved from prototypes made from a different material.

As to the use of these drums, we can only guess. Helmet Loofs-Wissowa has suggested they were used as regalia by chiefs who wished to join an international elite, in much the same way as their successors adopted Indian and then the Islamic religions. Most of the drums have simply been found in villages rather than excavated, but in recent years there have been two interesting archaeological finds in Central Java. At Plawangan, a drum was found buried upside-down with the crouched skeleton of a child inside. A similar child burial was found beneath a Dong Son drum which was interred on top of a second bronze drum of the Indonesian Pejeng type. The latter contained beads of glass, carnelian and gold, a four-legged bronze container with a typical Dong Son circle and tangent ornament on its lid, other bronze vessels, a gold necklace, an iron spearhead and chisels, bracelets of gypsum and wood, pottery, and a few human bones.

Other Bronze Artefacts

Bronze-casting industries in Java and Bali flourished early in the first millennium AD, and were probably responsible for the manufacture of the numerous swallow-tail socketed bronze axes of Java, the splendid flasks from Kerinci and Lampung (both in Sumatra) and Madura, and the flamboyant and unique ceremonial axes of Roti.

The Pejeng-type drums, named after the site in Bali where the first example of this type was found, were cast in Java and Bali, and they differ from the original Dong Son specimens in that they were made in two pieces with mantles and tympana cast separately by the lost wax method. Negatively-incised stone moulds or stamps, such as one found at Manuaba in Bali, were used to form a relief decoration on the wax surface. Bali was only one of several centres of manufacture for these artefacts.

Origins of Indonesian Bronze Traditions

The tradition of casting large kettledrums is most probably of Vietnamese origin. However, hundreds of heart-shaped copper axes very similar to those found in Balinese sarcophagi have recently been excavated from layers dated *ca.* 700–500 BC near Lopburi in central Thailand. This suggests that a single origin in mainland Asia for Indonesian metal-working is unlikely. Indonesian metallurgy may have been created by societies with links to several areas.

Furthermore, many of the dates for pre-classic style bronzes in Indonesia overlap with the earliest evidence for Indian contact in western Indonesia. Recent research in Bali, north Sulawesi and north Maluku reveals that such artefacts as copper/bronze and iron tools, glass beads and pottery with distinct, incised patterns spread widely, almost as far as Irian Jaya, by the 1st or 2nd century AD. Was the spread of bronze in Indonesia related to rapid growth of mercantile activity as the civilisations of the Old World began to demand spices?

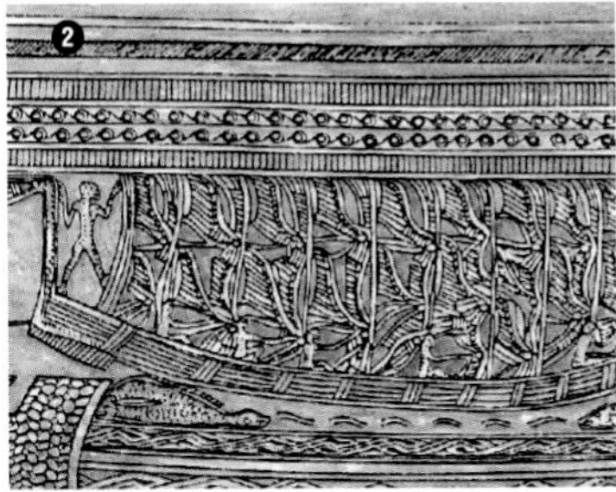

Baked clay moulds for casting copper or bronze socketed axes, Leang Buidane, Talaud, ca. *500 AD.*

Scenes of Bronze Age Mythology
(Left) The Makalamau drum from Sangeang Island (MNI 3364) is decorated with a series of scenes apparently depicting one or more legends. (Illustrations after Marcia Bakey, Smithsonian Institution.)
❶ *Domestic scene from top of drum.*
❷ *Boats and humans from upper cordex zone of drum.*
❸ *Animals and human with sword from side of drum.*
❹ *Human, horse, and elephant rider figures from bottom zone of drum.*

Social Complexity in Late Prehistoric Java

There is much evidence to prove that Javanese society had reached a high level of complexity by late prehistoric times. Elaborate works of art in metal and stone, and sanctuaries utilising arrangements of terraces and monoliths, hint at a rich ceremonial and political life.

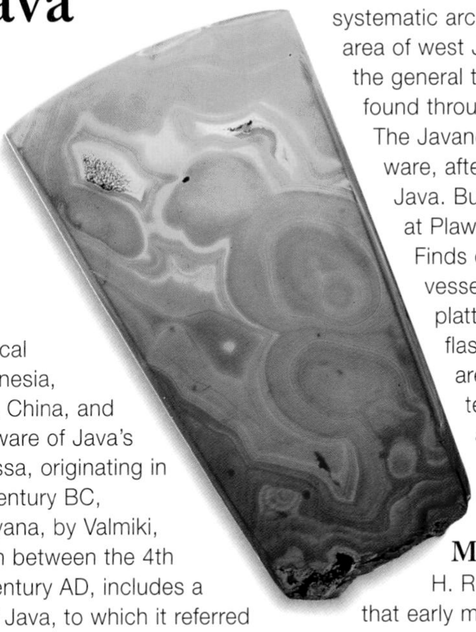

»Adze of semi-precious stone. This artefact may have been used as a symbol of rank rather than a tool.

Foreign Sources

Several centuries before local inscriptions appear in Indonesia, foreign merchants of India, China, and the Roman Empire were aware of Java's existence. The Maha Nidessa, originating in India during the mid-3rd century BC, mentions Java. The Ramayana, by Valmiki, which was probably written between the 4th century BC and the 2nd century AD, includes a description of the island of Java, to which it referred as Yavadvipa (Barley Island in Sanskrit) and described it as having seven kingdoms. A Chinese report, the *Nan zhou i wu chih*, written by Wan Zhen (222–280 AD) mentions the volcanoes of *Si-tiao*, its fertile soil, and its population who wore clothing made from bark. *Si-tiao* was almost certainly a reference to Java. The *Geographia* of Ptolemy, an Alexandrian Greek astronomer who lived around 100 AD, refers to a place named *labadiou*. This toponym may possibly be derived from the word Yavadivu, the Prakrit form of Yavadvipa. This source says that labadiou was fertile and that its capital *Argyre* (which was also mentioned in Indian sources) was located in the west.

PREHISTORIC JAVANESE SITES

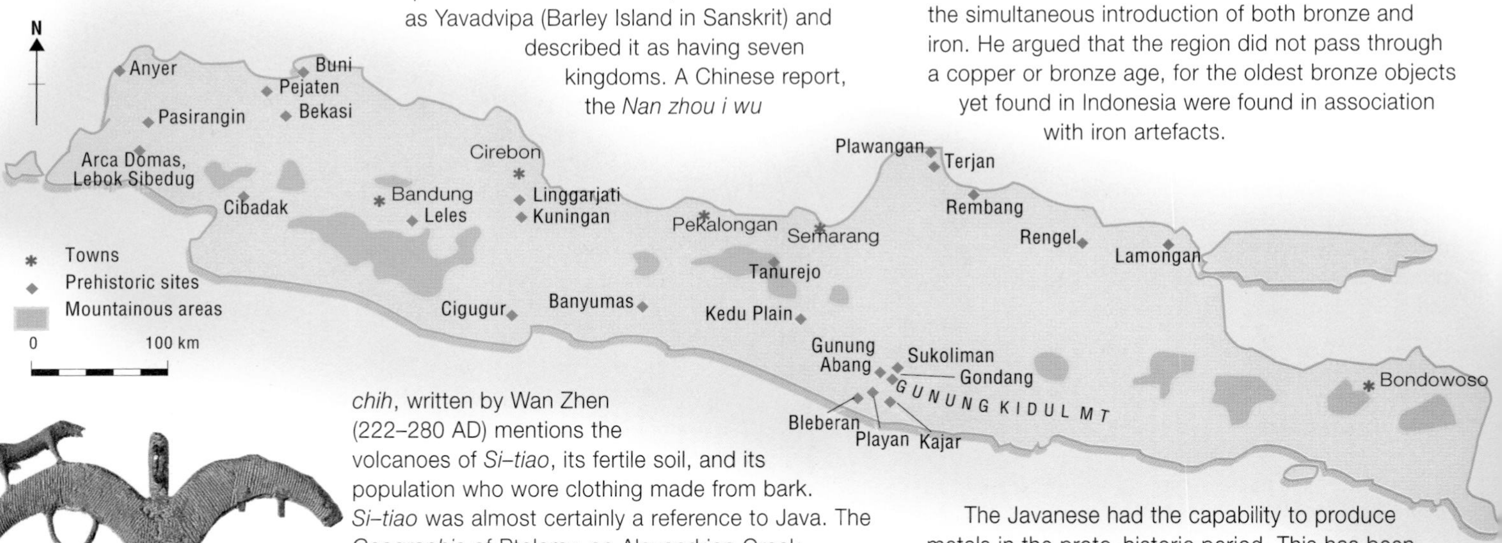

Archaeological Discoveries: Buni Culture

The discovery of rouletted Indian pottery at Kobak Kendal and Cibadak in west Java is the earliest evidence for contact between India and Java. Similar pottery found in south India dates from the 1st and 2nd centuries AD. However, the exact period when this pottery arrived in Java cannot be ascertained, for the specimens of this ware said to have been discovered in Java were not found in systematic archaeological research. The Bekasi area of west Java has yielded pottery belonging to the general type known as Sahuynh–Kalanay found throughout most of island Southeast Asia. The Javanese variety is referred to as Buni ware, after one of the principal sites in west Java. Buni-type pottery has also been found at Plawangan, central Java, and in Bali. Finds of this pottery type include globular vessels with inverted rims, bowls and platters, open bowls on pedestals, and flasks with lids. Many of these examples are decorated using a number of techniques. These include impressed and incised designs, red slipping, burnishing, and, on the pedestals of some vessels, cut-out decorations.

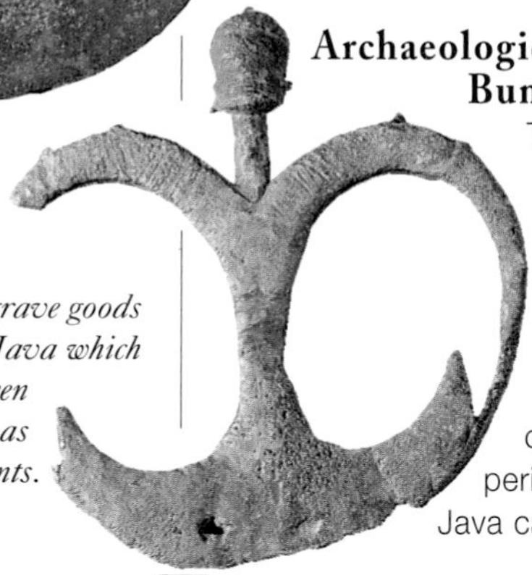

Bronze grave goods found in Java which may have been used as pendants.

Metal

H. R. van Heekeren concluded in 1958 that early metalworking in Indonesia began with the simultaneous introduction of both bronze and iron. He argued that the region did not pass through a copper or bronze age, for the oldest bronze objects yet found in Indonesia were found in association with iron artefacts.

The Javanese had the capability to produce metals in the proto-historic period. This has been proved by the discovery of clay moulds for metalworking at various sites in the Bandung area and at Pejaten, south of Jakarta, indicating that a group of specialised metal workers existed in protohistoric times. It is also highly probable that other occupational specialities including pottery-making developed in Javanese society in the protohistoric period.

Bronze drums of the Dong Son-style Heger I type have been found at nine sites in Java. These include: Cibadak, Cirebon, Pekalongan, Banyumas, Semarang, Kedu, Tanurejo, Rengel, and Lamongan. These drums are in the style associated with the art of north Vietnam, which flourished between 2,000 and 2,500 years ago. Such finds indicate that Java had established contact with mainland Southeast Asia by late prehistoric times. These drums and other bronze objects probably displayed the high social status of their owners.

Burial Customs

Javanese society in the early centuries AD had a relatively complex organisation. The burial system, which included both jar burial and the use of stone sarcophagi, reflects ranking or social stratification. Individuals buried in containers with grave goods probably had a different social identity from those buried without coffins. Jar burial was specifically associated with coastal Java. The most important burials of this type have been found at Anyer, west Java, and Plawangan, near Rembang, north central Java. It should be noted, however that jar burials are not unique to Java. Similar finds have been discovered in various coastal sites of Indonesia, including Gilimanuk in west Bali and Melolo in east Sumba. Burials utilising stone sarcophagi have been discovered in Bali, Sumatra, and Sulawesi.

Structures which archaeologists have interpreted as graves have been found at Cigugur and Kuningan, in west Java. However no skeletal materials were discovered in them. Artefacts such as quadrangular adzes, stone bracelets, and earthenware pottery were found there, and these may have been burial offerings. The fact that stone tools were still being made, or at least being used as offerings during the Early Metal period, suggests that they may have been valued as heirlooms.

In 1935, the archaeologist Th. a Th. van der Hoop reported finding a number of stone cist graves at sites at Kajar, Gunungabang, Sukaliman and Bleberan in the Gunungkidul area near the south coast of central Java. At Kajar and Bleberan, the skeletons in these graves were discovered in an extended position. They were accompanied by iron tools, bronze bracelets, and beads of glass and carnelian. Iron tools have also been discovered in various burial sites throughout Java. They consist mainly of iron axes, knives, sickles, swords, hoes and spearheads. These were probably used as agricultural implements, and as weapons.

Several stone-lined graves and sarcophagi have also been found near Bondowoso, east Java, mainly in the vicinity of Pakauman. One of these burials contained 9th century Chinese ceramics and is undoubtedly of a much later period than the prehistoric sites. This and similar finds demonstrate that prehistoric traditions such as burial in stone chambers persisted into the historic period, particularly in eastern Java.

Belief Systems

Protohistoric burial customs suggest belief in a world of ancestor spirits who were located on high places, especially on mountains. Megalithic remains in the form of *punden* (shrines associated with village founders), pre-Indic statuary, and menhirs (erect naturally shaped monoliths) have been found in various areas of Java. Terraced *punden* have been discovered in several parts of west Java. These sites include Arca Domas, Lebak Sibedug, Leles, Kuningan, and Pasirangin. Menhirs have also been discovered at Sukoliman, Gondang, and Playen, Gunung Kidul, Terjan and Rembang, central Java. The tradition of using terraced *punden* apparently continued throughout the classic period, to judge from such sites as Sukuh and Ceto, dating from the 15th century, when a probable archaising tendency brought this form of sanctuary back to prominence. It is not known how this practice survived during the centuries between late prehistory and the late classic era. Possibly some sanctuaries such as those on and around the summit of Mount Lawu, on the border between central and east Java, remained in use by the common people throughout the classic era at the same time as the upper classes were busily engaged in erecting temples in the Hindu and Buddhist traditions.

«Bronze axe found at Bandung. Although it looks like a weapon, its elegant blade is not strong enough for any practical use in warfare, nor could it be used as a tool for agricultural purposes. Its most likely use was as a ceremonial object.

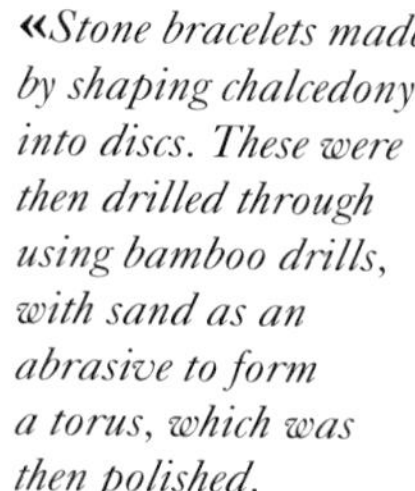

«Stone bracelets made by shaping chalcedony into discs. These were then drilled through using bamboo drills, with sand as an abrasive to form a torus, which was then polished.

PUNDEN NEAR THE SUMMIT OF MOUNT ARGAPURA, EAST JAVA

(After de Jonge)
This site displays aspects of both late prehistoric and late classic ceremonial structures of Java.

Late Prehistoric Bali

The distinctive character of Balinese culture within the general sphere of Indonesian culture was already well–established by the late prehistoric period. Late prehistoric Bali was marked by general similarities indicative of relative cultural homogenity and intra–island communication.

»» Prehistoric Burial Offerings. These heart–shaped bronze axes or spear points and the dimpled earthenware pot were found in Gilimanuk, site of a large prehistoric burial ground and village at Bali's western tip. With the introduction of Hinduism and Buddhism, the custom of burial was replaced by cremation.

Burial

One of ancient Bali's distinct features is manifested in its burial practice. Elaborate stone sarcophagi have been found at Margatengah, Batukaang, Pludu, Taked, Blanga, Plaga, and Tigawasa. Recent excavations at Gilimanuk in west Bali discovered two sarcophagus burials indicating that sarcophagus burial was practised in coastal areas despite the lack of tuffaceous rock. This discovery suggests that links existed between coastal and inland sites in Bali during the Early Metal Period. A different system of earthenware jar burials and burials without coffins has also been discovered. Skeletons were found in various positions, some buried alone, others in pairs, or with a later burial on top. The burial system may reflect social stratification, those buried in sarcophagi probably being of higher status. Small sarcophagi for infants at Celuk, Ambiarsari, and Busungbiu, suggest that status was obtained at birth.

Sarcophagus burials are the least common type of burial in Southeast Asia generally, and in Bali the size and overall shape of many of the sarcophagi are unique. The most common ones, which are small (84 to 134 centimetres), are designed for a single corpse, although very small examples containing bones from earlier burials are also in evidence. Many of the larger sarcophagi have rounded, disc–shaped, square, rectangular or septilateral–shaped knobs protruding from the longer sides. Although these knobs appear to be purely decorative, they may have had a functional purpose also, such as binding the two halves of the sarcophagus together while transporting the heavy load to its final resting place. Bernet Kempers has further suggested that by binding the two halves together, the dead would be prevented from disturbing the living. Belief that the dead possibly bear malevolent attitudes towards their descendants is widely attested by ethnographic sources from eastern Indonesia. Related customs included covering parts of the faces of corpses,

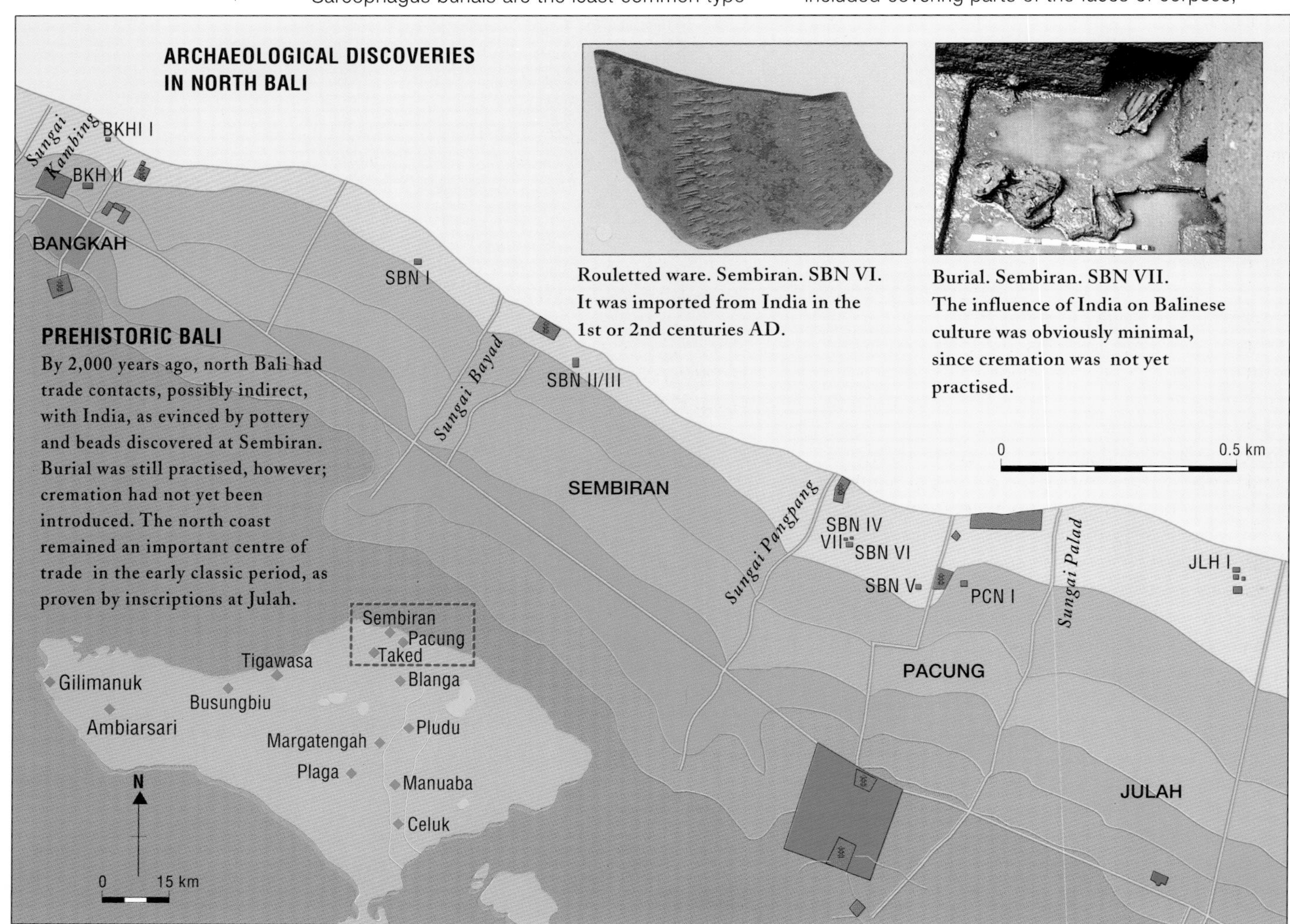

PREHISTORIC BALI

By 2,000 years ago, north Bali had trade contacts, possibly indirect, with India, as evinced by pottery and beads discovered at Sembiran. Burial was still practised, however; cremation had not yet been introduced. The north coast remained an important centre of trade in the early classic period, as proven by inscriptions at Julah.

Rouletted ware. Sembiran. SBN VI. It was imported from India in the 1st or 2nd centuries AD.

Burial. Sembiran. SBN VII. The influence of India on Balinese culture was obviously minimal, since cremation was not yet practised.

including the eyes, nose and mouth, with gold foil. Some sarcophagi have masks or human heads carved on them. One of the most unusual examples is the sarcophagus found at Taman Bali depicting a human head with the curved back of a zoo–anthropomorphic figure.

Grave Goods

Many sarcophagi appear to have been robbed of their contents before archaeologists were able to study them scientifically. At Gilimanuk grave goods included bronze wristlets, anklets and earrings. Also found, but possibly of a later date, were glass wristlets and beads, and simple tools made of shell. Metal artefacts and glass and carnelian beads found in burials both in Gilimanuk on the coast and in the hinterland indicate intra–island connections about 2,000 years ago. Crescentic and heart–shaped bronze axes are found both in the sarcophagi and the Gilimanuk burials, and were probably made in Bali though their moulds have not been found.

Early Metalworking and Trade

The best known and most impressive metal artefacts from this period are bronze kettledrums, the most famous being 'The Moon of Pejeng'. Other drums of this type have been found elsewhere in Indonesia. What is significant, however, is that the Balinese examples were undoubtedly made in Bali. Fragments of moulds which were used in the manufacture of the drums, and with patterns imprinted on them, have been found at Manuaba; a stone fragment possibly meant for the same purpose was found at Sembiran. Such enormous drums certainly would have had great social value for their possessors. This corresponds to the theory that the bronze drums of the Dong Son tradition functioned as status symbols. It should be remembered that no Heger I type drums have yet been discovered in Bali.

As neither copper nor tin, the raw materials for bronze making, are found in Bali, the existence of these huge bronzes indicates that there must have been intensive inter–island trade between Bali and other parts of Indonesia in prehistoric times. Indian pottery decorated with rouletted designs found at Sembiran and Pacung, north Bali, also attest to outside trade. These sherds were found at depths of 2.4 to 2.8 metres, and date from 2,000 years ago.

Agriculture

Archaeological research at Pacung recovered 2,000–year–old particles of rice husks. There is no firm evidence that irrigated rice was grown in Bali until the 9th century, when Balinese inscriptions refer to irrigation, but the importance of this technique in the earliest historic era suggests that it may have developed considerably earlier. The oldest Balinese inscriptions indicate that the Balinese classified land into a number of categories including irrigated and dry rice fields, dry fields for other crops, orchards, and grasslands. The mountain population may have practised dry land farming and exploited the forest for timber and game.

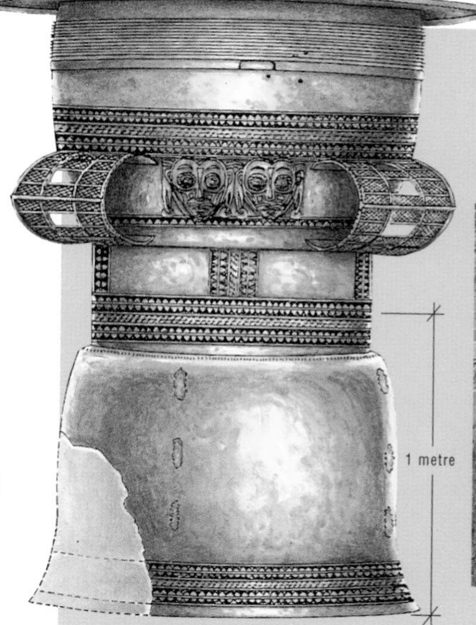

DETAIL OF THE "MOON OF PEJENG"

THE PEJENG DRUM

This artefact, the largest of its type found in Southeast Asia, is often called 'The Moon of Pejeng'. It differs from the Heger 1 type in that the tympanum protrudes about 25 centimetres beyond the body, and was probably cast separately from it. It may have been cast as recently as the first few centuries AD. Between its four, evenly spaced handles are unique decorative human mask motifs. These may symbolise a Balinese cosmic concept called *nawasanga*, connected with the nine divine guardians of the compass points.They possibly also had a protective function.

Excavations in Bali

The most important prehistoric site in Bali, Gilimanuk, was first investigated in 1963 by R.P. Soejono after pottery and Neolithic adzes were discovered nearby, at Cekik. He also found bones and pottery on an exposed cut through a beach ridge at Cekik. One of the most important types of artefact at Gilimanuk is the wide range of pottery, including jars, bowls, ewers and lids, decorated by impression, applique, red paint or slip, and burnishing. These earthenware vessels served as funerary goods for the hundred or so men, women and children whose skeletons were found at this site. The skulls of some were absent, and may have been preserved elsewhere prior to burial. The pottery is similar to the Sahuynh–Kalanay type found elsewhere in late prehistoric Southeast Asia.

Taman Bali sarcophagus, Pejeng Museum, Bedulu.

Late Prehistoric Culture in Sumatra

Sumatra has several attributes which would have encouraged civilisation to take root. These include a plethora of minerals, a variety of environments yielding a range of plant and animal products from fragrant wood to ivory, a long coast on the route between the Indian Ocean and South China Sea, and ethnic groups expert in exploiting different ecological niches, linked to each other through exchange relationships.

Stone slab tombs, Pasemah Plateau, South Sumatra.

Bronze figure from Bangkinang, South Sumatra (National Museum, Jakarta).

The Megalith Mystery

Sumatrans evolved the oldest complex of permanent symbolic art in Indonesia in the form of large sculpted stones, found not in lowlands near international trade routes, but in highland valleys. Groups in the highlands had contacts with the external world, but their art developed along its own unique path for centuries, before the taste in monumental art shifted to Indianised styles, whereupon centres of development moved to lowland riverbanks.

One of the more intractable problems in Indonesian archaeology concerns the interpretation of 'megalithic' remains. Monuments using large stones in a manner analogous to monuments found in prehistoric Europe have been built in Sumatra and elsewhere in Indonesia for over 2,000 years. The tradition has never died; it persists in many parts of Indonesia, including Nias, just off the west coast of Sumatra, as well as other islands such as Sumbawa in eastern Indonesia. Old theories postulated the idea of unilinear stylistic evolution, but they have been found inadequate. Dating megalithic material is extremely difficult. This fact, coupled with the variability of Sumatra's cultures and the lack of archaeological research there, makes it impossible to gain a clear picture of the role of these highly symbolic objects and sites in prehistoric Indonesia.

The Dong Son Style

We still have no information regarding such important subjects as the origins of Indonesian metalworking. Artefacts of the Dong Son style, which flourished between 2,000 and 2,500 years ago, are found over a wide arc of Southeast Asia, from Vietnam and Yunnan through the Malay Peninsula, Sumatra, Java, and the Lesser Sundas to northwest New Guinea. It is not known how or when they reached Sumatra, nor what role they played in the local cultures. The most distinctive Dong Son artefacts, bronze kettledrums, have been found in several locations in Sumatra. Our only reliable insight into the Sumatran cultures of late prehistory can be gleaned from the megalithic complex in Pasemah, south Sumatra, where a Dong Son connection can be established.

Another megalithic complex found several hundred kilometres away in west Sumatra may date from a different period, and possibly has an independent origin. These two areas illustrate a general and long-lasting Sumatran attitude toward the use of stone as a symbolic material, which may have persisted for centuries, separate from and parallel to the classic Indianised style.

Late Prehistoric Art of Pasemah, South Sumatra.

The Pasemah Plateau lies at an altitude of 600 metres. A large number of stone works of art lie around the plateau, on the slopes of Mounts Dempo and Gumai. Research was first conducted here during the colonial period, and since Independence Indonesian archaeologists have made many new discoveries. The most spectacular are subterranean chambers constructed of stone slabs, some with walls painted with pigments of yellow and red clay, charcoal, and haematite. Six such chambers have so far been discovered. The paintings depict complex themes. In one example, two black human figures with bent bodies and round eyes hold between them a drum of Dong Son style. Such drums are depicted in Pasemah stone carving as well, along with Dong Son-type swords, suggesting that this painting style flourished between 2,000–2,500 years ago. One stone chamber is decorated with a zoomorphic painting which may be a long-taloned owl. The owl is connected with death in Javanese culture. It has also been suggested that the animal

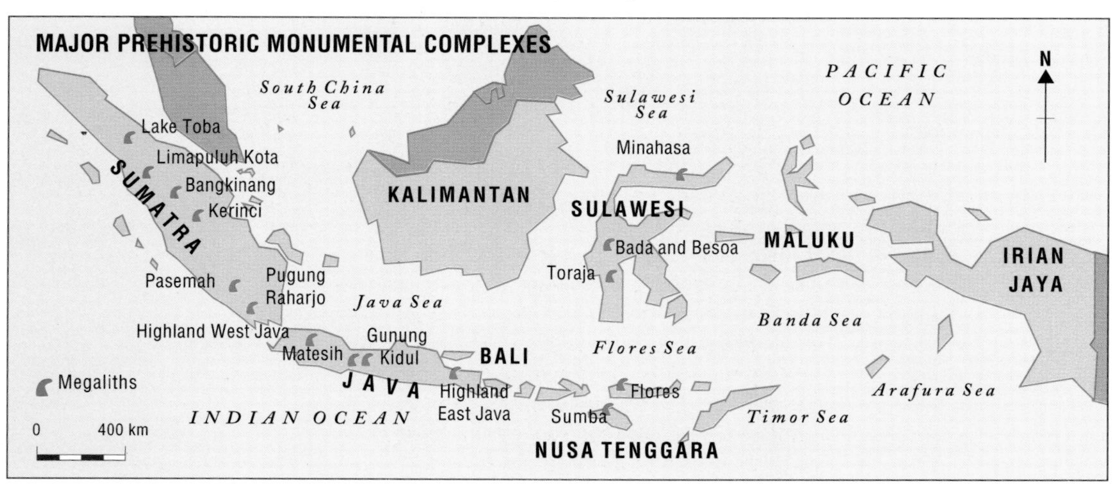

portrayed is a tiger; many tiger statues are found throughout this area.

Excavations carried out in 1991 revealed another stone chamber decorated with a painting of a zoomorphic head. The image with a wide mouth displaying sharp teeth and fangs may depict a supernatural rather than real being, perhaps analogous to a belief held by some groups in Nias regarding the *Lasara* or supernatural animal which protects humans.

Few artefacts have been discovered in these chambers other than corroded iron fragments and beads. No bones have been found, though it is believed that these chambers were tombs.

Another form of Pasemah's ancient art consists of carved boulders depicting humans seated on one another's shoulders, crocodiles, and heroic men grappling with buffalo, boar, elephants, or serpents. These are assumed to be the oldest stone sculptures yet discovered in Indonesia. Their functions are unknown. They may symbolise myths of powerful ancestors. Associated objects include stone 'mortars' which may have been used for agricultural rituals.

Two Dong Son drums found at Padang Peri, Bengkulu, west of Pasemah, suggest that the late prehistoric people from Pasemah had some links to the western coast. Folklore also preserves legends concerning relationships between Pasemah and the kingdom of Sriwijaya which evolved in the eastern lowlands in the 7th century AD. Pasemah probably formed a prehistoric centre of cultural development which supplied a necessary precondition enabling a sophisticated political and economic centre of Sriwijaya to develop at Palembang, to which Pasemah is linked by river.

Batu Tagak of West Sumatra

Megalithic remains in this area were reported in the early 20th century, but archaeological research only began in 1984. Hundreds of standing stones (*Batu Tagak* in Minang) are found in the Limapuluh Kota Regency. Some are plain, others carved with geometric and curvilinear designs. Local traditions assert that the decorated stones were used as burial markers for men, the plain ones denoting female graves. Excavation has demonstrated that skeletal remains do indeed lie beneath the stones. However, decoration on the stones is not correlated with the sex of the individuals buried beneath them. The skeletons are oriented southeast–northwest, with the heads at the northwest, beneath the stones.

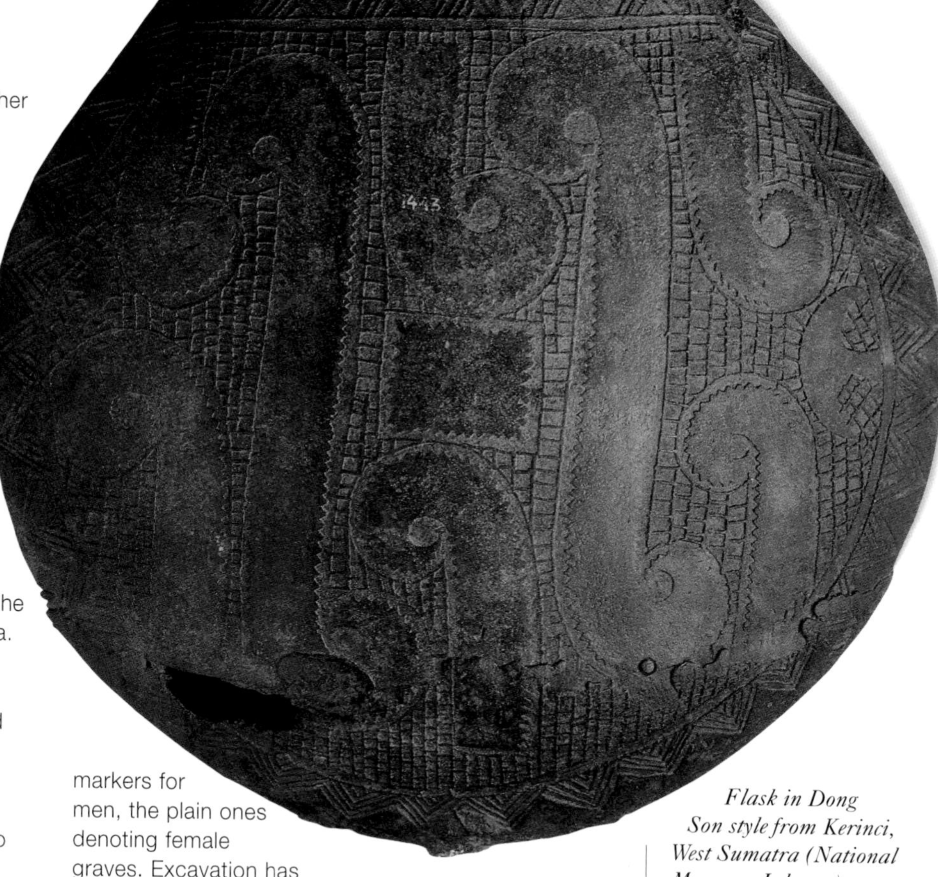

The skeletal material shows that, like the modern Balinese and most ancient Indonesians, the people of the West Sumatran megalithic tradition filed their teeth. The average age of death among those buried in the megalithic graves varied between 35 and 50 years. The burials resemble those of the Islamic period in that no burial offerings have been discovered: the corpses were laid in a chamber dug sideways, in an extended position, and were wedged in place. This raises the possibility that these burials date from the period of cultural transition when Islam began to penetrate this region, about 1500. However the burials are not oriented toward Mecca, but instead toward nearby Mount Sago, where some local inhabitants still believe that the spirits of their ancestors reside. Thus the age and duration of the West Sumatra complex remains a mystery. Other megalithic sites in west Sumatra are associated with 14th-century inscriptions. At the site of Kuburajo, near Batusangkar, three large stones decorated with pre-classic motifs are arranged to form backrests for stone seats. At the same site is an inscription erected by Adityavarman, who ruled from about 1343 to the 1370s. Such sites which combine megalithic and classic traits suggest that the West Sumatran megaliths represent several periods, rather than a single historical stage.

Flask in Dong Son style from Kerinci, West Sumatra (National Museum, Jakarta).

Zoomorphic painting in stone chamber, Pasemah, South Sumatra.

Prehistoric Sumatran Sculpture, Pasemah, South Sumatra.

THE PROTOHISTORIC ERA OF INDONESIA

The Protohistoric period began with the first inscriptions to be carved in Indonesia. These date from the late 4th or early 5th century. Technically history, the study of written documents, begins at this time. Unfortunately, for the first few centuries after Indonesians began to inscribe words on stone, this practice was relatively rare, and the topics dealt with in the inscriptions are limited to records of religious acts and prayers. Only in the late 7th and early 8th centuries do indigenous inscriptions begin to supply enough details to enable historians to piece together a coherent narrative of political and economic affairs in Indonesia. During the protohistoric period from 400 to 700 AD, we must rely largely on archaeological data and foreign sources to construct an image of conditions in the archipelago.

The protohistoric era is thus a transitional period when Indian artistic motifs and literary genres were becoming familiar to Indonesians. Indigenous practices and art styles continued to exist alongside them. The ship reliefs above, from the Lau Biang, North Sumatra, symbolise early Indonesian maritime exploration.

Bronze Buddha from Sikendeng, Sulawesi, 2nd to 5th centuries.

Visnu statue found at Cibuaya in west Java, 6th or 7th century.

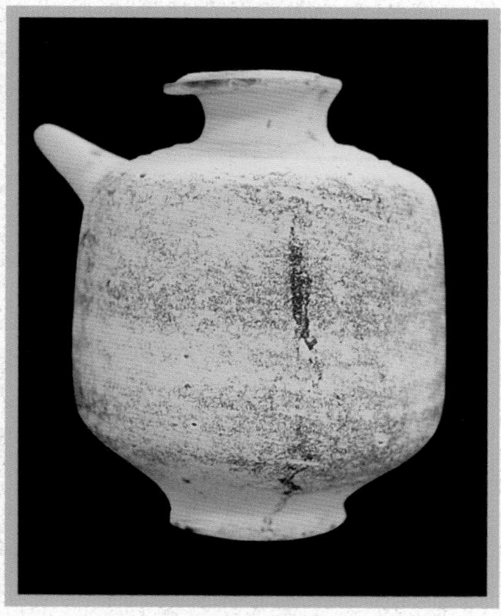

Spouted vessel found in Kerawang, west Java, possibly imported from elsewhere in Southeast Asia in the protohistoric period.

INDONESIA AT THE DAWN OF HISTORY

The oldest surviving Indonesian document, from Kutai in East Kalimantan, is dated around 400 AD. Writing appeared in the western part of the archipelago shortly thereafter. Inscriptions scattered from the highlands of southwest Java to the coast near Jakarta, outline a Hindu kingdom called Taruma. In the 7th century the appearance of numerous inscriptions in south Sumatra heralds the birth of the Buddhist kingdom of Sriwijaya.

Most early texts were undoubtedly written on perishable material. The production of inscribed stone monuments represented a specialised literary activity connected with political situations. These texts provide few details of political and religious history. Most information about the subjects must be inferred indirectly. These sources are written in a script derived from South Asia. Historians have long puzzled over the significance of this fact, and the subsequent appearance in Indonesia of South Asian style sculpture and architecture. It was originally assumed that direct Indian colonisation was responsible, but later analysts have focused their attention on interaction between Indian merchants and religious teachers of both South Asia and Indonesia as stimuli for the spread of Indianised culture and writing.

The inscriptions give abundant evidence of local initiatives in several parts of Indonesia, taken by a ruling class which found it useful to create more symbols to mark different levels of a social hierarchy in an increasingly complicated status system. The dispersed locations of the early inscriptions are evidence that mere proximity to India or to trade routes was neither a necessary nor a sufficient cause for writing's appearance in Indonesia, nor, in more general terms, for the formation of complex societies. As time passed, the gradual tendency of inscriptions to cluster around the trade routes does highlight the fact that, as social complexity increased, trade became an important factor in accentuating this process.

The oldest inscriptions from Kutai seem to have been a false dawn, since no other ancient inscriptions and few other remains have been found there. In west Java, the kingdom of Taruma was followed by a later phase in which the centre of Javanese civilisation moved eastward. At the end of the 7th century, Sriwijaya, a kingdom centred in southeast Sumatra, attained control over the Straits of Melaka, the main artery of maritime trade between two great mainland civilisations, India and China. This was to become Indonesia's first long-lived kingdom with influence over a broad area of coastline.

Phases of Early Indonesian History

In the early 20th century the Dutch scholar N.J. Krom introduced the term "Classic" to designate the period from the beginning of Indonesian history to the conversion to Islam. He divided the classic era into the Central Javanese and East Javanese phases. This periodization continued to be widely used among archaeologists, but disputes exist regarding both the appropriateness of the terms and their precise meanings.

Intricate carving at royal graveyard at Air Mata, Madura, early Islamic period. The tombstones of this site are unique; they are broad flat slabs rather than tall thin monoliths like other Muslim grave markers. The early Islamic art of north Java and Madura forms a transitional phase between Late Classic and Muslim art, often termed pesisir (coastal) style. The material used for carving was often soft limestone such as in this example.

Research and Evidence

Architectural remains of *candi* show that in the early historic period some Indonesian societies conducted a dialogue with sources of knowledge, especially religious, and other cultural elements originating outside their local areas. Although cultural remains bear marks of foreign influence, inscriptions and literary sources depict a society which evolved on the basis of indigenous values and norms formed before Hindu and Buddhist influences arrived. The search for the factor which stimulated the development of early historic Indonesian societies, formerly focused on discontinuity and the appearance of non-Indonesian elements, has now shifted its emphasis to continuity between historic and prehistoric elements.

Periodization based on clear criteria for the course of ancient Indonesian history still requires further research. At this moment, the channel in which ancient history flowed is still marked by historians' maps of royal dynasties. This method obviously contains a weakness in that it cannot present an integrated narrative. The connecting thread linking times and places still needs to be identified. Conventionally, the antiquities of Java were divided into the Central Javanese and Eastern Javanese periods. It is now felt that this division is inappropriate because there are examples of temples in east Java, such as Candi Badut, which date from the early period, and conversely there are temples in central Java, such as Candi Sukuh, which belong to the very Late Classic. To overcome this Soekmono uses the terms Early Classic style and Late Classic style, based on architectural decorative motifs. Early Classic, which lasted from *circa* 700–900 AD, is typified by strong emphasis on horizontal mouldings and particularly in the example of Hindu temples, the use of tapering, multi-storeyed roofs. Major decorative elements were placed at the corners and mid-points of each tier of the roof mouldings. In the Late Classic style, which began in the 13th century, the use of perspective effects was taken much further than before. The temple bodies were somewhat decreased in size, and the temple bases became higher. Roofs became even taller with many more tiers, and much smaller corner ornaments. These towers were also very unstable and tended to fall down. The Late Classic style first appears with Candi Kidal, which preserves no elements at all of the Early Classic style. There is an unexplained gap of over 300 years between the Early and Late Classic styles of architecture.

CANDI MOULDINGS (BUILT AROUND AD 800)
Mouldings on base of Candi Arjuna (early 700s) and Candi Kalasan (*ca.* 800). The important difference between them is the appearance of the semi-circular moulding➡, a chronological marker which distinguishes earlier from later temples of Early Classic Java.

Candi Arjuna

Candi Kalasan

Stylistic Changes

Because of the absence of inscribed dates, art historians and archaeologists have had to rely on stylistic changes to date Javanese works of art. A number of fixed elements were found on most Javanese temples. These standard elements however did not remain

GEDONG SONGO: An example of the Early Classic style of architecture, built in the mid-8th century in north central Java. The spires on this temple are sometimes called false lingga (lingga *semu*). The elaborate bases for these spires accentuate the horizontal roof tiers. The temple has a projecting vestibule with a separate roof, another Early Classic feature.

CANDI JAWI: A typical example of Late Classic architecture, built in east Java around 1300 AD and repaired after a lightning bolt struck its pinnacle in the mid 14th century. The roof is decorated with antefixes on a much smaller scale, with proportions which accentuate its height.

static throughout the long Classical period; they gradually evolved through certain stages.

The technique of seriation is well established in archaeology and art history, though it is subject to certain complications. It is assumed that most art motifs follow a similar trajectory, from the evolution of a simple introductory form through a phase of increasing elaboration to a peak of complexity, and then through a period of declining popularity during which the motif is again simplified, before it becomes extinct. There is, however, the problem of archaism in which an old motif is revived after a period of neglect. It is also common for some areas to retain art forms which have been abandoned elsewhere.

One of the main elements exploited to date Javanese classical art has been the mouldings of the temple foot. These were complicated patterns of flat, semi-circular, and bell-shaped projections which underwent a well-defined process of evolution over time. Another motif was the *kala* head found over the entrances to temples and above niches for statues. Often the *kala* was combined with the *makara.* The *kala* heads of the Early Classic period were depicted without a lower jaw, in conformity with Indian literary tradition. In the Late Classic the *kala* was often given a lower jaw, and portrayed in an increasingly stylised manner. The *makara* vanished.

Sumatra and Bali

Neither Sumatra nor Bali can be fitted into this framework. Bali has its own brand of architecture seen in the candi form of buildings carved into cliffs, for example at Gunung Kawi, from the late 11th century. The candi bodies of Gunung Kawi display similarities to the Early Classic of Java, while the roofs are more like those of the Late Classic. The overall impression of Sumatran classic architecture is reminiscent of Javanese Late Classic style. However, Sumatran candi still have *makara* decorations at the bottom of the stairs, an element found in Javanese Early Classic.

Social Evolution

When inscriptions first make their appearance in Indonesian history, between the 6th and 8th centuries, they depict a culture that already contained both Hindu and Buddhist elements, and that was in the process of consolidation around a few main centres of power. Apparently the ancestors previously associated with power had been replaced by gods. Although power was becoming centralised, it is quite possible that real authority still depended on the voluntary submission of the populace.

Dynastic Formation

In the next stage it became possible for dynasties to form. In central Java candi associated with rajas or dynasties became increasingly common. The ruling class clearly appears at this time, distinct from the main population. The mass of society was still governed by the traditional system in which leaders were only *primus inter pares*, resolving affairs according to local custom.

Early Classic relief carving from Borobudur displaying the naturalistic, rounded style of the Early Classic period.

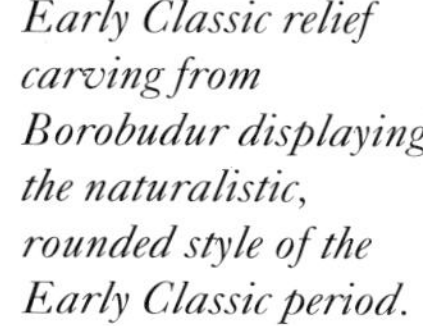

Then something happened which cannot be satisfactorily explained: the capital moved from central to east Java. A variety of causes may have been responsible; volcanic activity in central Java, increasing population and trade in the east. This shift was accompanied by social evolution. Governmental organisation became stronger, including provision for communication between court and villages. Complex bureaucracy arose.

«Sendang Duwur Gateway, east Java, part of a 15th century Muslim grave complex in which pre-Islamic motifs such as the makara (a sculptured form of mythical beast or sea monster) are still visible at the stairways.

The End of Antiquity

During the period between 1500 and 1800 various outside powers were beginning to extend their presence in the region: Europeans, West Asians, and East Asians. The most prominent feature of this period is the spread of Islam. Areas which had previously been unimportant emerged due to their role in expanding trade and spreading Islam.

Islam brought with it a great number of social changes. However many of the cultural traits that had been formed in ancient times were not immediately replaced. In areas where Indian influence had never appeared, social forms which had developed uninterrupted since prehistory continued to evolve, however sometimes in adaptation to Islam. Despite the great number of external influences, local cultural evolution has continued along different paths in various parts of Indonesia through Independence and right up until the present.

Gunung Kawi, Bali. This series of rock-cut temples in relief is unique in Indonesia. Some bear short inscriptions in a script which suggests that they were carved in the late 11th century. Stone caskets for foundation deposits were found with them.

Early Trade Patterns

Indonesians began to conduct long-distance sea trade in prehistoric times, but little information is available to clarify its nature. Circumstantial evidence of this activity takes such forms as gold artefacts in Java where gold sources are few and were probably not exploited in prehistoric times, and locally-cast bronze drums in islands such as Bali where copper and tin are not found. Romano-Indian rouletted ware in Bali, and a reference to Java in a 3rd century BC source, tell us that Indonesians were also in regular contact with India.

Coral beads are important early trading items between Indonesia and China.

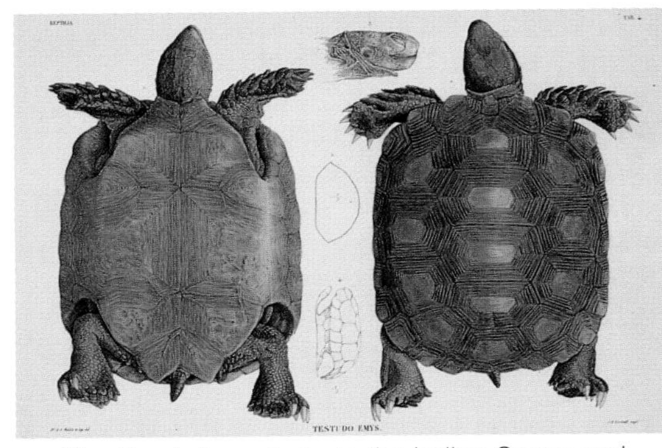

Tortoise-shell was an Indonesian product imported by China.

Redrawn medieval map of Southeast Asia; the original was itself based on Greek sources of the 2nd century AD.

Maps and Written Evidence

Early evidence for Indonesian traffic in the Indian Ocean comes from a Greek astronomer named Claudius Ptolemaeus who lived in Alexandria, Egypt, in the 1st century AD. He wrote *Guide to Geography*, the oldest known manuscript of which contains tables of latitudes and longitudes of places. It is not known when this table was compiled; its final form was probably given to it by a Byzantine monk around 1000 AD. Maps attached to the manuscript may have been made even later, around 1300 AD, so we cannot be sure that the ancient Greek astronomer knew everything in the manuscript bearing his name. It seems likely that he had at least some knowledge of western Indonesia. South of a peninsula called the Aurea Chersonnesus are names such as Barosae, Sinda, Sabadiba, and Iabadium. These probably correspond to Barus, an important port in northwest Sumatra; Sunda, west Java; Suvarnadvipa, the ancient Sanskrit name for Sumatra; and Java.

The Greeks' proximity to the Indian Ocean and their proclivity for sea trade led them to the Indian subcontinent, where they established trading colonies in the 1st century AD. Some of the information in Claudius Ptolemaeus' *Geography* could have come from Graeco-Roman traders, who are also mentioned in Indian sources.

Another source from the early Mediterranean is the *Sailor's Guide to the Erythraean Sea*, the old Greek term for the Indian Ocean. *The Sailor's Guide* mentions some 27 ports where foreign trade was conducted according to a uniform set of commercial practices, including the levying of customs duties. Graeco-Roman merchants did not sail east of India, but the *Sailor's Guide* describes great ships coming from the direction of India carrying cargoes of pepper and other goods.

Trade with India

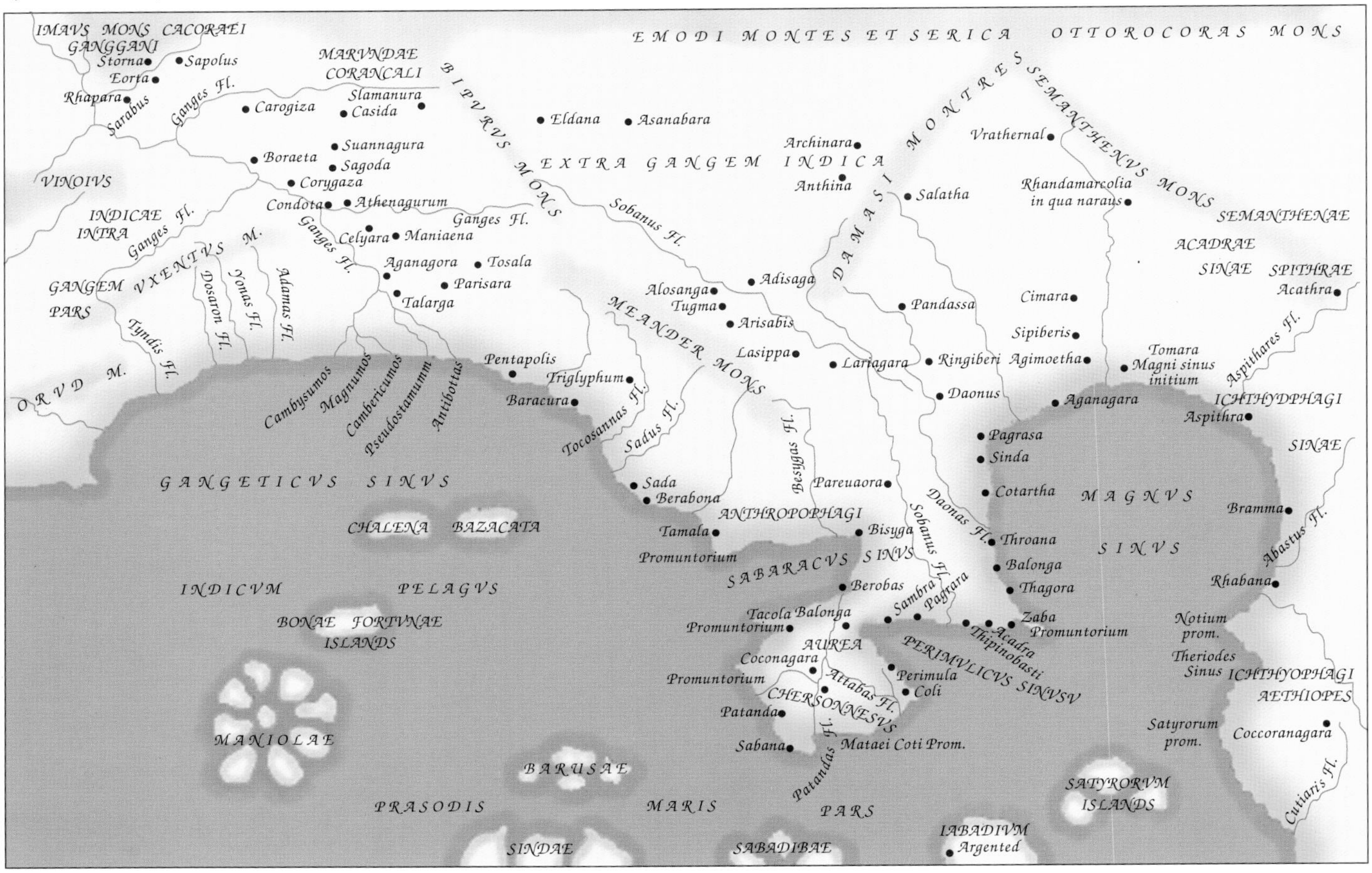

Ancient Indian sources portray Java and Sumatra as lands where junior princes might go to seek their fortunes, though they contain no details of specific people or places in Indonesia. Indian interest in Indonesia surged around the 2nd century AD at the same time that gold in India was in short supply due to the exhaustion of Indian mines and disturbances along the overland routes bringing gold from Central Asia. The Graeco-Romans paid for their spices and other purchases in India with gold and silver. Indian stone and glass beads may have reached the archipelago in the late centuries BC.

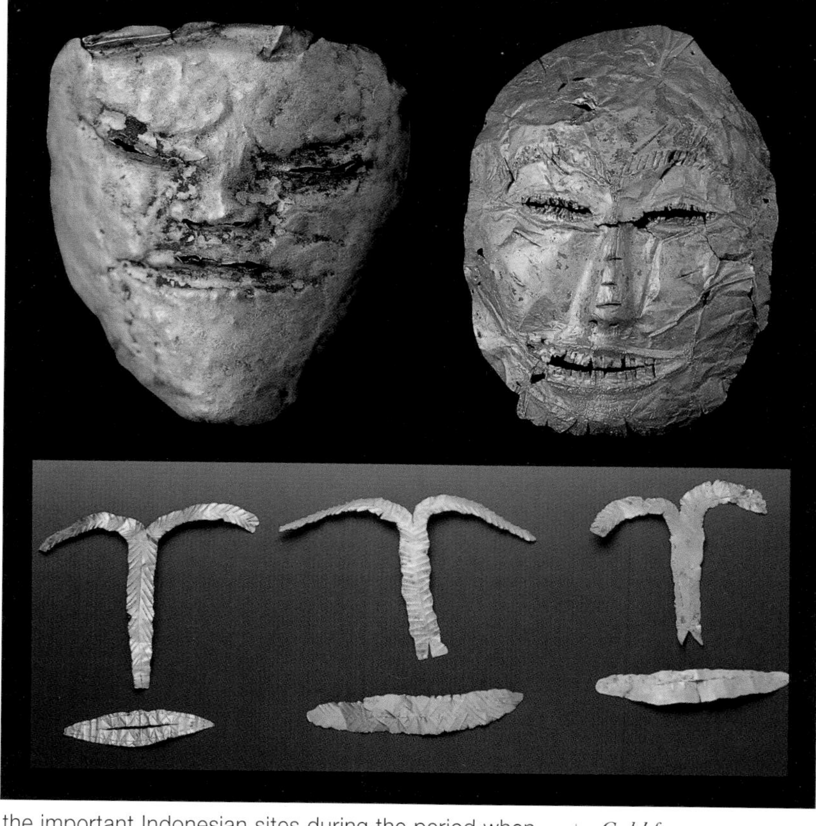

Gold face covers (ca. 500 BC–500 AD) from East Java, part of a prehistoric tradition of burial. Gold to make such artefacts was imported to Java in late prehistoric times.

Indonesian Commerce

Linguistic evidence indicates that Indonesians reached Madagascar by the early part of the first millennium AD. Their language includes few words of Sanskrit origin, suggesting that their ancestors migrated to the island before their language had absorbed much Indian influence. The Roman historian Pliny described people who brought cinnamon to East Africa after a long voyage across the Indian Ocean. They took back in exchange glass, bronze, clothing, brooches, armlets, and necklaces.

It used to be assumed that Indians played the active role in stimulating early Indonesian commerce, an assumption now shown to be false. The Greek descriptions of major trading ships as non-Indian, the evidence that Indonesian rather than Indian migrants populated Madagascar, and slightly later Chinese sources, all reinforce the conclusion that Southeast Asian ships formed the backbone of the transport system in the early Indian Ocean. Indonesian commodities such as cloves were reaching the north Chinese court of the Han 2,000 years ago, Rome by 70 AD, and Mesopotamia perhaps as early as 1,700 BC.

Trade with China

Direct trade with China began between 250 and 400 AD. Chinese missions were sometimes sent abroad to search for 'rare and precious objects' for the court. During the Han dynasty (206 BC–220 AD) the south coast of China was incorporated into the empire. The imperial government took control of the luxury trade of Canton before 100 BC. Official envoys were sent abroad by the Wu and Wei courts after the Han fell. Envoys from Indonesia began to visit China, possibly to ensure the continued recognition of their trading rights. A Chinese account from 414 AD is the first proof that ships were sailing directly from Indonesia to China. The main commodities exchanged were pearls and tortoise shell for the emperor's own use, and incense and rare perfumes for religious ceremonies, due to the increasing popularity of Mahayana Buddhism.

Unfortunately most of the materials involved in early Indonesian trade were perishables such as spices, clothing, incense and birds' feathers. The locations of the important Indonesian sites during the period when Indonesia first forged links with India and China are therefore largely unknown. We can conclude that oceanic trade and communications had been in existence for several hundred years before any important cultural changes occurred in Indonesia. Trade routes provide channels along which commodities, people and ideas travel; but trade alone is not a sufficient explanation for the developments which led to the Classical Period in Indonesia. Independent social evolution must also have been occurring which laid the foundation for the classical art of the 7th and later centuries.

Trade within Southeast Asia must have been occurring long before Indonesians began trading with India and China. Early Chinese sources suggest the coasts of the South China Sea were linked by an active trading network. The kingdom of Funan, at the southern tip of Vietnam, had strong connections with India by the 1st century AD. Probably Indonesian sailors were among the merchants to be found there. Historical and archaeological evidence suggest that some of the commodities exchanged among the various Southeast Asian parties to the trade in late pre-historic times were metals: iron, copper, tin, and gold. Various parts of Indonesia possessed supplies of these metals which were exploited in antiquity for coinage and status goods.

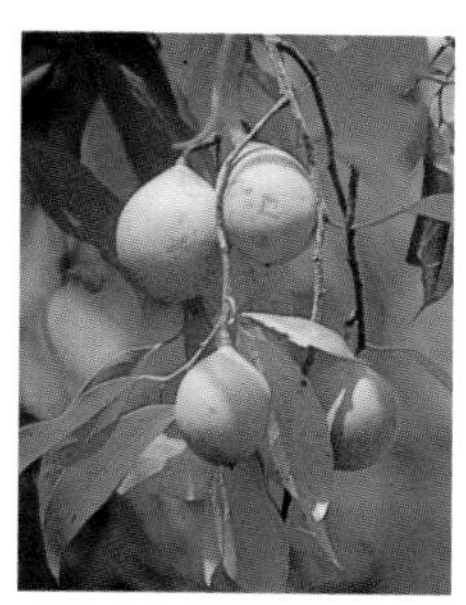

Nutmegs and cloves from Maluku were traded from an early period. Until 1800 cloves grew only in Maluku. In the Chinese court 2,000 years ago, petitioners admitted to the emperor's presence had to chew cloves first to sweeten the breath.

«The search for cloves and nutmeg stimulated the early European voyages of discovery.

Early Indonesian Inscriptions

Early inscriptions written in a script designated as 'Pallava' (after the name of a South Indian dynasty which issued inscriptions in this type of script) and dated from the 4th to the 8th century AD have been found in many parts of Southeast Asia. As the inscriptions before the 7th century bear no dates, only approximate ages, based on palaeographic comparisons with dated examples in South India, can be given for them.

Tarumanagara Inscription, west Java. The earliest known kingdom in Java, Taruma, during the 5th century had its capital somewhere in the Bogor region.

Kutai Inscription. The oldest surviving written documents from Indonesia, dated about 350–400 AD, are seven inscribed stones from East Kalimantan. They record the sacrifice of animals in a ritual characteristic of archaic Hindu religion. Why the first inscriptions in Indonesia should have been erected in such a remote area, far from known trade routes linking the archipelago with India, is still a mystery.

The Language of Early Inscriptions

The earliest inscriptions discovered in Indonesia are written not in a local language, but in Sanskrit. Sanskrit was the ancient language of learning throughout India, used mainly by scholars and religious specialists.The local Indian languages such as Tamil appear to have made little impact in Indonesia. This suggests that the process of adoption of Indian cultural elements proceeded mainly as a conscious intellectual exercise rather than through frequent contact at the middle level of society, between such groups as merchants or warriors.

Inscribed Pillars of Kutai

In the lower Mahakam river valley of east Kalimantan, seven stone pillars described as *yupa,* to which sacrificial animals were tethered, have been found. They are inscribed with Sanskrit verses which commemorate lavish gifts. These gifts consisted mainly of cattle, but also other animals such as horses, given to brahmins as rewards for the performance of rituals on behalf of a king named Mulavarman. These rituals appear to have been characteristic of archaic Hindu practices in India. The script of these pillars points to a date in the second half of the 4th century AD, but a genealogy included in the text indicates that the kingdom may have been founded half a century earlier. No information about the origin of Mulavarman's kingdom, which is one of the earliest in Southeast Asia, is given. It also remains a mystery as to why the first inscriptions in Indonesia were erected in an area which in succeeding centuries was far off the beaten paths of international communication, and where few other traces of classical art have been found.

Carved Boulders from Taruma

The kingdom of Taruma, comprising part of west Java, flourished under King Purnavarman during the 5th century. The name of this king is recorded on a number of inscribed stones, one of which was found on a large boulder in the middle of a streambed. The king's footprints were engraved on the boulder, and may indicate conquest or occupation of the area. In ancient India, footprints were commonly used as a symbol of divine beings. In the text of the inscription, King Purnavarman compares his footprints to those of the Hindu god Visnu. One stone shows the footprints of the royal elephant, which was presumably transported there from Sumatra since no wild elephants have existed in Java since prehistoric times. The inscription grandiosely compares the footprints to those of the mythical elephant Airawata, the mount of Indra, king of the Vedic deities. By implication the king of west Java was of the same stature as Indra. Purnavarman's principal fame rests, however, on a canal which he had built to the north–east of Jakarta. It was probably intended for drainage of the area which was subject to flooding.

West Malaysia

Though this region is situated outside the modern boundaries of Indonesia, during this early period the people of west Malaysia were undoubtedly so closely related to those of Indonesia that any separation would be artificial. There do exist a small number of Sanskrit inscriptions from Kedah, west Malaysia, dating from the 5th century AD. Perhaps the most interesting of these are two stelae with superficially engraved *stupa.* On one of these, brief Sanskrit inscriptions mention a sea captain named Buddhagupta, inhabitant of a place called 'Red Earth'. He was a merchant and also a pious Buddhist. This is the earliest evidence of the presence of Buddhism in Southeast Asia. Kedah, which is mentioned by name by the famous Chinese Buddhist pilgrim I–Ching, circa 670 AD, came under

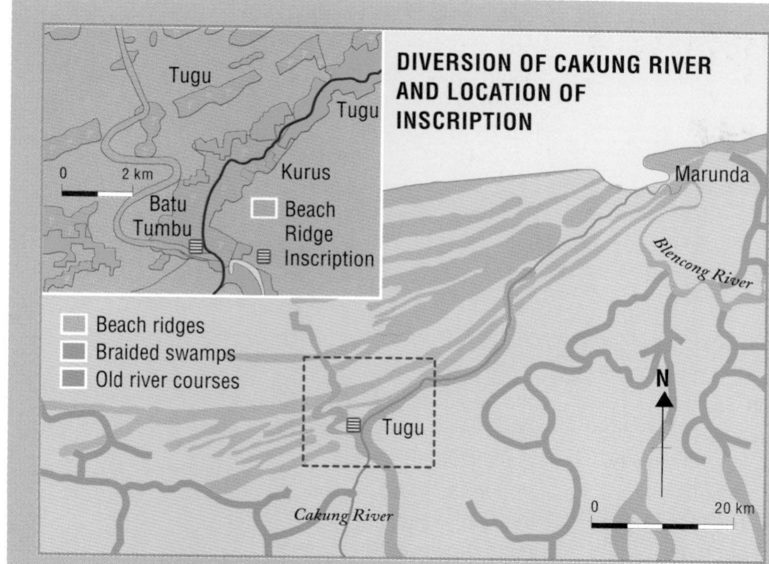

PURNAVARMAN'S INSCRIPTION AT TUGU

The Tugu inscription was found at the junction of the present course of the Cakung River with a probable ancient course, now silted in. The topographic map of the Tugu area of Jakarta with its particular configuration of beach ridges marking former shore lines, levees or banks of older rivers, and modern creeks, shows that the older coastlines have been cut away by wave erosion in the Marunda area to the northeast.

"Formerly the Candrabhaga dug by the king of kings, the strong-armed Guru, after having reached the famous town, went into the ocean. In the 22nd year of his increasing, prosperous reign the illustrious Purnavarman – who shineth forth by prosperity and virtue and who is the banner of the rulers of men – hath dug the charming river Gomati pure of water, – long six thousand, one hundred and twenty two bows, dug in 21 days, having begun it in the bright half of the 8th lunar day of the dark half of Phalguna and completed it on the 13th lunar day of Caitra. That river which had torn asunder the camping ground of the Grandfather and Royal Sage, now floweth forth, after having been endowed by the Brahmins with a gift of a thousand kine".

the control of the Sumatran kingdom of Sriwijaya before the end of the 7th century.

Other inscriptions have been discovered in the same general area. These include two Buddhist verses in Sanskrit found at Bukit Meriam. In addition seven stone fragments, part of yet another Sanskrit inscription, have been unearthed at Cerok Tekun.

Sriwijaya

The first great Indonesian empire emerged before 683 AD, the date of its earliest inscription, near Palembang, south Sumatra. By then Sriwijaya was already building up the empire which was to dominate the Straits of Malacca and adjoining areas for centuries. The earliest inscriptions of Sriwijaya, 683, 684 and 686 AD, are the oldest in Old Malay. The first two were found in the vicinity of present-day Palembang, the last on Bangka island. They are the first evidence of the presence in Southeast Asia of Mahayana Buddhism, which became the prevalent form of Buddhism in Indonesia. One of the Palembang inscriptions is a pious vow pronounced by the king that he will pursue to its end the arduous path ultimately leading to the attainment of the perfection of Buddhahood.

The inscription of Bangka is a lengthy imprecation directed against potential rebels and traitors. This oath of loyalty was engraved when the fleet of Sriwijaya passed along the coast of Bangka on the way to west Java, an area not loyal to Sriwijaya. A more elaborate, but undated, version of this imprecation was found at Sabukingking, Palembang. This 7th century inscription was meant both to be read and to be used. Water was poured over the heads of the seven naga, or water spirits, carved at the top of the stone. Naga were important in Sumatran religion. According to a Chinese 7th century visitor, these creatures were worshipped. This practice was probably a survival of prehistoric religion; similar references relating to the importance of naga at the dawn of history are found in Chinese references to several areas of Southeast Asia. The water then flowed over the words chiselled into the stone, and was collected from the spout at the bottom. The inscription states that whosoever drank the 'imprecation water' and subsequently broke his oath of loyalty would be poisoned by the water of the curse. The practice of 'drinking oaths' was common throughout Southeast Asia, and has persisted until recent times. Other versions of the same oath have been found at Karang Berahi, far upstream in modern Jambi, and at two sites in the far south of the island. This distribution is suggestive of the extent of Sriwijaya's control.

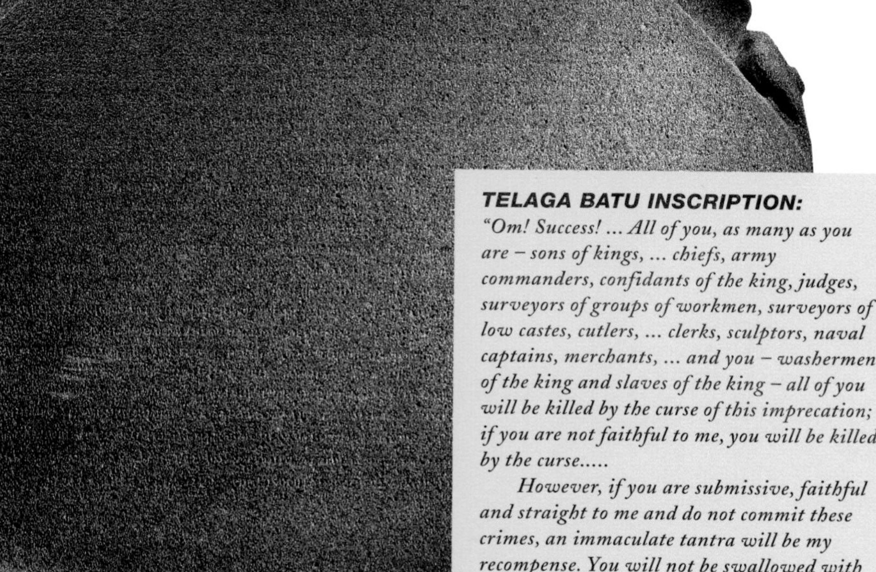

Telaga Batu Inscription (National Museum, Jakarta), from Sabukingking, Palembang. This 7th-century inscription, composed by a Sriwijayan ruler records an oath of loyalty. The motifs atop the stone symbolise a seven-headed naga, symbol of water and fertility.

TELAGA BATU INSCRIPTION:

"Om! Success! ... All of you, as many as you are – sons of kings, ... chiefs, army commanders, confidants of the king, judges, surveyors of groups of workmen, surveyors of low castes, cutlers, ... clerks, sculptors, naval captains, merchants, ... and you – washermen of the king and slaves of the king – all of you will be killed by the curse of this imprecation; if you are not faithful to me, you will be killed by the curse.....

However, if you are submissive, faithful and straight to me and do not commit these crimes, an immaculate tantra will be my recompense. You will not be swallowed with your children and wives. ... Eternal peace will be the fruit produced by this curse which is drunk by you. ...

The Early Archaeology of Sriwijaya

During the 6th and 7th centuries, steady growth in maritime trade made a profound impact on Southeast Asia's burgeoning kingdoms. The southeast coast of Sumatra became the centre of Indonesia's most advanced early kingdom, which exploited trade routes between the Indian Ocean, the South China Sea and the Spice Islands.

Votive stupika made of clay from a bronze mould found at Palembang.

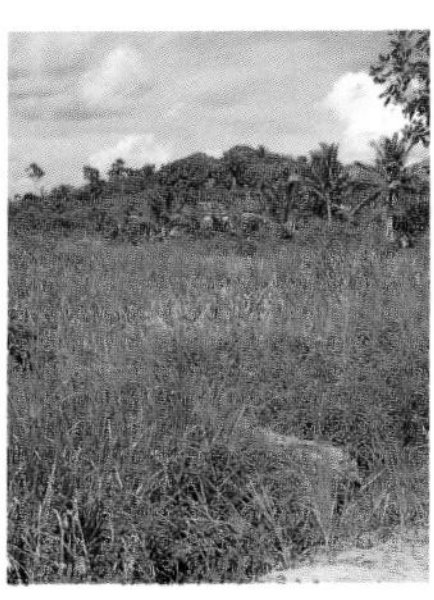

Seguntang Hill, Palembang, site of probable Sriwijayan Buddhist monuments.

The Rise of Sriwijaya

Asian maritime trade prospered at the expense of the overland Silk Route between China, the Middle East and India. The reunification of China under the Sui and Tang dynasties in the 7th century, and the demise of long-distance Persian trade, benefited the emerging Southeast Asian kingdoms. A huge Chinese market was suddenly opened up to Southeast Asian commodities, and Southeast Asia also began to supply many goods previously obtained from India .

Several small kingdoms that existed in Java and Sumatra, in the early 7th century, which were already probably spearheads of intense commercial activity, sent a flurry of embassies to China. After 670 AD, however, the fever suddenly abated and only one kingdom, identified as *Shi–li–fo–shih* by Chinese sources, continued to send embassies. Chinese texts described this kingdom as one of the major trading operators of the South Seas. Camphor, oleo–resins, and benzoin from Sumatra and the Malay Peninsula became standard commodities in trading with China alongside spices and pepper. Simultaneously the name of this polity appeared in various texts written by Chinese Buddhist monks. On the way to India to collect canonical texts needed to codify the Chinese practice of this religion, these monks travelled on Southeast Asian–owned ships, and often stopped off in *Shi–li–fo–shih*, sometimes staying there for years to learn Sanskrit, while residing in a large religious community of local and Indian colleagues. The famous Chinese monk I–Ching spent some ten years there between 671 and 695 AD. Writing about the city of Sriwijaya, he said 'there are more than a thousand Buddhist priests whose minds are bent on study and good works; their rules and ceremonies are identical with those of India'.

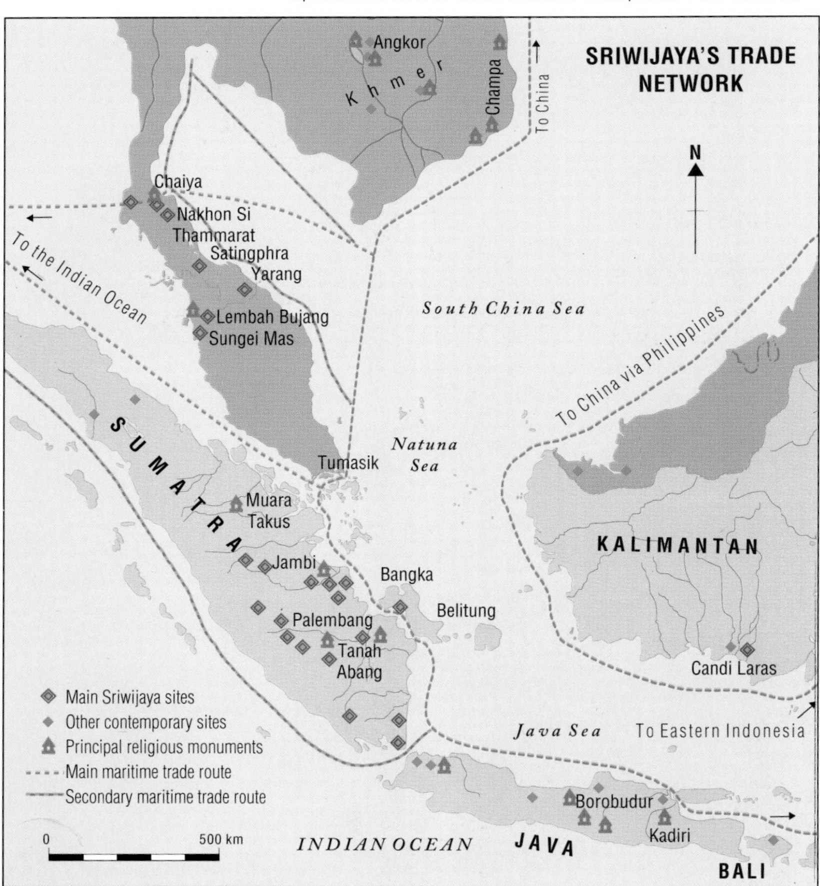

Early Findings

In 1918, the eminent French historian G. Coedes linked these foreign sources to a group of stone inscriptions found in South Sumatra and written in the Old Malay language and a form of Indic script termed Pallava. These inscriptions, carved between 683 and 686 AD, described a polity named Sriwijaya, for which *Shi–li–fo–shih* was the logical Chinese transcription. Most of these crucial records were found at Palembang, now the capital of the province of South Sumatra. Other inscriptions were found on the southern tip of Sumatra, the island of Bangka, and on the upper reaches of the Batang Hari river. Palembang emerged in Coedes' theory as a centre of political power. By combining the evidence of local inscriptions and Buddhist and Hindu statues found scattered in Palembang and its vicinity with evidence from foreign sources, Coedes concluded that the centre and birthplace of prosperous Sriwijaya could only have been located at modern Palembang.

The Search for Sriwijaya

No recollection of the name Sriwijaya is known to exist in oral traditions from South Sumatra, or from anywhere within the Malay realm. Chronicles compiled at Melaka several hundred years later did, however, preserve memories of a nameless kingdom which was said to have prospered near Palembang in the area of Seguntang Hill.

This hill, now located within the boundary of the modern city of Palembang, still holds strong significance for local residents. Various stories connected to it abound, functioning as origin–myths for the Malay people. These stories correspond so well with the topography of modern Palembang, and the recent archaeological and historical discoveries relating to Sriwijaya, that it is difficult not to associate them with an actual historical process and with memories of the formative stages of a state such as Sriwijaya, which grew prosperous by controlling the

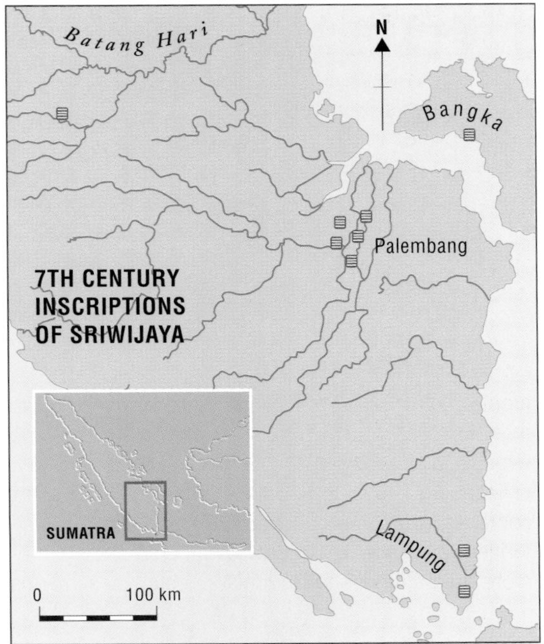

Straits of Melaka, the crossroads of the main sea routes of ancient Asia.

For a long time, however, Palembang stubbornly refused to provide enough solid evidence to enable archaeologists to confirm the inference that this site had once played a major role in Asian history. Over the years, various other sites, mainly on the isthmus of the Malay Peninsula, yielded enough archaeological vestiges such as trade goods, inscriptions, and statuary, to lay claim to the status of Sriwijaya's capital. This situation continues to nurture vigorous scholarly debate.

Archaeological Discoveries at Palembang

It was only in the 1980s that archaeologists began to unearth substantial evidence of economic and religious activity in Palembang during the period of Sriwijaya's prominence as attested in foreign sources (7th to 13th centuries). New inscriptions and statues were found during archaeological surveys and excavations, at times also during construction work in the city. For the earliest phase of Sriwijaya, though, evidence other than inscriptions and statuary remains scarce. A few dates resulting from carbon 14 analysis of charcoal and wood samples recovered in the deepest layers of archaeological sites indicate that people had settled in Palembang between the late 6th and 9th centuries. Trade had taken place there: remains of ships dating to the 6th–7th centuries have been found, one of them at the foot of Seguntang Hill, all built with purely Southeast Asian techniques, and clearly indicating local economic activity. For a variety of reasons, identification of confirmed archaeological sites of this early period at Palembang remains ambiguous: during this period the Chinese ceramics which serve so well as archaeological sign-posts for later sites in Indonesia were not yet being exported from China. Their absence does not facilitate the work of archaeologists in a very disturbed environment. Construction and other activities highly destructive of archaeological evidence are known to have been conducted in the Seguntang Hill area over the past century. Other probable early sites which once existed in the eastern suburbs of Palembang near a modern fertiliser factory are also known to have been destroyed. Considering the fact that the modern city of Palembang, now containing over one million inhabitants, is steadily encroaching upon the few remaining surrounding areas where sites may still exist, archaeologists have little chance of ever uncovering a reasonably complete picture of this earliest phase of Sriwijaya's development.

HIKAYAT HANG TUAH

"And so it became known among all nations that Seguntang Hill had a king whose demeanor was exceedingly kind and courteous, and who cared for all foreigners. After this was heard in all countries, people from all places started gathering at Seguntang Hill, and they came from overseas as well as from overland to visit this king. And so much homage was paid to him that his name became famous among all countries neighbouring Palembang. And Seguntang Hill thus became an exceedingly active harbour and a large country that had civil and military officers and lords and people". (Hikayat Hang Tuah, a classical Malay epic).

Speculations

What type of remains might archaeologists expect to find from early Sriwijaya if Chinese ceramics have been unavailable, and brick temples have been demolished? Much depends on Sriwijaya's settlement pattern. If the early population followed the same custom as many modern residents of Palembang and other parts of Sumatra, they would have built their houses out over the water. Palembang was described by A.R. Wallace in the mid-1800s as 'a populous city several miles long but one house wide, all dwellings being built on piles at the edge of the water'. Most artefacts would have fallen into the mud, and would be buried ever more deeply by gradual sedimentation.

Glass beads, Sabukingking, Palembang.

Short inscription in Old Malay recently discovered at Kambang Unglen, Palembang, 7th century.

Raft dwellings in 19th century Sumatra, a traditional form of housing which existed in Sriwijaya.

Buddha image over two metres high dating to approximately the 8th century. Seguntang Hill, Palembang.

Adoption of Buddhism and Hinduism

The period of Indonesian cultural history termed 'Classic' by many writers is marked by the predominantly Hindu and/or Buddhist character of its archaeological remains. This character is found in temple architecture and related statuary, the use of Sanskrit in many inscriptions, and adherence to Indian prosody, to name only a few features.

»» Buddhist Fables. Stories in which animals took on human characteristics to exemplify moral qualities were popular subjects for temple reliefs in ancient Java.

Cultural Elements

Hinduism and Buddhism were not introduced to the Indonesian archipelago through force or conquest. Nor were they introduced by traders as was formerly argued. Cultural and religious circumstances, the introduction of Sanskrit for writing, and the adoption of Buddhist and Hindu mythology were not the domain of traders. It is more likely that the princes who ruled small Indonesian kingdoms were influenced by priests and Brahmins from India. These priests would have been responsible for introducing a religion that allowed the king to identify himself with a deity or bodhisattva, reinforcing his temporal power. More abstract cultural elements also played a role, such as the concepts of the *cakravartin* (universal ruler), *warna* or social class, the existence of a supreme supernatural power, *rasa* in aesthetics, and all the detailed artistic renderings of those concepts.

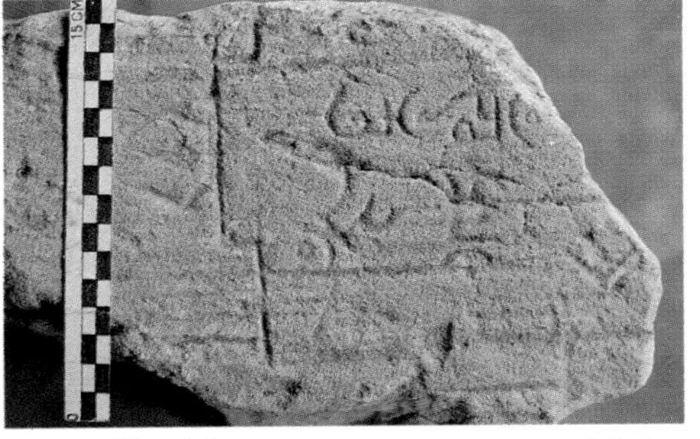

Mandalas were inscribed on temple bricks in Sumatra. The form of Buddhism which became popular in Indonesia, Mahayana or Greater Vehicle, advocates belief in multiple Buddhas and aids to salvation such as mandalas. The unique stupas on Borobudur shelter images of a deity who may be Vairocana.

Kingdoms that adopted Indic concepts of kingship were found in Kalimantan, Java, Sumatra and Bali. Archaeological and historical data have revealed that each island was home to local kingdoms which flourished for varying spans of time. Hindu kingdoms in east Kalimantan and west Java were among the oldest and are believed to have flourished around the end of the 4th and the beginning of the 5th centuries respectively. Both were ruled by kings who had adopted Hinduism of a Vedic character. Historians know about both kingdoms today because Sanskrit inscriptions they left behind have been discovered. Remains of sculpture from both kingdoms are quite scarce in number and rudimentary in style, so it is difficult to be certain whether specific statues found in those areas date from this formative period.

»Cross–section of a perforated stupa on an upper terrace of Borobudur, as drawn by one of Raffles' draughtsman in the early 19th century. The stupa is an important Buddhist icon, but few free standing stupa have been discovered in Indonesia.

Hindu and Buddhist Kingdoms

The ancient Hindu and Buddhist kings of central Java ruled from the 8th to the 10th centuries AD under two dynasties: the Sanjaya and Sailendra. The Sanjayas were Sivaistic Hindus, while the Sailendras were Buddhists of the Mahayana or Vajrayana schools. Both dynasties demonstrated a capacity for religious conceptualisation as well as for organising their society to create a large number of temples displaying a complex symbolism. Other lesser kingdoms existed simultaneously in central Java, which may not have been related to either dynasty, particularly the builders of temple complexes in such mountainous areas as Dieng and Gedong Songo.

Temple Complexes

The largest temple complexes were found in the lowlands of south central Java. Borobudur houses a series of Buddha statues of the serenest appearance related to the Gupta style of India. The Sewu and Kalasan complexes once housed huge bronze statues in their main chambers, but unfortunately only traces of them still remain; the originals were probably melted down centuries ago. The great Hindu complex of Lara Jonggrang, Prambanan, centres on three tower–like buildings. The central shrine houses a statue of Siva, the northern one a statue of Visnu, and the southern one contains a Brahma image. Many other temples of this period are scattered over central and east Java, but the Early Classic style of sculpture is best represented by central Javanese examples.

Narrative Reliefs

The earliest Indonesian narrative reliefs were made for Buddhist temples. Temples such as Mendut and Sajiwan, however, did not have series of narrative reliefs, instead they had individual scenes, mostly recalling tales from the Jataka, mainly animal fables. The reliefs on Candi Jago consist both of texts brought in from India — the Jataka and Tantris — and also purely Javanese literature — the Arjunawiwaha. These stories are arranged according to Javanese belief in the favourable or ill omens associated with different compass directions, and high and low positions. In early Indonesian Buddhism, the sequence of reliefs leads the worshipper around the shrine in a clockwise direction so that the monument is always on the right. This circumambulation called *pradakshina* in itself constituted an act of worship. Later, in east Java, many narrative reliefs required the worshipper to walk counterclockwise in a manner termed *prasawya*. This seems to have been associated with the introduction of Tantric ideas.

The Kingdom as a Mandala

Despite differences in symbolism, all Indonesian kings, Buddhist or Hindu, shared the same fundamental assumptions about the ideal political structure. Inscriptions refer to kingdoms as mandalas, a word which incorporates a wide range of meanings. The simplest meaning is a circle. In a religious sense, the term refers to a symmetrical arrangement of deities in concentric circles, surrounded by an enclosing wall. Mandalas drawn on the ground were believed to create spaces within which religious devotees could meditate, free from the danger of disturbance by evil spirits. Temples were designed as three–dimensional mandalas.

In a political sense, the ideal kingdom would be a gigantic mandala from which all evil forces were excluded. At the centre would be the supreme being, surrounded by rings of officials, each of whom in turn formed the centre of a smaller ring. Economically, this concept seems to have had a strong influence in Java: villages were arranged in groups of four around a central place, and markets were held in each village once every five days. The five–day calendar keyed to the market cycle is still important in Java, both in economic terms and also in compiling *pawukon,* predictive devices meant to determine favourable and unfavourable days for various activities.

Kings styled themselves as *cakra–vartin*, wheel–turners. This term was linked to the assumption that there could only be a single, supreme universal ruler, who obtained his position through spiritual power. In practice, this meant that rulers who aspired to be *cakravartin* sought to entice chiefs of neighbouring areas to ac–knowledge them as supreme ruler through a combination of threats and persuasion. For most subordinate rulers, such recog–nition meant no more than providing occasional tribute and paying court on important occasions. On a daily basis, central rulers of mandalas did not, or could not, intervene in local affairs. Such political organisations depended to a great extent on the personal qualities of the central ruler. Thus centres of political power in Indonesia tended to shift frequently, with alliances regularly forming only to dissolve again. The ideal of the *cakravartin* was difficult to attain, and even more difficult to maintain.

«Siva on Nandin. In this archaic statue from the Dieng Plateau, dating from the early 8th century, Siva's mount is depicted as a human with a bull's head. During the earliest phase of central Javanese art, represented by the architecture and sculpture of Dieng, Javanese artists experimented with numerous ways of expressing Indian-derived religious concepts.

THE LINGGA IN INDONESIA

The gold lingga–yoni ❶ which is only 10.5 centimetres high, was not used in lustration ceremonies as the spout is non– functional, having no hole. It was probably meant as a royal offering to some Sivaite establishment. Yoni ❷ is from Java, where some examples were highly decorated. This one from the National Museum in Jakarta has an additional feature in that the turtle stands on three nagas, and in turn supports a figure of the winged gana, originally winged demons in Indian mythology. They were subdued by Ganesha and condemned to support temples (the mountains of the gods) and *yoni*, among other things.

The *lingga* consists of a cylinder which modulates into an octagon which blends into a square base ❸ . The lingga may be further elaborated with such designs as an anthropomorphic face in which case it is termed a *mukalingga* ❹ . The *lingga* stands on a base called a *yoni* which consists of a square plinth with a spout at one side. The spout often has decorations beneath it, often consisting of a tortoise and a serpent. This is a symbolic reference to the churning of the ocean of milk to produce the elixir of immortality. This is all connected with the ritual use of the *lingga* and *yoni* wherein the lingga is worshipped by lustrating it with various fluids which then run out of the spout of the *yoni.*

By the 15th century the worship of the lingga in Java had taken on new forms. For example at Candi Sukuh on Mount Lawu which appears to be unique is the naturalistic relief of male and female genitalia carved on the floor of the main entrance gate, over which all who entered the complex had to pass ❺ . Another instance of the use of the *lingga–yoni* at Candi Sukuh, is that the main shrine was surmounted by a lingga over two metres high ❻ and bearing an inscription, and the upper part of the shaft is decorated with four spheres which some have connected to a Southeast Asian custom whereby little balls were inserted under skin of the penis.

❷

❸

❹

❺

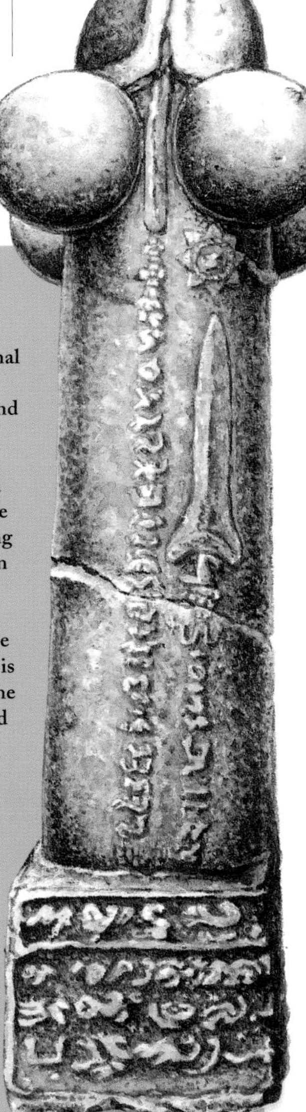

❻

Candi: Symbol of the Universe

Between the 7th and 15th centuries, hundreds of religious structures were constructed of brick and stone in Java, Sumatra and Bali. These are called candi. The term refers to other pre–Islamic structures including gateways and even bathing places, but its principal manifestation is the religious shrine.

Balinese religious architecture is characterised by multi–storeyed temple roofs, which always total odd numbers. They are called meru, after the cosmic mountain, and symbolise the axis of the universe.

Function of the Candi

The word *candi* is generally considered to have been derived from the term *candikagrha* denoting the dwelling place of Candika, Goddess of Death, and consort of Lord Siva. Candi are linked to death: they were frequently constructed to glorify a deceased king or queen. Literally this could be interpreted to mean that the candi is a building used for burial purposes, or even a tomb, but in fact candi are associated with death in a very different way.

They were built as shrines to glorify deceased rulers. The monarchs were believed to be manifestations of particular deities, earthly representatives of the deities, who ruled over the people to protect the cosmic order on behalf of the deity. In death, the monarchs had become reunited with their divine patrons and were immortalised as statues depicting

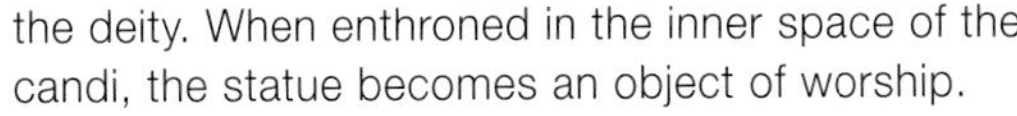

the deity. When enthroned in the inner space of the candi, the statue becomes an object of worship.

One primary function of the candi was to protect this statue from the elements, and from the view of commoners. The essence of the deity was not believed to reside in the statue at all times. The deity had to be invited, through invocations, to descend and temporarily occupy the image. On such occasions the statue could be viewed by worshippers, but only the priests were actually allowed in the shrine room.

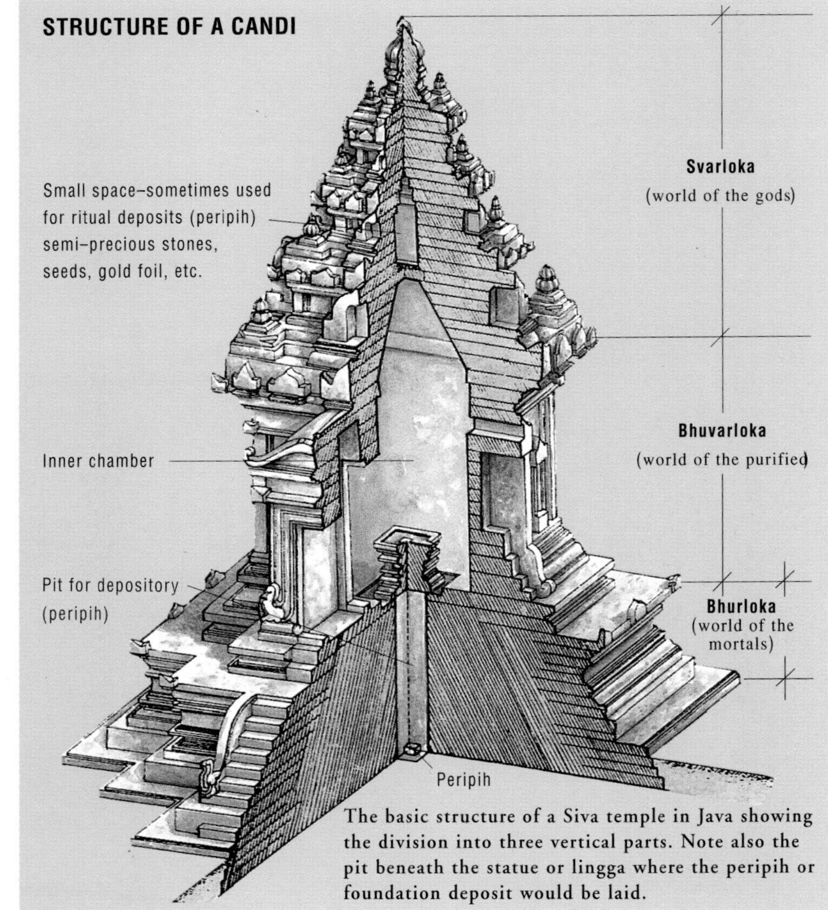

The basic structure of a Siva temple in Java showing the division into three vertical parts. Note also the pit beneath the statue or lingga where the peripih or foundation deposit would be laid.

The Temple Mountain

Early Javanese inscriptions sometimes referred to temples as mountains. Javanese reverence for mountains began in prehistoric times, and Indic mythology contains elements which the Javanese would have found instantly recognisable. In Hindu–Buddhist mythology, Mount Meru is a cosmic mountain situated at the centre of the cosmos that constitutes the axis of the world. It rises from the very bottom of the earth up to the highest levels of heaven. It is also the abode of the gods. The cosmic mountain is thus a symbol for the universe. The candi and its architectural details can be interpreted in terms of this symbolism.

The three levels of the candi represent the *triloka*. These consist of the three superimposed worlds believed to make up the universe. The base of the candi represents the world of mortals, and is called Bhurloka. One level up, the body of the candi represents the Bhuvarloka or world of the purified. It is here that the devotee can communicate with a deity and in turn, the deity receives homage. At the highest level, the roof of the candi represents the world of the gods, or Svarloka.

The architectural features of the candi are designed to accentuate its symbolic meaning as a replica of Mount Meru. The base of the candi is dominated by a series of horizontal mouldings. Carvings here are largely confined to geometric patterns and floral designs. In complete contrast, the walls of the temple body are richly decorated with all manner of ornamental designs, the aim of which is to create an other–worldly atmosphere.

Elements like the *kala–makara* frame the entrance and the niches. According to one story, Kala was a legendary being created by Siva to kill a titan. In another version Kala is a representation of a demon called Rahu, who stole the elixir of immortality. He was beheaded by a god, but because he had already swallowed some of the elixir, he could not be killed. Hence in early sculpture Kala is depicted without a lower jaw; in later times his jaw reappears. Variations appear, such as paws; other variants include highly stylised depictions with one eye. *Makara* are mythical beasts with an elephant's trunk, a lion's mane, parrot's beak, and fish's tail. They are water symbols, and also symbols of sexual desire. The pennant symbolising Kamadeva, god of love, is emblazoned with a *makara*. Images of *makara* were found at the entrances to most Early Classic temples. In Late Classic temples of Java they were

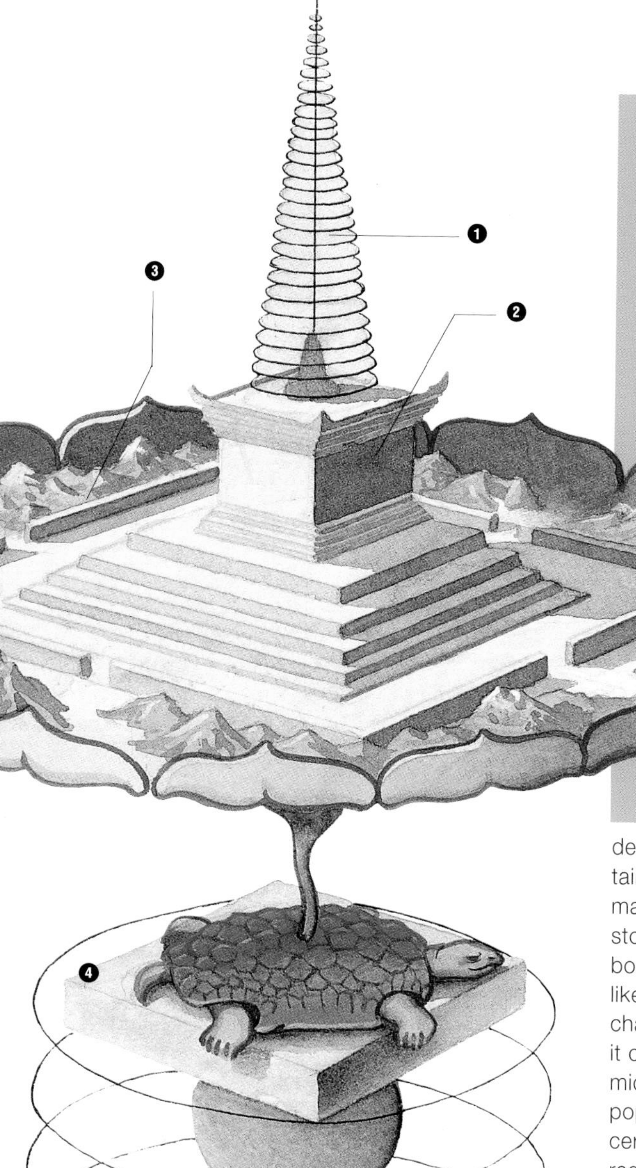

THE MANDALA OF THE UNIVERSE

1 Svarloka: consists of 27 heavens. In descending order, the gods who inhabit these heavens range from pure thought, to deities with more and more corporeal ties, and who have not yet completely relinquished their material forms. Twenty of these heavens are above the earth, and the lower seven are on the slopes of Mount Meru. Mount Meru is like a pivot around which all planes of existence rotate. It is also like a nail which stabilises the world, keeping it from spinning away uncontrollably. Two of the former ruling princes of Central Java, the Pakubuwono of Solo (Surakarta) and Pakualam of Yogyakarta, incorporate this concept in their names, both of which mean 'nail of the world'. This signifies the idea that without some kind of anchor, anarchy will ensue.

2 Mount Meru: mountain on which the gods of the lower levels of heaven reside like hermits in caves. The ruler of the summit of Meru is named Indra. Many Javanese kings depicted themselves as linked to Indra, often incorporating the name as part of his own.

3 Around Mount Meru are seven concentric rings of mountains and oceans. In the outermost ocean are four continents. Humans live on the southernmost continent.

4 Beneath the world of men are various layers of underworlds, inhabited by demons, ghosts, and souls of the damned. The entire edifice, in turn, rests on the back of a giant turtle envisaged as swimming eternally in a boundless sea of ether.

rare, but in Sumatra they continued to be used at places such as Padang Lawas.

The scenes depicting *gandharva*, *vidyadhara* and various other celestial beings floating in the air, rows of nagas supporting garlands of lotus rosettes, elaborate carvings on panels and antefixes, and many other decorative items are meant to depict the world beyond. The three stages of the roof, and their many tops arranged around and beneath the pinnacle, depict the top of Mount Meru.

Foundation Deposits (*Peripih*)

Beneath the centre of the candi is a pit for the *peripih*. Formerly it was widely thought that the *peripih* were containers to inter the ashes of the deceased monarch. The *peripih* is, in fact, a container in which are placed elements symbolising the material world: gold, silver, bronze, semi-precious stones and seeds. The *peripih* was usually a stone box divided into sections arranged in a *mandala*-like pattern, sometimes with nine, sometimes 25 chambers. The number nine is significant because it corresponds to the four cardinal directions, four mid points, and the zenith. Certain Tantric texts popular in ancient Java contain instructions for ceremonies used in creating a sacred space which require ritual objects to be buried. This may be the origin of the practice of creating these *peripih*.

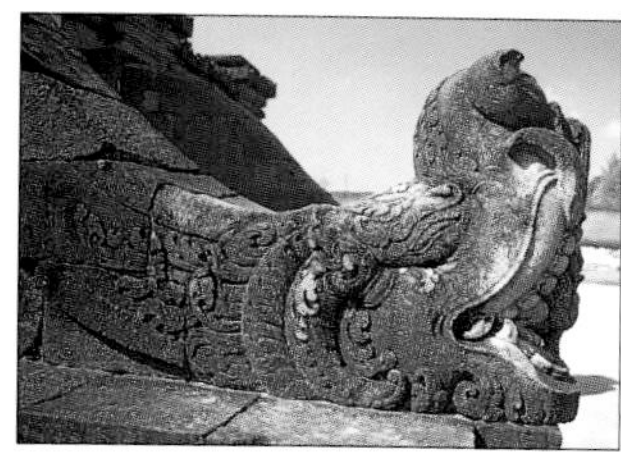

Makara (mythical sea monster), Candi Sambisari. A common ornament on both Hindu and Buddhist temples.

The statue of the deity is enthroned in the inner chamber above the *peripih*. A small hole is pierced in the ceiling of the chamber, above which is another small space — the temporary abode of the deity. During the *pranapratistha* ceremonies, which were held to animate the statues, the deity was invoked and was believed by its devotees to descend from heaven to occupy its residence in the roof of the candi. The deity then travels further down into the chamber beneath to imbue the statue with its spirit. At the same time, the earthly elements of the temple which had been deposited in the pit were activated upon contact with holy water from the ablution of the statue. This water flowed through the spout in the pedestal of the statue, and thence through the cracks of the floor stones down into the temple pit, where it finally came into contact with the *peripih*. The statue was now deemed to be alive and able to receive homage as well as to communicate with devotees.

Peripih (ritual deposit box) of stone. Central Java.

EARLY CLASSIC ART

The early classic period lasted for only two centuries, but was characterised by an outpouring of monumental art. Classical art made its first appearance in Bali late in this period. Archaeologists and art historians are now able to divide the Early Classic into sub-phases. In the first of these, Hinduism predominated, and the Javanese temple acquired a basic form which it retained with slight modification for several centuries. The rise of Hinduism was connected with a ruling family who called themselves the Sanjaya, after the first known ruler of central Java. In the late 8th century, Buddhism came into ascendancy, associated with the family known as the Sailendra. This phase is represented by the "hidden foot" of Borobudur, which was covered in a subsequent phase of construction. The parrot motif appeared on both Hindu and Buddhist temples by about 830 AD and forms a useful dating marker. The god Kuvera, associated with wealth, was popular among both Hindus and Buddhists. Perhaps notions of wealth already formed an important element in the Javanese social structure by this time.

EARLY CLASSIC PERIOD

Hindu temple. Gedong Songo, central Java, early 8th century.

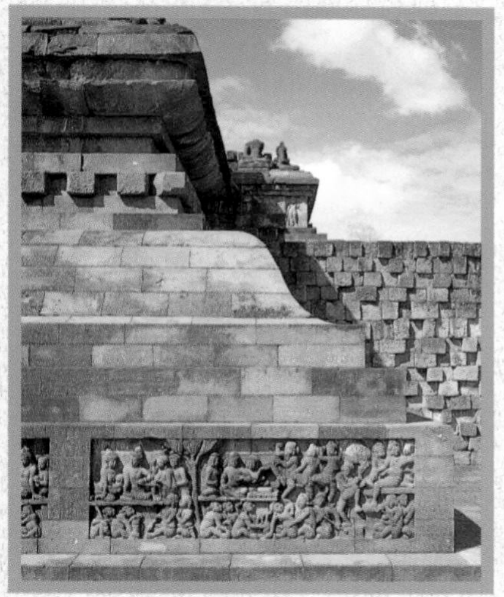

Borobudur, profile of the so–called hidden foot, 8th century.

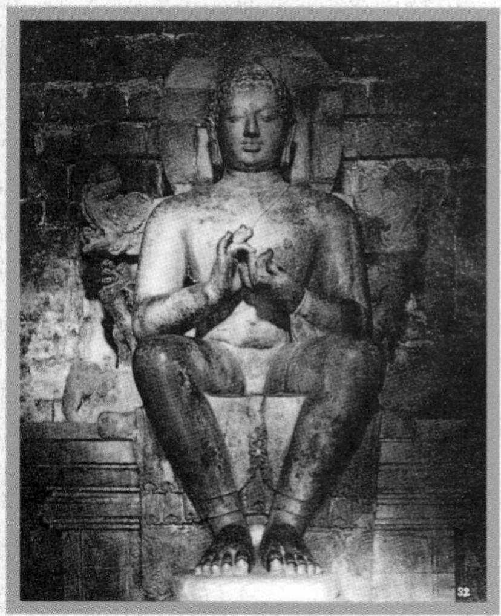

Buddha, Candi Mendut, near Borobudur, 8th century.

Although writing appeared in Indonesia in the 4th century, it was not part of a general process of Indianisation. Indonesian societies utilised different elements of South Asian culture at various times for local ends. Indonesians probably began to adapt South Asian sculptural and architectural styles for the same reason they adopted monumental writing: increasing elaboration of Indonesian social hierarchies. The patronage of religious edifices became an additional instrument for use by emerging elites aspiring to distinguish themselves from their followers and competitors.

As in the example of writing, the earliest examples of Indonesian adaptations of South Indian sculptural and architectural styles are lost, partly because they must have been made of wood. Early brick structures may have been built in south Sumatra, but an archaeological expedition to Palembang reported in 1920 that many ancient brick ruins had been quarried for road building material. The oldest known Indonesian monuments are those built of stone. The oldest known Indonesian classical monuments were erected in Java in the 8th century. These are the oldest standing structures of their type anywhere in Southeast Asia. The time lag between the appearance of writing and the appearance of stone masonry is not an absolutely reliable indicator of the true history of cultural development in Indonesia, but it is reliable evidence that these techniques were adopted in Indonesia at different times, as part of a gradual process of local development. Thus it is more appropriate to examine how South Asian culture was Indonesianised rather than the reverse.

There are no clear signposts along the path of Indonesian cultural evolution. The appearance of writing and Indic art indicate processes of development under way, rather than points marking sudden changes in direction or trajectory. Indonesian cultural history is best viewed as a gradual evolutionary process, marked by strong continuity. Chronological periods are in an important sense arbitrary.

As data become more plentiful during the 8th and 9th centuries, we note that societies in western Indonesia were well–integrated into an extensive international network bound by religious and commercial ties.

The following sections delineate our knowledge of the early Classic period, defined as the span of time during which the people of Indonesia began to apply theories of universal beauty, fixed proportions, standardised iconography, and harmony to art and architecture.

Early Classic History

The beginning of the Early Classic period of Indonesian history is marked by the sudden emergence of two political centres: Sriwijaya in southeast Sumatra, and Mataram in south central Java. Of these two, Sriwijaya ('Glorious Victory' in Sanskrit) is the older. The kingdom of Mataram appeared approximately 50 years later. The two kingdoms represent different types of polities; Sriwijaya depended on sea trade, Mataram on agriculture. The two kingdoms clashed frequently during the period 700–900 AD.

CENTRAL JAVANESE CANDI

The major temple complexes of the Early Classic period in central Java are distributed in an arc around the southern foot of Mount Merapi, an active volcano almost 3,000 metres in elevation.

Dieng 1
Gedong Songo 2
Ngempon 3
Pringapus 4
Selogriyo 5
Borobudur 6
Pawon 7
Mendut 8
Canggal 9
Pendem 10
Asu 11
Kuning 12
Lawang 13
Morangan 14
Candi 15
Palgading 16
Gebang 17
Sambisari 18
Kalasan 19
Sari 20
Sewu 21
Plaosan 22
Lara Jonggrang 23
Ratu Boko 24
Dawungsari 25
Miri 26
Barong 27
Ijo 28
Banyunibo 29
Watu Gudik 30
Nagasari 31
Abang 32
Parangtretes 33

The city of modern Yogyakarta, just south of Palgading, is indicated for reference.

The first evidence of Sriwijaya's existence appears in the memoirs of the Chinese Buddhist pilgrim, I-Ching, who knew of it in 672 AD, when it was already a centre for Buddhist learning. Between 682 and 686 AD the rulers erected several stone inscriptions near the capital which lay in the vicinity of modern Palembang, in other parts of Sumatra, and on the island of Bangka. These inscriptions tell us that Sriwijaya quickly became the mistress of strategic points along the Straits of Malacca, and laid the foundations for several centuries of prosperity based on maritime trade. It is strange that the last known Sriwijayan embassy to China was sent in 742 AD, for the kingdom certainly continued to exist, even establishing a temple in Canton in the 11th century. The history of Sriwijaya's dominance of maritime trade is a subject about which only archaeology can hope to enlighten us, and research in South Sumatra is still in a preliminary stage.

The history of central Java can also be dated to the late 7th century, when an inscription was carved on the north slope of Mount Merbabu. It consists of a few lines in praise of a source of water, Tuk Mas (Golden Spring). In the year 732 AD an inscription was carved at Candi Canggal, on the top of Gunung Wukir. It is a hymn of praise for a ruler named Sanjaya, whose line established its influence over a large area of central Java. They were probably responsible for the construction of the Hinduistic temple complexes of Dieng and Gedong Songo, delineating a sphere of influence over a territory at least 100 kilometres wide from north to south.

The custom of setting up stone inscriptions quickly spread to east Java. In 760 AD a stone was erected at Dinoyo, near Malang. The connection between Dinoyo and the central Javanese Sanjaya is unclear; the inscription may have been erected by a separate but related ruling group.

In 767 AD Vietnamese annals record an invasion by men from Java and the 'Southern Islands'. In 775 AD the maharaja of Sriwijaya set up an inscription at Ligor, Southern Thailand, where he probably held some sort of suzerainty. In 787 AD a Cham inscription records that an invading army from Java burnt a temple in what is now south Vietnam. An Indonesian kingdom even seems to have acquired temporary power over Cambodia around this time.

In Java another ruling elite rose to challenge the Sanjaya: the Sailendra (a Sanskrit term meaning 'Lord of the Mountain'). They were Buddhist; the inauguration of the construction of the Buddhist shrine of Candi Kalasan in 778 AD is the first evidence we have that they had reached a position of ascendancy in Java. During the next 50 years they relegated the Hindu descendants of Sanjaya to a subordinate position. They constructed Borobudur and many other elaborate Buddhist monuments.

The last inscription of the Sailendra rulers in central Java dates from 824 AD. Thereafter the Sailendra and Sanjaya families seem to have merged through marriage. In 842 AD Java's supreme ruler, entitled Rakai Pikatan, was a Hindu married to a Buddhist queen. During his reign Hindu and Buddhist temples received royal sponsorship. The principal achieve–

ment of this era was the construction of the Hindu temple complex of Lara Jonggrang at Prambanan, consecrated in 856 AD.

We know little about the internal politics of this era. One piece of information, the charter of Nalanda, a Buddhist centre in northeast India, tells us that in about 860 AD a Sailendra, Balaputra, was ruling in Sumatra. It suggests that he had originally come from central Java. Evidence suggests that he had rebelled against Rakai Pikatan, had been defeated, and managed to become ruler of Sriwijaya.

After the completion of the Lara Jonggrang temples, the great spate of temple building activity in central Java seems to have ground to a halt. Inscriptions continued to be carved, however, and they give no hint of any major disruption in Javanese economy or society. Nevertheless, the historical record of central Java suddenly falls silent in 919 AD. By 928 AD the Javanese rulers were based in east Java. Why artistic and literary activity ceased so abruptly in a region which had accomplished so much in a short time is completely unknown. Theories for the kingdom's eastward move range from volcanic eruptions, to epidemics, to attack from Sriwijaya, but no evidence has yet confirmed or refuted any of these explanations.

A *Candi Bima, Dieng Plateau, named after one of the Pandawa.*
B *Candi Asu (Dog temple), so named after the unfinished makara by the steps.*
C *Candi Selogriyo, built during the 9th century Hindu revival.*
D *One of the Nine Temples (Gedong Songo) on Mount Ungaran.*

The Oldest Buildings in Indonesia

The single largest contributor to the origin of religious architecture in Southeast Asia was southern India. This contribution took place at the beginning of the Christian era but the oldest vestiges visible today, found on the Dieng Plateau in central Java, date from the early 8th century. By this time the original model had undergone considerable alterations and therefore the links of the oldest Javanese monuments to those of India were already tenuous.

»»Siva lingga in Candi Badut, the oldest known temple in east Java.

Exterior of Candi Badut. Although originally erected in the 8th century, the form which we see today bears traces of later modification.

Wooden architecture depicted on Borobudur, late 8th century.

Indian Influences

The oldest permanent structures in Indonesia are temples built to house statues of Indian deities. In the early part of the 20th century, archaeologists spent much time pursuing the precise source of the earliest influences which led the Javanese to introduce this new practice. None of the structures now found in Indonesia precisely resemble any known buildings found in India. This difficulty was no doubt due partly to an evolutionary process which had already been under way for some time in Indonesia before the oldest known temples were built, but from this formative stage no structures have been preserved. Another reason for this situation is that Indonesian architects would have assimilated ideas from several different parts of India. Nevertheless, the temples of southeast India display the greatest number of similarities with the earliest Javanese examples, strongly suggesting that this region, which is geographically nearest to Indonesia, had the most frequent contact with the Javanese temple builders.

If we admit that nothing is known of the earliest Indonesian stone or brick buildings, it must be noted that our knowledge of the first temples built by the Pallava kings of south India is also very poor, consisting only of what is reflected in sculpted cave temples found in India. Nevertheless we can create models for some of the earliest temples, now vanished, which were probably made of wood, on the basis of two main sources: the architecture depicted on the reliefs of Borobudur which reproduce an architecture earlier than that of the monument, and the temples of the Pallava kingdom in south India. The reliefs depicted on Borobudur, carved in the very last years of the 8th century, show a large number of wooden buildings several of which can be linked to Pallava architecture. The primary example is a building located on a panel of the first gallery, on the upper row (eastern side, south aisle). This edifice has one peculiarity: its supporting structure is on the outside, resting on pillars with bases shaped like lions standing on their hind legs.

Similar pillars decorate the walls of temples built by the Pallava, at Mahabalipuram and Panamalai for example, where the supporting structure rests on zoomorphic bases. As on the edifice shown on Borobudur, the pillars are visible but instead of being detached from the body of the structure they are stuck against it and no longer support anything. However these monuments, like those depicted on Borobudur, originated from a model which can be reconstructed in the following manner: at each corner of a stone foundation, with a ground-plan either square or cruciform, a wooden pillar was erected with the lower part a zoomorphic shape sculpted in the stone; on these supports rest horizontal beams which support the roof and upper storeys.

Building in Stone

In Java, when construction in stone began, probably at the beginning of the 8th century, the model had already been transformed. One can observe, among the monuments depicted on Borobudur, some wooden structures which were inspired by the original form, retaining the essential principle (the exterior framework still found among the simplest rural houses of Java), but the pillars have no zoomorphic bases and sometimes the upper storeys are supported by another row of recessed pillars. The wooden temples have all vanished, but a more

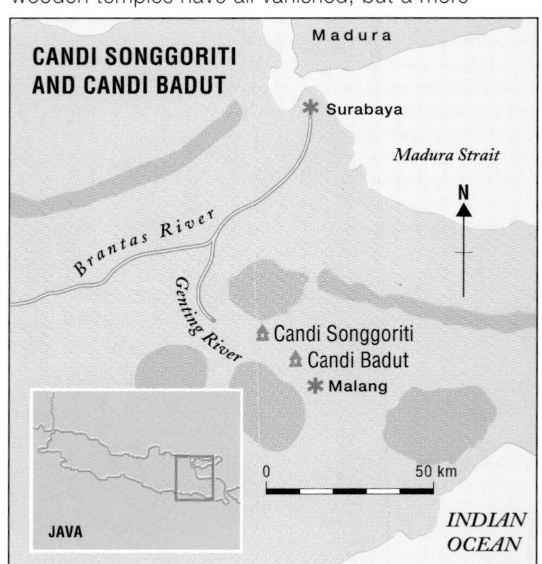

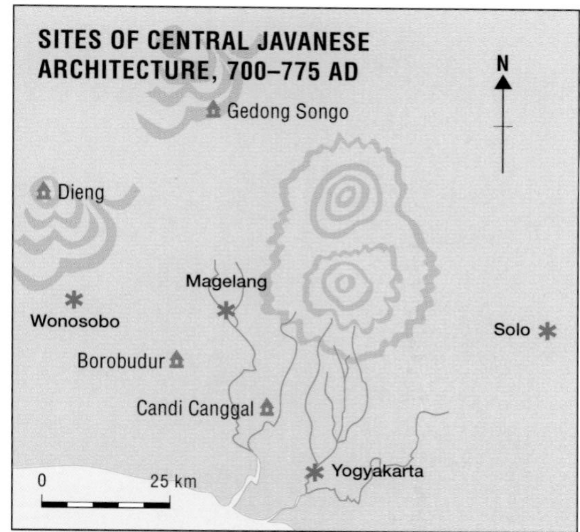

resistant material, stone, began to be used in a well defined region, the north part of central Java. This transition brought more changes to the original model, due to the different techniques that were required for stone, which permitted architects to realise more vertical designs.

Earliest Monuments

The oldest known monument dates from this period. It was erected on Mount Wukir, where an inscription of the Sanjaya Dynasty, dated 732 AD, has been found. The extant ruins, Candi Canggal, derive from the second half of the 9th century. On the Dieng Plateau ('Abode of the Gods') stands a group of sanctuaries built in two different phases, one before, the other after 750 AD. At Gedong Songo, on the outer slope of another volcano where a stream springing from a volcanic hot spring runs between the ruins, the monuments are contemporary with the second Dieng phase.

The first stage of Borobudur, a terraced pyramid without reliefs, must have been under construction around 775 AD, but it was never finished. This stage was probably meant for a non-Buddhist structure, dedicated to Hinduism or possibly a non-Indic religion. The terraced form would seem to indicate that the original plan for a structure on this site was based on a prehistoric Indonesian practice of terracing similar to that found on some Polynesian islands and in some Indonesian megalithic complexes.

The expansion of Buddhism interrupted the evolution of Hindu architecture in the region for nearly half a century. The Borobudur site itself seems to have been left abandoned for some time before the Buddhists revived the work here; they were not directly responsible for the cessation of construction on the original structure.

There was at least one other Hindu enclave at this time, near Malang in east Java, which left several traces, such as Candi Badut and Candi Songgoriti, which is related to the Dinoyo inscription of 760 AD. The Dinoyo inscription, which is written in Sanskrit, records the construction of a temple dedicated to Agastya by the son of a king named Devasingha ruling a kingdom called Kanjuruhan. Another inscription was discovered in east Java which may be even older to judge from its writing style. Unfortunately it contains no date, and therefore this supposition cannot be proven. It is, however, possible that this kingdom was linked to that of the Sanjaya of central Java, since the style of the architecture and the religious affiliation were very similar in the two areas. Again, unfortunately, this cannot be proven. Nevertheless, the two isolated structures of Badut and the two inscriptions give a tantalising impression that east Java was not merely an underdeveloped area on the fringe of central Javanese civilisation. On the contrary, it was probably more integrated into a larger polity and culture than present remains suggest. Unfortunately no significant new data has emerged to help us to resolve this question. In east Java, Candi Badut is larger than the temples of Dieng or Gedong Songo but the structure takes its inspiration from the same source. The extant ruins show the effects of major alterations (in the 9th and probably again in the 13th century). Candi Songgoriti has a plan and proportions very much like those of Candi Sembadra at Dieng; very likely it formed part of a larger group.

In spite of the scarcity of remains dating from this period, these monuments were very important to Javanese religious architecture. Their legacy for later Javanese temples, as well as those of Sumatra and Bali, remained influential for a very long time. Right up until the 14th century, they formed a sort of mandatory reference for all Javanese architects of religious buildings.

Candi Canggal, built on the site of the 732 inscription. This is a Hindu temple with a lingga sanctuary at the right and the remains of a nandin shrine to the left.

Group III, Gedong Songo. This group forms a direct continuation of the architectural experiments first undertaken on the Dieng Plateau. At Gedong Songo the Javanese architects formalised a style which persisted with refinements for centuries.

GEDONG SONGO

The monuments of Gedong Songo (left) display greater unity and with the exception of the later Group I, must have been built in one period between 750 and 775 AD. Although the architectural compositions are similar to Dieng, the site plans of the groups are quite varied, and later exerted an influence on monuments of a much larger scale. Group III includes three main shrines oriented toward the west, dedicated to the three gods of the Trimurti: in the centre Siva, on the north Visnu, on the south Brahma. In front of the Siva sanctuary a small building sheltered the vehicle of Siva, the bull Nandin. This latter edifice (right) is particularly interesting because it shows that a manual was used in its design. Because the proportions of this edifice were designed for a larger structure, the entrance would have been only one metre high. To avoid this inconvenience, the architect lowered the base of the opening so that it cut through the mouldings of the temple foot. This detail shows how, despite variations and alterations, the architects wished to conform to Indian texts which governed architecture.

Temples of the Dieng Plateau

The name 'Dieng' is derived from the archaic words Di Hyang, meaning 'Place of the Ancestors'. The association between this place and the oldest temples of Indonesia reinforces the conclusion that the Javanese melded Brahmanic ideas from India with pre-existing belief in the importance of ancestor spirits to create a new religion.

»»Dieng Plateau shrouded in early morning mist.

»»Telaga Warna. The peninsula in the upper centre contains meditation caves, one of which yielded an inscription dated 1210. This is the only inscription in central Java written after 919 AD.

Site and Situation

The Dieng Plateau, 2,000 metres above sea level, is shaped like a bowl enclosed within high mountain walls. When rediscovered in the early 19th century after having been long abandoned, the plateau was covered with swamp forest. As the forest was felled, dozens of stone ruins appeared. Almost all were carted away for building materials. Some such as Candi Parikesit, on the slope of Prahu, were photographed by a Dutch explorer in 1873 when the temple was already in ruins but still recognisable. Now all the stones have been taken away, so that even the site's location cannot be rediscovered.

The plateau probably attracted attention because of its height, remoteness, and the volcanic phenomena unique to the place: jets of steam, sulphur-tinted lakes, and bubbling mud cauldrons. At this elevation no tropical food crops could be grown, so all food would have to have been carried up the steep outer slope of the massif which encloses it. Probably the site was the scene of occasional pilgrimages by royalty and commoners. At other times, probably only a few priests shivering in the cold air watched over the shrines.

A few inscriptions give us independent dates for the site. Thirteen inscriptions found on and near the ruins are written in very old Kawi script. One bears a date corresponding to 809 AD. The same archaic script is found on golden plates of the temple deposits from one of the sanctuaries. In general, however, the ages of the temples can only be estimated on the basis of their structure.

Individual Monuments

The oldest monument on the Dieng Plateau is Candi Arjuna, consecrated to Siva, near in form to the original Indian model. Although it contains no cult object, it might once have housed a statue or lingga which would have been ceremonially bathed, for the organisation of the cella with the drainage channel leading the holy water through the wall made it possible to practise the Sivaite ritual in the same way as it was performed in Pallava temples of south India. The interior wall of Candi Arjuna has niches which were possibly meant to hold lamps. Decorations on the outside include *kala-makara* motifs over niches for statues on each of three sides.

Slightly later, and in the same line, were built Candi Puntadewa in its first stage, Candi Srikandi and, on a different part of the plateau, Candi Gatotkaca. After 750 AD Candi Puntadewa was remodelled. It originally was surrounded by a raised

CANDI ARJUNA

This temple forms part of the largest remaining architectural complex on the Dieng Plateau. The interior houses a Siva lingga and yoni. The shrine is equipped with a makara-headed spout which was meant to channel the fluids used to lustrate the lingga from inside the shrine to the outside. In this way, commoners who were not allowed into the shrine's interior could still benefit from the ceremonies held inside by collecting the water which flowed from this conduit, believed to be full of supernatural fertility and other qualities. This feature is common in Indian temples but in Indonesia only Candi Arjuna possesses such a *sutasoma*. This suggests that Candi Arjuna may be the oldest surviving building in Java, and perhaps even in all of Southeast Asia. The structure is relatively complete except for the pinnacle which has vanished.

foot which has disappeared. Another temple, Candi Bima, is unique in Java. For this temple the model was probably derived from the northeast Indian province of Orissa, but this building was also considerably modified around 800 AD, probably to adapt it to Buddhist use.

At the time when the Dieng shrines were built, the model for the Javanese temple had not yet been standardised. The spout for holy water was quickly abandoned. At Candi Srikandi, a new experiment was tried. The exterior of the temple was decorated on three sides with bas-relief figures of the Hindu Trimurti: Brahma on the south wall, Visnu on the north, and Siva on the east. This iconographic scheme does not seem to have been repeated either. On later Hindu temples such as Gedong Songo it was replaced by a Durga–Ganesha–Agastya group, with Durga on the north, Ganesha on the side opposite the entrance (which could be either east or west), and Agastya on the south. Candi Bima represents yet another trial which yielded aesthetically satisfying results, but which was not repeated. The upper levels are divided into three tiers from which sculpted faces gaze out. The temple, which stood on an octagonal base, faces east. This contrasts with most of the temples at Dieng which face west. Besides these buildings there is an underground tunnel named Aswatama, with ventilation holes at intervals, which stretches from the Arjuna complex in a northwesterly direction to the edge of the plateau and undoubtedly was for drainage.

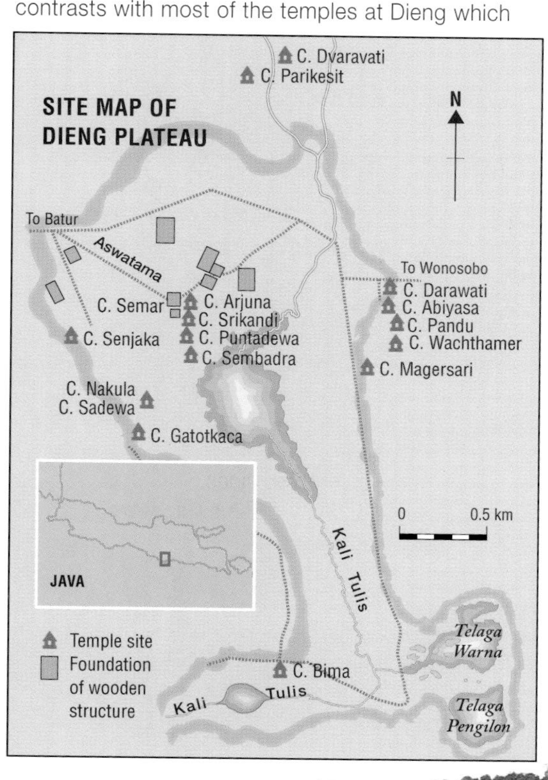

Remaining Research

Much remains to be learned about the sites of the Dieng Plateau. Few archaeological excavations have yet been conducted there. Finds of Chinese ceramics of the Tang Dynasty suggest that it may be possible to discover information regarding the implements used in rituals, and possible monastic life on the plateau. The small shrine, Puntadewa, at the south end of the row of four temples from Candi Arjuna, is unique among the group in that it has no surrounding wall. Excavations were conducted here to discover whether a wall had once surrounded it. A trench was dug between Puntadewa and neighbouring Sembadra. No definite remains of a stone wall were found, but soil discolouration suggested that a wall might once have existed here, only to be removed at some later date, perhaps by stone robbers. Further excavations along the course of this soil disturbance might help to resolve this problem.

The Dieng Plateau and its temples enjoyed a long life, with numerous construction phases. The last dated inscription on the site was carved in 1210. This is the only known inscription written in central Java after the early 10th century. It is important as it indicates that the east Javanese were not unaware of the existence of older sites in Central Java.

IMAGES OF DIENG
❶ Kinnari (half-human, half-bird heavenly musician of a type which inhabits the slopes of Mount Meru, eternally making music for the gods who dwell there).
❷ Kala head, Candi Sembadra.
❸ Head, Candi Bima
❹ Ganesha supported by figures of gana. Ganesha literally means "Lord of the Gana". (Jakarta, National Museum).

A general view of the Arjuna group – Candi Arjuna with Candi Semar to the right, and Candi Srikandi, Puntadewa and Sembadra in the background.

Early Buddhist Temples of Java

It is not easy to determine when Buddhism came to Indonesia, because early Buddhism produced no epigraphic remains comparable to those for early Hinduism. Large bronze statues discovered at Sempaga on the west coast of Sulawesi and Jember in east Java indicate that Buddhism may have reached Indonesia in the first centuries AD. The images are stylistically very similar to those found at the great Buddhist centre of Amaravati and were possibly imported from Sri Lanka or south India.

»»Candi Kalasan, Java's oldest Buddhist temple, was enlarged around 800 AD.

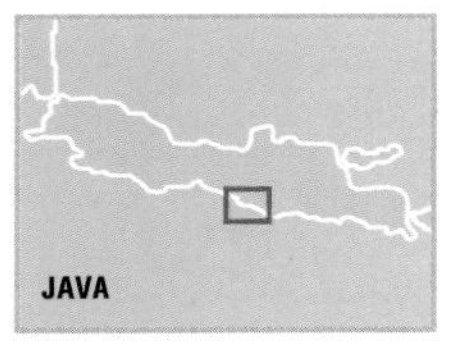

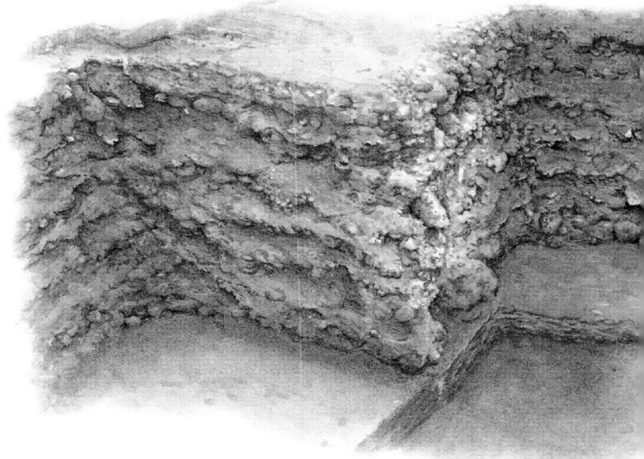

Candi Sewu: excavation displaying alternating layers of sand and cobblestones reinforcing the temple foundation.

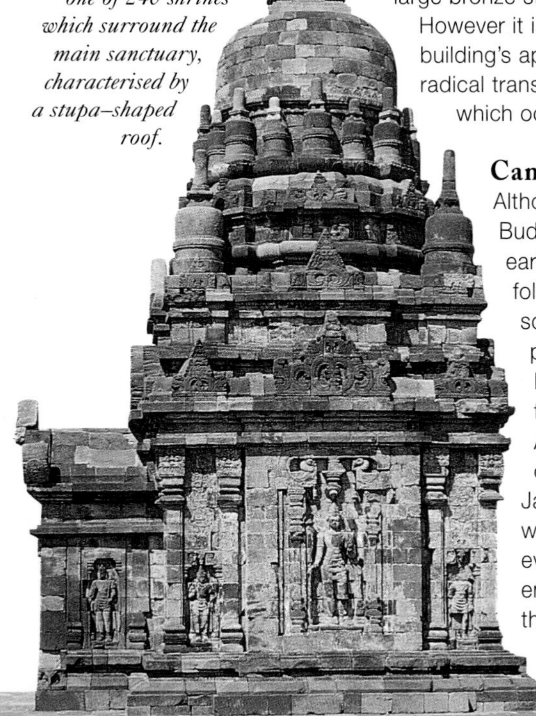

Candi Sewu chapel: one of 240 shrines which surround the main sanctuary, characterised by a stupa-shaped roof.

Candi Kalasan

Buddhism was established in Java by the 5th century AD, but no Buddhist edifices of this period have yet been discovered. The oldest Buddhist statues found in Indonesia date from around this time, but no architectural remains were found with them, so that we know nothing about this early conversion except that it occurred. The oldest known Buddhist structure dates from the mid-8th century; the first stage of Candi Kalasan in central Java, consecrated in 778 AD. The sanctuary has a square plan with one large and three small chambers. The large chamber contains an altar that once supported the main image, believed to have been a large bronze statue of the female deity, Tara. However it is impossible to reconstruct the building's appearance because of the radical transformation of the structure which occurred around 800 AD.

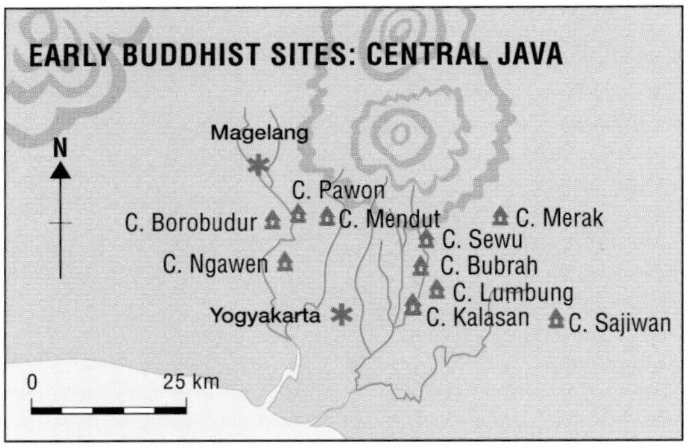

EARLY BUDDHIST SITES: CENTRAL JAVA

N
Magelang
C. Pawon
C. Borobudur
C. Mendut
C. Merak
C. Sewu
C. Ngawen
C. Bubrah
C. Lumbung
Yogyakarta
C. Kalasan
C. Sajiwan
0
25 km

Candi Sewu

Although we know the version of Buddhism that was practised in the early Javanese complexes followed a Mahayanist philosophy, it is difficult to specify the precise nature of early Javanese Buddhism. A profound change took place around the year 800 AD, which resulted in the complete remodelling of all Javanese Buddhist temples, wiping out all archaeological evidence which would have enabled scholars to reconstruct the earlier forms of ritual practised. It was around 775 AD, that the Sailendra ruling elite were installed in south-central Java and began to build a huge temple, Candi Sewu. This site was profoundly modified later but its first stage is more easily reconstructed than that of Kalasan. It consisted of a main monument in the centre comprising five elements standing on the same foot. This group was surrounded by 240 chapels arranged in four concentric squares; between the second and third squares a wide area was reserved for eight temples appreciably larger than the chapels, which may no longer be in their original form. The name Candi Sewu literally means '1000 temples'. Although there were never so many structures as this, the number of images in the shrine may well have exceeded that number. This particular plan attempted to generate harmony in the kingdom by creating a replica of the world in miniature. Two types of chapels were built: one for the first and fourth squares, the other for the second and third. In their first stage, the chapels were simple square cellas, resting on a foot with no staircase.

Rituals of Construction

Excavations conducted by Indonesian archaeologists have made it possible to reconstitute much of the ritual which preceded the construction of the central temple. It would appear that a huge square with sides 41 metres long was laid out and then dug to a variable depth of up to 2 metres. This hole was then filled in with alternating layers of sand and coarse pebbles up to about 60 centimetres beneath the surface of the ground; on the last layer of sand fill a geometric diagram, a mandala, was laid out, the corners of which were determined by small stones sunk into the sand. In each of the spaces thus demarcated, symbols of various Buddhist deities were buried. For example Tara, the consort of Avalokitesvara to whom Candi Kalasan is dedicated, was symbolised by her musical instrument, a lyre, made of mud. The mandala was then covered by more layers of sand and pebbles. Beneath the last sand layer, at the centre of the excavation, a brick altar was built, then encased inside a stone platform. On top of the platform a very high stone plinth was erected on which a statue was placed, then gradually enclosed and covered by the temple. The proportions of this platform conform to those of altars recommended for a Vedic ritual. This shows that at the end of the 8th century, the ruling Sailendra dynasty was still closely acquainted with the rituals of India, even if stylistically they were rather detached from Indian models.

Candi Sewu did not have a long life in its first stage; an Old Malay inscription of 792 AD shows that the temple had already been modified. One could draw this conclusion from the monument itself: the square central temple has been transformed into a cruciform edifice, incorporating the side chapels, and the iconography of the 240 chapels had been completely changed from a triad to a system of five *jina* ('Conqueror') Buddhas oriented toward the cardinal points and the centre. This transformation also affected Candi Kalasan, which was similarly modified to become cruciform. At this time a huge programme of new construction was undertaken, including the temples associated with Candi Sewu, such as Candi Bubrah and Candi Lumbung. Candi Sajiwan was erected in the south, also on a cruciform plan. The

Ngawen temple inserted into a set of three shrines originally designed to hold Siva, Visnu and Brahma in order to convert the complex into a sanctuary for the five Jina (Conqueror) Buddhas.

interior of this sanctuary was designed to facilitate the bathing of the main statue. Similar facilities were provided in the second stage of Candi Sewu, Candi Kalasan, and Candi Mendut. To this group should be added numerous other temples at Bogem and Bugisan, in the Prambanan area, which are now partially or completely destroyed.

Expansion of Buddhist Sites

During the course of the second half of the 8th century, Buddhism began to expand toward the north, an expansion which probably took place at the expense of Hinduism. This fact is demonstrated by

Subsidiary chapels, at Candi Sewu, first row, with a stone faced courtyard surrounding main sanctuary.

the sanctuary of Ngawen, west of Muntilan. This shrine consists of five buildings of which there are two types — three square buildings, between which have been inserted two cruciform structures of different style. Only the three square temples are correctly aligned. These probably originally formed a group for the statues of the Hindu Trimurti (Siva, Visnu, and Brahma) (similar to those at Gedong Songo III) which the Buddhists during their expansion transformed into temples for the five Jina or "Conqueror" Buddhas. They did this by inserting two more sanctuaries with cruciform bases between the three existing shrines.

At nearly the same time Buddhism reached the upper course of the Progo river where Borobudur was under construction. In its first stage Borobudur would have consisted of a terraced stone pyramid surrounded by brick monuments reminiscent of the Sivaite Khmer temple of Bakong (beginning of the 9th century) at Roluos in Cambodia. The first stage of Candi Mendut, on Borobudur's east-west axis, was not destroyed but simply taken over. The stone structure which the Buddhists built completely engulfed the Hindu structure of brick, as can be seen particularly clearly for the mouldings of the temple's foot. The essence of this approach was applied to Borobudur itself.

At the end of the 8th century, the domain of Buddhist stone architecture covered all of south central Java as far as the upper valley of the Progo. On the edges of this core, numerous wooden or brick sanctuaries probably provided the villagers with opportunities to follow their own individual, religious cults and practices. It is important to note, finally, that within a five kilometre radius of Borobudur, some 30 sites have been discovered, mainly Hindu, further attesting to the existence of the two religions side by side. No large settlements have been discovered in this area, only villages.

Three-branched niche from the interior of a chapel from the first iconographic system at Candi Sewu.

Bali During the Early Classic Period

The late prehistoric and early historic periods are difficult to disentangle in Bali. Sites have remained in continual use since late prehistory, and have been frequently altered, though some original patterns may remain.

»»Statue of Bhatara Da Tonta, Trunyan. From Nieuwenkamp's 'Zwerftochten op Bali', 1912.

Megalithic Practices

In the area between the Petanu and Pakerisan rivers Balinese megalithic culture is still visible in architectural form. The custom of placing large stones in the pavilion of a temple is one example. Terraced structures still exist in some temples at Sanur. Examples of the terracing tradition including the use of menhirs can be seen at Selulung and Sembiran; stone seats are found in Gelgel, Klungkung; and stone paths in villages classified as Bali Aga including Tenganan Pegeringsingan, Trunyan, and Julah can be seen as expressions of a megalithic tradition.

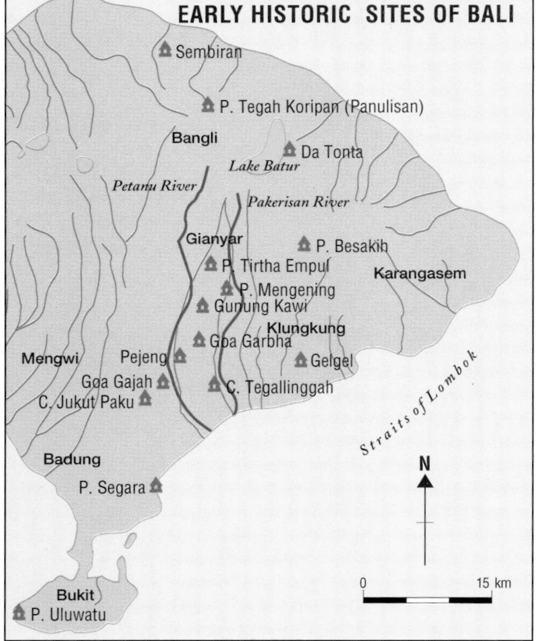

The Role of Water

Water, symbolising purity and fertility, already played an important part in Balinese culture in the Early Classic period. Many remains from that period are found near springs or riverbanks, especially of the Petanu and Pakerisan. These remains include Tirta Empul, Gunung Kawi, Goa Garbha and Tegallinggah, Goa Gajah, Candi Jukut Paku, and Candi Jehem. Water was channelled through the temple body and then into a river used to irrigate fields downstream. This can be interpreted as a design intended to fertilise the water with blessings.

Ancestor Worship

Ancestor worship is another prehistoric tradition which still persists in Bali. In the largest temple in Bali, the Besakih complex, is a pavilion termed *pedharman* which is used for prayers to the ancestors. Besakih's terraced groundplan conforms to prehistoric tradition. The village of Trunyan, on the shore of Lake Batur, maintains several traditions which may represent continuity with prehistory. Corpses are usually conveyed to their final resting place by row boat, a practice reminiscent of the canoe motif believed to portray spirit boats found on bronze drums of the Preclassic era.

Inscriptions

Documentary evidence shows that Trunyan had come into contact with Hindu cultural influence by the 9th century. The oldest inscription mentioning Trunyan dated 911 AD refers to the repair of a sacred shrine for Bhatara Da Tonta, a name which is not Sanskrit. The word Da is an honorific, while Tonta is the name of a deified local personage. A four-metre tall statue now kept in a *meru* in the Pura Desa of Trunyan is called Dewa Ratu Gede Pancering Jagat or 'the great god who is the centre of the world'. This statue can be interpreted as an ancestor of the founder of the village and not a Hindu deity. Worship of ancestral spirits and local gods in Trunyan is very active and may indicate continuity with prehistoric traditions.

Inscriptions show that candi were erected for various rulers. Portrait statues from the classical period are also frequently found in Bali. These statues may portray royalty or other important figures. Collections of them are found in some temples including Tegah Koripan and Panulisan.

Reconstructing Settlement Patterns

Balinese architectural remains of the Early Classic period are confined to religious structures. No remains of habitations have ever been recovered. The houses of the classic era must have been built of perishable materials. Some artificial caves carved at Gunung Kawi display details that probably imitate aspects of wooden construction, but it is difficult to reconstruct the settlement pattern of early classic Bali. Archaeological remains of candi, statuary, and other religious artefacts tend to be concentrated in the same areas as prehistoric remains, from which it can be inferred that there was continuity of settlement. The huge bronze drums, stone sarcophagi, clay seals bearing Buddhist mantras, statuary, and architecture show that Pejeng has been an important settlement area for 2,000 years.

It is common in modern times for settlements to be located in the direction of *kelod* or *teben* (west/south or toward the sea), relative to sacred edifices which are located in the direction of *kaja* or *luwan* (east/north or toward the mountain). The *kaja–kelod* or *luwan–teben* concept in

Stone seats like these at Gelgel, are found in several parts of Indonesia, probably constructed at many different periods. The custom of using stone seats for respected individuals on public occasions probably existed in many prehistoric Indonesian cultures.

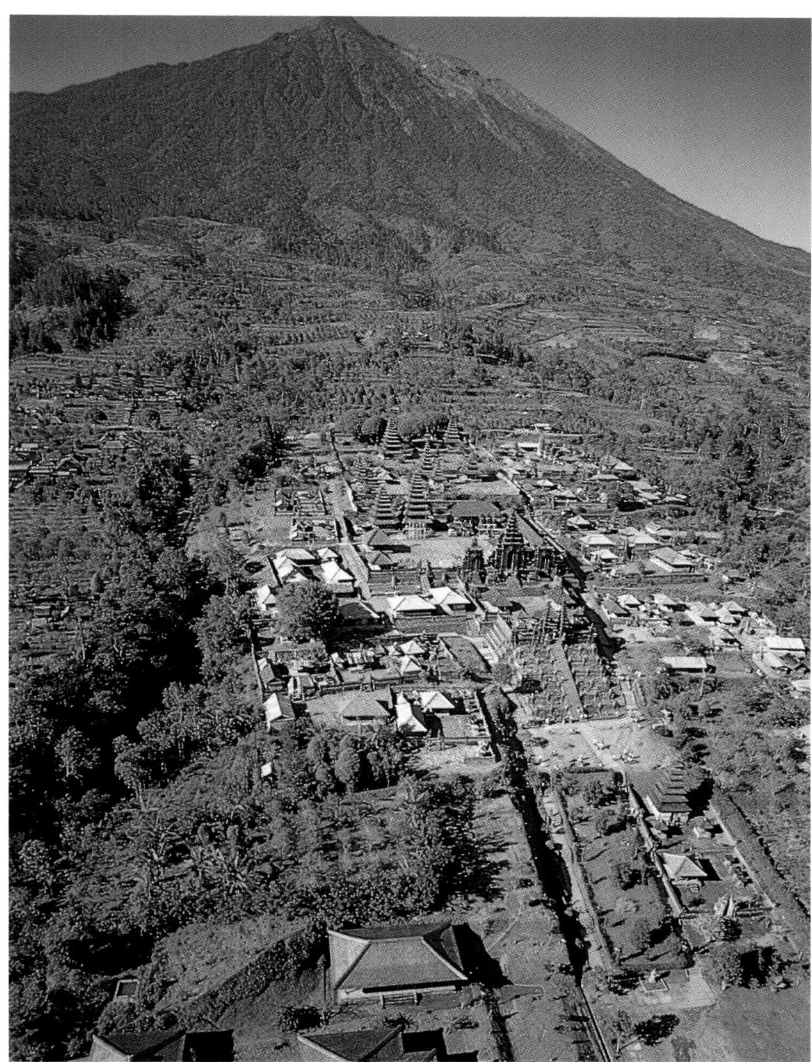

««*The great Besakih complex on the slope of Mount Agung, site of some of Bali's largest religious ceremonies. (Below) Plan of its terraces.*

modern Bali can be used as a guide to understanding settlement patterns in classic Bali.

Social Stucture

Old Balinese inscriptions provide an insight into the social and political units in early historic Bali. The oldest inscriptions from 882–975 AD use the title sang Ratu (Indonesian for maharaja) to refer to the highest political authority. The title Sri Maharaja first appears in the Gobleg inscription, dated 983 AD. In later times the number of royal officials increased, as Balinese society became more complex. The next level of authority beneath the kingdom was the village, where inscriptions mention a number of officials whose authority and responsibilities are not clear except for that of the scribe. One term, *kabayan*, is still used today in some mountain villages as a title for the village head. However, it is not clear whether this also applies to the ancient Balinese.

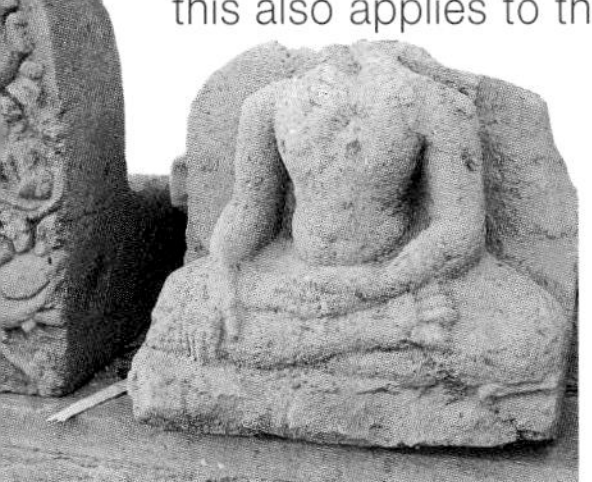

Statues at Pegulingan accidentally uncovered during excavations for a new pura show that a Buddhist stupa once stood here, probably during the Early Classic Period.

Economic Base

Rice cultivation has long been the main economic basis of Balinese society. Sarcophagus burials, over 150 of which have been found, required a great input of time and energy, and the provision of burial goods, which would have depended on a rice surplus. This notion is supported by the distribution of sarcophagi which are found in predominantly wet rice areas.

Inscriptions dating from the 9th and 10th centuries mention *sawah* (wet rice fields), *pagagan* (dry rice field), *parlak* (dry field), *mmal* (garden) and *padang* (grassland). The intensification of agriculture may have been facilitated through the construction of dikes and irrigation canals, and also by the introduction of the plough. The terms *suwak* or *kasuwakan* meaning an 'irrigation system' were already being recorded in Balinese inscriptions dating from the 11th century. New areas of land were also being opened for agriculture.

Several domesticated plants, including taro, coriander, rice, cotton, bananas, coconut, onion and garlic, are also mentioned in these inscriptions. So too are domesticated animals such as the buffalo, horse, goat, dog, duck, chicken and pig. Horse breeding was practised at this time, and cockfighting, which was taxed, was also popular. Cultivated land, irrigation water and domestic animals were also taxed.

Agricultural produce was bought and sold at village markets. The three day market system is mentioned in the inscriptions, a system which still persists today, and is known as *pasah, beteng* and *kajeng*. A market official called a *Ser pasar* was also mentioned in these old inscriptions, as were several coinages, including *suwarna, masaka, kupang, saga* or *piling*. Inter–island trade, already in evidence during the Prehistoric period, was known to have continued into the Early Classic period.

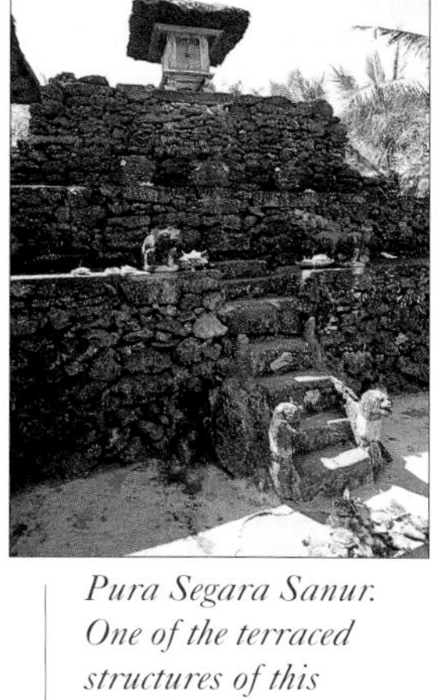

Pura Segara Sanur. One of the terraced structures of this temple, built of unworked stone. This temple contains several such miniature versions of a type of sacred edifice which probably was introduced by the first Austronesians. Analogous sacred sites called marae were also built in Polynesia.

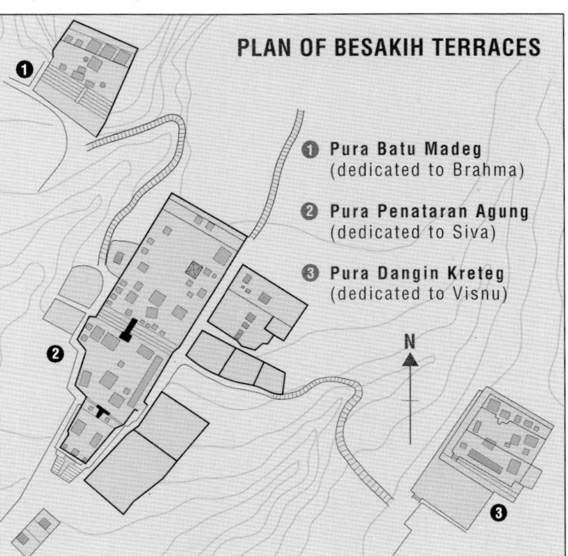

Borobudur and the Rise of Buddhism

Buddhism was a popular religion in central Java for only about a century, between circa 750 AD and 850 AD. Despite the relative brevity of its popularity, Buddhism fostered a number of great monuments. Borobudur, the best known of these, is interesting both for its beauty and for the light it sheds on the evolution of the Buddhist faith beyond India.

↲ Worshippers at Borobudur.

15 cm

Bronze vajra, a symbol of the thunderbolt excavated at Borobudur, used in esoteric Buddhist rituals.

The reliefs of Borobudur were probably used as teaching aids by ancient monks.

Mahayana Buddhism in Indonesia

The earliest evidence of Buddhism in Indonesia is found in an account of the voyage of a Chinese monk Faxien, who went to India to obtain scriptures and returned on a merchant ship via Java in 414 AD. At that time he reports that "Brahmanism" was flourishing, and Buddhism nearly non-existent.

By the 14th century Indonesian Buddhism had developed in a parallel direction to those Tantric versions still found in Tibet. Inscriptions from Java and Sumatra refer to Buddhist ceremonies which included intoxication, dancing on cremation grounds, and ritual love-making.

Buddhist visitors during the 7th and 8th centuries described Java and Sumatra as major centres of Buddhist scholarship. I-Ching, a Chinese monk, spent six months in Sriwijaya in 671 AD, and lived there for five years between 686 and 691 AD. He was impressed by the high standard of Buddhist scholarship. He noticed that Sumatran Buddhism possessed some unique characteristics which included praying to serpent deities (*naga*). I-Ching mentioned that many other Chinese pilgrims went to study in Indonesia. Indonesia also attracted famous Indian teachers. Monks from as far away as Sichuan in China and from north Vietnam went to Java in order to study under a famous teacher. Around 600 AD Mahayana Buddhism developed variants based on the idea that certain people can shorten the path to enlightenment by using appropriate techniques. These doctrines were in the early stage when Buddhism spread to Indonesia. The Way of the Thunderbolt (Vajrayana) which promises quick liberation with practices from Tantric manuals became popular by the end of the 9th century. These ideas associated with esoteric Buddhism were still evolving when Borobudur was designed.

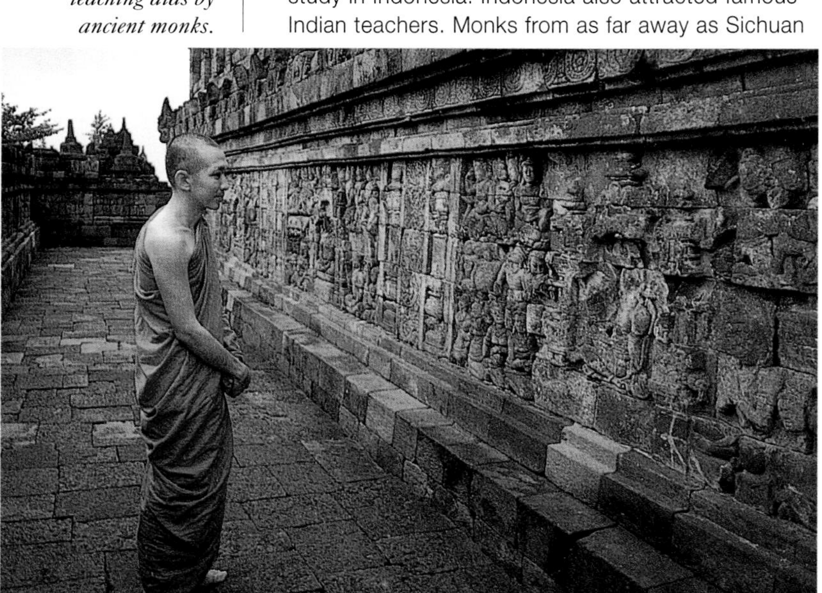

The Role of Buddhist Teachers

One of the most important Indian Buddhist teachers of the 8th century, Vajrabodhi, sailed to Sumatra in 717 AD, and then to Java where he met a Sri Lankan monk named Amoghavajra who had come to Java on a visit with his uncle, a trader. Amoghavajra became Vajrabodhi's pupil and accompanied him to China in 719 AD. They stayed in China until Vajrabodhi died in 741 AD. Amoghavajra returned to Java and collected new scriptures which he brought to China to translate into Chinese. Amoghavajra attracted many disciples, one of whom, Huiguo (746–805), taught both a Javanese and a Japanese who later founded Shingon (True Word) Buddhism in Japan. Scholars believe that Shingon and ancient Javanese Buddhism were closely related. A study of modern Shingon Buddhism can give some hint of the nature of Buddhism in early Java. The emphasis on the use of mandalas is one trait which modern Japanese and ancient Javanese Buddhism share. Unlike Java and Bali, Buddhism remained an important religion in Sumatra until the arrival of Islam. In 1013 an Indian named Atisa travelled to Sriwijaya in order to study with a famous teacher there. After Atisa had lived in Sriwijaya for 20 years he was invited to Tibet where he is credited with reshaping Tibetan Buddhism.

Buddhism and Borobudur

Buddhism was not in a static condition during the 8th and 9th centuries when Borobudur was built. This was a period of religious ferment. Buddhists felt deep respect for philosophers who advanced new religious theories and methods. Indonesians must have contributed concepts to Buddhism in addition to helping to disseminate Indian ideas to China and Japan, but very little information has survived to show us what they were. Javanese and Sumatran centres of Buddhist learning must have had important libraries like those elsewhere, but since the main writing materials were palm leaves and other perishable materials, nothing is left of them. Only a few short texts preserved on other materials, and manuscripts written in Java after Borobudur's time had passed, give us some clue as to what they contained.

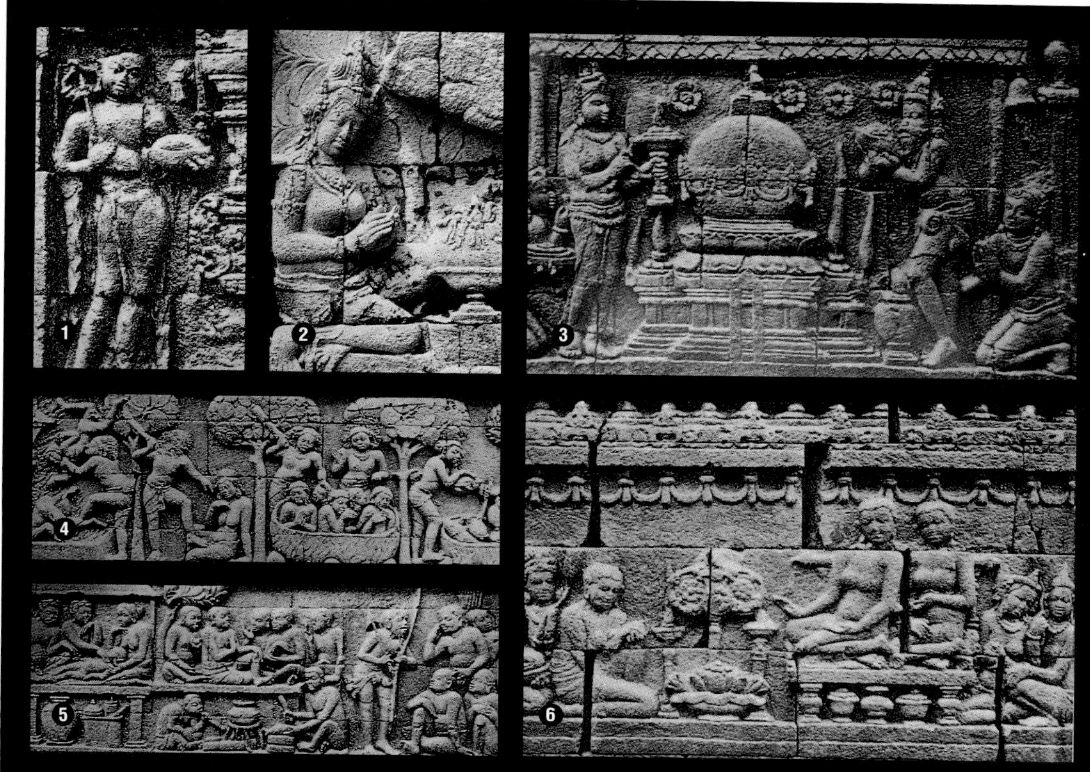

Scenes of Buddhist Devotion on Borobudur
❶ Monk
❷ A Buddhist lady making an offering of food.
❸ Revering a stupa.
❹ – ❺ Evil deeds and their punishments in hell.
❻ Initiation rite of Buddhist nun.

Buddhist Texts

The oldest surviving Buddhist text composed in Indonesia was written on 11 gold plates. From the writing style we can infer that the inscription on the plates was copied from an older version sometime between 650 and 800 AD. The scripture which they contain probably reached Java in the early 5th century; in fact it may have been brought by Prince Gunavarman. The text is written in simplified Sanskrit, perhaps devised for common people. Eight of the plates are inscribed on both sides with verses from a well-known Buddhist treatise which describes 12 causes of suffering and the link between them; it concludes that if one of the causes can be eliminated, then the chain will be broken and the others will vanish as well. Two plates are inscribed with shorter Buddhist credos. The last plate is incised with some mystical signs. The entire set of 11 plates was probably meant to be deposited in a monument such as a stupa, rather than to be read. The next oldest Javanese text on Buddhism, 'The Venerable Great Vehicle' or *Sang Hyang Kamahayanikan*, was written around 925–950 AD. It consists of 42 Sanskrit verses with Javanese commentary.

Most of the monastery libraries in Java and Sumatra in the 9th century probably contained a copy of *Great Vairocana*, the preaching of a deity known as Vairocana, literally 'Universal Light'. *Great Vairocana* is aimed at those who believe in using such aids to rapid enlightenment as mandalas and tantras. This scripture also became popular in central Java by 900 AD after Borobudur was completed.

Historians have discovered only two documents which may have been written about Borobudur while it was a centre of activity. One inscription dated 824 AD mentions a religious edifice referring to a structure divided into ten parts, a number symbolising the stages of development through which an 'Enlightened Being' must pass to become a Bodhisattva.

The second inscription discovered records an occasion in 842 AD when a queen allocated revenue from a village to support a sanctuary named Bhumisambhara. If the sanctuary had had the suffix *bhaudhara*, 'mountain', then the name Borobudur might have been derived from the phrase *bhara[bhaudhara],* meaning "the mountain of the accumulation of virtue on the [ten] stages [on the way to becoming a Bodhisattva]".

Archaeology of the Borobudur area. There are 30 sites within 5 kilometres of Borobudur, mostly of Hindu temples. Many Javanese continued to worship Hindu gods in the shadow of Borobudur. An excavation 4 kilometres northwest of Borobudur uncovered over 1,000 potsherds, fragments of bronze, iron, beads, and even a stone adze. This may have been a relatively large village.

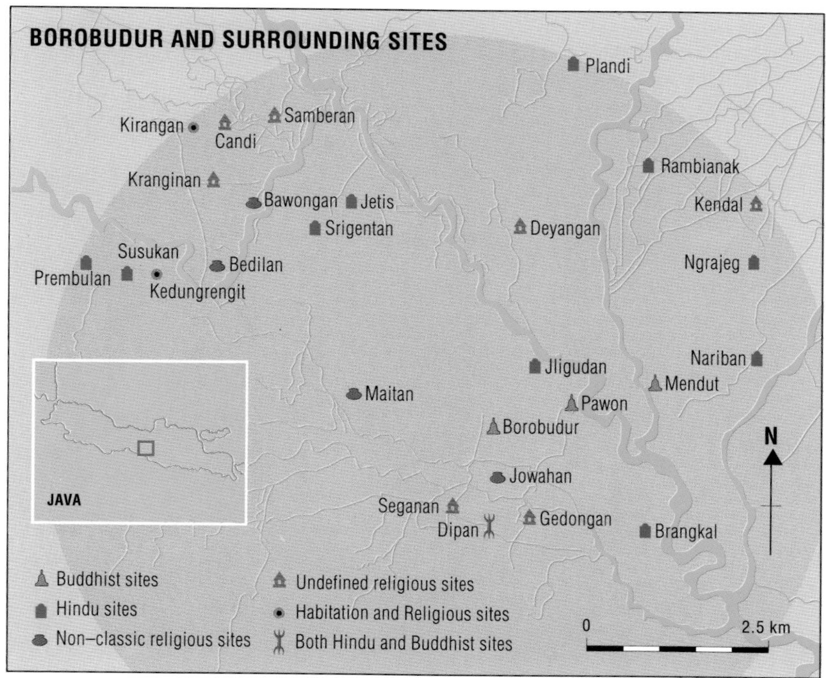

Borobudur: Form and Symbolism

Among the ruins of ancient Indonesia, Borobudur is unique. It contains no interior room analogous to the principal component of most Indonesian candi. Its shape can only be explained as the fusion of a number of elements both foreign and local.

STAGE ONE
The first stage began probably in 780 AD. In the first stage, a small structure three terraces high was erected on which another structure was begun and then destroyed. The structure may have been initially designed as a stepped pyramid.

STAGE TWO
The second stage saw the widening of Borobudur's foundation and the number of terraces was increased to include two more square terraces and one round one.

STAGE THREE
More thorough changes were made whereby the top round terrace was removed and replaced with a new set of three round terraces. Stupa were also built on top of these terraces.

STAGE FOUR & FIVE
There were minor changes to the monument including the addition of new reliefs and changes in the stairways and archways. In spite of these, the symbolism of the monument remained the same and alterations were mainly decorative.

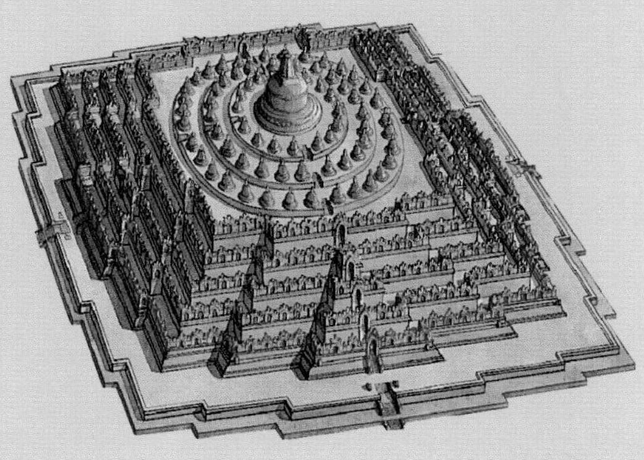

Symbolic Dimensions of Borobudur

At the summit of Borobudur stands a stupa. Some scholars have decided that Borobudur is this stupa, and all the accompanying components — the smaller stupa, the hundreds of statues, the thousands of relief panels — are mere embellishments, ancillary details without which the monument would still retain its fundamental significance. The lower storeys would thus be no more than a pedestal for the crowning motif at the structure's apex.

This explanation seems to give too little weight to the continuity between the multi-tiered lower storeys and the terraced shrines of the Preclassic era, associated with megaliths and probably designed for rituals connected with worship of ancestral spirits. The Buddhists who designed Borobudur occupied a site which, as J. Dumarçay has shown, had already been subjected to preliminary landscaping aimed at constructing a terraced landform (stage one).

It may be coincidental that the Buddhists chose this same site, and accommodated their design to the pre-existing landform merely to save time, but an alternative explanation is that the designers of Borobudur chose to build on this place precisely in order to associate themselves with the symbolism already established there.

Stages of Construction

The construction of the Buddhist monument on Borobudur's hill began when Buddhism was still quite underdeveloped in Java in comparison with Hinduism. Thus the stupa on the summit of the older stepped pyramid can be read as a fusion of Pre-classic and Classic icons.

Borobudur's construction took about 50 years, during which the design was altered. In stage two, stairways were changed and the base of the monument was extended, hiding the original foot. In stage three, circular terraces at the summit were added. In the final stages, only minor alterations were made.

Statues and Mandalas

The combination of motifs at Borobudur does not end at two. The groundplan of the monument seen from above clearly forms a mandala pattern. Mandalas are diagrams in which deities are placed in particular locations forming rings or concentric circles. These diagrams come in many types (over 2,000) and have multiple purposes, including such functions as aiding meditation, and delineating sacred space from which evil forces are excluded.

On Borobudur there are six different types of Buddha image. On the east, visitors are greeted by three tiers of walls atop which sit Buddhas in Dharmacakramudra (gesture signifying the conquest of illusion). On the south are three tiers of images in Varamudra (gesture of charity). On the west, three tiers of statues display Dhyanamudra, meditation, while those on the north are in Abhayamudra, dispelling fear.

The fourth tier on all four sides depicts a Buddha in Vitarkamudra — the preaching pose. Beyond this level are three more round terraces surmounted by perforated stupas in which can be seen Buddhas in Dharmacakramudra. This pose symbolises Sakyamuni's first sermon in the deer park at Benares. One of Borobudur's unsolved mysteries is that this set of six Buddhas corresponds to no known mandala.

Narrative Reliefs

The final symbolic dimension of Borobudur stems from the reliefs narrating Buddhist texts which adorn the walls of its four rectangular galleries. In the monument's first stage, there was another series of reliefs at the structure's foot. The text illustrated here is taken from the Karmavibhangga, the Law of Cause and Effect. The text takes the form of illustrations of good deeds and their rewards, but concentrates more attention on the terrible punishments which await those who perpetrate evil deeds such as killing animals, fighting, or adultery.

This series was covered up with added stonework and it was completely carved. The reason for this measure, as Dumarçay has shown, is structural: the designers miscalculated the width of the base needed to support the monument, and had to add more stone, which obscured the first series of reliefs. Perhaps as a kind of replacement, a second row of reliefs was added to the inner face of the balustrade on the first terrace.

The walls of the first gallery are decorated with four series of reliefs: two on the wall of the balustrade, and two on the main wall. Both series on the balustrade wall are taken from texts called Jatakas, or Birth Stories. These depict tales from from the lives of Sakyamuni, the historical Buddha, in various incarnations before his final birth as a human being. The theme of these stories is that of self-sacrifice as a means to gaining merit and a better birth in the next life, with the attainment of non-being (nirvana) as the ultimate goal.

The lower level of the main wall is adorned with another series of birth stories, this time depicting scenes from the lives of the other people in addition to Sakyamuni who also attained enlightenment. In contrast to Theravada Buddhism, in which it is believed that only one being has attained enlightenment in this era, Mahayana Buddhists believe that many beings have attained this stage. These texts are called Avadanas.

The upper level of the main wall, first gallery, displays reliefs depicting the life of Sakyamuni (Siddharta Gautama) during his life as a prince who became an ascetic teacher. The reliefs begin with the Buddha-to-be in heaven before his last reincarnation, and end with his first sermon in the deer park in Benares.

The fifth and last series occupies the upper three galleries of Borobudur. The text used for the source of inspiration is called the Gandavyuha. This scripture contains the story of a young man, son of a merchant, named Sudhana who goes from teacher to teacher in the search of enlightenment. The majority of reliefs show scenes of the boy alternately travelling by various conveyances including chariots and elephant, and scenes of him kneeling reverently in front of the various teachers (kalayanamitra, or "good friends") who include men, women, children, and Bodhisattvas. At the end of his quest Sudhana is admitted to the palace of Maitreya, Buddha of the Future, atop Mount Sumeru, wherein he is given more lessons and has various visions. The last series of reliefs on the upper terrace is taken from a sequel to this text, called the Bhadracari, in which Sudhana vows to become a Bodhisattva and to follow the example of a particular Bodhisattva named Samantabhadra.

The placement of this latter series at the uppermost level of the monument seems to indicate that this was the most respected text by the builders of Borobudur. The sequence of reliefs seems designed to encourage pilgrims to follow Sudhana's example while simultaneously climbing a symbolic mountain, the summit of which is thus portrayed as the goal and source or residence of the highest wisdom.

LOCATION OF RELIEFS ON BOROBUDUR

The placement of reliefs on Borobudur seems to follow a deliberate progression from the most obvious lessons at the foot, consisting of graphic punishments and rewards, to the most abstract at the uppermost level, the bliss of being a bodhisattva.

Borobudur is actually a shell of stone a few metres thick laid over a natural hill. Rain-water percolating through the structure nearly caused the collapse of the monument.

Buddhism and Architectural Change

By the time Buddhism reached its maximum extent, briefly attaining the Dieng Plateau in the 9th century, Javanese Buddhist rites had been profoundly modified and Buddhist temple architecture fundamentally transformed. They developed elaborate three dimensional mandalas.

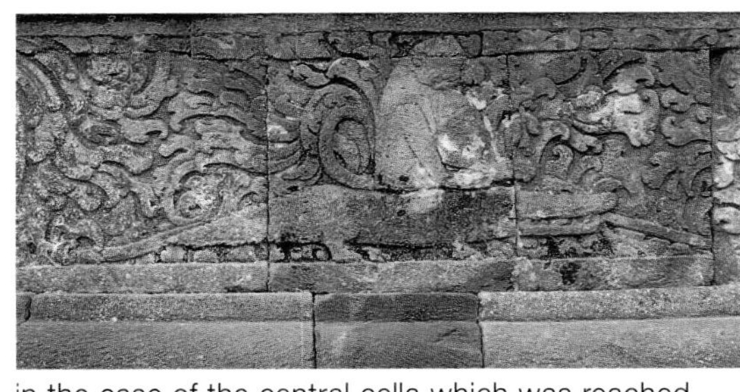

Candi Sajiwan: detail of narrative relief, depicting the story of the clever monkey who deceived the crocodile into taking him across the stream.

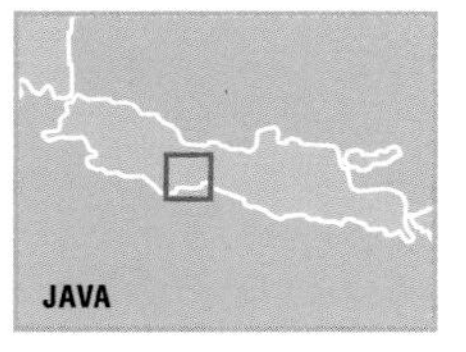

Architectural Modifications

Javanese Buddhist temples adopted the cruciform plan around 790 AD when the cult of the five Jina (Buddhas of the four cardinal points and the centre) was introduced. This plan provided separate rooms for the images, and the use of cella open to the exterior was retained for a short time so that the statues could be seen by the uninitiated from outside the shrine. Around 800 AD, the cella were closed by doors inserted into the entrances, sometimes requiring major modifications — for example at Candi Sewu. At Candi Lumbung on the central building of the complex, the cruciform plan is only perfunctorily symbolised by niches on the south, west, and north façades, which makes it difficult to add doors. This was nevertheless carried out; but rather than doors which opened inward as elsewhere, they opened outward.

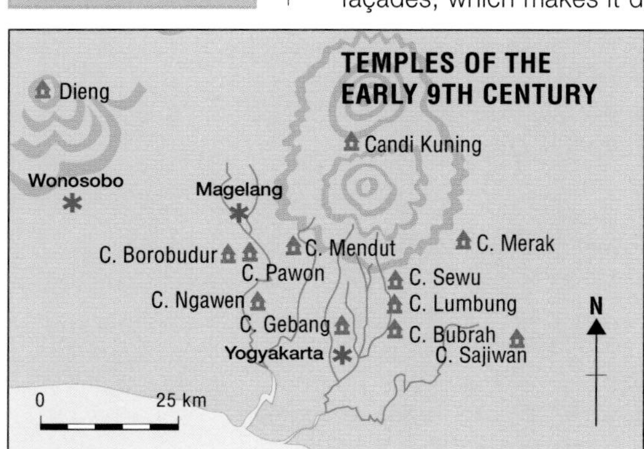

These architectural reforms were carried out in a very short time. In 775 AD we find the first construction with a square base, the adoption of the cruciform plan in 790 AD, and the closing of the cellas in 800 AD, allowing a chronology for Buddhist architecture to be established.

Candi Bubrah was built when the cruciform plan had been adopted but not the changed access; this detail is not without interest for it shows that Candi Bubrah was not associated with the first plan for Candi Sewu but rather the second. This also shows how the sequence began: the niches had been designed for standing images whereas the statues representing the Jina are in seated postures. It was thus necessary to decrease the height of the niches by inserting stones. The entrance of Candi Sajiwan, cruciform in shape, was redesigned; it is probably quite contemporary with Candi Bubrah.

The reform had the greatest effect on Candi Sewu where the entrances on the central temple had to be inserted into a monument which was to be significantly transformed. This caused great problems in the case of the central cella which was reached directly by a broad staircase; it was necessary to thicken the walls and shorten the landing. On the chapels, not only was a door added but also a vestibule and, wherever possible, a staircase to enable one to climb over the temple foot.

This reform was not only applied to major monuments, but also to minor ones, such as Candi Gebang (later transformed into a Hindu monument) and Candi Bima, at Dieng, altered when the Sailendra reached this region: a vestibule was attached to the east wall, covering part of the niches meant for the guardian statues of the original temple.

Candi Sewu: plan of the central precinct indicating the redesigned cruciform main shrine and the first row of surrounding chapels.

AXONOMETRIC DRAWING OF CANDI SEWU WITH DIFFERENT STAGES

Reunification of Central Java

When the Hindu Sanjaya reunited central Java, they showed themselves to be tolerant and the Buddhist sanctuaries were not touched. This is in contrast with the Buddhists who took over and altered several Hindu temples during their expansion (for example Candi Ngawen and Candi Bima). The Sanjaya even allowed Buddhists to continue their projects, although one can conclude (if the Dutch restoration has not altered the structure too seriously) that Candi Mendut was transformed by the addition of a vestibule, built with characteristic Hindu construction techniques which were introduced no earlier than 830 AD.

What the Evidence Suggests

The term revolution may be too strong for a situation which, architecturally speaking is quite trivial, but the addition of the doors to the cella at Buddhist temples nevertheless has great historic meaning. The epigraphic documents from this period are often very brief and they take for granted information which we no longer possess, since it was unnecessary to spell out facts which were commonly known at the time. Architecture provides a source of knowledge which in other circumstances would not assume such importance.

We do know from textual sources that esoteric Buddhism was making its influence increasingly felt in Java around 800 AD. At Borobudur, in the early stages of construction, only the top of the stairways at the transition between the square terraces with narrative reliefs and the round terraces bearing the perforated stupas were furnished with gates. In a later phase gates were added to the lower levels where the stairways reached a new terrace. This feature seems to emphasise the importance of the moment when pilgrims reached a new series of reliefs. There is, however, no evidence that these gates were ever equipped with doors that could be closed.

As esoteric Buddhism evolved, eventually four different levels of believers were distinguished, according to their assumed level of spiritual awareness. We do not know how the different levels of religious merit were correlated with different levels of the social hierarchy, but it is not unlikely that the two tended to parallel each other closely. Thus it is possible that the architectural developments of the early 9th century had both religious and social connotations. In the religious sphere, the utilisation of mandalas signifies a greater interest in various aids to quicker enlightenment than was promised by the non-esoteric form of belief. In the social sphere the addition of doors shows that Buddhism, in 800 AD, imitating Hinduism, required the closing of doors to the interior of the cella (the only exception is that of Candi Lumbung), probably during the ceremonies which consisted of bathing the statues, and this ritual could not be seen by any but the faithful.

The length of time taken to implement this reform could not have been short in view of the fact that different techniques were used to insert the doors. It is possible that the first temple to be reformed was Candi Sewu, around 800 AD, and Candi Mendut, one of the last, around 840 AD. This is a relatively long time which indicates that this reform was not easily accepted, whereas the change to a cruciform plan was quickly adopted, Candi Sewu and Kalasan having been transformed in 790 AD and from this time until 830 AD no other plan was used. Only after the Sanjayas' return did Buddhist architecture undergo further evolution.

Detail of devotee at Candi Mendut.

«Candi Bima, Dieng: the only temple of this type in Indonesia which takes its inspiration from Orissa, north India. In the 9th century it was altered by Buddhists during their brief period of influence at Dieng.

Candi Mendut. During restoration in the early 20th century it was discovered that a brick structure (in red) lies within the stone exterior.

0 10 m

«««Candi Sewu: around 800 AD the original building composed of a simple square was redesigned as a cruciform shape to accommodate the symbolism of the five Jina Buddhas.

Prambanan and Architecture

Buddhism attained its greatest extent at the start of the 9th century when the power of the Hindu Sanjaya dynasty was in decline. However, in 825 AD a reaction against Buddhism began, fuelled by a new cultural impetus from India. Part of this impetus consisted of new technical practices for laying out and constructing monuments. As a result, when Hinduism was revived it was accompanied by a great architectural renewal, centred southeast of Mount Merapi.

»»Plaosan Lor: main sanctuary, flanked by chapel on left, stupa on right.

(Below) Location of temples during the Hindu revival.

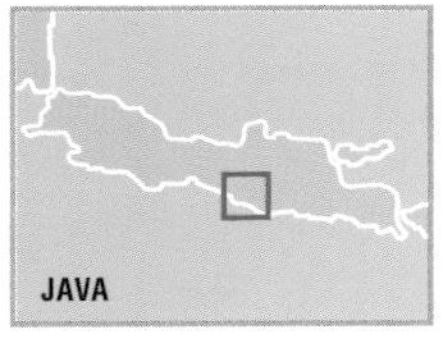

Banyunibo. The roof of this stone sanctuary seems to reproduce a type of thatched roof possibly used for ancient wooden shrines in Java.

The Prambanan Complex

One of the most important manifestations of the new political order established around 825 AD was the construction of the complex known as Lara Jonggrang at Prambanan, which was finished in 856 AD. The central part of the complex consists of three main shrines dedicated to the gods of the Trimurti. The temple of Siva stands in the centre, that of Visnu on the north, and that of Brahma to the south. In front of each of these main temples stands another, smaller temple, constructed to contain a statue of the mount of each god. This ensemble is completed by two annexes, the 'Candi Apit' or 'flanking temples', and nine small shrines to shelter the stones demarcating the compound within which the temple complex stands. The central shrine, perhaps dedicated to the local god of the soil, rests on a projection from the base of Candi Siva, thus forcing the complex's layout to be asymmetrical. This central shrine, a small and unobtrusive monument with a niche perhaps meant for the insertion of offerings, is set against the south side of the east staircase leading to the main sanctuary of Candi Siva.

This new principle for laying out temple complexes was copied not only at other Hindu sites, but also at Buddhist ones, both in central and east Java. When Candi Badut (near Malang) was rebuilt, the central space of the complex was already covered by the main sanctuary. Since it was impossible to move the monument, the centre of the complex had to be changed so that the centre of the new compound could be left free.

The main terrace of Prambanan is surrounded by four concentric squares of chapels on the lower terraces, at least some of which once bore a painted inscription. These inscriptions have now almost completely vanished, but the epigrapher J. G. de Casparis has compared them with the carved inscriptions found in similar locations on Candi Plaosan. These short inscriptions show that each of the smaller chapels was donated by a high ranking noble to the temple in which the main god was depicted in the king's image. The location of the donor's chapel within the complex seems to correspond to the actual location of that noble's domain within the geographical structure of the kingdom. The temple complex as a whole thus becomes an ideal representation of the kingdom — a veritable mandala, symbolising a harmonious symmetry between heaven and earth.

Lara Jonggrang Complex, Prambanan. (Left to right) Candi Apit; Candi Perwara, Candi Siva; Candi Visnu and Candi Apit.

Other Temples

The Hindu revival, in the second half of the 9th century, was not limited to the Prambanan region but was manifested by a reoccupation of all central Java. This took the physical form of a major construction campaign, primarily in the region where Buddhism had made its most striking progress. For example, just as Prambanan was erected near Candi Sewu, a temple dedicated to the Trimurti was built near Borobudur: Candi Banon, now completely destroyed.

Even more effort was expended along what had once been the border between the different zones of influence of the two great religions. Candi Pringapus, dedicated to Nandin the mount of Siva, was situated in front of a triple sanctuary consecrated to the Trimurti. Usually, however, the temples were limited to a single edifice dedicated to Siva, who was symbolised within by a lingga, facing three chapels. Examples include the second stage of Candi Canggal and Candi Sambisari.

Sambisari is well preserved because it was situated on low-lying ground near a river and was buried by eruptions of Mount Merapi. The site was accidentally brought to light in 1966. Almost 95 per

cent of the structure was recovered, thanks to the 6.5 metres of sand and gravel which accumulated on top of the temple courtyard. Its proportions are unusually squat. Its form is a consequence of the fact that its main edifice, built of stone, was covered by a roof which rested on wooden pillars, the bases for which have been preserved at the temple's foot. Not only were new buildings erected but old temples were renovated. For example, at Dieng, the outer wall of Candi Arjuna was rebuilt and Candi Gatotkaca was duplicated by expanding its foundation and adding a second temple.

The Sanjaya did not merely undertake numerous Hindu projects; they also showed themselves tolerant toward Buddhism. They reappropriated Borobudur, transforming the doors of the first level and extended the added foot. They left Candi Mendut, Pawon, and Ngawen intact, as well as Candi Sewu and associated temples, despite their proximity to Prambanan. They went further however when they built a Buddhist temple, Candi Plaosan, on top of an older building.

Plaosan Complex

The Plaosan complex consists of three parts which are enclosed within a double wall of volcanic tuff. The three parts are called Plaosan Lor (North Plaosan), Plaosan Kidul (South Plaosan), and Sanctuary C. The two sanctuaries of Plaosan Lor each contain two floors with three rooms on each storey, connected by doorways and illuminated by windows. Surrounding the complex are 58 chapels and 116 stupas which are arranged in three rows. This section was originally elevated above the surrounding plain on a terrace about one and a half metres high. Volcanic eruptions have raised the surrounding soil level so that today it appears to be of the same height. Unfortunately the plan of Plaosan Kidul cannot now be reconstructed, but it probably contained a central structure which has long since been destroyed. This would almost certainly have been surrounded by chapels. Sanctuary C stood further north, on the same axis as the main shrines of Plaosan Lor. This was a huge building covering an area of about 400 square metres. This structure, which was erected around 870 AD, marked the return to the use of wood for the purpose of religious construction. After such a considerable building effort in a relatively short period, some 40 years, it was necessary to return to a swifter and easier method of construction.

Other Buddhist Candi

Candi Plaosan was not the only Buddhist edifice built during this period; there are numerous examples near Prambanan, such as Candi Sari and Candi Banyunibo. The stone roof of the latter temple depicts four thatched panels. Beyond this region, Buddhist monuments of this period are rare; Candi Bendo, in the Solo area, near Sukarejo, built of limestone, follows the Plaosan Lor model on a smaller scale.

The architectural effort of the late 9th century was probably over-ambitious considering the country's economic power. A return to such massive projects had to wait until the 13th century, and even then none attained the scale of those of Prambanan.

Prambanan in the late 19th century, before restoration.

««*Sambisari, preserved almost intact under volcanic debris.*

ELEVATION OF CANDI APIT, One of the large shrines of unknown function flanking the north and south entrances to Lara Jonggrang's upper terrace.

Ratu Boko

The site, known to modern Javanese as Kraton Ratu Boko, 'King Boko's Palace', is located on a plateau, about three kilometres south of the Lara Jonggrang complex at Prambanan. The site covers 16 hectares in two hamlets (Dawung and Sambireja) of the village of Bokoharjo, Prambanan. In striking contrast to other Classic–period sites in Central Java and Yogyakarta, which are remains of temples, Ratu Boko displays attributes of an occupation or settlement site, although its precise function is unknown.

»» Gateway leading to the paseban group of ruins on the third terrace.

» Gold foil inscribed in old Javanese script, 'Om Rudrayana puh swaha', meaning: 'This is the way of the god Rudra who destroys heaven.'

Archaeological Remains

At Ratu Boko traces of probable secular structures were erected on a plateau divided into terraces separated from each other by stone walls and stone–faced ramparts *(talud)*. The site was reached by a steep path up the northwest slope of the plateau, in the direction of Prambanan.

The first of the three terraces is reached through a massive gateway built on two levels. On the western edge of this terrace is a high *talud* of soft white limestone. The second terrace, separated from the first by an andesite wall, is reached through a gateway in *paduraksa* form consisting of three doors, a larger central one flanked by two of lesser dimensions. The third terrace, the largest, contains the richest concentration of archaeological remains. Another *talud* and andesite wall separate the third terrace from the second terrace, with another connecting gateway of *paduraksa* form, this time consisting of five doors, again the central one having larger dimensions than the two which flank it.

The structural remains on this terrace consist of places with folk names connected with palaces such as *paseban* (reception hall), *pendopo* (audience pavilion) and *keputren* (women's quarters). A pool complex lies on a terrace adjoining the east side of the *pendopo*. A group of artificial caves, probably for meditation, lies to the north, isolated from the rest of the site.

Ratu Boko has yielded many smaller artefacts including statues, both Hindu (Durga, Ganesha, Garuda, a *lingga* and a *yoni*) and Buddhist (three unfinished Dhyani Buddhas). Other finds include ceramics and inscriptions. Despite the large quantity and variety of remains found there, the function of the Ratu Boko site is still unknown. Some believe it was the former palace of ancient Mataram; other scholars interpret this site as a monastery, while a third group holds that it was a place for rest and recreation. Inscriptions show that the site was occupied at least during the 8th and 9th centuries AD. Five inscriptions in pre–Nagari script and Sanskrit describe the construction of a shrine for Avalokitesvara. One inscription refers to the construction of a Buddhist monastery modelled after Abhayagiri in Srilanka, where a group of ascetic forest dwelling monks resided. Three dated inscriptions in Old Javanese and poetic Sanskrit recount the erection of two *lingga,* and bear the date 778 Saka or 856 AD. Another undated inscription mentions the erection of the *lingga* named Hara at the order of King Kalasodbhawa.

THE LEGEND OF KING BOKO

Bandung Bondowoso, King Boko's son, loved the princess Lara Jonggrang, but she rejected his proposal of marriage. King Boko defeated Lara Jonggrang's father in battle, and to save her father she was forced to agree to the union, but she posed one condition: that Bandung build her a thousand temples in one night. He entered into meditation and conjured up a multitude of genies from the earth. They succeeded in building 999 temples. Lara Jonggrang then aroused her palace maids and ordered them to begin pounding rice. This awoke the roosters, who began to crow. The genies, hearing these sounds of morning, believed the sun was about to rise and so disappeared back into the ground. Thus the prince was foiled, but in revenge he cursed the princess and turned her into a stone statue. According to tradition, she is the image of Durga in the north cella of the Siva temple at Prambanan, which is still known as Lara Jonggrang or 'Slender Maiden'. The mural at Adisutjipto Airport, Yogyakarta, depicts the main scenes from the legend.

Restored exterior wall surrounding the double meditation platform in the eastern sector of the Ratu Boko complex.

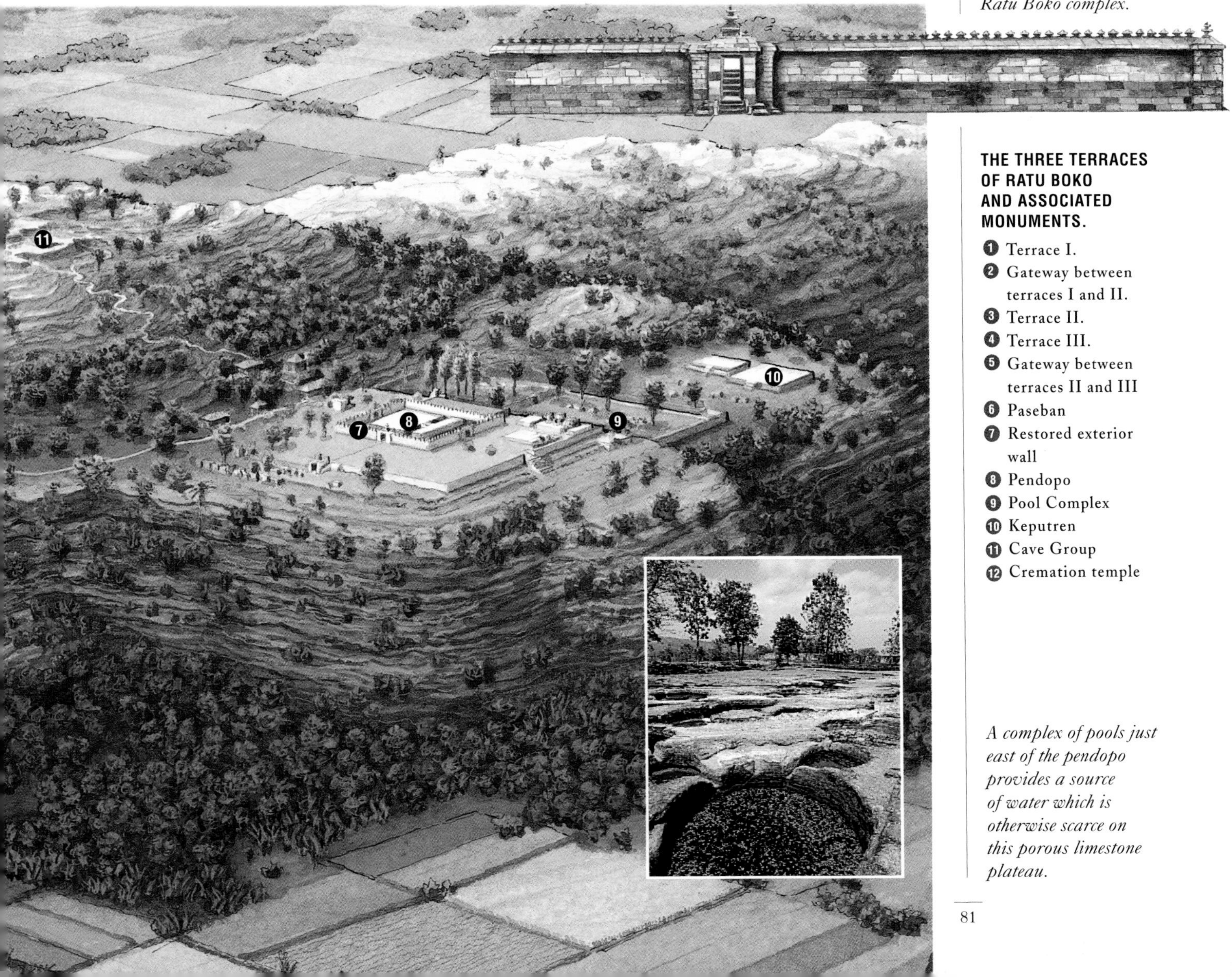

THE THREE TERRACES OF RATU BOKO AND ASSOCIATED MONUMENTS.

1. Terrace I.
2. Gateway between terraces I and II.
3. Terrace II.
4. Terrace III.
5. Gateway between terraces II and III
6. Paseban
7. Restored exterior wall
8. Pendopo
9. Pool Complex
10. Keputren
11. Cave Group
12. Cremation temple

A complex of pools just east of the pendopo provides a source of water which is otherwise scarce on this porous limestone plateau.

Sriwijaya's Golden Age

Early Sriwijaya, known by the Chinese as Shi-li-fo-shih, *sent its last embassy to China in 742 AD, half a century after it was founded in southern Sumatra. For the following century, no clear indications of the kingdom's activities have been found in south Sumatra. The kingdom however did not disappear. On the contrary, the 10th century may have been Sriwijaya's most prosperous era.*

A bronze Maitreya from Komering (Palembang), National Museum, Jakarta.

The Era of Balaputra

An inscription at Nakhon Si Thammarat in the Malay Peninsula, dated 775 AD, mentions that several Buddhist sanctuaries were founded by a king of Sriwijaya, who may have fathered a princess named Tara who later married a king of Java, a member of the Sailendra family, and begot a younger son (Balaputra). A Buddhist prince called Balaputra was defeated in battle in central Java sometime between 832 and 856 AD; he was probably the same person. Soon after this setback, the name Balaputra appears again, this time in an inscription from Bengal, northeast India, which states that he ruled over Swarna-dwipa, or the "Island of Gold", which was a common Indian name for Sumatra at that time. This inscription also said that he had a sanctuary built in the famous Buddhist centre of Bengal, Nalanda. While the data are still ambiguous, it is likely that the Hindu Sanjaya enforced their rule in Java at the expense of the Buddhist Sailendra, Balaputra left Java and emerged as a Sailendra king ruling Sriwijaya.

Recent archaeological excavations at sites in western Palembang, to the south of Seguntang Hill, have provided evidence that commercial activity was taking place on a significant scale by the early 9th century, particularly trade with China. During the second half of the 9th century, precisely when Bala-putra appears in Sumatra, that economic activity seems to have attained a grand scale. Excavations at the heart of modern Palembang have unearthed a riverine settlement that would have been prominent during the 10th–11th centuries. This is clearly evinced by large quantities of Chinese ceramics unearthed there.

»Excavation of a ca. 10th century building on Seguntang Hill.

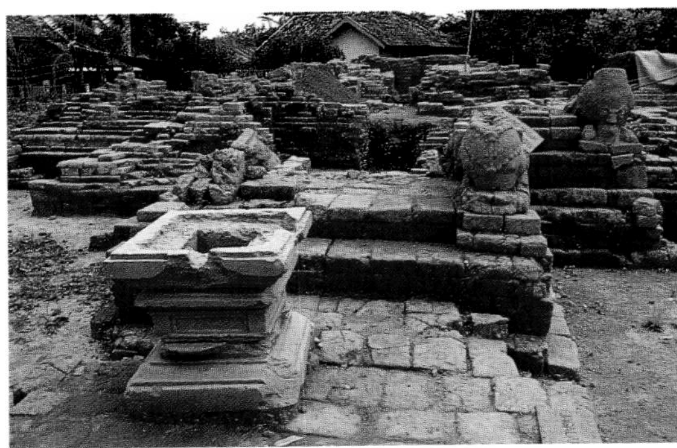

»Siva temple at Bumiayu (Tanah Abang) during restoration.

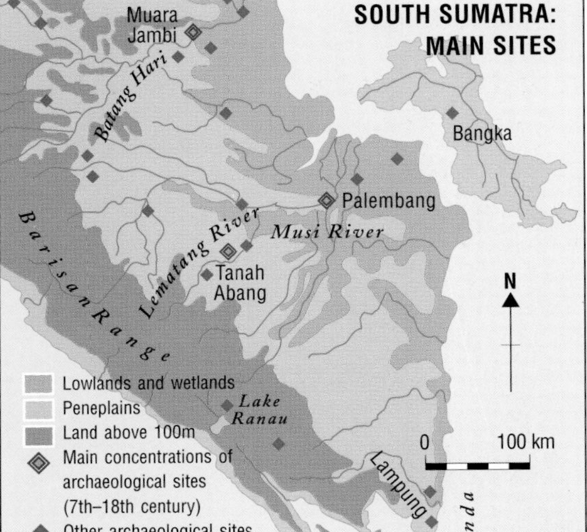

The Pinnacle of Prosperity: the 10th Century

We now enter the most prosperous period of Sriwijaya's history, when the power and fame of the maharaja of Sriwijaya attained their greatest height. Merchants from Arabia, and merchants and geographers from Baghdad always mention the Maharaja of Zabag among the powerful rulers that thrived upon the wealthiest maritime trade routes that existed at that time. The location of Zabag is uncertain, but several scholars have argued that it referred to Sumatra or Sriwijaya. He was then said to rule over Kedah, on the Malay Peninsula, where contemporary archaeological sites have indeed been found.

Sriwijaya's influence over the Malay Peninsula appears to have extended as far north as the Isthmus of Kra. What exactly this influence may have consisted of, however, is difficult to say. In 775 AD an inscription in Sanskrit was carved in that region. It came to light in the early 20th century when it was found to have been preserved in a Buddhist monas-tery, Wat Sema Muang. It mentions the victorious king of Sriwijaya, who had built five brick edifices for Buddhist deities, and three stupa. Another face of the same stone bears an inscription which mentions the head of the Sailendra family; but the relationship between this inscription and that on the first face is still in dispute. They do not seem to have been carved at the same time.

Conflicts with Java occur repeatedly during the 10th century. They appear to have been concerned with control of the produce of the Spice Islands. The Chinese received numerous embassies from the Malay rulers of Sumatra, now using the term *San-fo-qi* to designate this restored Sriwijaya.

Buddhism was still practised by the inhabitants of the Sriwijayan kingdom. During this period Buddhist temples were known to have been built on behalf of the Maharaja of Sriwijaya in China and India. However archaeological research has recently also brought to light a complex of twelve temples dedicated to the Hindu god Siva, at Tanah Abang in the hinterland of the Lematang River valley. Con-struction of these shrines was begun in the 10th century. A number of other sanctuaries, both Bud-dhist and Hindu, have been located along the valleys

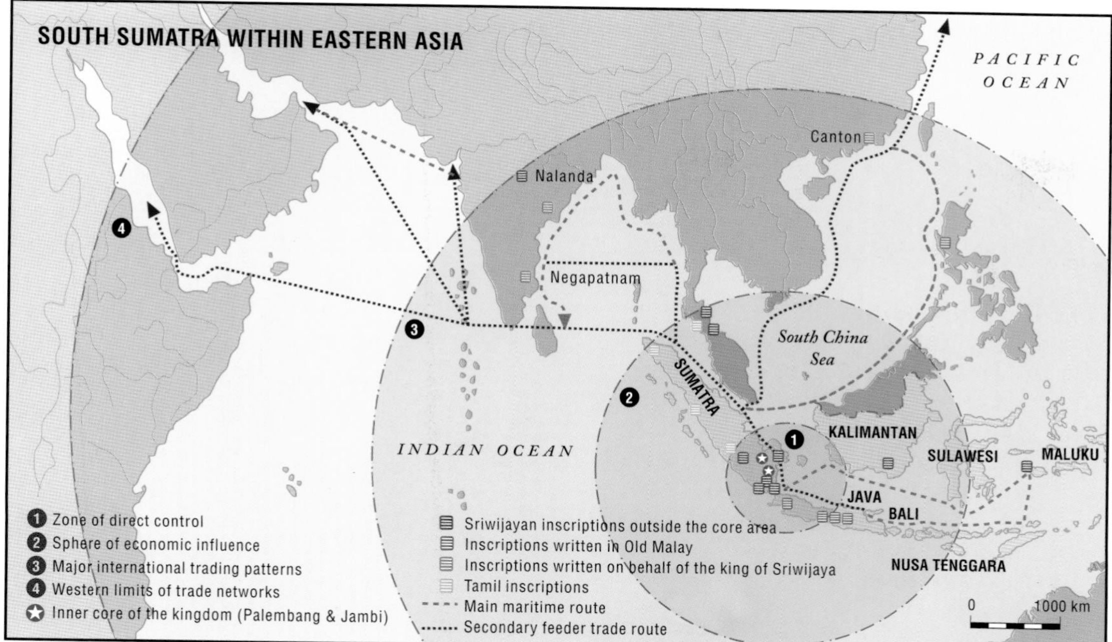

upstream from Palembang, as far west as the foot of the Barisan mountain range.

This no doubt indicates the political and economic centre at Palembang exerted a measure of influence over the vast Musi River basin. This region yielded forest products like timber and oleo-resins, alluvial gold, and possibly rice. The Sriwijaya rulers appear not to have satisfied themselves with simple entrepot trade in the harbours of western Indonesia. They fed local products into the maritime network, from their own hinterland in south Sumatra, as well as from other regions in Sumatra, Malaysia, west Java, and probably Kalimantan.

It is unfortunate that due to the paucity of written sources, historians have been unable to discover the structure of the Sriwijayan government. Sriwijaya must have been primarily a harbour-kingdom. Its direct territorial control would have been limited to the immediate environment of the ruler's abode at Palembang. However, there is no doubt that Sriwijaya also commanded a vast sphere of economic influence. The accumulated prestige and profits of an intricate web of kinship, religious and political ties to most of western Indonesia, accrued to the centre as though drawn by a magnet. The repeated building of temples by Sriwijayan rulers in more distant regions 'marked' the limits of their sphere of commercial enterprise; in India, the transfer of sanctuaries from Nalanda to Negapatnam followed the 11th century shift of power from the Palas of Bengal in the northeast, to the Cholas in the south.

Sriwijaya's Decline and the Rise of Competitors

This flourishing state of affairs, however, appears to have attracted the attention of rising neighbouring powers. Twice, in 1017 and 1025, fleets of the Chola king from south India are known to have raided the harbours under Sriwijayan control in the Straits of Melaka. They captured the king of Sriwijaya himself. The Chola appear to have played an active role in Sumatran politics for the rest of the 11th century, and no doubt it was they who encouraged the increased presence of Tamil merchant guilds in the region. These guilds left behind inscriptions in Sumatra and the Malay Peninsula.

The Chinese used more peaceful means to extract a larger share of the profits generated by Indonesian commerce. Unified under the Song Dynasty in the 11th and 12th centuries, China concentrated her economic power on a robust maritime commercial expansion. It began building its first overseas merchant navy and took a far more active part in the South China Sea trade. At this time Javanese influence increased in South Sumatra, to judge from bronze statues of East Javanese style associated with 11th-century additions to the temple complex at Tanah Abang. Sriwijaya's economic clout deteriorated under the blows received from east and west. In the last quarter of the 11th century, the political centre moved from Palembang to Jambi.

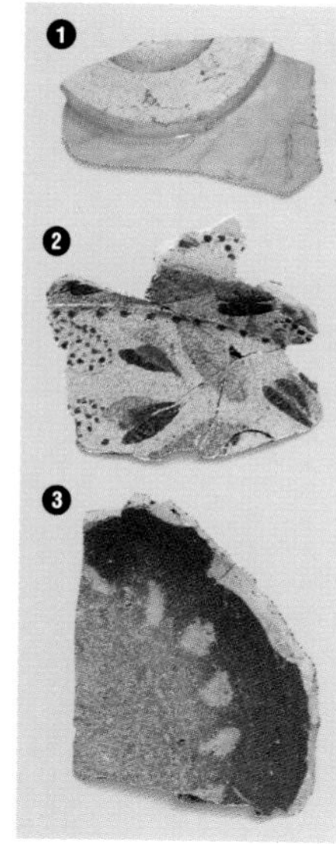

Ceramics:
❶ *Sherd of Tang opaque white ware, from Palembang excavations, 9th century.*
❷ *Islamic lustre ware excavated at Palembang, 10th–11th century.*
❸ *Fragment of Yue bowl, dated to about 840 AD.*

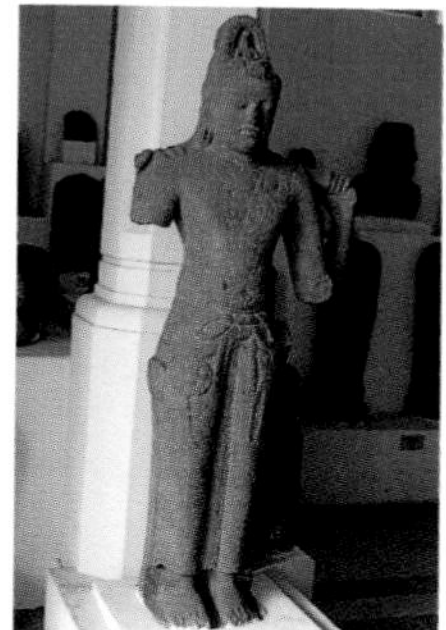

Avalokitesvara statue discovered at Palembang

««A small bronze Buddha from Seguntang Hill, Museum Balaputra Dewa, Palembang.

Photograph taken by the Javanese photographer, Cephas in 1895, showing Prambanan in ruins.

Reinforcements of the ancient foundations of Prambanan, discovered during reconstruction work.

Relief from Prambanan showing a scene from the Ramayana story in which Rama utilises his prowess in archery to slay a demon.

Bearded man, perhaps a rsi or heroic teacher and ascetic, recovered from the Dieng Plateau, probably early 8th century.

Durga slaying the demon, Mardini. This is one of the archaic images typical of Dieng style sculpture of the early 8th century, before the Javanese had formulated standard conventions for depicting Hindu themes.

LIFE IN EARLY CLASSIC INDONESIA

During the 9th century, the Hindu religion gradually asserted its claim to the loyalty of the majority Javanese population, in place of Buddhism. In Sumatra Buddhism remained predominant, but archaeologists have discovered traces of Hindu sanctuaries in various parts of the island, even near the centre of the strongly Buddhist kingdom of Sriwijaya. The 9th century witnessed the construction of the largest single Hindu edifice ever built in Java: the Siva temple at Prambanan, central Java. During the 8th century, power in Java had been contested between two families: the Sanjaya and Sailendra. This competition was apparently brought to a conclusion in about 832–856 AD by the marriage of a Buddhist Sailendra princess to a Hindu Sanjaya prince. A younger son, Balaputra, of the Sailendra line appears to have attempted to arrogate the rulership to himself; failing to achieve his aim in an armed struggle, he managed to install himself as ruler of the Buddhist Sumatran kingdom of Sriwijaya.

The newly unified ruling elite of Java exemplified the practice of religious tolerance. The rulers sponsored the construction of both Hindu and Buddhist sanctuaries. The complex of Plaosan with its elaborate mandala design, was erected at the same time as the Hindu temples at Prambanan, also laid out according to mandala principles. After these no more temples on such a huge scale were built in Indonesia. A kingdom continued to rule and issue inscriptions from central Java until 919 AD. Although there are no indications in the written sources of any decline, there seems to be a lack of new temple construction after the late 9th century. Then all traces of the central Javanese civilisation come to an abrupt end. Aside from one or two possible exceptions, no stone temples were built in Java for three centuries. The end of the 9th century is therefore an important watershed in the history of Java.

In Sumatra, the kingdom of Sriwijaya appears to have continued to prosper until the 11th century. Although it apparently sent no more embassies to China after the mid–9th century, reports from various sources indicate that the kingdom remained wealthy. Recent archaeological research in south Sumatra has finally begun to lift this veil. Bali makes its first appearance in the written sources during this era. Inscriptions found there show that this island had begun to adopt elements of Indic culture long before the formation of the kingdom of Majapahit, which Balinese folklore has credited with introducing classical civilisation to Bali.

The Javanisation of Hindu and Buddhist Art

In Indonesia's cultural history, the 9th century is the time when the fruits of acculturation with Hindu–Buddhist traditions from India reached maturity. Hindu–Buddhist concepts and technical expertise were localised and re–interpreted, becoming distinctly Indonesian. Material examples from India were never taken at face value and the same applies to religious and social concepts. They were not simply copied, but were adapted to the needs of the Indonesians themselves.

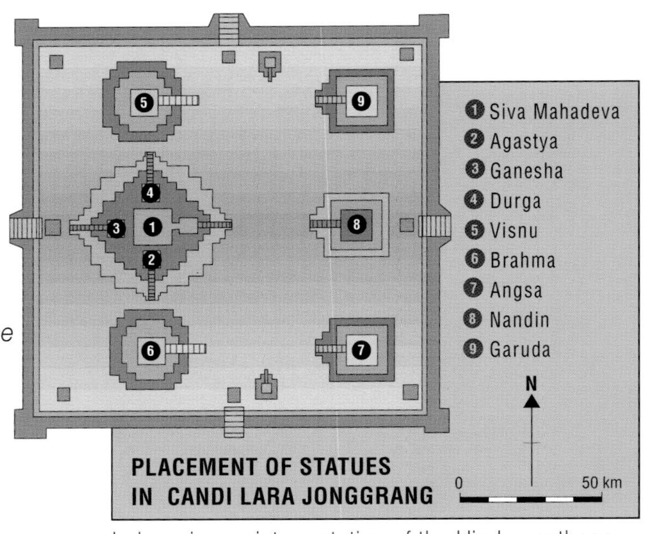

PLACEMENT OF STATUES IN CANDI LARA JONGGRANG

Sculpture of Prambanan. Siva and his three emanations (Durga, Ganesha and Agastya) formed a long–lasting unit in Java. This is an example of the Javanising process; this combination is not significant in India. The provision of a separate temple for Brahma is another point at which Javanese Hinduism had a different emphasis from the Indian model.

Central Javanese Sculpture

In the late 9th century, although Hinduism and Buddhism coexisted with no obvious sign of hostility, the two religions had separate belief systems and rituals. This contrasts with their development in the later 'East Javanese Period', from the end of the 13th century, when the two religions coalesced in what was called the Siva–Buddha school of thought. The Prambanan and Plaosan complexes are the two major religious edifices of the late 9th century. Prambanan contains examples of sculpture underlain by certain Hindu religious concepts, while Plaosan may stand for the Buddhist relationship between art and religion.

The Sculpture of Prambanan

Prambanan is the name of a village where the Lara Jonggrang complex is found. The Javanese call the temple group Lara Jonggrang, after a maiden in a local legend. A statue of the goddess Durga Mahisha–suramardini in the north chamber of the main Siva temple is believed to be the image of the maiden, who was turned to stone by a curse after deceiving her suitor. The central chamber of Lara Jonggrang contains a representation of Siva in anthropomorphic form rather than the more common lingga standing on a yoni, a speci–fically Sivaitic pedestal. The image faces east, where the main entrance to the temple is located. The same building contains separate chambers for three other deities: the aforementioned Durga Mahishasuramardini in the northern cella, Ganesha on the west, and the *rsi* or wise teacher Agastya in the south.

This composition of three particular deities in specific positions relative to Siva as principal god was an ancient Indonesian re–interpretation of the Hindu pantheon. The four deities in Indonesia became a permanent set, a practice which exists in no other Hindu lands, neither India nor other parts of Southeast Asia. Once established, this set of deities was maintained con–tinuously throughout the Hindu period. Other deities were frequently added to this core set in Javanese temples. These additions belonged to two different levels. The first consisted of the level of supreme gods: Siva accompanied by Visnu and Brahma, the three together constituting the Trimurti or 'The Three Forms' of the highest Hindu deity. At another level, two gate guardians were frequently added. These guardians, according to inference from relevant writ–ten sources, were called Mahakala and Nandisvara.

This pantheon was often further enlarged by adding yet more deities. A frequently encountered group, which is still considered relevant by modern Javanese, is the group of eight *lokapala*, led by the god Indra who resides in the east. The other members of the group reside at the remaining cardinal directions and intermediate points of the compass. The *lokapala*, led by Indra, became a symbol for the world of the gods. It was clearly differentiated from the supreme supernatural entity identified as Siva or Batara Guru. The Javanese believed that the powers of the *lokapala* were symbolically incorporated into the powers of the Javanese kings.

Other peculiarities of late central Javanese Hinduism include an emphasis on Brahma, to the extent that he was allocated his own temple at the Lara Jonggrang complex. Temples to Brahma are rare in India. In Indonesia he seems to have been associated with volcanoes, which do not exist in India. Temples to the vehicles or *vahana* of the gods such as those at Lara Jonggrang are also uncommon in India. The system of placing rows of smaller shrines in concentric squares around the central complex as at Prambanan is also not found in India. At Prambanan, it may have been adopted from the nearby Buddhist complex of Candi Sewu.

One of the most interesting aspects of the Lara Jonggrang complex is that the centre of the main compound is not used for the placement of the icon of the main deity, in this case the statue of Siva. In–stead the complex is so arranged that the midpoint is located in the spot at which the south side of the

DEITIES OF LARA JONGGRANG

Durga, the image which in Javanese folklore is the princess Lara Jonggrang (slender maiden) turned to stone by the curse of her disappointed suitor. North cella, main sanctuary.

Agastya, teacher and ascetic, south cella, main sanctuary.

Visnu, main cella, north sanctuary.

Ganesha, the overcomer of obstacles. West cella, main sanctuary.

stair leading to the Siva temple joins the base of the main temple. At this corner is a small unobtrusive shrine. Judging from the inscription which records the complex's consecration in 856 AD, the shrine was perhaps dedicated to the local gods of the soil, to prevent them from disturbing rituals.

Whereas some gods occupying minor roles in India became more prominent in Indonesia, the opposite process also occurred: some iconographic forms popular and widespread in India are seldom or never found in Indonesia. For example, one of the most popular and powerful images of Siva in India is Siva in the form of Nataraja, 'Lord of the Dance'. Bronze figures of four-armed Siva in a particular dance posture with one leg raised, surrounded by a round flame border, are and have been common in India for centuries. For unknown reasons this image was never introduced to Indonesia. It has not yet been possible to detect a pattern in the rise and fall of various Hindu deities in Indonesia, but perhaps it will be possible to reconstruct the principles which governed Indonesians' decisions to favour some Indian deities and cast others into disfavour.

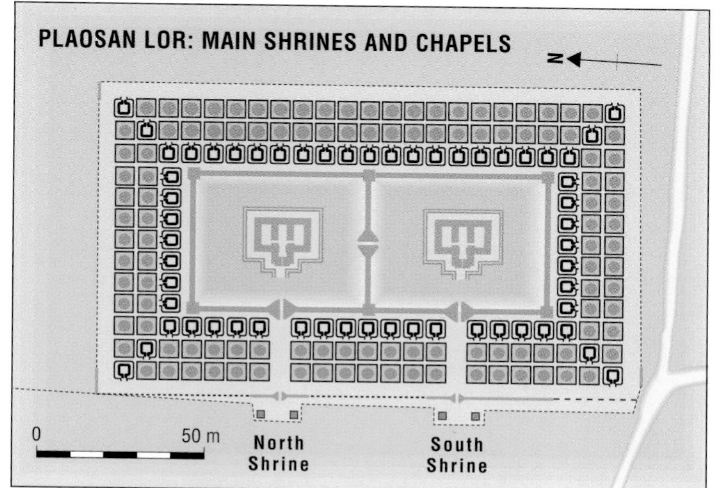

Relief Carving

Old Javanese poetry of the 9th or 10th century expounds a doctrine called *astabrata,* meaning 'eighth vow' by which kings may acquire the powers of the guardians of the eight directions. This phrase still occurs in *wayang kulit* (shadow-puppet) performances. The deities of this group are: Kuvera, Vayu, Isana Candra, Varuna, Indra, Nairrta/Surya, Agni, and Yama. This series of deities is depicted in relief on Prambanan.

The Lara Jonggrang complex is built on three levels. The uppermost level contains the main buildings, including the three temples of the Trimurti. Each of these three buildings faces smaller temples called the Vahana (vehicle) temples, since the central one contains a statue of Nandin, vehicle of Siva. The outer walls of the plinths of all six main buildings bear carvings depicting heavenly beings such as *kinnara* and *kinnari* (half-human, half-bird creatures) and heavenly trees full of miraculous flowers and fruit. It may be surmised that the whole central courtyard with all the buildings on it represents the abode of the gods on Mount Meru.

Symbolism of Plaosan

Plaosan is also a symbol, but of another concept. While Prambanan symbolises the Hindu cosmos, Plaosan symbolises the spiritual path to be taken by the religious pilgrim. Plaosan consists of two complexes, a northern and a southern one. The northern complex once contained three main sanctuaries. One of these, constructed largely of wood, has left few traces. The other two sanctuaries were nearly identical structures built of stone, each containing three chambers. Each chamber contained three statues: a Buddha in the middle, flanked by two Bodhisattvas, "enlightening beings". The set symbolised the Buddhist principle, the ultimate truth and source of enlightenment, flanked by his spiritual soldiers who have the task of descending to earth to save all creatures. Buddha was put on a higher platform than the Bodhisattvas. The Bodhisattvas each have one leg dangling down; pilgrims seated in front of them will have their eyes on the same level as the statues' feet, symbolising the accessibility of the Bodhisattva saviours. The statue of the Bud-dha is higher, symbolising that the ab-stract Buddha principle re-mains beyond the reach of human senses.

Figure of Maitreya from the northern chamber of the north shrine, Plaosan. The dangling leg may symbolise the Bodhisattva's accessibility to pilgrims.

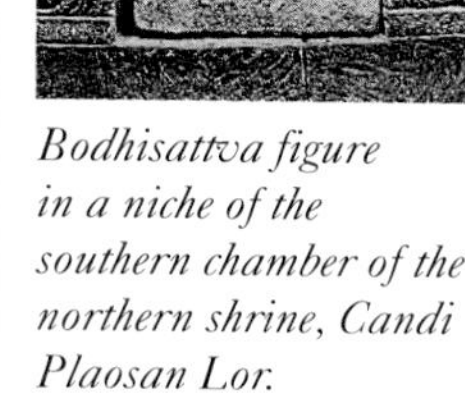
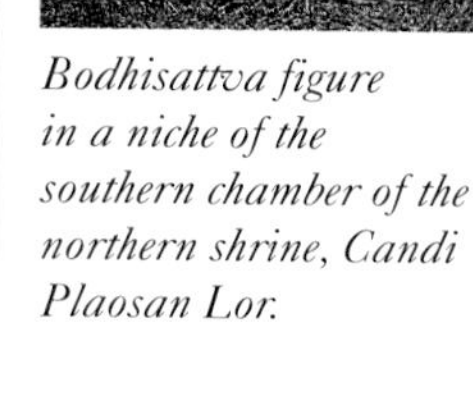

Bodhisattva figure in a niche of the southern chamber of the northern shrine, Candi Plaosan Lor.

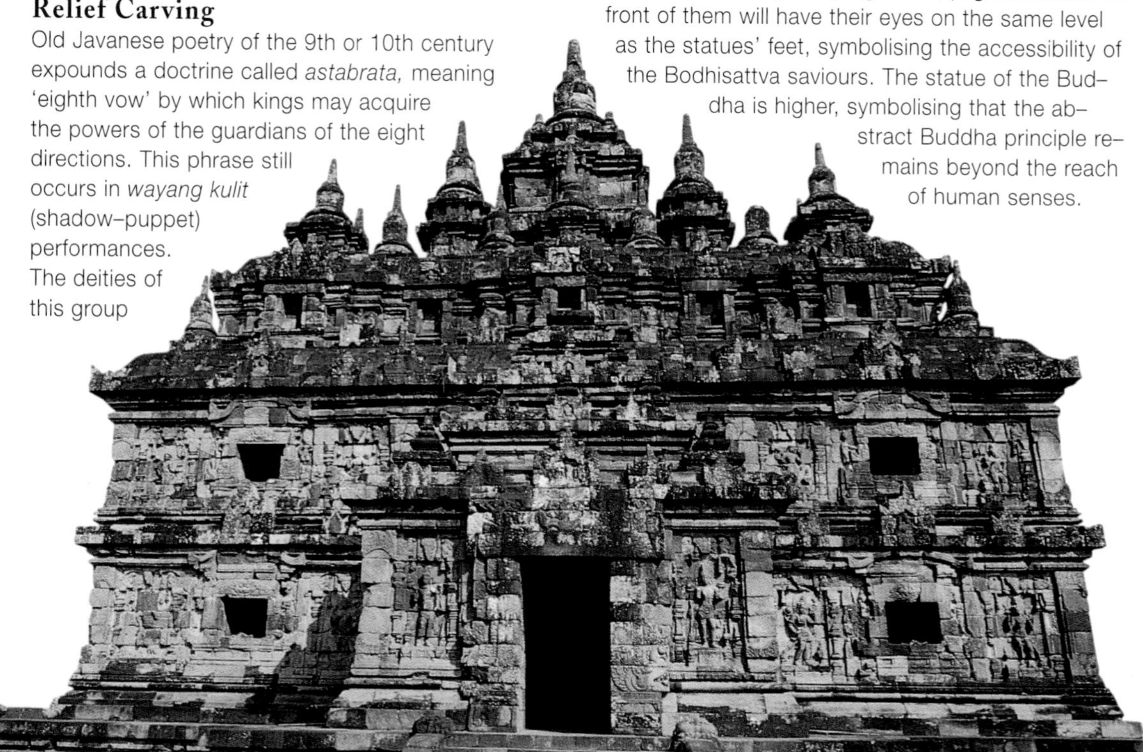

«Two-storied Candi Plaosan. The purpose of the double storey is possibly to create a three-dimensional mandala. The inner floor, built of wood, disappeared long ago.

Early Classic Sculpture

The oldest sculptural remains of the Early Classic period found in Kutai, east Kalimantan, and Tarumanagara, west Java, date from the late 4th to early 5th centuries. These examples are rudimentary, and it is the somewhat later Central Javanese statuary that is more representative of the period, displaying a maturity of development, as is lavishly demonstrated on contemporary temples.

Statue of Siva discovered in east Kalimantan and now in the National Museum, Jakarta. Its unusual style makes it difficult to date.

Bodhisattva entering Queen Maya's womb. Narrative relief from Borobudur.

Gautama with his first five disciples. Narrative relief from Borobudur.

Javanese Classic Sculpture

Early Classic sculpture can be best represented by the sculpture of the so–called Central Javanese Period, when mature development was achieved and lavishly demonstrated on central Javanese temples. High technical and artistic qualities are demonstrated by both Hindu and Buddhist temples. After a period of neglect, supposedly because of the adoption of another religion, Islam, in the 16th century, most of these temples have been restored and are maintained by the Indonesian Directorate for the Preservation and Protection of the National Heritage.

Buddhist Sculpture

Borobudur represents the peak achievement of early classic sculpture. The Buddha figures found here conform to the style of the Indian Gupta period.

Unfortunately the bronze statue of the female Bodhisattva Tara which once stood in the central room of Candi Kalasan long ago disappeared, like many other early large bronze statues which no doubt once existed. Almost all of these have been melted down; only a few fragments remain. Early Classic bronze casters were masters of their art, as demonstrated by many smaller sculptures representing a wide range of Hindu and Buddhist deities which have escaped destruction. In the early period the deities of both religions were usually portrayed standing; by the 9th century most Buddhist deities were depicted in a seated position. In addition to small bronzes and larger andesite sculptures, other beautiful examples of Buddhist sculpture include heavenly beings floating on clouds sculpted on the outer walls over niches. In some of these niches individual figures in elegant poses were installed.

Hindu Sculpture

The huge statues of the Hindu Trimurti (Siva, Visnu and Brahma) which are housed in Prambanan along with the various gods and goddesses also found in the temple conform to criteria for beauty expounded in Sanskrit manuals. These manuals governed the form that religious images could take, and consequently the statues found in central Javanese temples display the same curvilinearity as is found on ancient Indian sculpture. The bodies of these divine figures have been given a fleshy and rounded form by delineating the contours with curving lines. The Javanese statues show a tendency to minimise the voluptuousness of the figures, in effect making them more restrained. We can infer that this tendency was governed by innate Javanese taste where slimness of figure was a condition for beauty.

Borobudur and Kalasan may be regarded as representing the peak period of early classic sculpture. Earlier sculptural examples which represent the beginning of this period are some of the gold plaques and statues that were found in the region of Wonosobo

CLASSIC PERIOD METAL SCULPTURE (NATIONAL MUSEUM, JAKARTA)

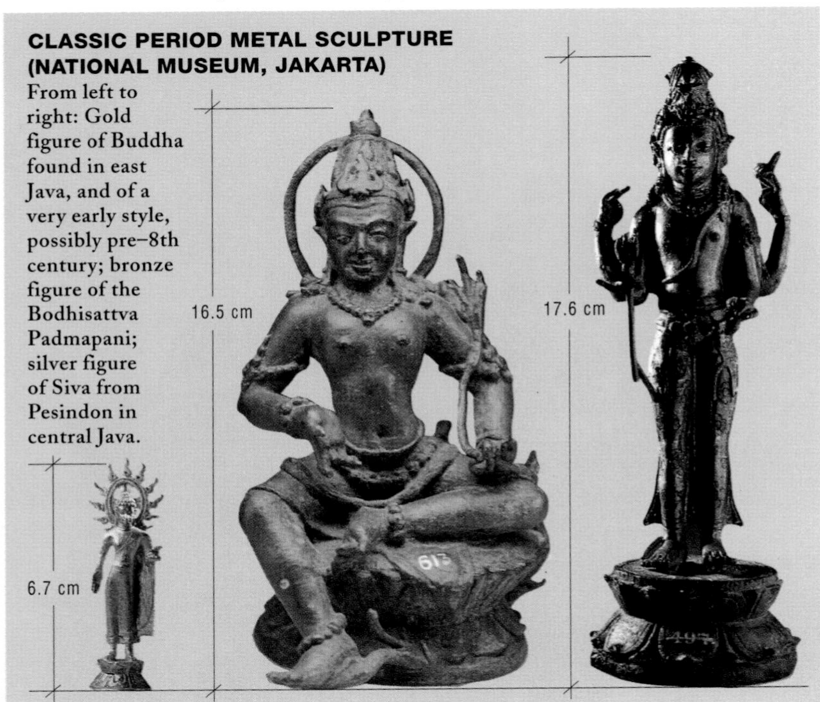

From left to right: Gold figure of Buddha found in east Java, and of a very early style, possibly pre–8th century; bronze figure of the Bodhisattva Padmapani; silver figure of Siva from Pesindon in central Java.

and Banyumas in central Java. These gold plaques have figures of either Siva, Visnu or Harihara depicted on them. The last mentioned figure combines Siva and Visnu within one body. The predominance of these figures reminds one of early statues found in mainland Southeast Asia. These earliest figures must represent a phase before the definite choice of Sivaism was taken by the then reigning kings and followed faithfully by their descendants.

Relief Carving

Early Classic sculpture is also distinguished by remarkable achievements in the art of stone relief carving. Several Hindu and Buddhist shrines in central Java have been carved with compositions obviously depicting scenes or episodes found in Hindu or Buddhist religious texts. At the temples of Mendut and Sajiwan, for example, are found panels on which are depicted scenes readily identifiable as episodes from the Jataka tales. These are stories mainly of self-sacrifice performed by Buddha in his various earlier lives. The tradition of using relief carvings to depict religious texts is not unique to Java; the practice had already appeared in India several centuries earlier. What is unique to Indonesia is the practice of placing a large number of reliefs in a series to depict an entire narrative in linear fashion.

This concept was first employed in Indonesia at Buddhist Borobudur in the late 8th century, and was later repeated at the Hindu complex of Lara Jonggrang in the mid-9th century when panels were arranged to tell the story of the Ramayana. The relief panels of Prambanan and Borobudur are arranged as pictorial narratives and the placement of the reliefs is such that religious and ritual demands are met. They follow a clockwise sequence, probably in order to conform to the practice of circumambulation or *pradaksina*, of the monument worshipped in a clockwise direction, so that the votive object or temple is always on the right of the devotee. These narrative scenes use all the modes of portraying a figure as expounded in Hindu manuals, comprising frontal figures, complete backviews, and bodies in frontal position but heads in profile.

At the same time, contemporary social and cultural, and natural settings are reflected and these scenes have provided us with a great deal of useful information about the everyday life of the Javanese people during that period. These include domestic practices such as pottery manufacture and food preparation and also various agricultural activities, jewellery, performing arts such as dancing and music making, as well as plants in their particular environments, and different animal species.

««Durga, initially the deity created from the combined forces of the mightiest Hindu gods in order to defeat the demon, Mardini, became closely associated with Siva in Java and was normally housed in a niche on the north side of Siva sanctuaries such as this one at Sambisari.

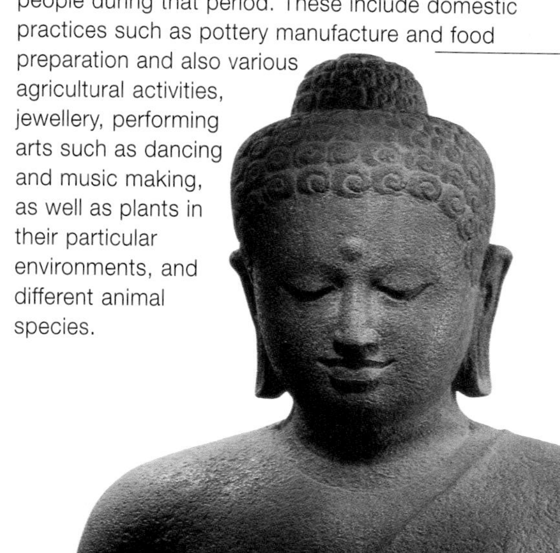

Buddhist sculpture from the top row of the square galleries of Borobudur in the vitarka (teaching) mudra. Sculptures of Borobudur display many similarities with Indian statues of the Gupta period; smooth curving contours, convex body lines, and the serene impression of the gentle smiling faces are typical.

106 cm

The Agricultural Basis of Classic Java

Little is known of ancient Indonesian agricultural development, but intensive rice cultivation must have been introduced at an early date. Large numbers of stone tools have been found that would have been used for making agricultural implements. Iron tools, which came into widespread use in the Early Classic period, would have enabled Indonesians to develop a more complex civilisation.

»» Relief from Candi Lara Jonggrang of Rama shooting the golden deer. At the right of the main scene is a detail which the Indian epic poem Ramayana does not mention: terraced rice fields with two bamboo pipes from which water is pouring. This detail added by the Javanese sculptor probably portrays a common local sight.

East Javanese temple relief depicting a rural landscape in which wet rice fields formed a prominent feature. They are juxtaposed with a scene of forested hills. Perhaps the composition was meant to emphasise the distinction between the natural and man-made scenery.

Early Javanese Farmers

The apparent density of population on the island at the beginning of the Classic era is a significant mark of the success of the early Javanese farmers. In his endeavours the Javanese farmer was assisted by favourable environmental conditions, such as the rich soil and mild climate, with which he had to work. These factors do not explain why the Javanese alone among the early Indonesians devoted great effort to developing a sophisticated and flexible combination of irrigation and dry land farming.

Scholars have begun to examine information regarding agriculture contained in classic sources. No agricultural implements such as hoes or ploughs from the Early Classic Period have yet been discovered, but temple reliefs, inscriptions, and other literary sources give us a partial image of the agricultural practices in Java during the Classic era.

Evidence from Inscriptions

The Tugu inscription found near Jakarta contains the oldest reference to water management in Indonesia. The inscription, written at the command of Purnavarman, is in Sanskrit language and Pallava script dated to the 5th century. The inscription reports Purnavarman's order to dig a channel about 11 kilometres long to the residence of his grandfather. The inscription also mentions a similar project which had been conducted previously. This inscription has two different interpretations. According to one, the king dug a new channel. An alternative suggestion is that he simply deepened or diverted an old river course which had become silted up. The project may have been meant to control flooding. The channel was dug in the month of *Caitra* approximately corresponding to April, the beginning of Java's dry season. Perhaps this time was selected because during the rainy season the river was subject to flooding.

Sima inscriptions, which commemorate the establishment of zones that had been freed from paying taxes to the government in return for providing services to religious establishments, often mention the types of land which are included in the zones in question. The categories usually include dry fields (*tegal*), orchards (*kebun*), and irrigated rice land (*sawah*). Some inscriptions, including some from east Java, mention contributions made by kings to the construction of dams and canals. These may have had several functions, including drainage, irrigation, defence, and transportation. The central government in ancient Java does not appear to have played a major role in building or maintaining irrigation works. Water control officials mentioned in inscriptions seem to have formed part of village level government.

It seems also that when areas were declared *sima* more irrigation facilities were installed. This may be due to the fact that irrigated rice land was heavily taxed, so that under the *sima* system farmers had more incentive to intensify production.

Land Use

In addition to irrigated rice fields, dry land was used to plant upland rice (called *gaga*). Unirrigated fields were also planted with such crops as *mowi*, *suda*, taro, and other roots and vegetables (*gangan*). Vegetables could also be planted in gardens (*kubwan*) between fruit trees. Cultivated fruits included *kajar-kajar*, durian, rambutan, *kapundung*, langsat, *ambawang* (onions?) and *duwit*. Unfortunately, researchers are unable to match old names for many crops with their modern equivalents.

Literary Sources

Literary sources, in particular the Arjunawijaya and Sutasoma, both written by Mpu Tantular, have added some details to our knowledge of Javanese agriculture during the Classic era, most specifically during the reign of King Rajasanagara in the fluorescent period of Majapahit. The Arjunawijaya mentions that dams could be made of stone, tree trunks, or branches. Water was then distributed from these dams to bunded rice fields. The first fields which received water from the dams were called *pasimpangan* (Arjunawijaya 38:6c). From these fields water was spread further, and siphoned into fields divided by *galeng* (bunds) (Arjunawijaya 22:5). Irrigated rice fields lay just beyond the boundaries of the capital. The Sutasoma provides us with a description of farmers weeding their rice fields.

The descriptions found in these poems obtain confirmation from the Longan Tambahan inscription written in Old Javanese and issued by King Sri Dharmawangsa Wardhana–Marakata–Pangkaje–Sthanottunggadewa in 1023. The inscription gives the stages in rice cultivation. These include *amabaki* (clearing the field before ploughing), *amaluku* (ploughing), *atanam* (planting), *amatun* (weeding), *ahani* (harvesting), and *anutu* (pounding the rice).

Relief panels from Javanese temples showing agricultural scenes:
❶ Bullock pulling a plough
❷ Seedlings being transplanted in paddy fields.
❸ Harvested rice being carried on shoulder poles.
❹ Rice being pounded.

««Bamboo pipes used in west Java to distribute water between fields. This old technique is still in use today.

Reliefs

Reliefs on Javanese temples illustrate idealised situations and moral fables. However, scenes mirroring what must have been common sights in agrarian life are found on several sites, such as Borobudur and Prambanan in Central Java. Although no ancient ploughs have yet been discovered, we can conclude from a relief at Borobudur showing a farmer ploughing with a yoke of oxen that such a practice was indeed employed in ancient Java. Other panels at Borobudur show such agrarian activities as rice being carried on a shoulder pole. In the background of reliefs from the Lara Jonggrang temple at Prambanan rice milling can be seen. Probably the first sound heard in most ancient Javanese villages each morning was the thumping of women pounding rice for the day's meals.

In the later Classic period, narrative reliefs are more numerous, and the role of agriculture becomes much more a part of the foreground. Unfortunately many of the reliefs from the later Classic have not been deciphered, so the precise significance of these depictions is unknown. Scenes of villages and their surrounding fields seen as if from the air are common. Sometimes individuals are shown planting or harvesting rice. The dominance of activities related to rice-growing in these scenes, and the scarcity of depictions of other agricultural or subsistence pursuits, suggests that the Javanese thought of themselves first and foremost as rice growers. By the 13th century, if not before, Javanese rice was exported to Sumatra and possibly other parts of the Archipelago, according to Chinese historical accounts.

Ethnographic Evidence

Ethnographic analogy provides us with a final insight into the probable nature of ancient Javanese rice-growing practices. Like farmers of an earlier era, some farmers today still use traditional technology and methods. Rice harvesting, traditionally a woman's job, in some areas is still carried out with the finger knife which probably was introduced in prehistoric times. Many farmers still make use of ritual methods including complex astrological calculations to determine the proper times to plant and to harvest. Other ceremonies are still conducted in many villages during the growing season to safeguard the crop from pests, diseases, and inclement weather, and during the off-season to clear the irrigation infrastructure. Offerings are sometimes placed around the fields to honour Dewi Sri, goddess of rice, particularly in West Java Province. These customs seem in many instances to preserve elements of folk culture which must have been prevalent in Java a thousand years ago.

The Rhythm of Rice. Although agricultural modernisation is rapidly changing farming methods, traditional techniques such as the use of the finger knife for harvesting and shoulder pole for transporting rice are still retained in parts of Java.

Ploughing

Planting

Winnowing

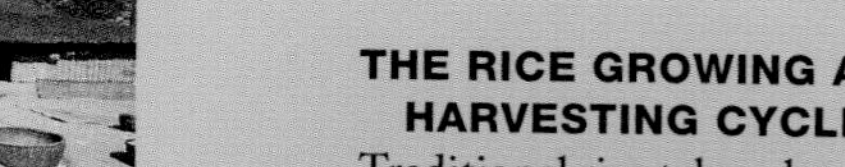

THE RICE GROWING AND HARVESTING CYCLE.

Traditional rice takes about six months to mature. New varieties ripen in as short a period as three months. The various activities at the different stages of rice cultivation dictated many aspects of Classic social life and ritual.

Pounding

Bunding

Harvesting

Patterns of Temple Distribution in Early Classical Java

Indonesian archaeologists have applied the new approach of spatial archaeology to several areas in Indonesia. An example is a study carried out in south central Java, in the area surrounding the city of Yogyakarta. This study is part of an attempt to discover the natural and cultural factors affecting the way people used space in the Classical period.

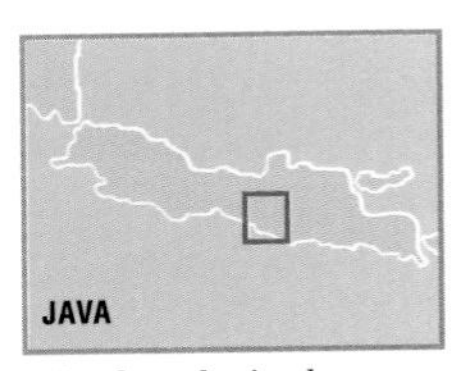

Archaeological survey on the south slope of Merapi volcano and the lowland plain stretching to the Indian Ocean revealed patterns of Classical site distribution which in some respects conform to stipulations in Indian texts but deviate from them in others.

Problems of the Study

Ideally, a study based on spatial archaeology would make use of data obtained from sites of several different kinds. Unfortunately, the only sites which are easy to find in Indonesia are religious sites, where stone or brick were used as building materials and for statuary. Village sites, in contrast, are extremely difficult to detect, due to the perishable nature of most materials used by the Javanese in everyday life. In addition there is a noticeable lack of well–defined pottery types which have proved so useful in similar studies elsewhere. Other problems that need to be taken into consideration include the dense modern population which may have disturbed most traces of earlier villages, and the frequent deposits of volcanic ash which have deeply buried earlier soil surfaces, to name only the most obvious obstacles.

The Javanese knew of an Indian text called the *Manasara Silpasastra*, which gives instructions on choosing temple sites. These stipulate that temples should be built on fertile soil and should be located near water; for water cleanses, purifies, and fertilises. The distribution pattern of ancient Javanese temples should, therefore, give some indication of the Javanese interpretation of these stipulations, insofar as they adhered faithfully to them. Indirectly this pattern provides us with an insight into the Javanese people's view of their environment. It also must have some relationship to the pattern according to which other activities were distributed especially the settlements of the people who built and used the temples, and supported the priests who officiated in them; thus the results of such studies can guide further research aimed at discovering the settlement patterns of early Java.

Survey Site

The area known to geographers as south Merapi was chosen for an experiment in spatial archaeology. It is a well–defined geographical region, but within it there

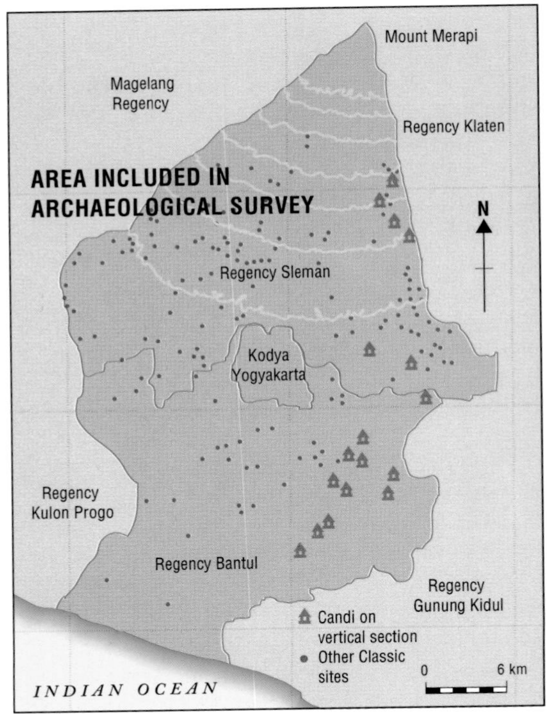

are numerous variations in natural resources. The study area is bounded by the Opak River on the east and by the Progo on the west. Both of these rivers have their sources at the peak of Mount Merapi and flow south until they reach the Indian Ocean. The area covered by the survey consists of slightly over 1,000 square kilometres; the central part, which is occupied by the city of Yogyakarta, was not included as any ancient sites there have been destroyed by modern construction. By studying the distribution pattern of ceremonial sites or *candi*, we can hope to discover some factors which governed the way ancient Javanese interacted with their environment.

Results

A total of 218 Classical temple sites were discovered by the survey. For each of these sites, a number of variables were recorded; soil type, fertility, groundwater resources, slope, elevation, distance from the nearest river, and the distance from the nearest water source.

Analysis of the collected data showed a significant difference between the two regencies included in the survey. In Sleman, the part of the survey area which includes Mount Merapi, sites were much more numerous and more evenly distributed than in Bantul, the lower part of the river valleys and the south coast. The largest number of sites clustered around the lower slopes of the mountain, lying below 200 metres, although some sites were found as high as 550 metres.

CROSS SECTION OF SURVEY AREA SHOWING RELATIVE ELEVATIONS OF IMPORTANT SITES (VERTICAL SCALE EXAGGERATED)

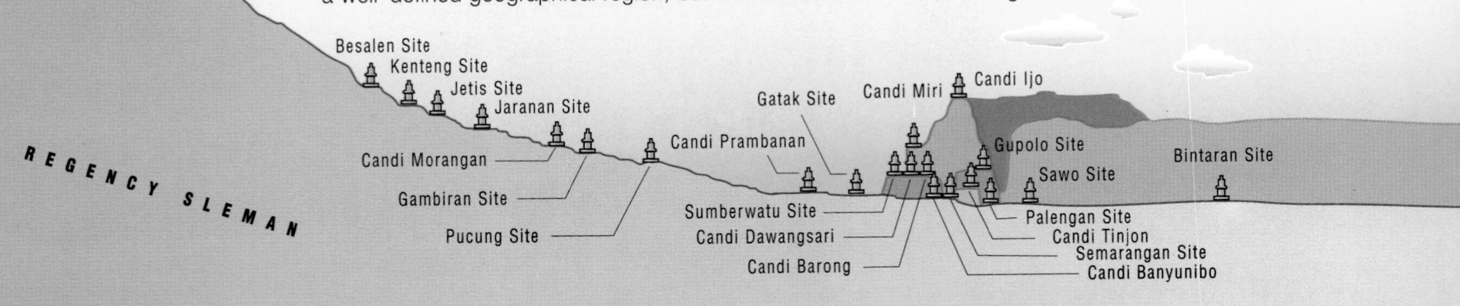

The candi showed a very strong tendency to occupy soils with high fertility, though not all types with high fertility were equally favoured, and alluvial soil only attracted 1.8 per cent of all candi. One possible explanation for this pattern is the likelihood of flooding on alluvial soil which replenishes the fertility of the soil but can cause severe damage to buildings.

In most other respects the survey results tended to confirm expectations based on the Indian manuals, except for one: groundwater. The sites favoured for temples had moderate rather than high groundwater levels. In other words, it would have been necessary to dig deeper wells to obtain water for the temples than if they had been situated elsewhere. This may indicate that the population relied more on rivers than on wells for their water supply. This conclusion is reinforced by the finding that 82 per cent of all candi were within 500 metres of a river, while only 11 per cent were within 500 metres of a spring.

The distribution of candi may be a good indicator of the sites of ancient villages, but of course this theory must be tested through more research. However, one group of 10 sites deviated significantly from the prescriptions of the Indian *sastra*, and thus were probably chosen according to quite different criteria from the other candi sites. These were located on the limestone hills known as the Siva Plateau on the east side of the survey area, and include the Ratu Boko group. One of the probable pre-Classic Javanese beliefs was that high places were associated with ancestral spirits.

Conclusion

Spatial analysis has already begun to hint that it can illuminate some hidden aspects of ancient Javanese culture. This approach has potential to contribute many more insights into the Indonesian heritage.

The region south of Mount Merapi is one of the most important in Indonesian history, but it is by no means certain that the correlation between the locations of temple sites and geographic features here is typical of other areas. If further surveys are conducted in other parts of Java and different patterns are detected, this will enable scholars to compare the relationships between religion and other activities at different times and places. Equally important is the search for settlement sites. If the locations of temples cluster near modern population, it is highly probable that ancient population centres existed in the same general areas. Another survey using different methods could then be designed to search for the sites of cities, towns, and villages, which are at present undiscovered.

INDIAN OCEAN

REGENCY BANTUL

FALSE COLOUR SATELLITE IMAGE OF MOUNT MERAPI AND SOUTH CENTRAL JAVA

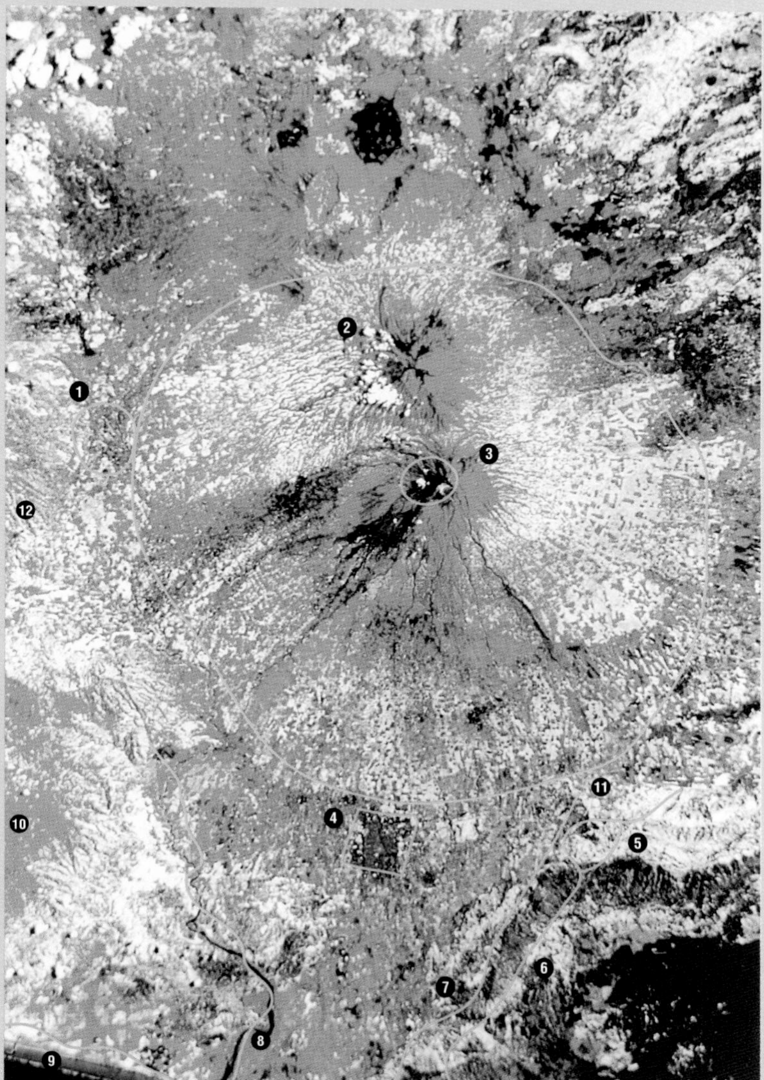

1 City of Magelang
2 Mount Merbabu
3 Mount Merapi
4 City of Yogyakarta
5 Siva Plateau/ Ratu Boko
6 Southern Mountains
7 Opak River
8 Progo River
9 Indian Ocean
10 Menoreh Hills
11 Lara Jonggrang
12 Kedu Plain

This satellite image depicts the area included in a systematic archaeological survey for classical archaeological sites as well as the surrounding region. The active peak of Mount Merapi occupies the centre of the photograph. The slopes of the volcano are largely uninhabited today, due both to their steep gradient and the constant threat of eruptions. The most recent eruption which resulted in fatalities occured in 1994. In the lower or southern part of the photograph, a fertile plain extends to the Indian Ocean, just visible at lower left. The lowland plain is fringed by two rivers, the Progo and the Opak, on the east and west sides. The rivers flow at the foot of limestone hills which extend for hundreds of kilometres along the south coast of Java. These hills are low in fertility and water is scarce. Thus they are sparsely populated. The densest populations occupy the fertile valley between the two rivers. The distribution of ancient temples occurs in the same area, with the exception of a group of sites along the hills at the southeastern border of the zone, called the Siva Plateau. The locations of these sites must have been determined by special considerations.

Volcanic activity is now concentrated on the west side of Merapi. There is no archaeological evidence of a single huge eruption over the past 2,000 years. Instead the pattern seems to be one of relatively frequent eruptions with damage limited to the immediate surrounding area. Many of the fatalities are caused by scalding steam and mud slides, rather than lava.

Material Aspects of Everyday Life

The archaeology of daily life in ancient Indonesia has not been pursued with the same intensity as research into temples and inscriptions, which reflect only part of the past. The discussion which follows must therefore depend on studies of temple reliefs and written records to reconstruct a picture of the material side of daily life in early Indonesia.

Modern craftsman in central Java making a copper dandang or rice cooker: the source of raw material is old recycled copper.

Tiny gold ornaments from 9th century Java. The largest is about 15 millimetres high.

Toe ring and textiles depicted on a 13th century statue.

Metal

One of the few materials which has survived to give us an idea of the aesthetic tastes of the everyday Indonesians, and to which attention has been devoted, is gold. Gold is a good indicator of changing fashions, as it was used for articles of personal adornment of types subject to frequent development of new styles. Gold has formed one of the primary media for Indonesian craftsmen since prehistoric times. Prehistoric burials, as well as those from later times in such places as Sulawesi where classic culture made little impact, were sometimes accompanied by pieces of shaped gold foil laid over the faces of the dead. In the protohistoric era craftsmen in many parts of Indonesia began to use gold for jewellery to adorn the living. Designs of similar type were used in a wide area of protohistoric Southeast Asia, including the Philippines and parts of the mainland, for finger rings, neck chains, and ear ornaments. In prehistoric times Javanese craftsmen limited themselves to beating gold with hammers. The use of heat to work gold began in the early centuries AD. Prehistoric bronze workers had already become masters of the lost wax technique, and this method was soon applied to jewellery. A range of other techniques including casting, carving, chiselling, and filigree was also used. Repoussé, or beating a design out in relief, was also popular and a highly developed art. Some of the jewellery designs used in early Java were imported from India. Examples are ear ornaments in the shape of the *makara,* a mythical sea monster which symbolised Kama, god of love. Most designs were local creations, many of impressive quality.

The sources from which the Javanese obtained their metals is still a mystery, for no archaeological studies of ancient mines have been conducted in Indonesia. Dutch explorers in Sumatra in the 19th century mention seeing remains of large-scale mine workings for gold and mercury, but most of these sites were later utilised by the Dutch, thus wiping out traces of all earlier activity. Metallic sources are rare in Java, so the raw material must have been imported. The Javanese did obtain sufficient supplies to make a wide variety of items. Copper was used for kitchen utensils: kettles, pots, rice steamers, storage vessels and serving trays. Iron was used for agricultural tools including axes, adzes, sickles, knives, machetes, swords and crowbars. Inscriptions mention several categories of metalsmiths classified according to the type of metal with which they worked. There was even a special term for craftsmen who made copper pots. The standard iron-working technique consisted of forging, that is heating and beating the raw metal into shape. Copper, with its lower melting point, could either be forged or cast by melting and then poured into a mould, prepared with the lost wax method. Although we have no quantitative information, we can infer that iron was sufficiently plentiful and cheap to enable most farmers to own at least a few metal tools.

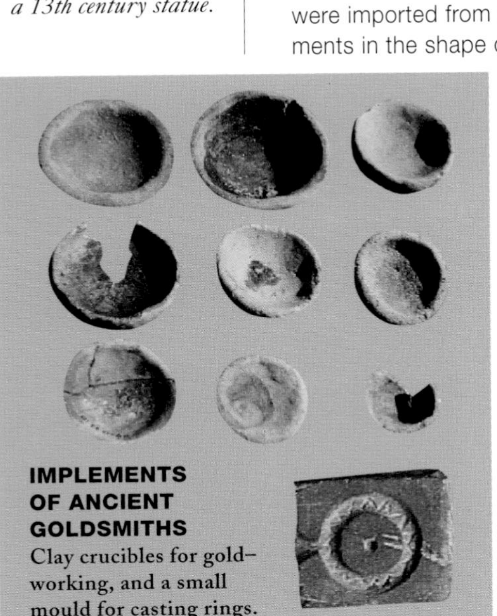

IMPLEMENTS OF ANCIENT GOLDSMITHS
Clay crucibles for gold-working, and a small mould for casting rings.

BIRD RINGS
So called because of their tiny dimensions, these small gold ornaments are decorated with glass beads. Such artefacts were very common in the Early Classic, and were made in many different forms. Their actual function is unknown.

Clay

Although pottery was a common material, very little archaeological effort has so far been devoted to the study of the use of this material in early Indonesia. The only exceptions are the clay containers used to contain the ceremonial deposits found beneath the temples. These containers can be of many shapes, such as vases, plates, cooking pots, saucers and jars; their shapes do not seem to be especially related to their ceremonial uses. From this we can reasonably conclude that the pottery used in everyday life was not too dissimilar in shape. Some pottery was perhaps made with the

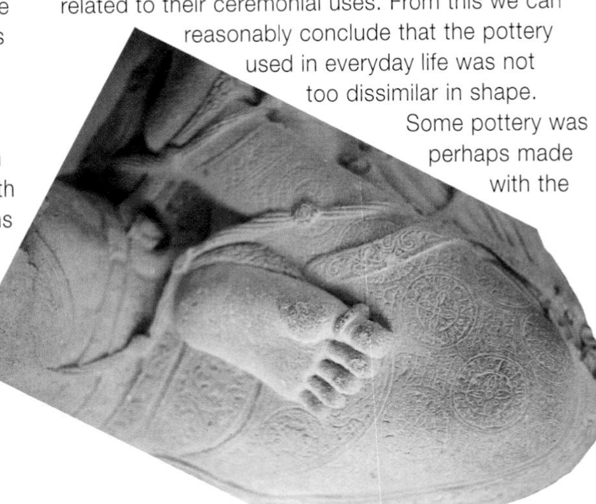

potter's wheel, but a great deal was probably hand formed. There are two reliefs on Borobudur that depict potters at work. They are using wooden paddles to harden and smooth the clay. As in many societies, the potters are female. The men's involvement in the process was to bring the clay, usually dug from paddy fields or river banks where suitable material was found, to the women. Another relief from Borobudur, from the Mahakarmawi–bhangga series (02) on the edifice's foot depicts a person cooking with a pot on a stove. Possibly the stove was also made of clay, as they are still in some parts of Java.

Clay was also used for making miniature stupas (called stupika), of which over 2,307 have been found, and votive tablets such as those found in large quantity just south of Borobudur. The stupika were made in moulds and the votive tablets were produced by stamping patterns into flat pieces of wet clay about six centimetres in diameter. The patterns consist of images of Buddha seated on a lotus.

Wood, Cloth and Bamboo

These materials are seldom found on archaeological sites due to their perishable nature, and we must fall back on inscriptions which mention carpenters, basketmakers, bamboo plaiters, and decoration makers for houses or roofs for ceremonies.

Javanese inscriptions mention a wide variety of textiles and clothing types. There are references to weavers and dyers, especially makers of red dye. They mention a wide range of clothing, differentiated according to pattern, colour, and possibly other factors, indicating that clothing was an important matter for the early Javanese, and that much variety existed. Depictions on temple reliefs show common people dressed simply, wearing only a sarong. Royalty dressed in a similar way, without shirts or blouses, and can be distinguished by the wearing of jewellery. Inscriptions mention itinerant goldsmiths who worked in markets, and examples of jewellery made of bronze have been discovered, suggesting that commoners too sometimes wore jewellery. Cloth had an important ceremonial meaning in early Java, to judge from inscriptions describing temple founding ceremonies. Gifts were given out to those attending the ceremony; these consisted of gold, silver, and pieces of cloth or sets of clothing and iron tools.

House forms can only be reconstructed by looking at temple reliefs found on Borobudur and Prambanan. No ordinary dwelling sites have yet been discovered dating from the Early Classic era. Houses depicted in these reliefs display several striking differences when compared with modern Javanese rural dwellings. They resemble the house types of Sumatra, among the Batak and Minangkabau, and on Sulawesi among the Toraja. The houses are built on stilts to enable people to use the ground beneath the floors. The roofs have curved ridges. This form indicates that the technique of construction made use of the stressed roof-beam. The top of the roof consisted of a long horizontal piece of wood, the sides of the roof being held up by leaning other

Sexual division of labour: this relief from the late 8th century depicts men carrying clay while seated women make cooking pots with wooden paddles. The same sexual division still exists in Javanese villages where pottery is produced.

pieces of wood against this beam, sloping down. The roof covering, straw, wood or clay tiles, was laid on these sloping members. The weight of these beams and their coverings inevitably caused the top of the roof to curve down, pushing the ends upwards and creating the characteristic curvature still found in the outer islands. Stone models of such houses, perhaps used for offerings to the rice goddess Dewi Sri, are also known from Java. It is not known when or why this type was replaced by the modern Javanese house built on the ground and using different construction techniques.

Stone house models and depictions in temple reliefs demonstrate that houses with curved roofs, now associated mainly with Sumatra and Sulawesi, were once found on Java.

Popular Beliefs

In addition to the worship of Buddhist and Hindu deities, inscriptions indicate that belief in local spirits was still powerful. Javanese inscriptions were usually set up to record the establishment of special zones called *sima* with certain rights and duties concerning religious centres, These inscriptions contain curses on those who would disturb the peace of the special zones, and invoke the spirits of mountains and other local supernatural beings. The Kuti inscription of 840 AD invokes six types of spirit.

In the temple–founding ceremonies the main activity is the presentation of agricultural implements, metal pots, and such ordinary objects to a stone called the *sima* stone or *sang hyang kulumpang*, possibly a reference to a stone mortar such as has long been used to pound rice. Supernatural beliefs seem to have been connected with stone mortars in prehistoric Indonesian culture. In this way we may note the probable importance of symbols and beliefs linked to the agrarian way of life.

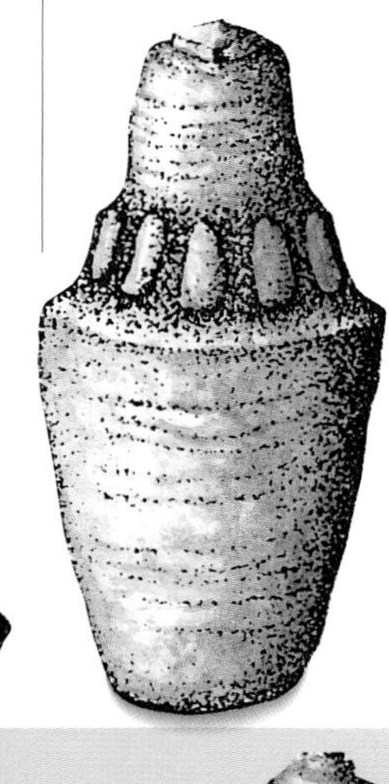

STUPIKA

Various types of stupika, miniature Buddhist stupa, between four and 13.5 centimetres high, were found in a pit southwest of Borobudur in 1974. They were made in moulds; some were inscribed with Buddhist formulae. They were probably made at important religious sites and distributed to pilgrims who carried them away, perhaps as talismans. They are examples of everyday objects found in Sumatra, Java and Bali.

Javanese Gold: The Wonoboyo Hoard

Gold has formed one of the primary media for Javanese craftsmen since prehistoric times, when some burials were accompanied by pieces of shaped gold foil laid over the faces of the dead. Most discoveries of antique Javanese gold have come to light as a result of chance finds, as was the case with the striking find now known as the Wonoboyo hoard.

»»Water dipper that copies the form of palm leaf containers still used by villagers.

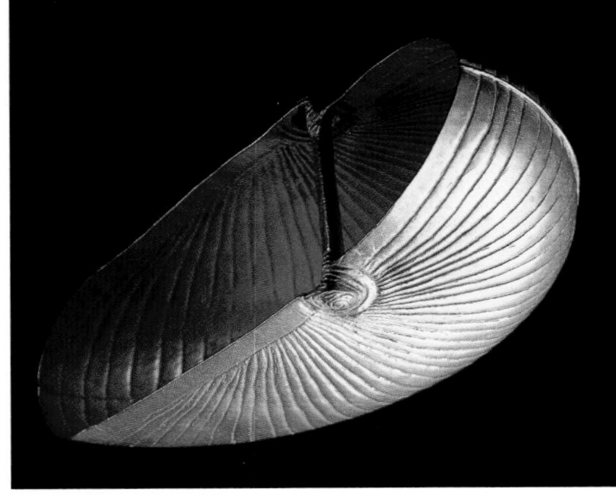

The Wonoboyo Gold

In October 1990, six men were at work levelling land for agricultural purposes when they discovered a Chinese jar, buried in the ground at a depth of 2.75 metres. On examination, the the jar was found to contain 12.5 kilograms of gold objects and 3.95 kilograms of silver objects. This particular discovery occurred in the village of Wonoboyo, which lies only five kilometres from the Lara Jonggrang temple complex at Prambanan. The discoverers on this occasion were, fortunately for science, aware of the potential significance of their find.

A report was made by local officials, and quickly reached the relevant archaeological authorities who were able to visit the location right away and record the exact find spot. It was immediately apparent that the artefacts in the hoard, including coins, jewellery, and ritual objects, were of great importance both for the study of Javanese goldwork and for the wider interpretation of ancient Javanese culture and economy. The discovery of this first hoard was quickly followed by a second, consisting of 6,396 gold coins, and yet a third, including jewellery. The total weight of gold and silver recovered was 35.8 kilograms, the largest hoard ever reported in Java.

This golden box with gold wire suspension cord is identical to rattan, wood, and bamboo cases still used in Lombok and Tibet for carrying scrolls bearing religious formulae or holy amulets.

Unravelling History

Several of the objects bear short inscriptions which have enabled archaeologists to determine the approximate date of the hoard's burial, which has been put at around 900 AD. The inscriptions and the nature of the finds themselves suggest that the hoard would have originally belonged to a member of the nobility.

Many of the objects in the hoard are unique. Some of the items imitate other materials. A water dipper weighing 228.3 grams of 16 carat gold, for example, takes the form of a simple village dipper made of palm leaf. An item connected with Visnu in the Wonoboyo hoard is a small elephant goad, one of the symbols of the universe depicted on Visnu's footprints. One of the most unusual items is a golden box decorated with symbols of the god Visnu: a winged conch, a sword, club, bow, discus, and umbrella. As Rama was an incarnation of Visnu, it is tempting to conclude that these items, including the gold bowl below, were all used for Visnu worship.

The excellent state of preservation of the Wonoboyo gold enables us to refine our interpretation of other objects already in museum collections. For example a gold object in the collection of the National Museum, Jakarta can now

One of the most spectacular finds is a gold bowl, four–lobed in shape, bearing repoussê decoration showing scenes from the Ramayana. Given the religious nature of the subject, the bowl might have been an important ritual object. Perhaps it was used to contain ingredients such as flowers for ceremonies.

LOST WAX

In prehistoric times Javanese craftsmen limited themselves to beating gold with hammers. The use of heat to work gold only began in the early centuries AD. Javanese statue makers became masters of the lost wax technique and used this method for bronze and gold statues. They also made jewellery with a range of techniques including casting, carving, chiselling and filigree. Repoussé, or beating a design out in relief, was also popular and a highly developed art.

❶ The clay model is covered in wax. Casting point and air channels are provided.

❷ A layer of clay is applied over the wax model.

❸ The wax is melted and poured away.

❹ The hollow between the inner and outer forms (stabilised by connecting supports) is filled with molten gold.

❺ After breaking the outer form, the casting comes into view.

❻ Completed figure.

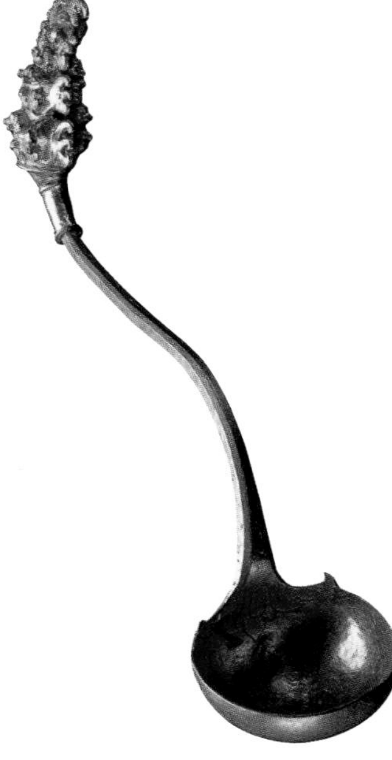

Gold ladle which was probably used for pouring oil on religious objects or ritual participants; the tip of the handle was made separately and decorated with foliage.

be identified as a sword handle. Most of the Wonoboyo items were found in jars, but some were disposed neatly outside them. The people who buried them were clearly not in a hurry. They were not buried very deeply, perhaps just under the ground surface at the time. They were later covered by a layer of volcanic sediment.

What Kind of Site was Wonoboyo?

The gold and silver items appear to have been hidden near the bank of a stream. About 60 to 100 metres away, archaeologists discovered a brick foundation, sherds of earthenware pottery, and animal bone in a soil layer which indicates that they date from the same period as the gold hoard. It is not clear whether this was a typical village or a more specialised site.

One possibility is that it was a hermitage established in a forest (this is suggested by the word *wono,* which is Sanskrit for forest) for a royal ascetic, perhaps even a king or queen who had abdicated to live as a hermit, an act which many texts present as the ideal goal for people in their old age. More research is needed before this theory can be proven. The proximity of the site to Prambanan raises many other possibilities as well; rather than a monastery, this may have been a royal treasury.

Touches of luxury (below left to right) covered bowl moulded in a lotus pattern ; spout for a pouring vessel in the form of a mythical sea monster; and gold finial perhaps for a royal parasol.

The Early Indonesian Economy

By the 10th century Java had one of the most complex economies in Southeast Asia. Rice farming was still the main occupation of most village households, and it continued to provide most of the tax income of the Javanese courts. However, with the upsurge in sea trade in Asian waters between the 10th and 13th centuries, trade played an increasingly prominent role in Java's economy.

TABLE OF CURRENCY WEIGHTS

NAME	WORD ORIGIN	WEIGHT	VALUE
Kati (ka)	local	750–768 grams	
Tahil (ta)	local	38 grams	20 tahil=1 kati
Suwarna (su)	Indian gold weight	38 grams	= 1 tahil; value of a buffalo
Dharana (dha)	Indian silver weight	38 grams	= 1 tahil = 20% same weight in
Masa (ma)	Indian gold and silver weight	2.4 grams	1/16 tahil; 1 goat = 4 silver ma
Atak	local	1.2 grams	1/2 masa
Kupang (ku)	local	0.6 grams	1/4 masa
Saga (sa)	local	0.1 gram	1/6 kupang

Indonesian merchant ships exported goods from the north coast ports of Java by the early first millennium AD.

»This copper plate inscription, dated 6th September 939 AD, says that King Sindok declared this land called Alasantan to be a sima. The land was purchased for 12 kati.

Documentary Evidence

Most of what we know about the early Javanese economy is derived from local documents composed after the beginning of the 9th century in Old Javanese language and preserved on stone or copper plate. Almost all of these inscriptions are financial documents. Some record debt settlements of individuals or judgements in court cases concerning financial or tax matters. However, the vast majority of the documents that have survived are charters of *sima* territories, that is, villages which were wholly or partially released from the obligation to pay taxes in return for paying tithes to specific temples or other religious foundations.

We know from these records that it was possible to buy land freehold by the 9th century, and that by the 10th century land could be leased or pawned against future redemption. In fact, the list of things which could not be bought and sold in 10th century Java was very short. There is even a record of the sale, in 934 AD, of a small, privately owned monastery.

Markets in Java

Most villagers had access to periodic markets, or *pkan*, which circulated on a five day schedule, as they do now. *Sima* charters provide a good deal of information about these rural periodic markets as, in order to prevent too many market traders from moving into *sima* territories to evade taxes, rulers began to place limits on the number of traders who could claim residence there and on the volume of trade that resident traders could conduct free of tax.

According to the charters, villagers regularly brought to their local markets not only rice, beans, vegetables and fruit, chickens and eggs, oil, cane sugar syrup, cooked snacks, and so forth, but also thatching fronds, lime, baskets, mats, various small items made of bamboo and wood, low–fired pottery items of different kinds, home–spun and dyed cotton yarn, and wild animals and birds, which members of farming households produced, collected or trapped in their spare time.

Professional pedlars and wholesale traders travelled more widely, and brought to the market a wide range of local foodstuffs. These included palm sugar and palm wine, tamarind, salt, shrimp paste, salt fish, sesame cake, red onions and various different spices, as well as betel nuts and betel boxes, kapok, combed cotton, cotton thread, dyestuffs, metal ingots and metal goods. Livestock dealers brought animals to market: buffalo, cattle, goats, pigs and ducks for sale, and cart–owners hired out their services for transporting goods. Artisans operating in these markets included professional weavers, blacksmiths, copper and bronze smiths, goldsmiths and potters. Large markets, located in the heavily populated Brantas River delta or where inland trade routes crossed, also drew jewellers, wire–makers, shield–makers, metal pot makers, metal casters, stonemasons, carpenters, painters, and, near the coast or rivers, boat builders.

Late 19th century market in Java. Periodic markets held according to a five–day rotation system already existed in Java over 1,000 years ago.

Ports and Sea Trade

The ports on the northern coasts of Java and Bali became the foci of a brisk export trade in local agricultural products and manufactures, in addition to spices and sandalwood from the eastern islands, which were brought in for trans–shipment to China, India and more distant markets. The impact of this port activity was felt throughout Javanese society by the later 10th century.

Farmers near the ports began to grow cash crops which they could sell to merchants for export.

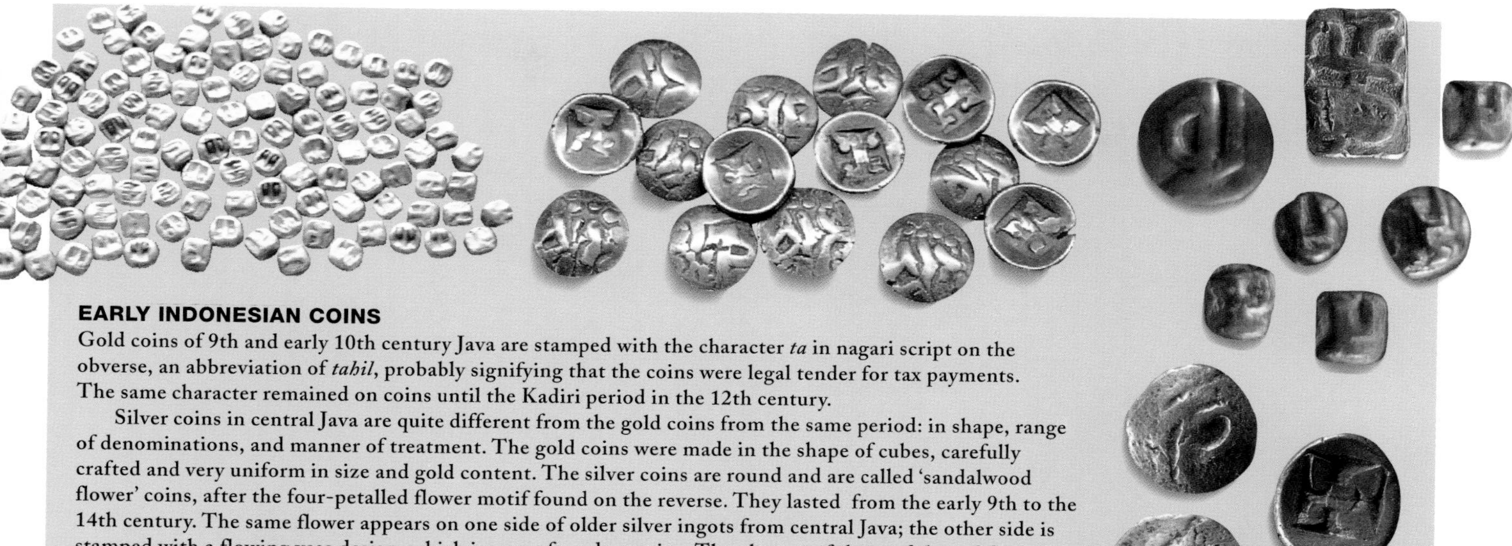

EARLY INDONESIAN COINS

Gold coins of 9th and early 10th century Java are stamped with the character *ta* in nagari script on the obverse, an abbreviation of *tahil*, probably signifying that the coins were legal tender for tax payments. The same character remained on coins until the Kadiri period in the 12th century.

Silver coins in central Java are quite different from the gold coins from the same period: in shape, range of denominations, and manner of treatment. The gold coins were made in the shape of cubes, carefully crafted and very uniform in size and gold content. The silver coins are round and are called 'sandalwood flower' coins, after the four-petalled flower motif found on the reverse. They lasted from the early 9th to the 14th century. The same flower appears on one side of older silver ingots from central Java; the other side is stamped with a flowing vase design, which is never found on coins. The obverse of the sandalwood flower coins bears the nagiri script character *ma*, (abb. *masa)*. This character degenerated quickly, perhaps because it is different from the *kawi* letter *ma*. The shape of the coin, its weight, and possibly its silver content all changed rapidly in about a century. The one *masa* coins shifted in the early 10th century from thick and flat to cup–shaped, and thin (about two millimetres). These coins presumably served as small change and were probably made by smiths in the markets for use in market transactions.

(Far left) One masa *gold coins: five millimetres diameter. (Second from left and lower right) Silver sandalwood flower coins: 11 millimetres diameter. (Top right) Gold coins of different denominations.*

Then the rulers began to allow tax farmers, who usually consisted of local and foreign merchants, to collect certain quantities of locally grown spices, dyestuffs, medicines, rice, beans and salt in return for annual payments to the court.

Cotton cloth, dyes and metal goods imported from India, and ceramics, lacquerware, silk cloth and silk thread from China began to filter into the village market circuit. These imports had a profound impact upon Javanese taste and technology. Indian printed cottons were so popular that local dyers began to copy them, and in so doing developed the technique of batik resist dyeing, which is mentioned in inscriptions by the 12th century. Javanese weavers were using silk as well as cotton by the 11th century, and gold leaf was being applied to cloth by the 13th century. The Chinese fast–wheel potting technology was copied by Javanese potters near the ports, who began to abandon the slower paddle and anvil technique by the end of the 10th century. Black pepper and the rose–coloured safflower dye, both native to southern India, were transplanted to Java during the 9th and 10th centuries, and by the 12th century Java had become China's major supplier of these crops, undercutting Indian exporters.

Currency

The increasing intensity of domestic trade called for a convenient currency. During the late 8th century money in Java appears to have taken the form of ingots made from gold and silver, and gold rings of specified weight, as well as bundles of iron bars. Weights and measures were standardised during the period 850–900. These were a combination of Indian and indigenous elements.

The *kati, tahil, masa,* and *kupang* units remained in use in a number of contexts until the Dutch period, although their weights changed over time. The Javanese word *wli,* which in modern Indonesian has become *beli*, meaning 'buy' appears in an inscription of 878 AD. The Sanskrit term *wyaya* (modern Indonesian *biaya*, 'expenses') appears in another inscription of 878 AD. There are no stylistic parallels between Javanese and Indian coins. Most coins, and most varieties, are from central Java; east Java has produced fewer finds.

From the end of the 10th century onward, as copper coins from China were imported in greater quantities, Chinese cash and local copies, which are called *pisis* in the inscriptions, began to displace the silver alloy coins as small denomination currency. By the mid–14th century, there were so many *pisis* in circulation, that the Javanese court recognised them as official currency for tax purposes.

Early Sumatran Coins

Coins may have been first minted in Sumatra at some time in the 11th century. Sandalwood flower coins much like those of Java, and made of gold, electrum, and silver alloy, have been found at several 11th century sites in Sumatra including Barus, Bengkulu, and Muara Jambi, and also in South Thailand. These examples were very well made in comparison with silver alloy examples found in Java. Silver coins are rare in Sumatra; most are made of gold. No ancient coins have yet been reported as having been found at Palembang, despite abundant evidence that this was the site of an important port for centuries. This suggests that coinage may have had a limited role in the early Sriwijayan economy. International trade was probably conducted either through the mechanism known as tributary trade, as in the case of China, or in another form known as administered trade. In this system, equivalencies were established between commodities through diplomatic negotiations rather than by bargaining.

This scene from Borobudur is meant to depict a merchant (seated at right) selling gold to a customer (standing at left). The Javanese artist has added elements to the scene which are not called for in the text on which this composition is based, for example the cloth draped over the railing in the background.

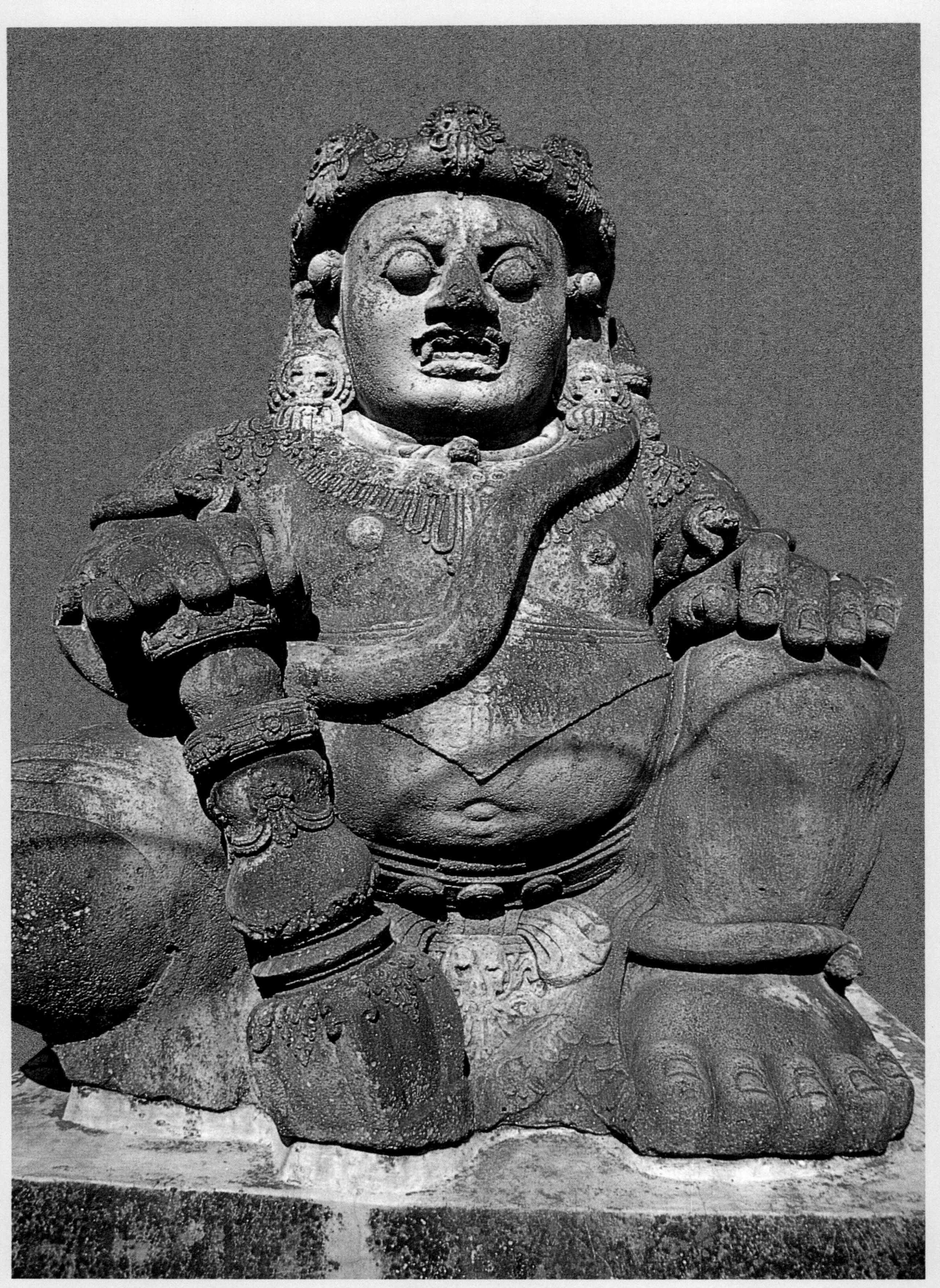

Tantric dancer on the staircase of Biaro Bahal I, Padang Lawas, north Sumatra, 13th century.

Bhrkuti, from Candi Jago, now in the National Museum of Jakarta. She is a Buddhist deity, a ferocious form of Tara, the female counterpart of Avalokitesvara, who appeared when he frowned.

«Guardian statue which may once have stood at the entrance to the palace of Singasari in the 13th century.

MIDDLE CLASSIC PERIOD

At the beginning of the 11th century, the Sumatran kingdom of Sriwijaya enjoyed supremacy in the Straits of Melaka and good relations with China and the Chola kingdom of south India. Chinese archives contain reports of hostile relations between Sumatra and Java. Then in 1025 the Chola attacked and captured Sriwijaya's ruler. Once Sriwijaya's power was broken, new trading ports grew up in Java and Sumatra, stimulated by the arrival of the first immigrants from China. The site of Kota Cina, 'Chinese stockade', in northeast Sumatra, which appeared in the late 11th century, is the oldest example of a city in Indonesia, with a wide range of occupations, evidence of active foreign trade, a multi–ethnic population, and a monetary economy.

At the same time an extensive complex of temples dedicated to esoteric Buddhism was under construction in the north Sumatran hinterland. This was the greatest florescence of brick architecture in Sumatran history, but we know nothing about the kingdom which was responsible for this activity.

North Sumatra had intensive contact with other trading centres around the Indian Ocean. An Islamic kingdom was established in Aceh in the late 13th century, but coastal change has destroyed evidence of the earliest sites.

In Java, several small kingdoms coexisted. The best known of these, Kadiri, is remembered for its important literary works and sculpture. The formation of the kingdom of Singasari in 1225 signalled the rise of an expansionist Javanese realm which succeeded in imposing temporary suzerainty over the principal Sumatran kingdom of Malayu. By the mid–14th century Singasari's successor state, Majapahit, under its famous prime minister Gajah Mada established Javanese overlordship on a firmer footing.

Indonesian sources for this period still pose difficult problems of reconstruction. The few sources we have suggest that a new Sumatran capital was formed in the mountainous western highlands. At least 35 inscriptions were erected there in the mid to late 14th century by a ruler who belonged to a Tantric Buddhist sect. Thereafter we have no more information until the beginning of the Islamic era.

The intermediate classic period did not produce any great architecture or sculpture, but extremely important social changes were in progress: urbanisation, expanding commerce, and the introduction of Islam. These factors were intertwined in a complex relationship with pre–existing traditions to produce the important events of the late Classic era.

The Twilight of Sriwijaya

A kingdom called Malayu, situated in the area of modern Jambi province, appeared briefly in Chinese sources in the early 7th century. It was probably absorbed by Sriwijaya a few decades thereafter and disappeared from history for several centuries. In the late 11th century it returned to prominence as the centre of Sumatra's paramount kingdom.

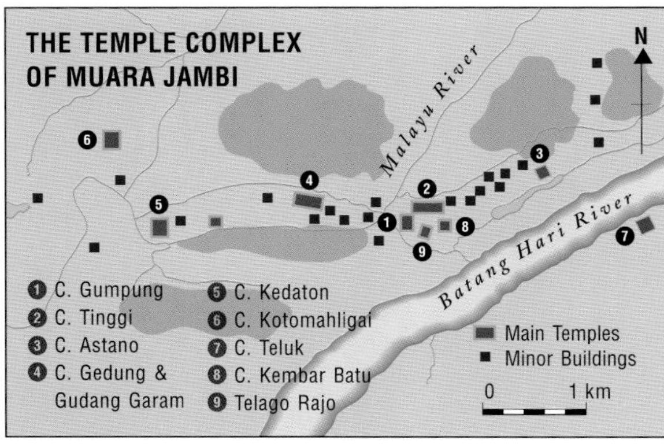

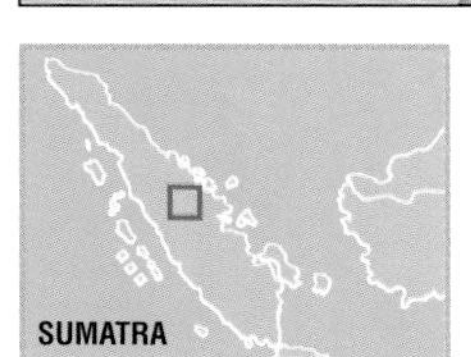

The Shift to Jambi

Malayu appears in 1030–31 in a Chola inscription which contains a list of ports in the Straits of Melaka raided by the South Indian fleet. A stone *makara* found in Jambi inscribed with a date corresponding to 1064 was almost certainly part of a large temple. This sculpture testifies to the re-emergence of a significant centre of power in Jambi in the early 11th century. Due to a number of factors, including Chinese and Indian economic and military inroads into the Sriwijayan scene during this century, and an antagonistic relationship with Java, it is believed that the centre of political dominance shifted from Palembang to Malayu's capital at Jambi around 1080. However, the Chinese continued to use the name San-fo-qi (formerly referring to Sriwijaya at Palembang) to designate the Sumatran realm at Jambi. This was perhaps an indication that the rulers there sought to reinforce their claims over the former vassals of Palembang by seeking to cloak themselves with the prestigious mantle of Sriwijaya.

Jambi sent many ambassadors to China, another sign of an ambitious polity, and secured support from the Chola kings for a temple in south India that had been established decades earlier at a time when Sriwijaya–Palembang dominated the region. In establishing an economically vibrant kingdom on the banks of the Batang Hari basin, the rulers of Malayu–Jambi exemplified the readiness of the maritime population to adapt to changing economic conditions.

»»Amoghapasa, a Buddhist deity, standing on a plinth with an inscription indicating that it was presented to Malayu by the ruler of East Java in the 13th century.

Chinese porcelain uncovered in excavations at Palembang. The sherds and 12th century Qingbai bottle are important evidence indicating that trading activity continued in Palembang until the end of the Classic period.

0 5 cm

The Archaeology of Jambi

Though a great deal still remains to be done before the archaeology of Jambi during this late Sriwijaya period is clear, we can conclude that Jambi was able to maintain its pre-eminence through the 12th and into the 13th century. Temples at the extensive complex of Muara Jambi were restored and enlarged during this period, which bears strong testimony to the kingdom's prosperity. This Buddhist centre, which has now been largely restored, comprises nine main brick temples and a multitude of smaller buildings which are distributed along a five kilometre stretch of the Batang Hari's left bank. Candi Gumpung, which is among the largest of these, yielded a masterpiece of Indonesian sculpture. The East Javanese style of this statue depicting Prajnaparamita, Buddhist deity of divine knowledge, attests to the likelihood that close political and religious bonds with the kingdom of Singasari were already established in the late 13th century.

Large quantities of Chinese ceramics dating mainly from the 12th to 14th centuries were found in Muara Jambi and at other sites along the Batang Hari. One

particularly important area which has been identified but which has not yet been excavated is to be found halfway between Muara Jambi and the present coastline, at the junction of the Batang Hari and its tributary the Kumpeh. Within this area, large deposits of sherds, many of Chinese origin, are exposed along the river banks. Bricks of large dimensions indicative of an early date are also in evidence and mark the presence of an early building, probably a temple.

Other isolated sites are found in the Batang Hari hinterland, where some Buddhist statuary has been discovered. On the upper Kampar River, a group of stupa at Muara Takus further testifies to the vigour of Buddhism in Sumatra during this period. Throughout the 12th and 13th centuries the old centre of Sriwijaya at Palembang, although a dependency of the Malayu–Jambi elite, continued to perform a role as a trading port. Recent archaeological excavations at Palembang have yielded Chinese sherds dating from this period.

The Statuary of Jambi

One of the most spectacular finds at Jambi is a statue of Amoghapasa Lokesvara which was discovered at Rambahan on the banks of the upper Batang Hari but was probably originally installed at Padang Roco. The Lokesvara is almost an exact copy of a statue found in east Java. Images of this Buddhist deity were favoured by King Krtanagara of Singasari. The lotuses flanking the main statue are frequently found on statues of the royal family of Singasari. The four deities in mid-air beside the main god have been identified as Syamatara, Sudhanakumara, Hayagriwa, and Bhrkuti, the same four gods found in the main sanctuary at Candi Jago in east Java. The connection between this statue and Java is further reinforced by the inscription engraved on its plinth. The inscription tells us that the statue was sent in 1286 from the land of Java to Suvarnabumi (Sumatra) at the instruction of Krtanagara, as a gift to King Srimat Tribuanaraja Mauliwarmadewa. The statue's installation in Sumatra was overseen by four high Javanese officials. Beneath the statue and above the writing is a frieze of reliefs. The images depicted are a horse, wheel, queen, jewel, a minister, general, and elephant. These figures are the 'seven jewels' (*sapta ratna*) the symbols of a universal ruler or *cakravartin* (literally 'one who turns the wheel'). Krtanagara may either have been asserting his suzerainty over recently conquered Malayu, or as the epigrapher Dr. J. G. de Casparis believes, he was cementing an alliance, presumably against the expansionist Mongol Yuan Dynasty in China that was making its presence increasingly known.

Muara Takus
This Buddhist site may represent a distant outpost of the kingdom of Malayu. The buildings were enlarged and modified after construction, indicating that the site was in use for a rather long period of time.

The Decline of Sriwijaya

As the 13th century began, forces of decay seem to have been at work in Sriwijaya. Chinese sources tell us that the king of Sriwijaya now had to use naval forces to coerce passing ships into his harbours, a possible sign of his diminishing appeal to traders and the rise of competing ports. On the Malay Peninsula the kingdom of Tambralinga now possessed sufficient independence to send fleets across the Bay of Bengal on two occasions to invade Sri Lanka. During the 13th century the Thai acquired suzerainty over many of Sriwijaya's former peninsular domains.

The east Javanese rulers seized the opportunity offered by Sriwijaya's waning control over sea routes to attain political ascendency in Sumatra. Javanese statues began to appear in the upper Batang Hari, evidence of Javanese hegemony. The Malay centre of political power now began to move inland, heralding Sriwijaya's final demise.

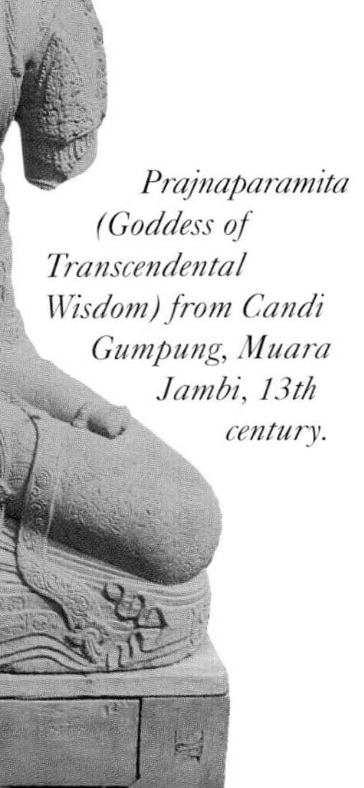

Prajnaparamita (Goddess of Transcendental Wisdom) from Candi Gumpung, Muara Jambi, 13th century.

Sumatran Kingdoms After Sriwijaya

The Javanese conquest of Malayu in 1260 reversed forever the ancient political relationship between Java and Sumatra. In earlier centuries Sriwijaya was able to keep the Javanese off balance, disrupt their trade and occasionally attack their palaces. After 1260 Sumatrans were continually on the defensive. The Javanese did not establish a permanent administration over Sumatran territory, but probably exacted tribute and recognition of ceremonial supremacy from local elites.

»» Dancing figures from a ruined Buddhist temple, Candi Pulo in Padang Lawas.

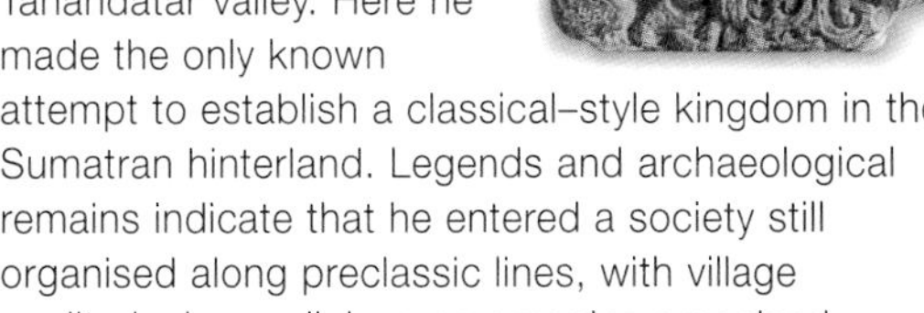

» A row of lions decorates the foundations, similar to those found on 12th century temple sites of Sri Lanka.

Adityavarman's Kingdom

According to a 16th century Javanese text, the *Pararaton* or 'Book of Kings', Javanese forces who conquered Malayu in 1260 took to Java a Malay princess. She later married a Javanese prince, and had a son, Adityavarman. Adityavarman is one of the few Sumatrans of the 14th century whose existence can be verified and of whom some details have been preserved. He left an inscription at the Buddhist Candi Jago near Malang, East Java, but about 30 inscriptions of his authorship have been found in Sumatra. The empire of Majapahit probably sent Adityavarman to Sumatra, perhaps as a kind of viceroy. The Javanese may have hoped that he would be accepted there due to his descent from a Sumatran mother.

Adityavarman's first Sumatran inscriptions were erected in Jambi, the territory of the kingdom of Malayu, but the majority which date from the subsequent period of his life, are found in the highlands of western Sumatra. He refers to himself in them as an independent ruler. We can infer that Adityavarman threw off allegiance to Java and moved his capital into Sumatra's mountainous hinterland. This move may have been partly dictated by the need to evade Javanese reprisals, partly by the attraction of gold mines; Adityavarman refers to himself in one inscription as Kanakamedinindra, 'Gold Land Lord'. Geologists have discovered much evidence of pre-colonial goldmining in the area.

Adityavarman as a Bhairawa, standing on a corpse which in turn lies upon a pile of skulls.

West Sumatra is, furthermore, the only part of the island to have developed intensive rice cultivation during the pre-colonial period. Undoubtedly this agricultural productivity and the consequent capacity for supporting a court helped to attract Adityavarman.

The majority of Adityavarman's inscriptions are found concentrated around the area of Pagarruyung, in the Tanahdatar valley. Here he made the only known attempt to establish a classical-style kingdom in the Sumatran hinterland. Legends and archaeological remains indicate that he entered a society still organised along preclassic lines, with village egalitarianism, religious ceremonies organised around megalithic monuments, and a strong matrilineal principle: irrigated riceland and houses were owned by women and inherited through the female line. Legends of the Minangkabau people from this region tell of a struggle between two warriors, one advocating an egalitarian society based on consensus, another espousing an aristocratic form of organisation. This may be an echo of Adityavarman's effort to transplant a Javanese-style court into the Sumatran highlands.

Archaeological Remains

Adityavarman's inscriptions and associated art indicate that he was a devotee of esoteric Buddhism. An enormous image has been discovered near the border between west Sumatra and Jambi. The statue depicts a Bhairawa, a demonic being embodying the negative impulses. People who are initiated into its special cult believed that these negative impulses could be transcended by indulgence in them. This statue is thought to be Adityavarman's portrait. It depicts a man holding a skull bowl and sacrificial knife, and standing on a pile of skulls and a victim. Inscriptions describe visions which Adityavarman is said to have experienced while inhaling the stench of burning bodies on a cremation ground.

Adityavarman's efforts to establish a Javanese-style kingdom did not outlive him. Although one of his inscriptions mentions a crown prince, there are no later inscriptions or other archaeological remains which would allow us to reconstruct events in west Sumatra after Adityavarman's last known inscription of 1374 until European sources appear.

Padang Lawas

Padang Lawas (the name means 'Broad Plain') is an environmental as well as archaeological anomaly. Here the long Barisan Chain of mountains comes to an end. Between the termination of this mountain wall and the rise of the northern Sumatran complex (termed the Batak Tumor) stretches a grassy plain covering several hundred square kilometres. This natural grassland is formed by dry winds which sweep through the gap.

Such a comparatively desolate landscape cannot support a dense population, but it does provide the most convenient communication route between the east and west coasts in the whole 1,750 kilometre-long island. Several rivers flow east from the plain. One of these, the Panai, could be connected with the kingdom of Pannei raided by the Cholas in 1025.

This is our only clue to the reason for the existence of at least 25 elaborate brick shrines for esoteric Buddhism built between the 11th and 13th centuries. Inscriptions from these sites mention no kingdoms, but the religion they espouse is identical to that practised by Adityavarman. The names of three of the Padang Lawas sites indicate connections with Nepal and Sri Lanka. These are Biaro Bahal I, II and III. Biaro is derived from *vihara*, meaning 'monastery'. Bahal is a term still used in Nepal to refer to two-storied temples of the Vajrayana sect, which was extremely influential in Indonesian Buddhism. Rampant lions carved on Biaro Bahal I are very similar to carvings at Polonnaruva, the capital of Sri Lanka in the 11th century.

SUMATRA: MAJOR ARCHAEOLOGICAL SITES

Pasai
Perlak
Tanjung Anom
Kota Cina
Kota Jawa
Deli Tua
Deli River
Straits of Malaka
Merbok Valley
PENINSULAR MALAYSIA
N
Melaka
Barus
Gunung Tua
Padang Lawas
Rokan River
Tanjung Medan
SINGAPORE
Karimun Island
Kampar River
Muara Takus
INDIAN OCEAN
Kuantan River
Batang Hari River
Muara Jambi
Karang Berahi
Pagarruyung
Langsat
Langsat River
Kota Kapur
Palembang
Musi River
Tanah Abang
Bengkulu
Jabung
Bawang Inscription
Batu Bedil; Ulu Belu
Palas Pasemah

Major temple, city site or inscription
Adityavarman inscriptions (14th century)
Land Above 100 metres
0 500 km

Urbanisation

While the Javanese were politically ascendant in Sumatra at this time, culturally and commercially the most important changes might have been due to early Chinese settlement. No large urban sites older than the 11th century have been discovered anywhere in the Archipelago, even in Java.

In the late 11th or early 12th centuries, we begin to obtain our first evidence that Chinese emigrants were residing permanently in Southeast Asia. At this time the Song dynasty was under great pressure from the Mongols and ancient strictures against private Chinese commerce with foreigners were not strictly enforced. With the relaxing of these laws, many Chinese married local wives and never returned to China.

The early Chinese merchants may have built fortified settlements to protect themselves. Marco Polo, who spent six months in northern Sumatra in 1292, on his return to Italy, recorded such a practice. With the decline of the strong monopolistic trading kingdoms of Sriwijaya and Malayu, many new trading centres sprang up in Sumatra, in most cases around a Chinese settlement. The most extensively excavated of these early sites is Kota Cina (Chinese Stockade). This site in northeast Sumatra has yielded carbon 14 dates and a wide range of artefacts from 1050 to 1300. Many areas of Sumatra with great potential to illuminate this complex and important historical era still remain to be explored.

One of the important regions most likely to yield further data is the coast of Aceh. A Tamil inscription that was recently discovered there may date from the 11th century, when Tamil trading guilds had already established themselves to the west of the Straits of Melaka in the wake of the Chola raids. The coast in this area has been sinking for centuries, and many important early sites no doubt are now submerged.

Buddha found by villagers at Kota Cina in the 1940s. Some villagers claimed the statue was of Indian origin. Some time later the head was stolen. The figure now has a replacement head. The style of the remaining portion indicates that it was carved in Sri Lanka or southern India about 1200 AD.

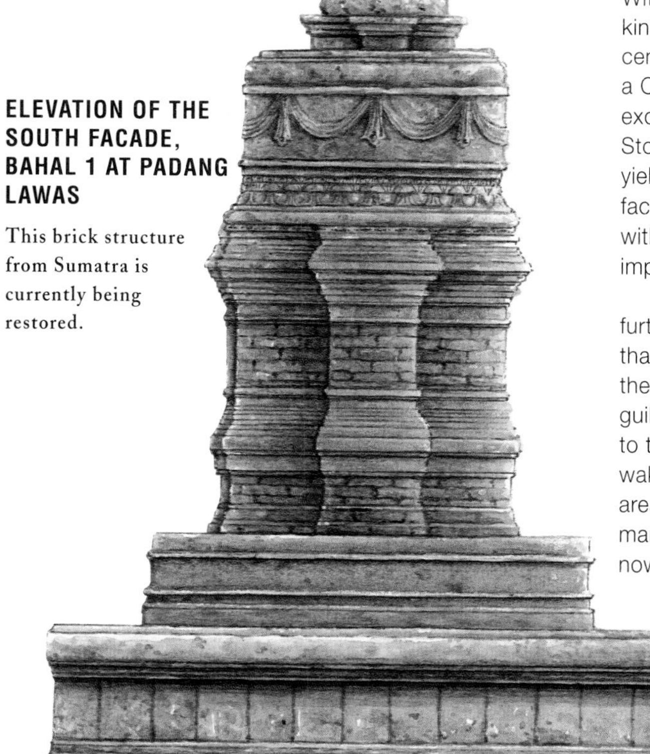

ELEVATION OF THE SOUTH FACADE, BAHAL 1 AT PADANG LAWAS

This brick structure from Sumatra is currently being restored.

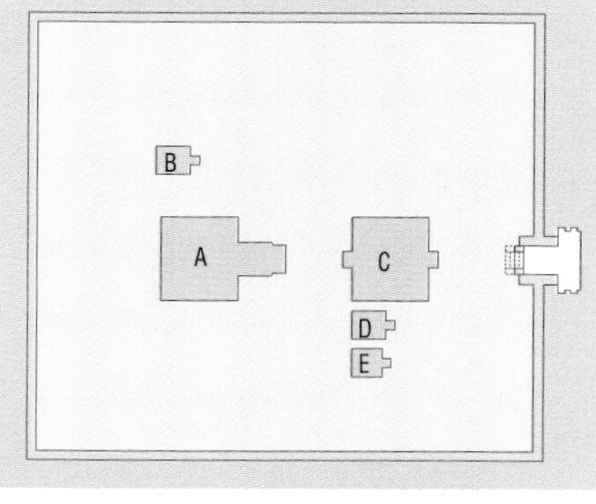

A. Bahal I
B. Stupa
C,D,E. Pendopos

Bali in the Middle Classic Period

In the late 10th century an East Javanese princess named Gunapriya married Udayana, a Balinese ruler of the Warmmadewa dynasty. After this marriage, Javanese cultural influence over Bali became very powerful. The Old Javanese language began to be used for official inscriptions, and a Javanese-style privy council was introduced, with members drawn from military commanders and from the Sivaite and Buddhist priesthood.

Durga statue from Kutri, possibly a representation of Queen Gunapriya.

Ancestor statue from Mount Panulisan, so called because these images have no attributes of specific deities.

»Goa Gajah. The face is surrounded by carvings representing a mountainous landscape with various animals, in a composition reminiscent of some scenes on Borobudur.

Old Balinese Art

The period from the 10th to 13th centuries corresponds to what the Dutch archaeologist W. F. Stutterheim termed the Old Balinese style, the second of three periods into which ancient Balinese art can be divided. The others are Hindu Balinese (8th–10th centuries), and Middle Balinese (13th–14th centuries). He assigned to the Old Balinese period the important sites of Panulisan, Goa Gajah, Kutri, and Gunung Kawi. It is extremely difficult to date Balinese monuments, which may well represent several different episodes of revision, so this periodization is only approximate. During the Old Balinese period Balinese art developed a character of its own, which evolved into the styles seen today.

The Rulers of Ancient Bali

Gunapriya and Udayana received posthumous titles meaning 'She who is immortalised *(dhinarma)* in Burwan' and 'He who is immortalised in Banuwka'. The name *Burwan* might be preserved in the village of Buruan, in Gianyar. In a nearby village, Kutri, three *pura* contain images probably connected with several ancient royal figures. The most famous of these images is that of Durga slaying the demon Mardini now kept in Pura Kedharman. This statue displays attributes of early East Javanese sculpture. Several scholars have suggested that this statue may be the memorial image of Gunapriya, though there is no direct evidence for such an association. The location of Banuwka is still unknown as no extant village bears such a name.

The connection between Java and Bali was strengthened when the eldest son of this couple, Airlangga, married a Javanese princess, daughter of Dharma-wangsa Teguh. After a struggle in which he defeated his enemies who had destroyed the kingdom of his father-in-law, Airlangga was installed as king of Java in 1037. Thus although Airlangga was born in Bali as the Balinese ruler's eldest son, he never ruled there. He attempted to have his own son installed as king of Bali, but his petition through a priestly envoy was rejected.

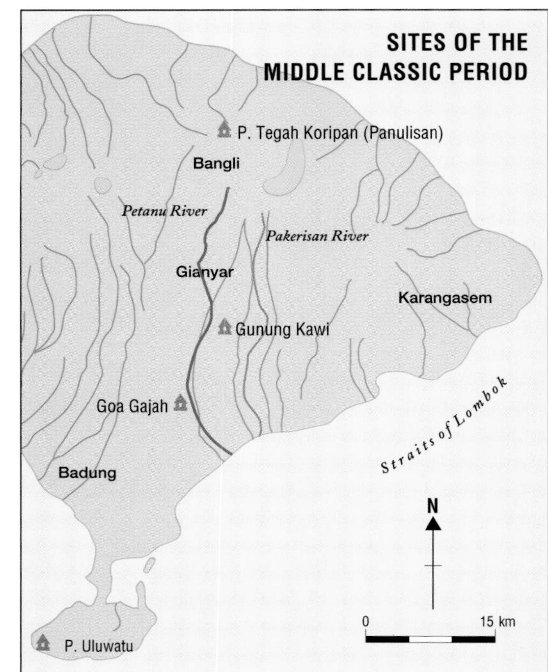

Dharmawangsa Marakata, Airlangga's younger brother ruled Bali between 1022 and 1025. His inscriptions depict Dharmawangsa as a protector of his people who was looked upon as a source of legal justice. A statue of the Bodhisattva Amoghapasa at Kutri has been associated with Dharmawangsa. Other statues connected with ancient royal figures from this period include a Ganesha and a pair of sandals on the same block of stone; the sandals denote a god or royal person who for some unknown reason was not depicted directly.

Anak Wungsu, the youngest child of Gunapriya and Udayana, then succeeded to the throne. However, the lapse of time between Dharmawangsa's

last inscription and Anak Wungsu's first is very long; nothing is heard of Anak Wungsu until 1049. We do not know whether other inscriptions existed which have not been discovered, or whether there was a real power vacuum during this time. Despite this long delay, Anak Wungsu issued a large number of inscriptions: 28 are known. They describe him as a compassionate ruler who always kept his mind on the perfection of the mandala of the island of Bali. His inscriptions have been found in south, central, and north Bali, demonstrating that his realm was geographically extensive.

On Mount Panulisan, at an elevation of 1,745 metres, the highest point of Mount Batur's enormous crater wall, stands a temple which has only been opened to non-Balinese in recent decades. Statues here bear dates corresponding to 1011, 1074, 1077 and 1254 (or 1257). A female portrait statue is inscribed on the rear with the name Bhatari Mandul and the date 999 (Saka; 1077 AD). Since this date falls into the reign of Anak Wungsu, Stutterheim suspected that the image depicted Anak Wungsu's queen.

Gunung Kawi and Anak Wungsu

The site of Gunung Kawi ('Poet Mountain') consists of a number of temple facades as well as a number of meditation complexes carved out of soft volcanic tuff. The complex is approached by a steep stairway and gate leading down into the narrow valley of the Pakerisan River, which like the Petanu has carved a deep, narrow course lined with rock faces which lend themselves to use as isolated ceremonial sites. On the north of the stairway, before crossing the river, is a group of four temple facades carved in relief. Across the stream is another group of five temple facades. One of these bears an inscription in Kadiri script: *haji lumah ing jalu,* the lord who died at Jalu. Jalu means kris or dagger, so the inscription may refer to this precise spot. Scholars associate this personage with Anak Wungsu, based purely on the fact that palaeography has dated the inscription to the approximate period of his reign. The temple facades themselves are mentioned in an inscription from Dharmawangsa as *Sanghyang katyagan ing pakrisan mangaran ning amarawati,* but perhaps the complex was not completed until the reign of Anak Wungsu. To the east of the temple facades is an ascetic's cloister and further east a long row of meditation niches.

Anak Wungsu was succeeded by Sri Maharaja Sri Walaprabhu, believed to have ruled between 1079 and 1088. We know little about this ruler, as he issued few inscriptions. His importance is that he first used the Sanskrit title Sri Maharaja, whereas the previous kings styled themselves Sang Ratu or Paduka Haji.

A Change of Dynasty

Before Walaprabhu, apparently all Balinese kings were descendants of Warmmadewa. Those who came after Walaprabhu seem to have belonged to a different dynasty. Their names and titles suggest a close connection with the rulers of East Java. The last king of this dynasty was Paduka Bhatara Parameswara Sri Hyang ning Hyang Adidewalancana (1260–1324).

During Adidewalancana's reign, in 1282, Bali was attacked and subjugated by the king of Singasari, Krtanagara. The inscriptions of Basangara (1296) and Sikawana (1300) refer to a non-royal official called Raja Patih Makakasir Kbo Parud. According to Goris, Kbo Parud was not a royal name, so it is possible that this individual was appointed by the Javanese to administer Bali as their representative.

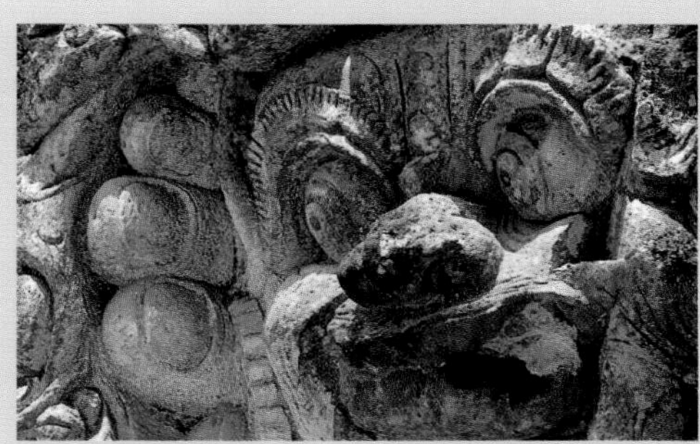

GOA GAJAH

The palaeography of graffiti on the entrance gives a date in the late 11th century. The interior contains Sivaite relics, but Buddhist statuary and collapsed fragments of rock–cut stupa indicate that Buddhists once revered this place as well. The identity of the face on the cave's entrance is controversial. A kala head would be conventional, but Bernet Kempers suggested that it depicts a witch equivalent to Rangda of modern dance, or the villain in the Calon Arang tale.

(Above) Ganesha statue, Goa Gajah.

«« Gunung Kawi. Royal tombs (top) and the main cloister (bottom). No such temples as these are known to have been constructed in Java. Interestingly, they were carved at a time when no temples were being built in Java. The main cloister consists of a central room surrounded by smaller chambers.

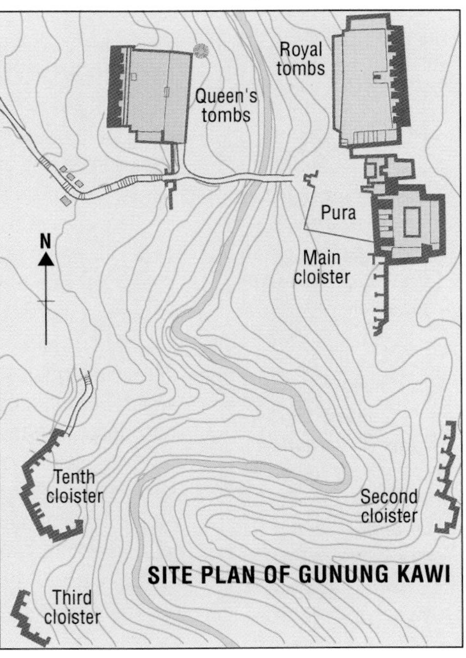

SITE PLAN OF GUNUNG KAWI

The Kingdoms of Kadiri and Singasari

According to legend, King Airlangga decided to retreat to a hermitage and to avoid a dispute over succession divided his kingdom between his two sons. For most of the 11th and 12th centuries, East Java was divided into a number of kingdoms. Kadiri is the best known because of its epigraphic and literary remains. The most important trading kingdom was known as Janggala. The rise of Singasari after 1222 marked the beginning of a major new phase in East Java's history.

»»Relief from Candi Jago depicting Kunjarakarna, a yaksa who has a vision of the underworld which is given to him by the Buddha, Vairocana. There he sees the demons and the punishments of the wicked, and resolves to avoid their fate by leading a righteous life.

The King's Divinity

In the kingdom of Kadiri, the sovereign was esteemed as the most eminent person in the kingdom. When people wanted to communicate with him they had to salute him with a *sembah* (both hands joined before the face) at 'the dust of his footwear'. He was regarded as the incarnation of a god, usually Visnu, who always rescues the world from danger. Many of the statues of the Kadiri period depict kings in their Visnu form. Indications of this belief are also found in inscriptions and literary works. The kings of Kadiri were identified with the 'state god', Visnu, and could also be identified with a god of their choice, an *istadewata.*

The Structure of the Kingdom

To what extent was the king's aura effective? This question cannot yet be answered. However, the Kadiri rulers' sovereignty was not projected purely in myth and story. There was another, pragmatic side of Kadiri state formation: improvement of the bureaucracy. Four points are worthy of note. First, the role of intermediary between the king and middle–ranking officials was intensified. Second, the status of intellectuals rose. Kings sought to attract poets and philosophers to court where they were seen as augmenting royal charisma. Third, military organisations were formed. Fourth, control was extended over water transport, probably in order to regulate the economy and facilitate military mobilisation. Water management for agricultural purposes seems to have remained under the control of local authorities although kings sometimes contributed funds for such projects as dam building.

There were two categories of intermediary in Kadiri. The first group comprised the *duwan* or *duhan,* officials at the village (*thani)* or central village (*dalem thani*) level, who received special dispensations from the king to avail themselves of special rank attributes. They were probably obligated to secure the flow of agricultural produce to the granaries of the capital. In the second category were the *sopana*, literally 'staircase' or 'mediator'. They were dignitaries surrounding the king, who on occasion assisted a middle–ranked official to ask a favour from the king, usually the right to display certain attributes of rank. Neither *duwan* or *sopana* or any other middlemen are mentioned in Airlangga's reign; they seem to have first appeared in Kadiri.

Another example of bureaucratic development in Kadiri was the elevation in rank of experts in religious and cultural affairs, who could act as *sopana* to convey the king's orders. These, along with the court poets who also surrounded the king, were placed there to enhance the cultural life of the court, and to augment the king's charisma and sovereignty.

Royal sovereignty was further secured by economic and military measures. A class of personnel with special proficiency in military skills included archers, lancers, battle–axe wielders, elephant drivers, and horse–mounted cavalry. Kadiri possessed a permanent professional army, and also a systematic means for mobilising the general population for war. The non–professional units were led by *thani* officials, and each had a special banner with emblems, usually depicting animals. State measures for economic control in Kadiri included fines, payable in gold, for trangressing state regulations. In earlier periods fines were mentioned but in general terms. More frequently inscriptions had referred to punishments in the form of curses. Taxes were collected on such activities as sale of cattle, metalwork, pottery, salt and oil, and even entertainment. The central government also controlled the building and use of boats.

The term *bhumi* expressed the idea of a territorial unit in Kadiri. Inscriptions state that 'the king reigns in *bhumi* Kadiri'. *Nagara* or *rajya* meant the capital. In the succeeding Singasari era, important changes occurred. The phrase '*bhumi* Kadiri', which had previously comprised the whole kingdom, in the Singasari era came to denote merely a province. Thus the Singasari period saw the formation of the first empire in Indonesian history. The process of centralised state formation began in Kadiri, and came to florescence in the Majapahit era.

COMMEMORATIVE STATUES

These three statues from the Kadiri period possibly depict two kings and a queen. The two male figures represent Siva; the first is dated between the 12th to 13th century, the second slightly later at around 1400. Some kings of Kadiri identified themselves with this deity as their personal god, as well as with Visnu. The female statue of Laksmi, consort of Visnu, dated between the 13th and 14th centuries, once served as a spout.

Sculptural Development

Although sculpture did not develop impressively during the Kadiri period, which seems to have been a time of trial and error in the stylistic development of the art, the *kakawin* Smaradahana is important for the study of sculpture of this era. It relates the story of the birth of the popular elephant-headed god Ganesha, and his exploits in defeating a demon who was the enemy of the gods. A full description of the god's appearance is given in the *kakawin*, and also a description of the weapon he used: an axe made from the concentrated powers of the gods.

The narrative relates how Ganesha picks up the heads of his decapitated enemies and brings them to his face to cool his tusk, broken in the fight. However, only in the succeeding Singasari period do the narratives of Ganesha seem to have been used faithfully as a reference for making statues. This is demonstrated by the depiction of Ganesha's two front hands holding skulls, and the overall terrifying appearance of the elephant-faced god, the axe held in his right hand, in conformity with the Smaradahana. Earlier Ganesha sculptures from Java, even during the Kadiri period, depict Ganesha's axe in his left hand.

Hindu and Buddhist Sculpture

There was an important difference between the Kadiri and Singasari periods in terms of religious preference. While the kings of Kadiri were definitely Hindus, with a strong inclination toward the veneration of Visnu, the kings of Singasari were more inclined toward Buddhism, with initial indications of Hindu–Buddhist syncretism. These differences were inevitably reflected in the sculptural traditions of the two kingdoms.

Relief Style

Candi Jago, constructed around 1280, is the oldest East Javanese temple with narrative reliefs. The style of its reliefs is considerably different from anything which existed previously. Early Classic reliefs were naturalistic and executed in high relief so that the figures, in some cases, almost became free-standing. In east Java the very earliest reliefs already show a very strong degree of stylisation. The depiction of humans resembles closely the shadow puppet shape; they are very flat and two-dimensional. The articulation of the limbs seems like that of leather puppets, and other details such as the headdresses are very reminiscent of those still found on *wayang kulit* today.

Another aspect of the Late Classic reliefs is that much larger natural scenes are depicted. The landscapes sometimes appear with no human figures at all, consisting mainly of stylised trees, bushes and resting places. The goal of the artist seems to have been to express the pleasure which the Javanese of this period took in contemplating rural scenery.

Sculptural Themes

The sculpture of Candi Jago demonstrates the combination of Hindu and Buddhist elements within a single temple. The main figure is Amoghapasa, a form of the Bodhisattva Avalokitesvara, accompanied by four lesser bodhisattvas: the fierce couple Hayagriwa and Bhrkuti, and the gentler couple Sudhanakumara and Syamatara. Smaller *dhyani* Buddha figures were also found in the temple precinct. All these figures have their names inscribed on their halos. The walls of Candi Jago bear several rows of narrative reliefs depicting stories of great interest because of their variety of religious references. The Buddhist Kunjarakarna story is found on the temple's lower part, while the upper parts bear stories from the Parthayajna and Arjunawiwaha. The Kunjarakarna has a *yaksa* as hero, converted by the teachings of Vairocana, a Dhyani Buddha or Tathagata. The second and third stories have Arjuna, the hero of the Hindu Mahabharata, as the main figure. All three tales have a similar dual theme coupling the search for ultimate truth with a release from danger, which may be threatened by sin or from worldly enemies. Candi Jago is therefore basically a Buddhist temple incorporating strong Hindu elements. The presence of popular Mahabharata stories might also indicate that the Javanese did not associate them specifically with Hinduism, but rather considered them part of the nation's common heritage. This blending of Hindu and Buddhist elements intensified during the succeeding Majapahit era, and continues into the present.

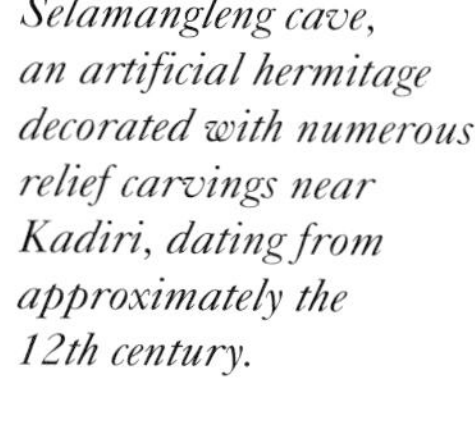

Kala head, from Selamangleng cave, an artificial hermitage decorated with numerous relief carvings near Kadiri, dating from approximately the 12th century.

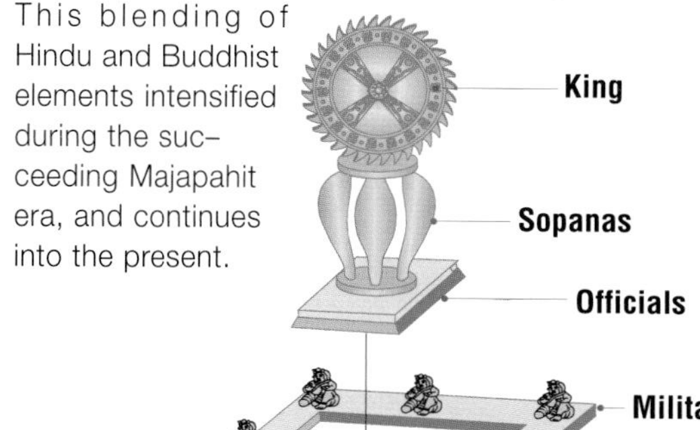

«Figure of Ganesha from Bara, near Blitar, perhaps originally from the site of Simping. It is inscribed with a chronogram equivalent to the date Saka 1161, or 1239 AD (Singasari period). Such Ganesha statues were often placed near river crossings. This may have been due to Ganesha's characteristic as the deity who enables his devotees to overcome all obstacles.

SCHEMATIC DIAGRAM OF THE KINGDOM OF KADIRI

The diagram depicts an ideal realm divided into four quarters with the king at the centre, symbolised by a cakra (discus), symbol of Visnu.

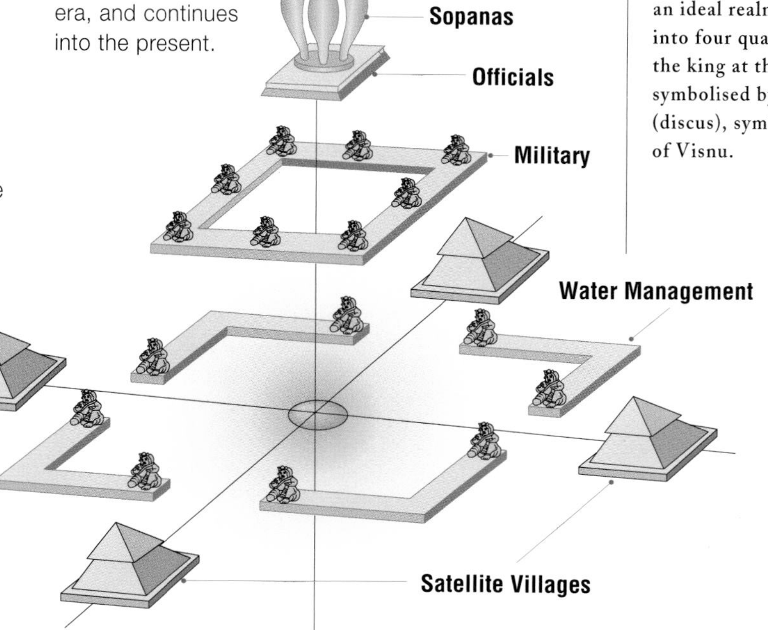

Head of Harihara, a combination of Visnu and Siva, from Candi Sumberjati, east Java, c. 1300. It is strongly suspected that this is a portrait statue of Majapahit's first ruler, Raden Wijaya.

Visnu clinging to Garuda for dear life, in a sculpture which exemplifies the naive style of Late Classic Javanese art. Candi Sukuh, central Java, 15th century.

INDONESIA IN THE LATE CLASSIC PERIOD

The Late Classic era witnessed the first unification of Indonesia under the empire of Majapahit. The most important archaeological remains of Majapahit are not temples nor sculptures but the evidence of early Javanese urbanisation. Research has only recently begun to concentrate on the search for ancient cities (see illustrations at right). Excavations aimed at uncovering aspects of the lives of the common city dwellers have recently been carried out at Majapahit's probable capital. Although data is still in the process of being analysed, it seems certain that this site was populated by several tens of thousands of people engaged in a wide range of economic activities in addition to religious and civil administration. Data from inscriptions also indicates that the relationship between the kingdom and religious establishments underwent a major change during the 14th century: efforts were made to separate the two organisations, suggesting a growing secularisation of government. Chinese and other foreigners came to constitute a larger proportion of the population, particularly of the coastal districts. Despite the growing differentiation between religious, economic, and adminstrative spheres, religious art still constitutes one of our major sources of information about this period. Rulers of the 14th century still had themselves commemorated in statues, such as the image of Harihara, which are not greatly inferior to the works of the Early Classic period. The sculpture of Candi Sukuh, and other stiff and highly conventional images carved 150 years later (see illustrations at top right) symbolise the decline of classic Indonesian civilisation, the gradual rise of new beliefs, and the shift of attention to new art forms. No large architectural complexes on the scale of those built in central Java 500 years earlier were ever attempted in east Java. Temple building was decentralised, resulting in buildings with smaller dimensions. The creativity of the Javanese artists had not diminished, however; the inspiration which produced such imaginative works as the one-eyed kala (*kala ekacaksu*) (above) provide evidence that the sculptors worked within an environment in which experimentation was valued.

Siva, east Java, 14th or 15th century. The hand posture and stiff attitude are typical of Javanese sculpture in the period when sculpture was gradually phased out.

Visnu, east Java, 15th century. The face and hands have been partially restored in recent times. Such images are normally associated with terraced mountain sanctuaries.

LATE CLASSIC PERIOD: 14TH TO 16TH CENTURIES

The Late Classic era was marked by the rise of Indonesia's greatest empire organised according to traditional models, and the simultaneous emergence of forces which ultimately shattered the ancient order on which that empire was based. These forces were urbanisation, conversion to Islam, and contact with Europe.

Majapahit became a shining symbol of Indonesia's ability to achieve unified self–government. During 350 years of Dutch encroachment into the archipelago, the memory of Majapahit made it possible for Indonesians from different islands to conceive of a unified country. The legacy of Majapahit is visible today. The national motto *Bhinneka tunggal ika*, 'unity in diversity', is extracted from a Majapahit poem. The name Palapa used for Indonesia's communications satellites is taken from an oath by Majapahit's chief minister, in which he swore he would not rest until he had united *nusantara*.

Even as these strides toward Indonesian unity were taken, traits which had been integral to Indonesia's ancient societies were disappearing. Thousand–year–old traditions of classic architecture and sculpture were sinking into oblivion. In the mountains simple terraces were built to accommodate powerful but comparatively crude images of deities with only tenuous links to Indic religions. In many instances no statues were used at all, as a new philosophy of imageless worship spread. We know little of the beliefs of the common people at this time; perhaps a religious vacuum existed into which Islam spread after 1500.

Some of the most important remains of this period are not monuments or works of art, but brass coins and sherds of earthenware pottery, the detritus of daily life. They signal the appearance of the first large city in Java. Before 1300, money was not in wide circulation, and even palaces probably were surrounded by villages whose inhabitants depended largely on agriculture for subsistence. During the 14th century Majapahit's capital grew into Indonesia's largest population centre of pre–modern times, inhabited by people whose lives acquired many of the characteristics of residents of modern urbanised societies: money–using, occupationally specialised, and fond of art.

Other important remnants from this period consist of literary works: poetry and prose which preserve a much wider range of feelings and situations than survive from earlier periods. These literary expressions enable us to see Indonesians of the late classic from many more sides than before.

Ruins of Candi Lor, east Java, 14th century.

Head of Kala, Candi Jawi, east Java, c. 1300

Mapping historic remains of an early city, Trowulan, east Java.

Archaeological excavation of an urban site, east Java.

The Kingdom of Majapahit

Majapahit, named after a fruit, succeeded Singasari as the dominant power in Indonesia in the late 13th century. Majapahit continued many of Singasari's policies, including the effort to exert greater control over areas beyond its heartland. The 14th century was remembered in later times as a "golden" age of political and cultural development. Historical figures and artistic motifs from this time remain popular.

Candi Berahu in a drawing made for Raffles' History of Java *around 1815.*

Majapahit potters produced kendis made of burnished red–slipped earthenware. Bronze kendis often took the same form. The bulging spouts and squat bodies are typical of the late classic period.

Majapahit's sunburst motif, with Surya the sun god mounted on his steed. Such stones are found at the peak of the ceilings on the interiors of Majapahit candi.

Gobog, copper coins or amulets cast during the Majapahit period. Some are decorated with wayang–style figures depicting the Javanese Damar Wulan myth.

Foundation of Majapahit

In Southeast Asian tradition, conquered principalities, usually corresponding to geographic units such as fertile river valleys were not assimilated into new kingdoms. Networks of kinship and patronage survived military defeat. East Java's history was dominated by two rival centres of power: one in the Kadiri area of the upper reaches of the Brantas River, the other near Malang. In 1222 Singasari defeated Kadiri. At the end of the 13th century Kadiri successfully challenged the domination of Singasari. This conflict is recounted in the *Nagarakrtagama* (correctly known as *Desawarnana)*, dated 1365, and the *Pararaton*, written in the 16th century. These two texts give different accounts of this famous event. One says Singasari's ruler was killed while engaged in a drunken orgy; the other says he died during a religious ceremony. These accounts may be reconcilable if he were conducting a Tantric ritual, perhaps to gain spiritual power over his enemies. Kadiri's victory was only momentary, as the conflict continued. A Singasari prince, Raden Wijaya, escaped to Madura. The Madura ruler advised him to pretend to offer submission to Kadiri's ruler in order to formulate a strategy for overthrowing him. Raden Wijaya requested and was granted permission to occupy a wilderness north of the Arjuna mountains and to start a new settlement there.

In 1293 a Mongol expedition sent to take revenge on Singasari's assassinated ruler for his defiance of Kublai Khan arrived in east Java. Raden Wijaya seized the opportunity to turn its members against Kadiri. Raden Wijaya then attacked the Mongols and succeeded in expelling them.

The Nagarakrtagama and Pararaton concur that Raden Wijaya had himself installed as ruler of a new kingdom called Majapahit ("Bitter Gourd") in 1294 AD. During the next few years he had to withstand several challenges, but he surmounted all opposition and ruled until his death in 1309 AD.

The next ruler died without issue and was succeeded by his sister Tribhuwanottunggadewi. She ruled the kingdom for 22 years before abdicating in 1350 and was succeeded by her 16–year–old son Hayam Wuruk. Both the queen and her son were advised by Gajah Mada, whose image has been preserved in Indonesian history as a brilliant statesman. To him is attributed the *Palapa* oath: he would not enjoy *palapa* until he had unified the whole Southeast Asian archipelago. *Palapa* has subsequently become a symbol of Indonesian unity and one of the cornerstones of modern Indonesia's self–image.

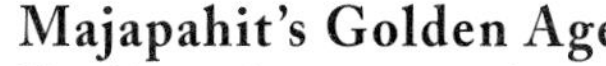

Majapahit's Golden Age

The Nagarakrtagama, written in 1365, depicts a sophisticated court with refined tastes in art and literature, and a complex system of religious rituals. The poet describes Majapahit as the centre of a huge mandala extending from New Guinea and Maluku to Sumatra and the Malay Peninsula. Local traditions in many parts of Indonesia retain accounts in more or less legendary form of 14th century Majapahit's power. Majapahit's direct administration did not extend beyond east Java and Bali, but challenges to Majapahit's claim to overlordship in the outer islands drew forceful responses.

A Chinese source reports that the Javanese commander and 30,000 troops were paid in gold. Majapahit may have developed a standing army, something which is rarely attested in ancient Southeast Asia. Although Javanese sources do not

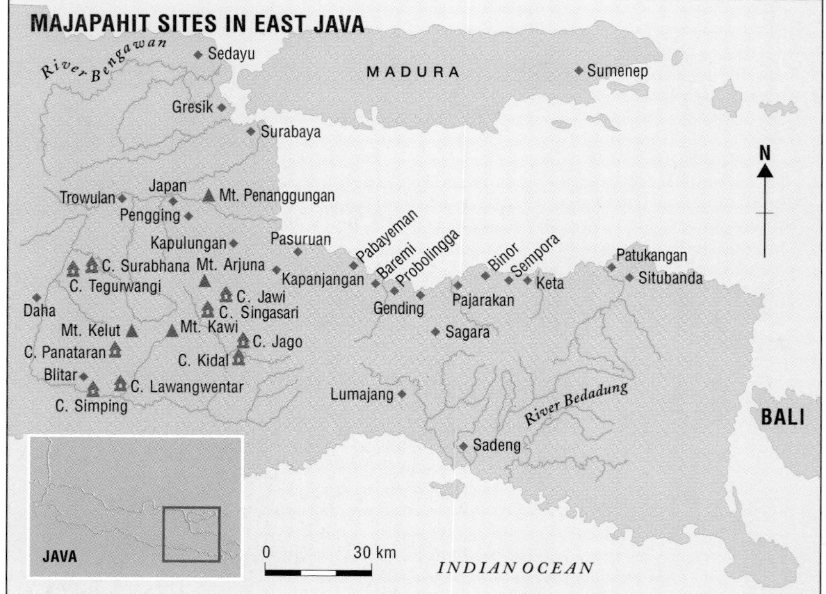

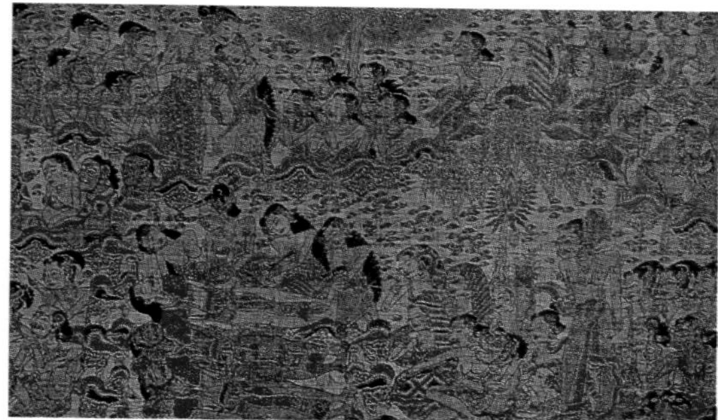

give details of Majapahit's military force, beyond praising its great fleet, it seems likely that it did indeed have a well-organised military structure.

The main event of the administrative calendar took place on the first day of the month of Caitra (March to April) when representatives of all territories paying tax or tribute to Majapahit came to the capital to pay court. Majapahit's territories were roughly divided into three types: the palace and its vicinity; the areas of east Java and Bali which were directly administered by officials appointed by the king; and the outer dependencies which enjoyed substantial internal autonomy.

Majapahit conducted an active program of diplomatic relations with countries on the Asian mainland. The Nagarakrtagama lists the kingdoms with which Majapahit had contacts. Vietnam is singled out as having been a particularly close ally. China at this time was still under the Mongol Yuan dynasty. Although diplomatic contacts with the Mongols were understandably cool after Raden Wijaya's expulsion of Kublai Khan's expedition, relations had been restored and missions were occasionally exchanged.

Contemporary sources from Majapahit which have survived are largely either religious or literary in nature, so that we know little of Majapahit's internal administration. We know the titles of many officials, but little concerning their duties. We cannot reconstruct the nature of the kingdom's bureaucracy. The evidence we have suggests that it must have possessed a complex structure, with a number of different levels, divided into religious, military, judicial, and financial sections.

Economy

Taxes and fines were paid in cash. Java's economy had been at least partly monetised since the late 8th century, using gold and silver coins. In about the year 1300, in the reign of Majapahit's first king, an important change took place: the indigenous coinage was completely replaced by imported Chinese copper cash. The reason for this is not given in any source, but most scholars assume it was due to the increasing complexity of the Javanese economy and a desire for a currency system that used much smaller denominations suitable for use in everyday market transactions. This was a role for which gold and silver are not well suited.

Some idea of the scale of the internal economy can be gathered from scattered data in inscriptions. The Canggu inscription dated 1358 mentions 78 ferry crossings in the country (*mandala Java*). Majapahit inscriptions mention a large number of occupational specialties, ranging from gold and silver smiths to drink vendors and butchers. Although many of these occupations had existed in earlier times, the proportion of the population earning an income from non-agrarian pursuits seems to have become even greater during the Majapahit era.

The great prosperity of Majapahit was probably due to two factors. Firstly, the northeast lowlands of Java were suitable for rice cultivation, and during Majapahit's prime numerous irrigation projects were undertaken, some with government assistance. Secondly, Majapahit's ports on the north coast were probably significant stations along the route to obtain the spices of Maluku, and as the spices passed through Java they would have provided an important source of income for Majapahit.

The Nagarakrtagama states that the fame of the ruler of Wilwatikta (a synonym for Majapahit) attracted foreign merchants from far and wide, including Indians, Khmers, Siamese, and Chinese among others. A special tax was levied against some foreigners, possibly those who had taken up semi-permanent residence in Java and conducted some type of enterprise other than foreign trade.

The Largest Southeast Asian Empire

In sum, Majapahit was the largest empire ever to form in Southeast Asia. Although its political power beyond the core area in east Java was diffuse, constituting mainly ceremonial recognition of suzerainty, Majapahit society developed a high degree of sophistication in both commercial and artistic activities. Its capital was inhabited by a cosmopolitan population among whom literature and art flourished. Most modern Indonesians view the political, literary, commercial, diplomatic, and artistic accomplishments of Majapahit as a source of great pride, and her foundation as the first expression of modern Indonesian nationhood.

An early 14th century sculpture of Visnu depicting this deity holding the standard attributes. This may be a royal portrait statue.

The Bubat Massacre of 1357 as depicted in a modern Balinese painting. Princess Citra Rashmi of Sunda was to marry King Hayam Wuruk of Majapahit, but a misunderstanding arose and a battle ensued on a field called Bubat in the Majapahit capital in which all the Sundanese were slain. The Sundanese king and his daughter appear above; below the bodies of the dead nobles are laid out.

Candi Jawi, funerary temple of Krtanagara, ruler of Singasari, assassinated in 1292. The foot of the temple bears reliefs, the meaning of which has not been determined. The tall slender form of the structure is typical of Javanese architecture of the 14th century.

Trowulan in Literature and Archaeology

The Nagarakrtagama*, written in 1365, contains a poetic description of the palace of Majapahit and its surroundings. Because some of its details are vague, scholars who have tried to compile a plan of the capital, Trowulan, have come to quite different conclusions. Prapanca, the author, only describes the royal and religious sectors. For glimpses of everyday life in this, one of Indonesia's first cities, we must turn to archaeology.*

Clay water pipes with multiple joints indicate that sophisticated water supply facilities probably existed in 14th century Trowulan.

Gold ornaments inlaid with precious gems.

Bronze lamp in the form of a pavilion with birds perched on the roof.

The Royal Compound

According to Prapanca's poem, the royal compound was surrounded by a thick, high wall of red brick. Nearby was a fortified guard post. The main gate into the palace, was located in the north wall, and was entered through huge doors made out of decorated iron. Outside the north gate was a long building where courtiers met once a year, a market place, and a sacred crossroad.

Just inside the north gate one entered a courtyard which contained religious buildings. On the western side of this courtyard were pavilions surrounded by a canal where people bathed. At the south end a gate led to rows of houses set on terraces in which palace servants lived. Passing through another gate, one entered a third courtyard crowded with houses and a great hall for those waiting to be admitted into the ruler's presence. The king's own quarters, which lay to the east of this courtyard, had pavilions on decorated red brick bases, ornately carved wooden pillars, and roofs decorated with clay ornaments.

Outside the palace were quarters for Siva priests, Buddhists, and other members of the nobility. Further away, and separated from the palace by open fields, were more royal compounds, including that of the redoubtable minister Gajah Mada. Here Prapanca's description ends.

A Chinese Account

A 15th century Chinese source describes the palace as being clean and well kept. It was said to have been enclosed within a brick wall more than 10 metres high and with a double gate. The houses inside were built on pillars and were 10 to 13 metres high, with wooden floors covered with fine mats on which people sat. Roofs were made from wood shingles. Dwellings of common people were covered with straw.

Settlement Pattern

A book on Majapahit court etiquette defines the capital as 'All where one can go out without passing through paddy fields.' Temple reliefs from Majapahit do not depict urban scenes, but some contain sketches of settlements indicated as pavilions enclosed within walls. The word *kuwu* in the *Nagarakrtagama* seems to refer to settlement units consisting of a group of buildings surrounded by a wall, in which a large number of people lived under the control of a nobleman. This pattern characterised 16th century coastal cities of Java described by early European visitors. Probably Majapahit's capital was composed of such units.

Artefacts from Daily Life

Trowulan, a village in east Java, is surrounded by a huge archaeological site covering approximately 100 square kilometres. This is probably the city described by Prapanca and the Chinese. Past research at Trowulan has concentrated on monumental remains: temples, tombs, and bathing places. Archaeological surveys and excavations have now found remains of industrial, commercial, and religious activity, habitation areas and water supply systems, all of which are evidence of a dense population during the 14th to 15th centuries.

Houses

Archaeological excavations have revealed brick floors and the walls of some dwellings. In certain cases two or even three layers of such buildings are superimposed. These dwellings were equipped with wells and drains. Traces of large reservoirs and wells lined with brick or clay have also been located.

Industries

Many pieces of gold jewellery from this period have been discovered in east Java. Although Java has no significant gold sources, imports from Sumatra, Borneo, and Sulawesi made it possible for many

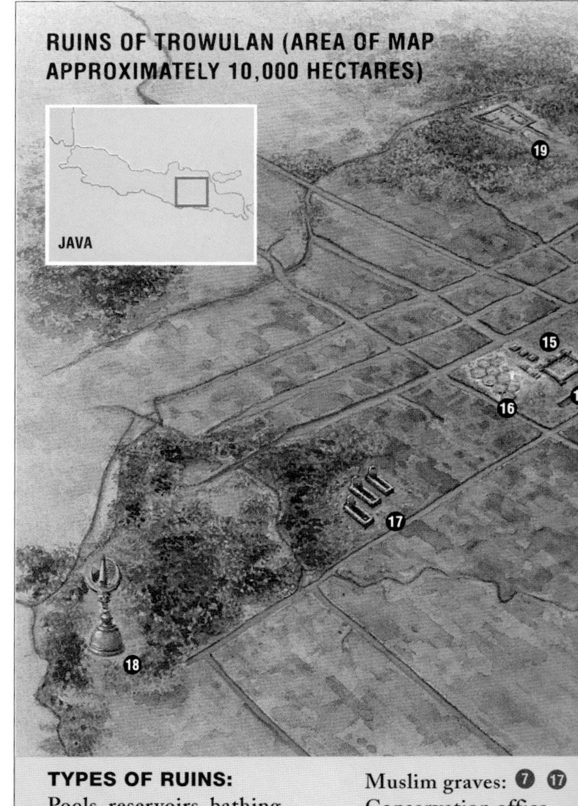

TYPES OF RUINS:
Pools, reservoirs, bathing places: 1 8 9 10
Gateways: 2 3
Temples: 4 5 6 19
Muslim graves: 7 17
Conservation office and museum: 11
Goldworking site: 12

goldsmiths to find work in Java.

One district of Trowulan is still called Kemasan, from the word *emas*, meaning 'gold'. Not only have gold ornaments been found in the vicinity of this area, but also the tools that were used for working the gold. Small clay cups might have been used for melting gold for use in lost wax casting. Bronze anvils and flat circular stones with three legs may have been used as work surfaces for chiselling and hammering metal. A large number of clay crucibles for melting bronze have been excavated at Pakis, in the southern part of the site. Some of the bronze was used to cast *uang gobog,* large coins or amulets, in stone moulds. Other metal objects include ornate bronze lamps, water containers, bells and other items probably used in religious ceremonies, and instruments usually called 'slit drums'. Similar objects made of wood or bamboo are still found in Javanese and Balinese villages. Many iron tools were used but most might have been imported since Java is poor in iron ore.

Money and Markets

The *Nawanatya* mentions a court official whose duty was to protect the markets. 'Eight thousand cash every day from the markets is the share' which was received by these officials. The 'cash' referred to in this text are Chinese bronze coins which in about 1300 became Majapahit's official currency, replacing gold and silver currency which had been in use for centuries. Apparently Chinese coins were preferable because they were available in small denominations, suitable for use in markets. This change suggests that economic life in Trowulan was marked by specialised occupations, wages, and acquisition of most daily needs by purchase. Important evidence for the 14th century Javanese perception of money comes in the form of clay piggy banks with slits in their backs large enough to admit a coin. The association between pigs as a form of wealth, and pig figurines as containers for saving money is obvious. Coin containers in other shapes are also found.

Products of the Potter

This craft was an important activity. Most pottery was intended for domestic use in cooking and storage with decoration limited to stripes of red paint. Lamps for coconut oil are another common find. The best pottery takes the form of vessels such as water ewers (*kendi*), with thin walled bodies, graceful shapes, and glossy red surfaces created by burnishing. These must have been made by professional potters. Water containers were one of the Majapahit potter's main products. Fragments of many large round water jars have been found. Rectangular water 'troughs' were decorated with aquatic motifs or other scenery. Terracotta figurines were produced in large quantities, representing many subjects: gods, humans, animals, buildings, and scenes. We do not know what they were used for. They may have served multiple purposes. Some may have been used in religious shrines attached to dwellings as in modern Bali. Examples of these terracottas in the forms of miniature buildings and animals have been found at shrines on Mount Penanggungan. Others such as humorous depictions of foreigners may simply have been meant as toys for children.

AN URBAN DWELLING

Part of a 14th century dwelling site unearthed near Balai Penyelamatan, Trowulan.

0 2 m

1. Drain
2. Floor of flat stones
3. Well
4. Large water jars
5. Grinding stone
6. Piggy banks
7. Brick floor
8. Statue
9. Cobblestone floor

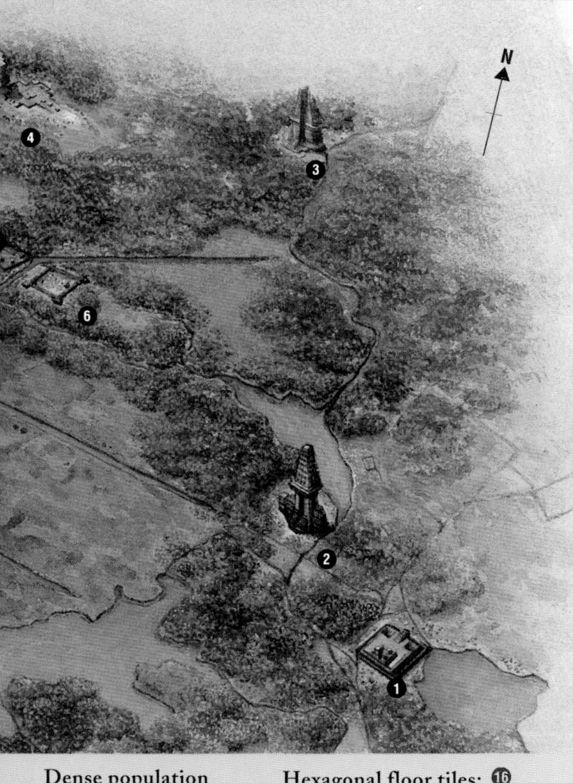

Dense population concentration: 13
Possible palace complex: 14
Stone pillar bases: 15
Hexagonal floor tiles: 16
Bronze working site: 18

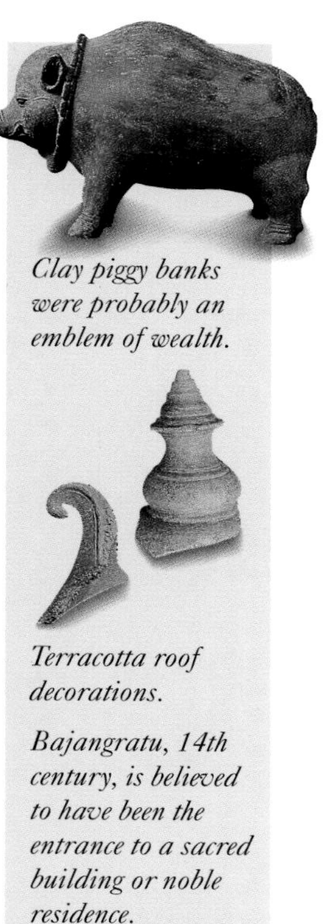

Clay piggy banks were probably an emblem of wealth.

Terracotta roof decorations.

Bajangratu, 14th century, is believed to have been the entrance to a sacred building or noble residence.

SITES OF TROWULAN

1. *Candi Tikus*
2. *Candi Bajangratu*
3. *Candi Wringin Lawang*
4. *Candi Gentong*
5. *Candi Berahu*
6. *Candi Menak Jingga*
7. *Makam Puteri Campa*
8. *Kolam Segaran*
9. *Balong Bunder*
10. *Balong*
11. *Balai Penyalamatan*
12. *Kemasan*
13. *Nglinguk*
14. *Candi Kedaton*
15. *Umpak*
16. *Sentonorejo*
17. *Tralaya*
18. *Pakis*
19. *Candi Sitinggil*

Mountain Sites of Lawu and Penanggungan

Several lines of evidence suggest that certain aspects of prehistoric Indonesian religious architecture underwent a revival in the late period of Hindu and Buddhist culture in Java. The principal characteristic of this architecture was a fascination with terraces on the high slopes of mountains. These terraces served as foundations for a variety of monuments, ranging from simple monoliths to pyramids. In modern Java these sites are termed punden berundak.

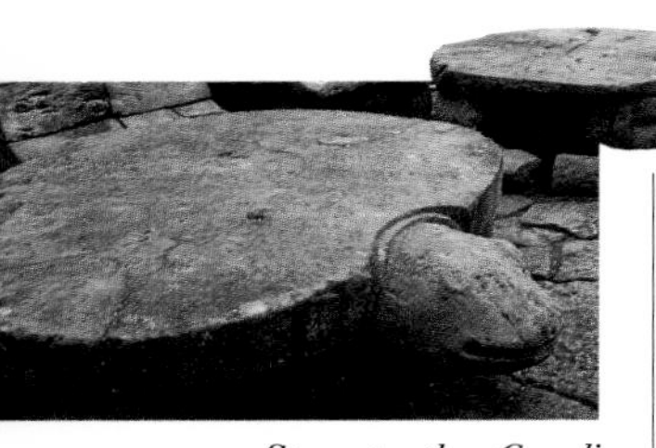

Stone turtles, Candi Sukuh. The turtle is associated with the elixir of immortality.

Penanggungan (in the middle), Gajahmungkur (left) and Bekel (right).

Mount Lawu (below), central Java.

Punden Berundak

The terrace temples of Java and Bali resemble structures called *marae* in Polynesia. It is highly probable that this similarity represents a common heritage derived from the culture of the early Austronesians. The nearest surviving analogues of the *marae* are structures found in highland west Java. Some sites such as Gunung Padang have been abandoned for centuries, but others in the south Banten area such as Arca Domas are still actively maintained by the Badui people, a remnant of the old Sundanese pre-Islamic kingdom whose capital, Pajajaran, was situated in the environs of Bogor. They resisted Islam and perpetuate a conservative culture. Their laws prohibit use of many modern innovations, including irrigation as an agricultural technique. Instead rice is grown on dry land.

Gunung Padang, Arca Domas, and other similar West Javanese sites are composed of artificial terraces on which once stood unworked monoliths. Some of these sites in west Java appear to have been constructed during the prehistoric period. However they seem to have been used intermittently for centuries, in some cases right up until the present. It is highly probable that these sites underwent occasional alterations after their inauguration, which makes it impossible to reconstruct their initial state without intensive excavation. Such excavations have yet to be conducted.

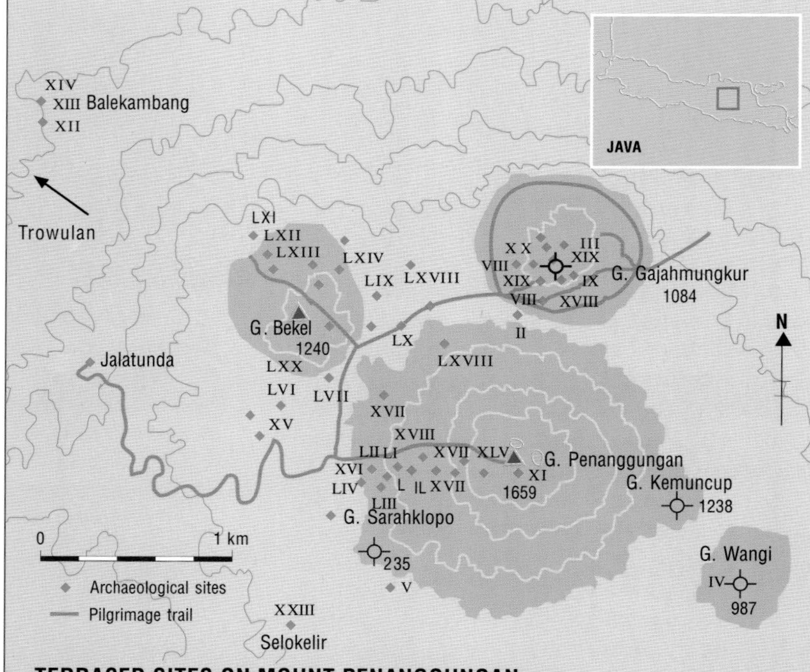

TERRACED SITES ON MOUNT PENANGGUNGAN

The main peak of Mount Penanggungan is surrounded by four subsidiary peaks with elevations approximately 600 metres beneath the main summit. Three of these (Bekel, Gajahmungkur, and Wangi) are so symmetrically distributed as to form an almost perfect replica of mythical Mount Sumeru. The ancient pilgrimage trail begins at Jalatunda bathing place on the west and climbs to the main peak, with side trails branching off to the other subordinate summits.

East Java's Terrace Temples

The largest concentration of terrace temples in Indonesia is found on Mount Penanggungan, east Java. Over 80 sites have been identified with inscriptions ranging from 977 AD to 1511. Penanggungan attains an elevation of 1,659 metres. Clearly visible looming behind it are the peaks of Mount Welirang (3,156 metres) and Mount Arjuna (3,339 metres). Its popularity may have stemmed from its form: an almost-perfect cone flanked by four lesser peaks distributed in such a uniform pattern as to suggest the mythical Mount Sumeru.

Most of the dated inscriptions found on Penanggungan fall into the period of the Majapahit kingdom, the probable capital of which was located only 25 kilometres to the west. It appears that during Majapahit's florescence the terraced temple became an

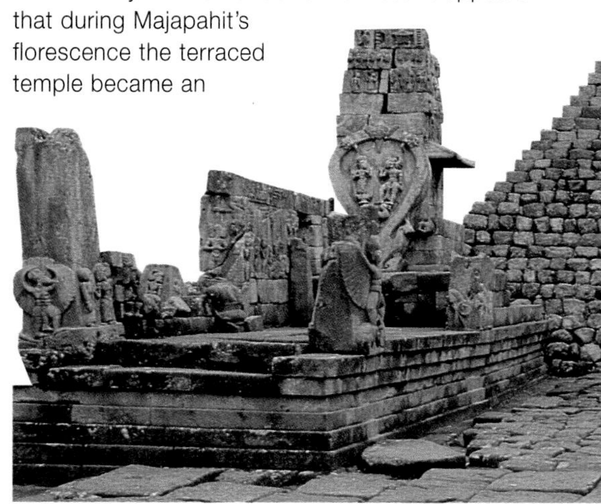

extremely important form of religious monument. Shrines built in the lowlands continued to evolve along the lines of the Indian inflected buildings consisting of brick or stone walled cellas. The mountain sites appear to have looked back to a prehistoric model. Where the Javanese of the 13th century obtained their inspiration for renewing this form we do not know. Probably some of the Singasari and Majapahit monuments made use of much older sites, but no excavations have been conducted which might confirm this.

It is likely that the ruins on Penanggungan were connected by a pilgrimage route. The oldest dated remain (977 AD) is the Jalatunda bathing place. From here pilgrims probably climbed to 1,000 metres to two monument clusters, one group on the peak of Bekel and the second on Gajahmungkur. A third cluster flanks the old route to the highest summit.

The main sites on the mountain consist of a series of terraces, usually five, a stairway on the central axis, and three altar-like constructions on the uppermost terrace. Some sites are decorated with carved reliefs illustrating narratives. In some cases the stories depicted have yet to be identified. One of the most popular compositions is easily recognisable: an illustration of a scene from the Arjunawiwaha in which Arjuna, the hero of the Mahabharata, is tempted by beautiful women. He is depicted flanked by beautiful nymphs. This image was a favourite of sculptors in east Java and is still popular in Bali.

Candi Sukuh

Other less elaborate *punden berundak* have been found on Mounts Arjuna, Welirang, and Argapura in east Java. The most famous monument of this class is found on Mount Lawu, which forms the border between the modern provinces of Central Java and East Java. The site, Candi Sukuh, consists of three terraces, together with associated remains. The largest of these is a truncated pyramid built of rectangular stone blocks on the highest terrace.

Inscriptions found on the site date from the mid-15th century. Unfortunately they give no clue as to the identity of the builders of the site. Important relics include reliefs depicting the Sudamala story; a foundation with obelisks decorated with reliefs from the Garudeya and Sudamala tales; a two metre-tall lingga surrounded by four spheres inscribed with a date corresponding to 1445 AD, which probably once stood on top of the pyramid; large statues of garudas, turtles, and guardians; and a three-panel relief depicting the deity Bima, as a *kris*-maker.

Jalatunda, with reliefs depicting the Adiparwa.

Bima seems to have been the most important deity worshipped at the mountain shrines. During the 15th century a cult devoted to Bima became popular among the Javanese, although worshippers were probably limited to the elite. Bima's role is that of a saviour who can restore life to the dead. Several similar sites lie within a few kilometres' radius of Candi Sukuh: Planggatan, Menggung, Cemara Bulus, and Ceto. In the 1970s worship at Ceto, situated at an elevation of over 1,400 metres, was revived by a group of Javanese mystics of high status. The symbolism of this site was very similar to that of Candi Sukuh, including an enormous lingga and a stone pyramid.

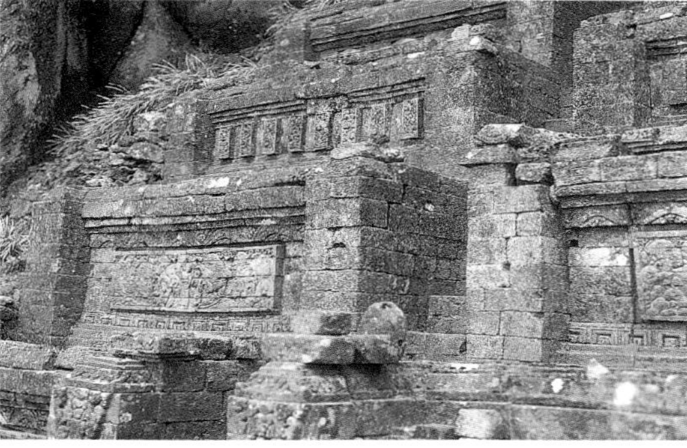

Candi Kendalisodo, a terraced site named after Hanuman's palace, decorated with reliefs depicting Arjuna and Bima.

Other Monuments

The largest group of monuments on Mount Lawu are clustered around the summit. No complete survey of the sites has been compiled, but there are approximately ten complexes. Some are of very large size, with the largest terrace being about 100 metres long and 20 metres wide, but all are constructed of unworked boulders, and no carved reliefs or statuary have been found on the sites. It is thus impossible to ascertain whether these terraces represent a final stage in the devolution of pre-Islamic Javanese mountain terraces, or a prehistoric group which survived unaltered due to their remoteness.

Candi Merak, typical terraced site from the Late Classic period on the upper slope of Mount Penanggungan.

In Bali the principal terrace temples are found at Sembiran, on the north coast, and at Besakih, still one of the most important Balinese temples. The number of structures built of perishable materials which now stand on the terraces gives some indication of what the Javanese sites may have looked like 500 years ago. Temple reliefs from East Java depict temple compounds much like Besakih.

Bima as the kris-maker, Candi Sukuh. Ironworking may have symbolised spiritual transformation.

Monuments of the Upper Brantas Valley

The upper Brantas valley was inhabited at the dawn of Indo–Javanese civilisation, and numerous archaeological sites are distributed between Malang and Kadiri. These sites can be divided into three periods, which are associated with different areas. The first building in this area, Candi Badut, dates from the 8th to 9th century. Buildings dating from the 13th century, are concentrated northeast of Malang (Candi Jago and Candi Kidal). The final phase dating from the second half of the 14th century is centred at Blitar.

Candi Tegurwangi. Relief panels depict the Sudamala legend. Sadewa is offered to a demoness, Durga, in exchange for assistance to defeat monsters. Sadewa exorcises Durga's curse and transforms her back into her true form.

View of Panataran complex. Visnu temple is seen in the right background, and the dated temple is on the left.

The Monuments

The monuments in the Brantas Valley area were used for quite long spans of time. Candi Badut, built in the 8th century, went through several stages and was remodelled for the last time in the 13th century. Candi Jago was built around 1280 and reconstructed in 1343. Some measure of unity is given to all these monuments by the predominant use of stone but there are some brick monuments.

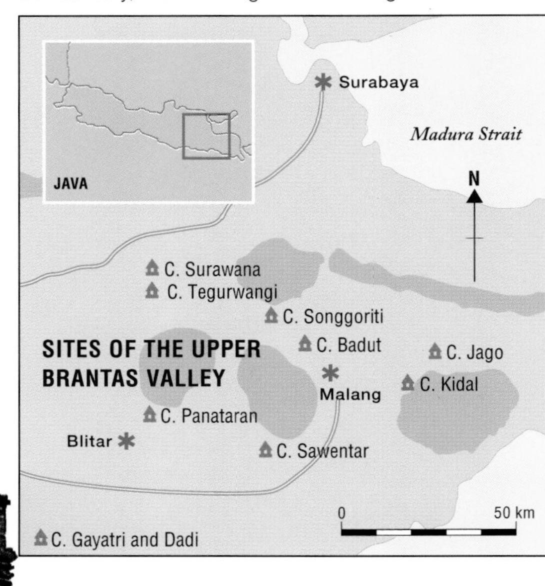

Panataran

The principal site built during the late period was the ensemble of Panataran. Numerous inscriptions from this era enable archaeologists to trace the period of construction activities to approximately 1345–1375. Work was not continuous; there were several pauses during which time a provisional enclosure would be built around the site. The temple grew incrementally, as if it were a palace, in contrast with the great monuments of the 8th and 9th centuries. Panataran and the other complexes of the 13th and 14th centuries had no predetermined plan and the growth of the monuments appears somewhat anarchic.

Work at Panataran probably began at the main terrace which supported a Visnu temple now destroyed, but the remaining base shows that the temple was depicted as a flying palace; the upper storey of the terrace is decorated with winged lions which seem to support the structure in the air. The two other storeys of the terrace are also decorated with reliefs depicting the Ramayana epic, in style and form very different than those found at Prambanan.

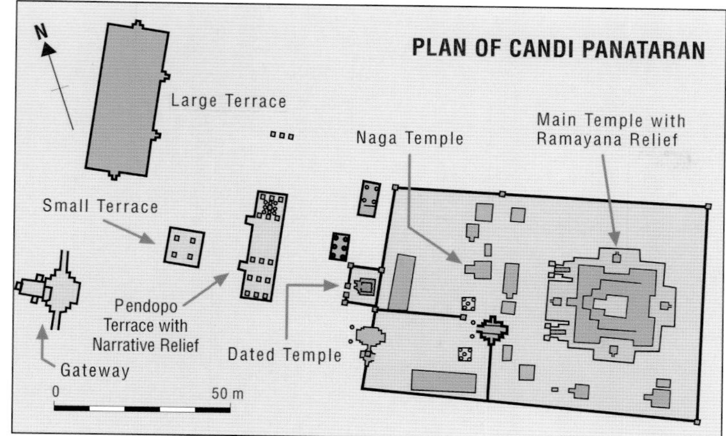

Surawana was visited by King Hayam Wuruk, the ruler of Majapahit, in 1361. This event is recorded in the Nagarakrtagama where it is related that the king stayed there overnight. The upper portion of the remains of this important shrine is decorated with scenes from the Arjunawiwaha, the Sri Tanjung story, and the tale of Bubuksa and Gagang-Aking, while the lower portion depicts scenes from Tantri fables. The stories which form the subjects for both sets of these reliefs were either completely Javanese compositions, or had only slender connections with their Indian originals. In the Arjunawiwaha, Arjuna is tempted by celestial nymphs who were sent by the god Indra. The Sri Tanjung story concerns a woman who is brought back to life after having been unjustly put to death by her husband. The legend of Bubuksha and Gagang-Aking compares two hermit brothers, to determine which of the two is more truly spiritual.

Candi Sawentar, one of the better preserved examples of the elongated east Javanese style candi.

Candi Jago, the Buddhist shrine erected during the late 13th century reign of Krtanagara.

In the second courtyard stands Candi Naga, oriented to the west; its walls decorated with human-like forms which carry the bodies of serpents, heads protruding from the corners. The roof of this structure was probably built of wood. Also in the same courtyard, on the west, rises a mass of masonry which evokes Balinese drum-towers (*bale kulkul*). Adjoining this wall, but on the other side, in the third courtyard, stands the 'dated temple', so-called because of the date 1369 carved over its doorway. The 'dated temple' belongs to the same type as Candi Kidal, but with a much simplified foot. There are many foundations which must have supported wooden structures, and the two bathing places.

«Candi Naga. The motif of the naga encircling this shrine at Panataran indicates Mt Meru, at the moment when the elixir of immortality, amrta, was churned by the gods and demons. This theme was extremely popular in east Java.

Candi Gayatri

Candi Gayatri near Tulungagung, comprises two structures, one on top of the other. They have been dated to between 1369 and 1389. Of the first temple, nothing but the foot is visible; the second is dedicated to the Buddhist goddess of wisdom, Prajnaparamita. The statue of the goddess is sheltered by a wooden pavilion with pillars held in stone bases buried among the bricks of the temple foot. Candi Dadi, also near Tulungagung, stands on a rocky promontory which dominates the whole valley. This candi is probably the base of a stupa, but its date of construction cannot be determined.

Tegurwangi and Surawana

Candi Tegurwangi, which lies in the Pare region of East Java, was built around 1370. Unfortunately, all that remains of this temple today is its high base, which was decorated with a series of interesting reliefs. Candi Surawana, in the same area, has also been reduced to its base. It is likewise decorated with reliefs illustrating a number of stories. The order of these reliefs, however, does not correspond to the sequence of the texts which they illustrate; instead the scenes are grouped according to themes. Those with demoniac associations are located on the west face, while those which depict asceticism are placed on the northeast. The iconographic symbolism appears to have been more important than the simple telling of stories.

The Religious Establishment

In 1269 King Krtanagara of Singasari published a charter which declared that the priesthood would have complete charge over the religious domain, without interference from either royalty or laymen. The relative modesty of the temples built after this time is probably a result of this charter. The clergy gained independence, but lost a great deal economically.

The clergy at this time recopied ancient inscriptions which recorded tax exemptions. By so doing they ensured, after a fashion, the survival of the religious establishments (temples, monasteries, and hermitages). As a result, the corpus of religious architecture built at the end of the 14th century is almost completely composed of works which are oriented toward the viewpoint of the spectator: the proportions, the false perspectives of these structures are all artifice, attempting to suggest that the structures are larger than they really are. This attempt did not continue; more diverse symbolism and rituals appeared, due to the independence of the clergy who now followed Krtanagara's charter, which gave them liberty to express their diverse religious sentiments and pursue visions of the creation of the world.

CANDI JAGO

The temple which was consecrated around 1280, is a complex structure designed to accommodate esoteric Buddhist rituals. Its foot is adorned with several series of narrative reliefs, marking the reappearance of this practice after a lapse of 400 years. The reliefs combine Buddhist, Hindu, and indigenous Javanese tales.

Sculpture and Reliefs of Majapahit

The sculpture of the Majapahit period displays a characteristically Javanese style. Characteristics of this style can be detected in both three–dimensional and semi–three–dimensional forms of sculpture. The three–dimensional form comprises sculpture in the round and depicts both divine and terrestial figures, whereas the semi–three–dimensional form is represented by reliefs on temple walls.

Panataran roundels with animals and birds.

Unidentified figure, east Java.

Portrait Sculpture

Among the Majapahit statues in the collection of the National Museum of Jakarta is an image which may be a posthumous figure of the first Majapahit king, found in Simping, Sumberjati, east Java. It depicts him as Harihara (Siva and Visnu in one body). A statue of Parvati from Rimbi is stylistically its female counterpart and is believed to be a commemorative statue of a Majapahit queen. Another famous statue is a female figure possibly portraying Suhita, one of the reigning queens of Majapahit, found at Jebuk, Tulungagung, east Java. Found in the same place is a statue of a couple seated side by side.

All these statues show a crystallised late Javanese model of anthropomorphic depiction. Bodies have a tubular form; the limbs are not detached from the torsos. Junctures between parts are smoothed, not emphasised. This tendency might have stemmed from a prehistoric idea that human images should be columnar, thereby emanating qualities of uprightness and strength. However, this style is quite distinct from Indian models of divinities. Indian models show voluptuous bodies with joints clearly indicated. Lotuses growing from vases, flanking a human image, are a typical Majapahit motif. Although firm evidence is lacking, it is believed that they represent rebirth or regeneration, hence their use on mortuary statues. Those who could be installed as deities were limited to kings and queens, their children, or warriors with proper credentials. For example King Krtarajasa was deified for his exemplary qualities: steadfastness, love of truth, good character, sharp mind, friendliness to people, valour in war, and wealth, particularly in gold, characteristics that identified him as a deity in human form.

The Nagarakrtagama of 1365 describes the ceremonies which attended the installation of such statues in their shrines; in this particular ritual a former queen of Majapahit was commemorated. 'The honoured, Illustrious Rajapatni is placed in a religious domain in Bhayalangu. The honoured holy Jnanawidhi was sent once more to perform worship, the ground purification ceremony and the pratastha establishing ceremony. It is called *Wishesa–pura* [Paramountcy Compound] because its construction was especially supervised by a great court official, Bhoja, young, diligent, and clever, who was ordered to take great care in it'. The pratistha was the image into which the spirit of the deceased king or queen could descend in order to be contacted by later generations and besought to give protection and assistance.

Bima Statues

Statues of the god Bima are found at various sacred edifices, especially in eastern Java, indicating that he was worshipped by many Javanese in the later pre–Islamic period. The Bima cult emerged in about the early 15th century, during the declining phase of Majapahit. The main feature of the cult seems to have been a concern with immortality, a kind of salvation.

Bima statues generally show such common features as a moustache, bulging eyes, stout body, long fingernails (*panacanaka*), wearing a particular 'crab's claw' form of curving headdress called *supit urang* in Javanese, wielding a club, and exposing part of the phallus.

Relief Sculpture

Figural sculptures of terrestial beings, as well as figures in Majapahit era narrative reliefs, show another set of characteristics which later developed into the standard style of Javanese figurative art. Terrestial figures in the round, and relief figures, show

Images of the Late Classic period (from left to right): terracotta fish, in the form of a stand for offering tray, probably symbolising the sea creature from the Sri Tanjung tale; white stone statue of unidentified deity and massive andesite statue of Garuda, from Menak Jingga, Trowulan; and the head of Bima with the characteristic "crab–claw" hairdo.

a strong tendency toward angularity, giving an impression of slenderness, litheness, and fragility. Almost without exception the shoulder line is strikingly horizontal, so that both arms seem to be suspended from a line. The same trait is found in the puppets used in Javanese shadow theatre.

Majapahit era temples with narrative reliefs include Panataran, Surawana, Tegurwangi, Jawi, and Kedaton. The Ramayana reliefs of Panataran give the most puppet-like impression, rendered in such low relief that they seem to have been worked out as relief *en creux*. Most faces had to be drawn in profile, like the leather puppets. Scenes are dominated by figures of monkeys and giants relating the story of Hanuman, the monkey hero, who went to Alengka, kingdom of Ravana, and the giants as Rama's envoy. Another special trait of the Panataran scenes is the density of decoration within the panels. Trees, plants and clouds fill all spaces around the actors. Besides the Ramayana reliefs at Panataran there is another set of reliefs on the foot of a stone terrace which once supported a wooden *pendopo*. They are reliefs of the Panji tales, though the precise storyline of this variant of the epic cannot be positively identified.

Majapahit reliefs do contain some hints that dramatic puppet performances indeed affected relief composition. Some of the scenes that appear in the reliefs are demarcated by depictions of trees, comparable to the wayang convention of using a puppet representing a (cosmic) tree to denote a change of scene. Another indirect reference to wayang performances is the organisation of Bhoma-kavya scenes on Candi Kedaton. The caste cord worn by figures runs through the right shoulder when the figure faces left, but when the same figure faces right the caste cord passes through the left shoulder, following the logic of a leather puppet in the puppeteer's hands. The existence of wayang performances themselves is indicated by inscriptions and literature from the 10th century.

The most frequently depicted story on temples is the Arjunawiwaha, in which Arjuna, the Mahabharata hero, performed penance, earned Siva's favour, received a supernatural weapon with which he vanquished the gods' demon adversary, and was rewarded with a marriage to heavenly nymphs. The *kakawin* narrating this story was written for king Airlangga in the 11th century. The popularity of this story is proven by its frequent relief depictions at Jago, Surawana, Kedaton, and artificial caves in Kadiri and Tulungagung both named Selamangleng. The most common depiction shows Arjuna doing penance while nymphs unsuccessfully try to seduce him. The Arjunawiwaha retains its popularity in both literary and dramatic forms among the modern Javanese and Balinese.

Relief sculpture of Majapahit also gives ample images of the environment. Very important visual data include depictions of different house types for various social classes. The reliefs function as a check on inscriptions which contain stipulations regarding the right to use certain architectural forms. Allied to Majapahit sculptures were also the abundant examples of terracotta figurines and toys found in and around Trowulan, hypothetical capital of the empire of Majapahit.

TERRACOTTA FIGURINES

The art of making terracotta figurines appears to have developed quite suddenly in the kingdom of Majapahit during the 14th century. Although no precedent is known in Indonesia, the Javanese craftsman displayed great skill and a wide range of emotions in their creations. These small items were produced in large quantities, sometimes even stamped out in moulds. They represent many subjects: gods, humans, animals, buildings, scenes. We do not know what they were used for; perhaps they had several functions. Many are humorous. Some represent mothers and children. Their heads are often missing; it has been suggested that these were perhaps made in order to be 'sacrificed' by breaking off the heads, thereby appeasing evil spirits who might otherwise disturb human mothers.

A common type depicts females with a characteristic hairstyle: piled in a heap on one side of the head. Many forms of buildings are depicted, ranging from simple dwellings to elaborate pavilions. The depictions of what appear to have been common dwellings and heads of average (non-royal) people provide one of our most poignant glimpses into the sights which must have been the norm in everyday life in ancient Indonesia. One potential subject which is seldom portrayed is religious imagery; very few terracottas of gods are known. Heads of people with un-Javanese characteristics, perhaps depicting foreign merchants, are rather common. Some examples of these terracottas have been found at religious sites on Mount Penanggungan. Many of these examples seem to represent miniature temples; others, such as a horse's head found in an artificial meditation cave, are difficult to connect with any known religious symbolism.

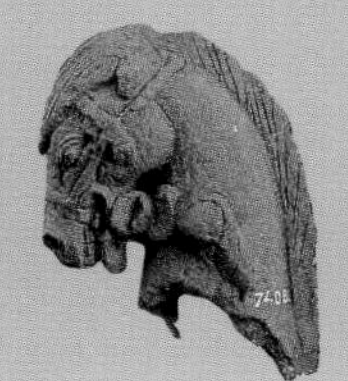

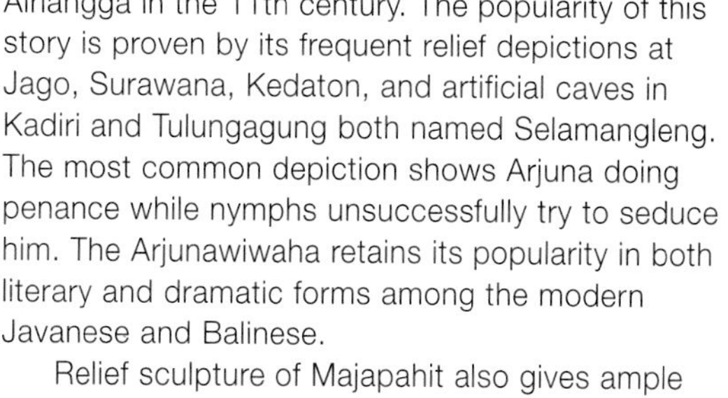

Bronze image possibly portraying Krishna, one of the few anthropomorphic bronzes of the Majapahit period.

Ramayana relief from Candi Tegurwangi, showing the use of puppet-like figures, with different scenes demarcated by building forms in the manner of the gunungan or kakayon in the shadow play.

Bali in the Late Classic Period

Bali's economy at the end of the Classic period had apparently not changed greatly since the beginning of the historic era. Agriculture was still the most important sector. In politics, religion, and coinage, Bali seems to have been under very intense Javanese influence. Legends refer to Javanese invasions, and later Javanese migration. The gradual disappearance of statuary from Balinese temples also parallels the evolution of religious practices in late Classic Java.

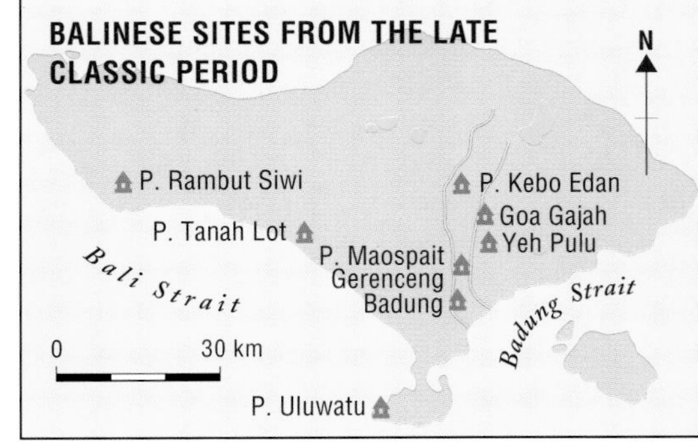

The paduraksa gateway, Ulu Watu. This gate has portions which may date from the Late Classic, including the kala head above the entrance and the two Ganesha-like elephant figures placed in the position normally reserved for door guardians (dwarapala).

The Economy

Inscriptions from the 11th century reign of Anak Wungsu contained explicit references to *kasuwakan* or traditional irrigation organisations, probably the modern Balinese *subak*. Inscriptions contain precise and detailed regulations regarding water taxes and construction of irrigation channels, as well as taxes on agriculture and animal husbandry. Other regulations concern the felling of protected trees and hunting.

The coinage system used in Bali was very similar to that of Java. The names for coins include *masaka* (or *masa*), *atak*, *kupang*, and *piling* (or *saga*). In the 14th century, copper coinage was used to pay taxes, as in Java. In Bali, this coinage was called *mahaji gung hartha* (great royal currency). Classic inscriptions also mention inter-village trade. The Dawan inscription of 1053 states that King Anak Wungsu bought 30 buffalo in Gurun which he donated to the inhabitants of Lutungan village. The Selumbung inscription dated 1328 states that the inhabitants of Selumbung were allowed to visit markets outside their village if they so desired.

Written Evidence

The Nagarakrtagama of 1365 says that King Krtanagara attacked Bali in 1284, and that the Majapahit army under the leadership of Chief Minister Gajah Mada attacked Bali again in 1343. The same source mentions two famous places in Bali: Badahulu and Lwa Gajah. Badahulu is reminiscent of the modern village of Bedulu, and Lwa Gajah is perhaps the same as Goa Gajah, in that village. Canto 79, stanza 3 of the Nagarakrtagama says that Bali followed the same traditions as Java. Local Balinese historical sources called *babad* or *pamancangah* say that a number of *arya* (great souls) came to Bali after the Majapahit conquest. The *arya* were led by Sri Arya Kepakisan, who became king of Bali and built his palace at Samprangan (Gianyar). Arya Kepakisan was accompanied by Arya Kenceng, Arya Dalancang, Arya Belog, Arya Kanuruhan, Arya Wangbang, Arya Kuta Waringin and three non-*arya* followers (Tan Kobar, Tan Kawur and Tan Mundur).

The last classical inscription which refers to Bali is dated 1384 and mentions King Kudamerta of Wengker. In the Pararaton he is styled Raden Kudamerta; the Nagarakrtagama calls him Wijayarajasa, the husband of Bhre Daha. At one time he had been the king of Matahun and Wengker, territories in east Java. He was the uncle and also father-in-law of Majapahit's illustrious king Hayam Wuruk (Rajasanagara). He may have played some role in Gajah Mada's 1343 expedition to Bali which could have resulted in him being called king or ruler in Bali, but this is unclear. Majapahit's decline in the 15th century is said to have caused some brahmans and others to flee to Bali. Danghyang Nirartha (or Danghyang Dwijendra or Pedanda Sakti Wawu Rauh) is one legendary character who came to Bali, taught religion, and erected several pura. Danghyang Nirartha is supposed to have come to Bali around 1550 during the reign of King Waturenggong of Gelgel. Local sources connect Nirartha with the construction of some of Bali's largest *pura*, including Uluwatu, Pura Peti Tenget (Badung), Pura Tanah Lot (Tabanan), and Pura Rambut Siwi (Jembrana). The legend of the arrival of the Majapahit people in Bali, mainly from the royal and religious classes, may be true. It is supported by the appearance of literary works and manuscripts written in Middle Javanese of the 15th and 16th centuries. *Palinggih Maospait* or sacred edifices used to worship Bhatara Maospait can be found in some family shrines and more important temples. One of the important temples in Denpasar,

»Kebo Edan. This statue may represent either a Bhairawa or Bima. The phallic character of this statue however is more consistent with an identification of the image as Bima. The hole in the penis was probably meant to enable a pin or peg to be inserted.

modern capital of Bali, is named Pura Maospait. It is possible that parts of the temple were constructed in the 14th century, but the name may be merely a reference to the presumed Javanese ancestry of some of the people who patronised the shrine. It should be remembered that Bali and Java had close contacts before Majapahit was founded.

Religious Developments

The thousands of *pura* or sacred edifices in Bali can be divided into two types: Pura Kahyangan, where God or Hyang Widhi Wasa is worshipped in all his manifestations, and Pura Pedharman where worship is dedicated to ancestors or people who are believed to have become gods or Bhatara and Bhatari. During the Majapahit period a new belief system spread through both Java and Bali. This belief was associated with the Siva-Siddhanta sect of Hinduism, which preached that statues were not necessary for enlightenment; the gods could manifest themselves in any form they chose, and individuals who were well along the path to enlightenment did not need physical depictions of deities. Thus statues were no longer carved. In modern Balinese temples, there are no statues of gods. Instead the main objects of worship are structures forming raised stone seats, where the gods can be invoked to manifest themselves invisibly during worship. Fortunately, old statues were not destroyed, but kept in storage, so that they may still be investigated for clues regarding early Balinese cultural and artistic evolution.

It is difficult to reconstruct the form of any Late Classic sites in Bali because they remained in continuous use and have been frequently remodelled.

Pura Uluwatu.
❶ *Mount Meru roof*
❷ *Paduraksa gateway*
❸ *Candi bentar*
This southernmost shrine may date from the 14th century. Its location on a high cliff overlooking the Indian Ocean belies the fact that for the Balinese the sea was a dangerous place to be avoided. Parts of the original shrine may have disappeared as a result of landslides. The temple is one of the sad kahyangan, *the group of Bali's most important temples.*

Goa Gajah is mentioned in the Nagarakrtagama, but dates from an earlier time. A massive stone statue popularly called Kebo Edan, 'Crazy Buffalo', bears attributes which link it either to Tantric worship of Bhairawa or to Bima, one of the five Pandawa brothers of the Mahabharata. Bima became popular in Java in the 15th century, and many images of him resemble Kebo Edan in that the sarong is carved so as to expose his phallus. It is also possible that this image merely portrays a generalised demonic figure.

YEH PULU RELIEFS

This is the only set of narrative reliefs known in Bali. The reliefs probably depict episodes from the life of Krishna, one of Visnu's incarnations. The entire relief is 25 metres long, with a hunter's cave at the end. The complex is associated with a simple hermitage. Possibly these reliefs were carved originally as an act of piety by an earlier hermit or group of ascetics. The location of the site is quite secluded.

❶ At far left is Krishna in the pose symbolising the lifting of Mount Govardana to shelter his playmates from a deluge sent by Indra to destroy them. The rest of the scene is difficult to interpret. It includes a man carrying a shoulder pole, a woman of high status, a half-opened doorway in which a woman stands, a hermit presenting a seated woman in a cave, another standing woman, and a seated dwarapala.
❷ In the forest, a man rides a horse. To his right is a scene of two men fighting a bear. One of the stories of Krishna concerns a fight with a bear and concludes with Krishna's capture of the bear's daughter. Above and to the right a man offers a jar to a woman.
❸ Two men carry a shoulder pole from which are hung two bears. This is followed by another scene of a man on horseback. Behind the horse is a standing figure this may represent the bear's daughter, whom Krishna eventually wed. The narrative concludes with an image of Siva's elephant-headed son, Ganesha in a niche.

Tombstone from the burial complex of Sunan Gunung Jati, Cirebon. Decorative motifs include stylised elephant–like makaras and Mount Meru.

Entrance to the 17th century Panjunan Mosque in Cirebon. The split gateway at the entrance emulates a pre–Islamic style.

Gateway to Sendang Duwur, an early Islamic tomb on Java's northeast coast with distinctive artistic motifs.

This semi-submerged early Muslim graveyard indicates that some Acehnese sites have been submerged by coastal change. Several ancient kingdoms are known to have been located along the Acehnese coast, but few remains of them have been located.

EARLY ISLAMIC PERIOD: 1300–1600

Islam was established in northernmost Sumatra in the late 13th century. From Pasai, north Sumatra, Islam spread to other ports in Indonesia, the Malay Peninsula, and the south Philippines. By the late 14th century Islam had made converts as far east as Trowulan in east Java. The conversion of the Melaka rulers in the early 15th century had a significant effect in popularising Islam in many ports along the trade route leading to the sources of spices in distant Maluku. When the Portuguese arrived in 1509, Islam was still mainly a minority religion, confined to the mercantile population of a few enclaves in trading ports. Islam's main expansion occurred during the 16th century, when the religion of the Prophet Muhammad gradually became popular among the agrarian villagers of the hinterlands of Java, Sumatra, and other islands. The process of conversion was not a single event with a single cause, but a series of occurrences effected by local factors.

In some examples the ruler's decision to convert was immediately followed as a matter of course by all his subjects; in others an appreciable proportion of the population seems to have converted first, followed by their ruler in what may have been a politically motivated act. Different agents were involved in different parts of Indonesia: sometimes itinerant merchant-missionaries of foreign or mixed parentage, in others conquering warriors, in still others charismatic teachers.

Different schools of Islam were popular in different areas. The Shi'a sect made converts in several areas, and traces of the mystical sect known as the Dervishes can still be seen in some parts of Indonesia. In general, the forms of Islam which received the readiest acceptance espoused a Sufi philosophy. Sufi-influenced believers can be divided into two groups: 'mystical orthodoxy' and less orthodox variants. Islam introduced new terms into Indonesian languages, and new symbols into architecture and art. However, the spread of Islam was accompanied by the same process of Indonesianisation as was the adoption of South Asian traits 1,000 years earlier.

The spread of Islam was often correlated with an increase in commercial activity. Islam contains many stipulations connected with trade. The integration of Islam into everyday life is an ongoing process in Indonesia today. As the world's most populous Islamic nation, the study of Indonesia's historical path to Islam and its evolution there deserves much more attention than it has received from scholars.

Early Mosques and Tombs

When Islamic cultural elements arrived, took root, and spread in Indonesia, they created a culture which took its ideology from the Qur'an and Hadiths, but in physical forms demonstrated continuity with pre-Islamic traits. The major ideological change involved the relative status of humans and God. The most enduring continuity concerned the elitist nature of Indonesian society, wherein the palace remained the central point of cultural reference, and the nobility remained the principal source of supply and demand for high art.

» Mosque at Bandung, from a hand-coloured lithograph from Kinloch's 'Rambles in Java and the Straits', 1852.

Carving on the tomb of Sunan Giri, one of the nine saints.

Royal Patronage

In addition to functioning as a centre of socio-political and economic power, the palace also provided an umbrella under which flourished other fields of scholarship: philosophy, education, and science. Islamic architecture provided forms which glorified the palaces of the sultans, and offered new shapes for public and religious structures, gardens and tombs. Calligraphy evolved in many styles, adapted to various media including stone, glass, leather, bamboo, palm leaves, textiles and wood.

Indonesian artists abstracted numerous Islamic concepts from their Arabian matrix, and adapted them to the local Indonesian contexts. These adaptations were apparent from Aceh to the Maluku Islands. In calligraphy for example, Indonesians created disguised anthropomorphic and zoomorphic forms, thus avoiding violation of the Islamic prohibition against depicting living things.

Mosques

Another adaptation was visible in the construction of Indonesian mosques with square plans, tiered roofs, and no minarets. The oldest surviving mosques, such as those at Demak, Sendang Duwur, Cirebon, and Banten, have such elements, as well as others including a pool around the *serambi,* or pavilion attached to the entrance where worshippers often gather before and after prayer for social motives. Another Indonesian custom affects the *mihrab* or marker on the wall indicating the direction of Mecca; the *mihrab* becomes a cave-like place large enough for one to sit inside and meditate, like the ascetic hermits of pre-Islamic times, and the *mihrab* is sometimes framed with a design recalling the *kala-makara* ornaments of earlier niches and doors of temples. The mosques and tombs are often enclosed within walls with one or more gateways in candi bentar or paduraksa form, again like temples.

Entrance to the grave of Sunan Bonang, one of the Wali Songo, at Tuban. Beyond the gateway is a wall or screen similar to those found in Balinese compounds.

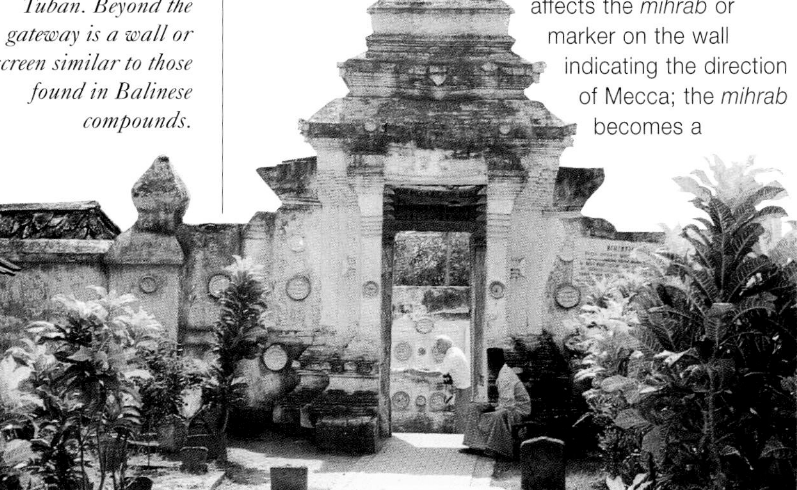

The mosque at Kudus is interesting because it incorporates a tall brick structure probably designed as a pre-Islamic temple, but adapted to use as a tower where the drum is beaten to announce that the call to prayer is about to begin. The tower is set with porcelain plates probably in imitation of classical Islamic tile decorations.

The use of decorative tiles on the exterior of both Indonesian mosques and tomb complexes may have been borrowed from a similar practice used for Islamic structures in the Near East, and in South and Central Asia. However, there is also some evidence that the use of such tiles was already known in pre-Islamic Indonesia. Blue and white Vietnamese tiles of various shapes, which date from the 15th century, adorn the exterior wall of the mosque at Demak which faces the *serambi*.

According to the *Babad Tanah Jawi*, the mosque at Demak was built by craftsmen from Majapahit who moved there after the Hindu kingdom succumbed to the Muslim forces of the Demak port kingdom. The Babad Tanah Jawi is a traditional chronicle which cannot always be taken literally, but archaeologists have discovered fragments of similar tiles at the site of Majapahit's capital at Trowulan. It is not known whether they were used to decorate sacred or secular structures there, but it is possible that they adorned the dwellings of nobles in a manner similar to the use of Dutch tiles in later Indonesian palaces. Porcelain plates have also been used to decorate the walls of some Balinese shrines.

The mosques of Demak, Cirebon, Banten and various other early Indonesian mosques incorporates four main pillars known as *soko guru*. These huge pillars are necessary to support the multi-tiered roofs of some Balinese shrines. These roofs are termed *meru* after the symbolic mountain at the centre of the universe and home to the gods in Hindu and Buddhist mythology.

Tombs

The oldest Muslim tombstone in Indonesia that we know of is dated AH 475 (1082 AD). It was found at Leran, west of Surabaya, east Java. The person buried there is a woman named Fatimah binti Maimun bin Habatallah; nothing more is known of her. She may not have been of Indonesian origin. In Aceh, Sumatra, the oldest known tombstone belonged to Malik al-Salih, a sultan who died in 1326.

By 1368 Islamic tombstones were being carved at the capital of Majapahit. The graveyard at Tralaya there contains unique examples with Islamic verses in Arabic script on one face and the Majapahit sunburst and other motifs with dates in Javanese numerals and Javanese year reckoning on the other.

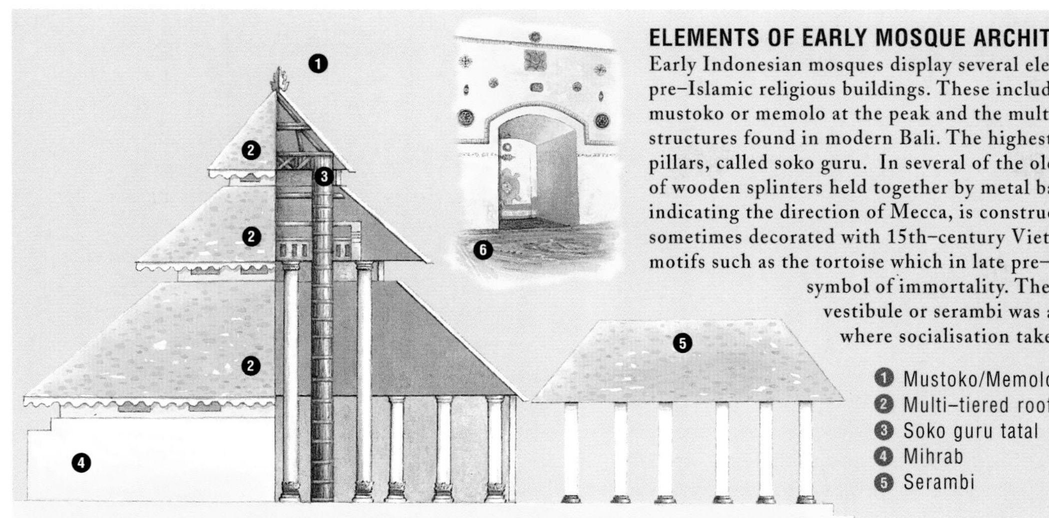

ELEMENTS OF EARLY MOSQUE ARCHITECTURE

Early Indonesian mosques display several elements suggestive of continuity with pre-Islamic religious buildings. These include the clay decoration called mustoko or memolo at the peak and the multi-tiered roof, identical to temple structures found in modern Bali. The highest roof tier is supported by four main pillars, called soko guru. In several of the oldest mosques, one of these is made of wooden splinters held together by metal bands. The mihrab, or wall niche indicating the direction of Mecca, is constructed as a deep cave-like place, sometimes decorated with 15th-century Vietnamese tiles (at Demak) and other motifs such as the tortoise which in late pre-Islamic Java was an important symbol of immortality. The mihrab may be a later addition. The vestibule or serambi was an important Indonesian addition, where socialisation takes place before and after prayers.

1. Mustoko/Memolo
2. Multi-tiered roof
3. Soko guru tatal
4. Mihrab
5. Serambi
6. Detail of mihrab from the great mosque of Demak. The mosque has been frequently renovated; the form of the original mihrab is unknown.

Graves were given architectural form and decorated with motifs formerly associated with temples. The tombs of the sultans and early Muslim proselytisers were given special treatment and became pilgrimage sites where people believed they could make requests of the dead for assistance in their own worldly affairs. These tombs have been frequently rebuilt by devotees, so that their original elements are sometimes impossible to reconstruct.

Some scholars have argued that the existence of a mystical form of Islam facilitated the penetration of this new religion into the formerly Hindu-Buddhist cultures of the archipelago. The practice of meditation at graves would have seemed to be a continuation of pre-Islamic practices of worshipping at temples containing statues of deceased royalty who become commemorated as Hindu-Buddhist deities.

Other scholars, however, now believe that pilgrimages to tombs did not derive from an older system of belief, but instead marked a new practice which had only indirect links to previous customs. Sufi and Shi'ite groups in other countries, including India, Pakistan, Iran, Iraq, and even Saudi Arabia, conduct similar pilgrimages. In pre-Islamic Indonesia there were no graves for descendants to venerate. Burial was not commonly practised, and the dead were mainly disposed of by cremation, and their ashes thrown into the sea or into the river. Furthermore, the idea that individual personalities persist after death certainly does not seem to have been common in pre-Islamic Indonesian thought; instead the doctrine of the soul's reunion with a greater consciousness after death seems to have been the standard form of belief.

Pilgrimage to Grave Sites

Some of the most important pilgrimage sites for Javanese Muslims are the tombs of the *Wali Songo*. These are the 'Nine Saints' who are widely credited with having introduced Islam to the island of Java. The number nine is numerologically significant for the Javanese, but there are local differences of opinion regarding the precise composition of the group of nine. Of those *wali* whom we are able to trace through historical sources, most lived in the 16th century. Their origins are obscure; legends give varying accounts of their ancestry. The same individual in different legends may be described as of Arabian, Indian, Indonesian, or even Chinese descent, or some combination of the above.

Of these sites associated with the Nine Saints, one of the most important is the tomb of Sunan Gunung Jati, just outside Cirebon, west Java. Other much-visited tomb complexes of the Saints include Sunan Kudus, Ratu Kalinyamat at Mantingan, near Jepara, Sunan Muria on Mount Muria, Sunan Bonang at Tuban, and Sunan Giri at Gresik, near Surabaya. The tomb complexes are often noted for their elaborately carved decorations of stone or wood; the wood carvings in particular are of great interest, since they may represent the oldest preserved examples of this art form in Indonesia. No detailed study of them has yet been compiled. Many Indonesians still make pilgrimages to these tombs in order to meditate, especially on important dates in the Muslim calendar.

The most important historical aspect of the belief in the *Wali Songo* is not the precise identities of the Nine Saints. Rather the important information to be extracted from these accounts is that the conversion to Islam was associated with the figures of itinerant preacher-teachers who sometimes supported themselves by trading. The stories of the lives of these saintly men (and significantly, women) indicate that the coasts of Java, Sumatra, Kalimantan, and the Malay Peninsula were linked by the existence of a cosmopolitan urban society, in which commerce, education, literature, and religion were important and related fields.

Decorative plaque from the Mantingan mosque, associated with the tomb of Ratu Kalinyamat, female saint.

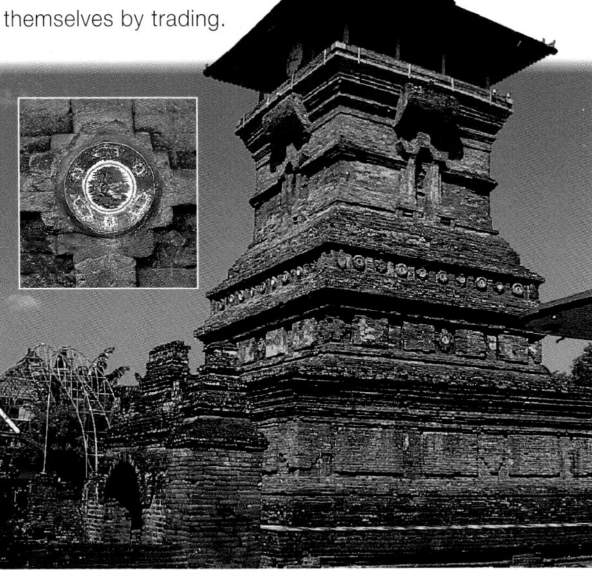

Menara Kudus, *a mosque's drum tower possibly converted from a pre-Islamic brick candi. (Inset) Blue and white ceramic decoration on the wall of the drum tower at Kudus.*

Palaces and Gardens

Palaces and gardens are numerous in Indonesia. Each potentate, great or small, built an architectural ensemble as a symbol of his glory and power. The rulers also desired to link themselves to the past, to show that the present dynasty descended from ancient kings, if not from ancient gods, and so they attempted to construct palaces in the image of those of the preceding dynasties. Subsequently several scholars have compared the description of the palace of Majapahit in the Nagarakrtagama, of the 14th century, with the 19th century palace of Yogyakarta.

»» Camouflaged garuda from Sunyaragi garden.

Remains

There are very few traces left of old Indonesian palaces. This is due to two factors: first to the impermanence of the materials used and also to the princes' habit of shifting their capitals. The only remains of the residence of Sultan Agung (1613–1645), at Kerta, near Yogyakarta, are a few pillar bases from the centrepiece. This was once a huge *pendopo* or pavilion covering nearly 1,000 square metres. A royal chronicle relates how fire destroyed the whole complex and that rather than rebuild on the same site, it was decided that it should be reconstructed nearby. This new capital was completed by Sultan Agung's son, Amangkurat I (1646–77), at Plered. The building of this new establishment was accompanied by irrigation works including a dam which destroyed part of the city when it gave way in 1660. In 1677 the capital was shifted again. The new capital, Kartasura, completed in 1680, lies in the valley of the Solo River. Large ruins exist but their overall pattern is not easy to reconstruct.

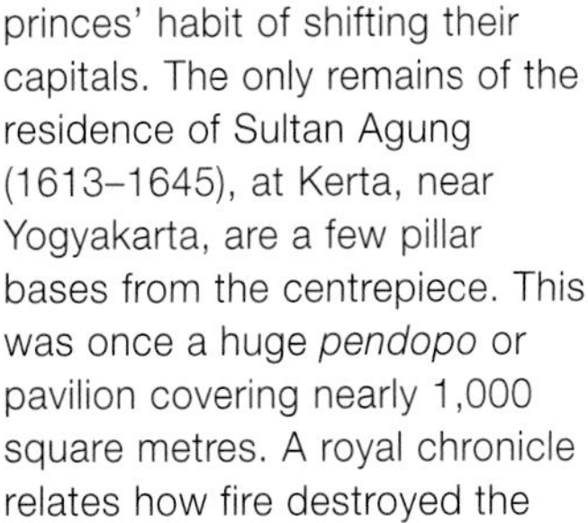

19th century painting of the Pulau Kenanga pavilion, Taman Sari garden, Yogyakarta.

Yogyakarta

Kartasura was abandoned a few years before 1755, when the realm was divided into two kingdoms and in its place two neighbouring capitals were created, Surakarta and Yogyakarta. Each of these newly created kingdoms built its own palaces. In Yogyakarta, Sultan Mangkubumi, who was a great builder, undertook a very ambitious palace construction project. This residence consists of a series of courtyards and pavilions, sometimes linked by covered galleries. The most charming aspect of the palace complex is a very beautiful garden, Taman Sari, or Fragrant Garden which was begun in 1759. It is sometimes referred to as the 'Water Palace'. Much of it was destroyed by the British attack of 1812, but was later rebuilt with many modifications. It occupies three levels and contains numerous pools with fountains and about 50 pavilions. The garden was intended for pleasure but also for meditation; for this end, a mosque was built on Kenanga Island in the pool, which was only accessible by two underwater tunnels.

Taman Sari water palace, Yogyakarta.

Under Sultan Mangkubumi's influence many other palaces were built around Yogyakarta, all sharing the same inspiration, combining architecture with water. One of the largest, at Banguntapan, east of Yogyakarta, covered 50 hectares and contained fountains shaped like Garuda, and secret baths in artificial caves, behind screens of sculpted stucco.

Cirebon

The oldest existing palace complex in Indonesia at Cirebon, west Java, was built on the site of the earlier Hindu Pakungwati Keraton. A gateway at the Keraton Kasepuhan (Elder Palace) is dated by a chronogram to 1445. The palace is enclosed by a brick wall. The eastern part of the wall may be part of the original complex. It is built without mortar, adhesion between bricks having been achieved by rubbing the bricks together until they fit exactly. This system was used in pre-Islamic Majapahit, and is still used today in Bali. In the front of the palace which borders a public square is a raised area with several pavilions each with a resounding historical name. These pavilions are constructed with varying numbers of pillars, which according to different

interpretations may symbolise either Islamic or pre-Islamic concepts. The pavilion with five pillars for example is called Pendawa Lima, the five brothers of the Mahabharata, but which can also stand for the five daily prayers. The palace has two gardens, one part of the main complex, the other several kilometres away, probably outside the border of the early city of Cirebon.

A large garden (built between 1720 and 1741) at Sunyaragi, in the suburbs of Cirebon is built on two levels. On the upper, a very large pool with an artificial island in the middle acts as a reservoir feeding the fountains of the garden which spouted amid stucco mountains of Chinese inspiration. Major elements include caves, and animals such as an elephant and garuda camouflaged in the rockwork.

The Kanoman Palace, also at Cirebon, was begun in the 17th century, but the extant structures date from the same period as the Kasepuhan and Yogyakarta palaces. The throne room is decorated with an imitation mountain. At Surakarta, one of the rooms at the Kasusuhunan Palace with the same type of decoration (in the Bale Retna) is called the Paradise of Indra.

The Balinese Palace

In Bali, the architects generally kept closer to the instructions in the architectural texts than did their Javanese counter–parts. The ground upon which the palace of Ubud stands is divided into nine equal parts. The central area contained a space reserved for the king. The palace chapel was located at the northwest corner of the entire complex.

This was not the only possible pattern: at Karangasem, the court is divided into two parts by two concentric walls of rectangular shape built on different levels. The central part, where the king lived, is higher than the space between the two walls, where the palace staff lived. In the inner space a pool was dug, in the midst of which a pavilion was constructed, called the Balai Kambang.

Indonesian palaces, despite local variations, had a certain conceptual unity. Although palace ceremonies are now rarely practised, palace designs still preserve an image of the kingdom similar to that which the architect of Prambanan wished to create.

«Amlapura Palace, Karangasem. The Balai Kambang or 'Floating Pavilion' was a common component of palaces throughout western Indonesia.

Kanoman, the entrance to the Sitinggil, or 'High Place' where the rulers sat on a raised pavilion. The gateway takes the form of a split gate or candi bentar inset with Chinese and European ceramics.

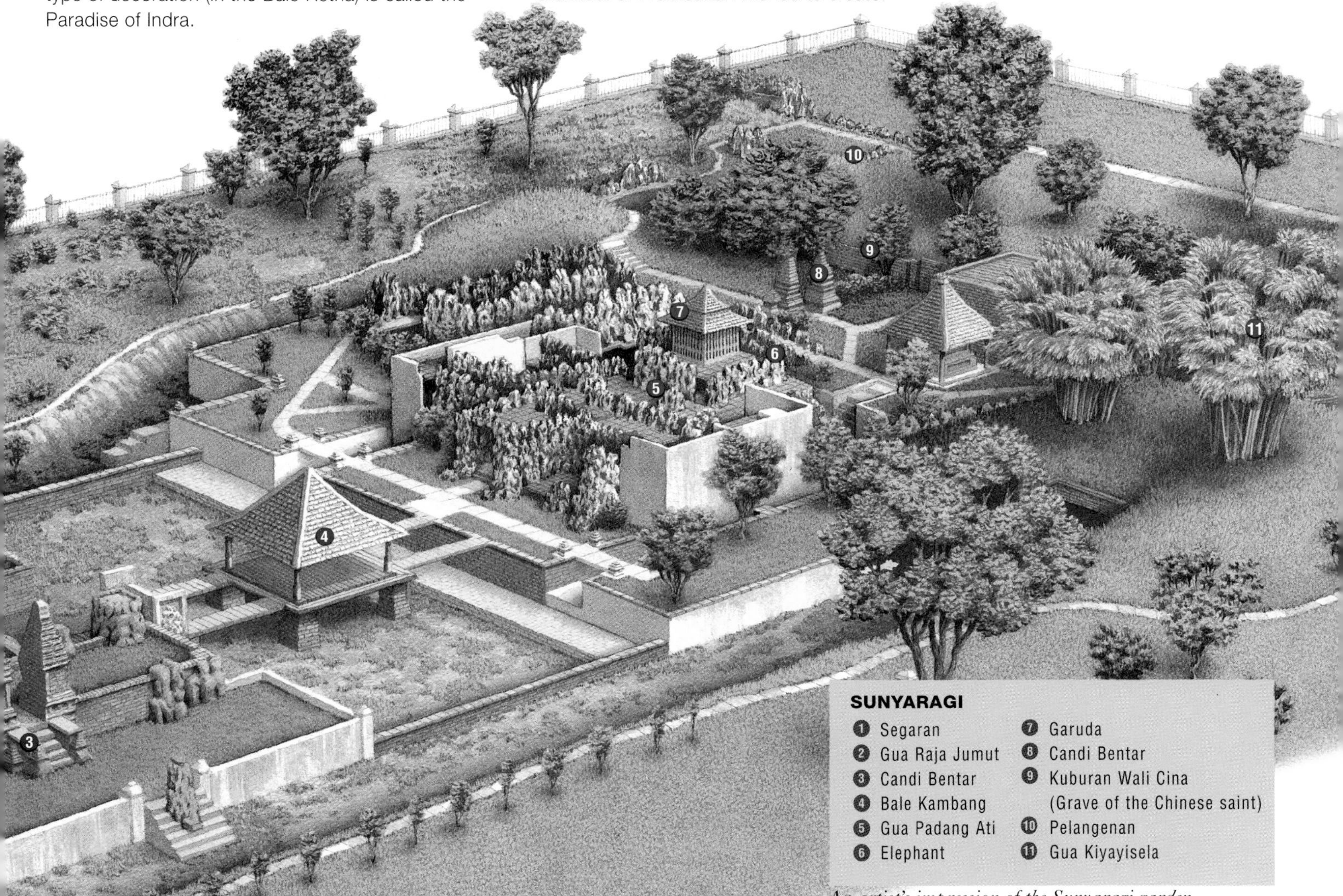

SUNYARAGI

1. Segaran
2. Gua Raja Jumut
3. Candi Bentar
4. Bale Kambang
5. Gua Padang Ati
6. Elephant
7. Garuda
8. Candi Bentar
9. Kuburan Wali Cina (Grave of the Chinese saint)
10. Pelangenan
11. Gua Kiyayisela

An artist's impression of the Sunyaragi garden.

Early Islamic Cities and Commercial Life

The rise and expansion of the Mongol empire in the 13th century had far reaching repercussions. New trade routes opened up through the Malay archipelago and with the increasing trade came the development and expansion of cities.

A CASH ECONOMY
The people of Indonesia were already familiar with coinage in the pre–Islamic era. The spread of Islam coincided with a major expansion in trade. Newly Islamised ports such as Pasai, Melaka, and Banten soon began to mint low–value coinage suitable for everyday use. These new coins were sometimes modelled after Muslim types from India and southwest Asia, sometimes after Chinese models. These coins were made of gold and silver, but more commonly of bronze, lead, or tin. The spread of these coins facilitated the evolution of new social institutions.

New Trade Routes and Traders

It is probably in Central Asia, that other region of the Ancient World situated, like Indonesia, at the intersection of many cultures, where we must seek the causes of the major changes which affected the societies of Southeast Asia beginning in the 13th century. Until then exchanges between the Far East and the Far West had been largely carried out by land, along the 'Silk Route' which Marco Polo followed to reach China in 1275. To be sure, the maritime route via the Indian Ocean fulfilled a parallel function, fostering the progressive 'Indianisation' of certain regions in Indochina and Insulinde and permitting the eastward diffusion of writing and Buddhism, but never before had this route achieved the same popularity.

In the 13th century Central Asia, which had been primarily a region through which travellers passed to reach another destination, became a true prime mover. In this zone and under the impulse of the Mongols arose a 'world system' which persisted for several decades and included much of Eurasia. Sino–Mongol pressure in the last years of the 13th century set in motion a series of military operations against Pagan, against Vietnam and Champa and, ultimately, against East Java. The storm passed rather quickly, but the weight of the North continued to make itself felt. Chinese from Fujian and Guangdong began to emigrate, forming 'overseas' communities in Southeast Asia, which played an increasingly essential economic role. Zhou Daguan tells us of a Chinese community in Cambodia toward the end of the 13th century, and Ma Huan describes several on the north coast of Java in the 15th century.

The Mongol order (which simultaneously destabilised the nations of Europe, India, and the Middle East) did not long endure. The rivalries born during the 14th century between the Turko–Mongol confederations hindered the ancient caravan traffic and the route through the Indian Ocean consequently assumed greater importance. This trade was primarily in spices, supplemented by the products of nearly all the Far East. In a complimentary sense, it was a trade of Muslims, supplemented by Christians. The 14th century witnessed the visit to Indonesia of the Moroccan khadi Ibn Battuta, who called at Pasai during his voyage from India to China, and the Italian Franciscan Odoric de Pordenone, who visited Java.

In this new situation, such ports as Barus, Kota Cina, Sriwijaya, and Banten Girang reacted

Banten market (1596)
A=Coconut sellers
B=Sugar and honey sellers
C=Bean sellers
D=Bamboo sellers
E=Weapon sellers
F=Men's cloth sellers
G=Women's cloth sellers
H=Spice sellers
I=Bengalis and Gujeratis selling ironwork and small utensils
K=Chinese stalls
L=Butchers
M=Fishmongers
N=Fruit sellers
O=Vegetable sellers
P=Pepper sellers
Q=Onion and leek sellers
R=Rice sellers
S=Merchants and travellers meet to discuss business
T=Jewellers
V=Ships with edibles
X=Chicken sellers

Annual procession of 10 Dzulhijah at the court of Aceh in 1637. The ceremony of which this procession formed a part commemorates Abraham's willingness to sacrifice his son. The artist, Peter Mundy, was an English sailor who visited Aceh the year after Aceh's greatest sultan, Iskandar Muda, died and was replaced by Iskandar Thani. The drawing shows the groups that comprised the cortege. On the left is the Great Mosque at Aceh, Bait ul–Rahman, with its four–tiered roof. The procession includes elephants, soldiers with pikes and firearms, cavalry, palace servants, and the sultan.

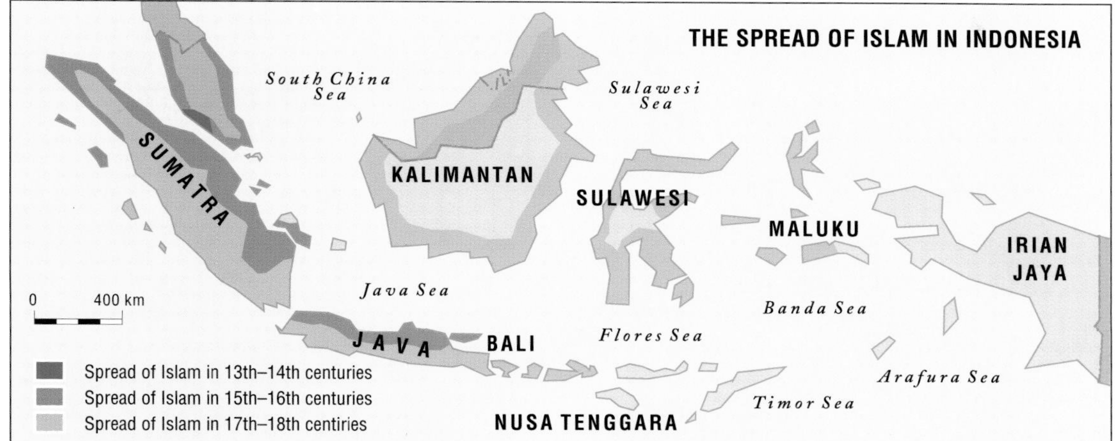

in remarkable fashion, playing the role of relay stations, supplementing the manufactured products from India and China with river gold and forest resources. Now the ports of the archipelago assumed a new role, that of active producers of goods for trade.

A new maritime route gradually appeared paralleling the route which traditionally led to the ports of Sumatra or Java and thence to China, stopping at Champa and Hainan. This new route allowed the integration of the Maluku producers of cloves and nutmegs, and all the islands of the 'Great East', into a greater commercial network. Along this new route to Canton or Quanzhou, appeared new ports such as Brunei and Manila. The knowledge which the western Indonesians possessed regarding the eastern part of their archipelago increased: a Javanese list of 1365 gives a whole series of toponyms corresponding to islands (or trading ports) located between Kalimantan and Irian Jaya. When the Magellan expedition passed through the Maluku islands in 1521, the local language of which the knight Antonio Pigafetta compiled the first lexicon was a form of Malay.

Commerce and Urbanisation

Increasing commercial activity was accompanied by true political and social florescence. The great kingdom of Majapahit was breached by the coastal merchants who gradually freed themselves from her suzerainty. The new Islamised cities which came into existence: Pasai and Tuban, Gresik and Surabaya, Melaka, Demak, Cirebon, Banten and Aceh, were all ports. In contrast to the large cities of the preceeding generation, with layouts geometrically organised according to the cardinal points and centred around the temple, mountain, or royal palace, the port cities evolved essentially from their function as wharves and markets. The principal sacred place became the mosque, the only edifice to keep a precise orientation (*kiblat*) with its *mihrab* pointing in the direction of Mecca. Except for some rare palatial or religious structures which have been preserved, as at Banten and Cirebon, there are today few remains of these merchant cities.

A new social structure also developed. The head of state was a sultan. The ancient nobilities which had constituted the framework of the agrarian societies were dismantled and gave way to the new elites, 'new men', commoners and cosmopolitan adventurers, whose notorious arrogance the Portuguese apothecary Tome Pires, describing Java around 1515, clearly noted (in his *Suma Oriental*): 'The lords of the coast who do not feel themselves as noble as those of the interior — for it has not been long since they were still slaves and merchants – never cease putting on airs and to demand respect as though they were the masters of the universe'. These gateway cities simultaneously developed collective festivals, now celebrated according to the Muslim calendar, designed to unify their hetero–genous populations around the person of the sultan. Many sultans became rich from trade.

PEPPER

The cultivation of pepper was developed in several parts of the western archipelago during the period of early urbanisation: first in Java, where it was mentioned by Zhao Rugua in the early 13th century (both in the country of Sunda as well as in Central Java, where the port of Sukitan exported large quantities), later in north Sumatra, in the region of Pasai (where Ma Huan described its cultivation in 1433), and in west Sumatra at Tiku (where a French vessel went to buy it in 1529). The plantation, aimed at systematic cultivation on a large scale of a product essentially destined for export, is well attested in Insulinde, long before the colonial economies were established in the archipelago.

Forms of Early Islamic Belief and Practice

The spread of Islam in Indonesia provides one of the rare examples of a process by which one world religion has displaced another in an extensive area. Indonesia is now the most populous Muslim country in the world. The process of Islamisation was not rapid or simple, and the steps by which this religion from the barren deserts of Arabia won converts in this fertile archipelago are still known only in vague outline. For the earliest period of Islamisation, very few written sources exist to assist scholars. Archaeology is and will remain an important source of knowledge regarding the causes and effects of the introduction of Islam to Indonesia.

 *Carved stonework from the tomb of Sunan Kudus.*

The Yogyakarta mosque, mid–18th century, is associated with the palace.

Gateway to the tomb of Sunan Gunung Jati near Cirebon, northwest Java. Porcelain plates are set into the walls to emulate classical Islamic tiled decorations.

Tombstones

The oldest traces of Islamisation in Indonesia are gravestones found on several islands. Their shapes and the contents of their inscriptions provide indications of the changes in religious practices brought about by Islam. The oldest gravestone of an Indonesian king, that of Sultan Malik al-Salih of Pasai (Sumatra), dates from 1297. It is also the oldest known specimen of a type of stone with 'wings', a style which has remained characteristic of Acehnese and Malay graveyards ever since. While these earliest examples of Islamic tombstones show strong local influences, other examples from Pasai, as well as the famous tombstone of Malik Ibrahim (dated 1419 AD) in Gresik, in the environs of Surabaya, east Java, seem to have been imported to the archipelago from Cambay (Gujarat in northwest India) at a slightly later time. This circumstance probably indicates one of the geographical sources of Indonesian Islam.

The conversion of the bulk of the Javanese population occurred much later. With the exception of the grave of a foreign lady (Fatimah binti Maimun, in Leran, dated AH475 [1082]), the oldest Islamic graves in Java (late 14th to 16th centuries) are those of dignitaries of the court of Majapahit at a time when that Hindu–Buddhist kingdom was still flourishing. These stones bear Arabic inscriptions, but are dated with Old Javanese numerals according to the Saka era. Their shape also indicates the syncretism of Islamic and Javanese practice, for they are shaped like the stones on which old Javanese religious charters were engraved. Other similar gravestones from the early 15th century have been found in the southwest (Matan) and the north of Borneo (Brunei).

Islamic architecture of the 15th century, such as the Sendang Duwur mausoleum, northeast Java (dated 1485), shows how much the monuments of the new faith owed to Hindu architecture. In the same way, the ornamental carved panels of Mantingan mosque (near Jepara in north central Java) proclaim the birth of an Islamic decorative art specifically Javanese, the development of which was halted by the economic situation caused by the Dutch colonisation of the island.

In the Malay-speaking area the oldest tombstones testify to a progressive transition from one culture to another. The stones of Minye Tujoh (Aceh, 1380) and Pengkalan Kempas (Malay Peninsula, 1467) bear Malay texts still written in script of a type derived from India. In the first years of the 14th century, the Trengganu charter (approximately dated 1303) was written in Jawi script, a new Malay alphabet adapted from Persian.

New Practices and Concepts

These early Islamic graves also indicate the approach of an important religious practice, namely a new way of disposing of the dead. Contrary to Hindu, Buddhist, or 'primitive' customs prevailing until then, corpses were now buried, wrapped in a shroud and facing Mecca. Islam was introducing a new concept of space, oriented no more according to eight universal directions around a central point but now with one centre located far away to the west of the archipelago. It is toward that direction that the dead must face, the same direction toward which Muslims bow during the five daily prayers.

This conception of the universe oriented toward a centre located outside the archipelago was not fully accepted however. We know for instance that several important people during the 15th and 16th centuries refused to make the pilgrimage to Mecca. The Sultan of Melaka was one of them, for he maintained that the centre of the Islamic world was in his own

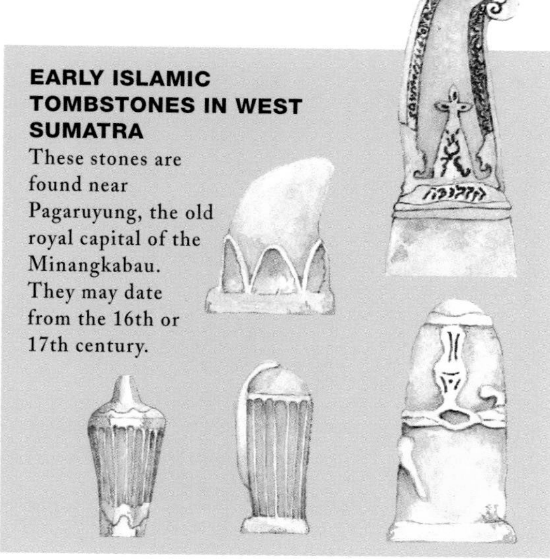

EARLY ISLAMIC TOMBSTONES IN WEST SUMATRA
These stones are found near Pagaruyung, the old royal capital of the Minangkabau. They may date from the 16th or 17th century.

kingdom. The *Hikayat Hang Tuah*, a famous Malay epic written in the 17th century, describes diplomatic and commercial missions undertaken by the hero Hang Tuah in the most important kingdoms of the time: China, India, Egypt and Constantinople. He makes the pilgrimage as if by chance on his way to the West, and it is clear that for him, as for his king, the centre of the world is not in Mecca.

One important Indonesian who made the haj and who visited some of the most prominent Islamic centres on his mystical quest, Hamzah Fansuri, was initiated into the Sufi Qadiriyya brotherhood. Sunan Gunung Jati, an enigmatic 16th century figure, one of the 'nine saints' of Java, according to some accounts is supposed to have been a member of the Naqshakandiyya and Shattariyya brotherhoods *(tarekat)*. In fact these brotherhoods did not develop in the archipelago until later, in the 17th century.

Mysticism, an Enduring Practice

The earliest adepts of the new faith were attracted by Islamic mysticism. The doctrine of the *wujudiyya* emerged as an important intellectual centre in the 16th century. According to that doctrine the universe was potentially contained in the eternal attributes of God which manifest themselves permanently in His creation. The universe, and man with it, participate in the divine essence. The universe is but a wave in the unfathomable ocean that is God. A Malay poem of the time urges: "Say, I am the supreme reality, do not be afraid. Then the wave becomes the sea". This is not far from the declaration which caused the Persian mystic Al-Hallaj to be put to death on the pyre in Baghdad in the early 10th century.

The *wujudiyya* adepts were promptly attacked and condemned by more orthodox scholars. Two legendary characters of early Javanese Islam have been compared to al-Hallaj, as both were condemned to be burned alive. They are Seh Siti Jenar, one of the 'nine saints' credited with the Islamisation of Java, and Sunan Panggung. Both were accused of blasphemy, but Javanese tradition consistently says that both of them were devotees of such high knowledge that their behaviour was misinterpreted.

Only a few Malay and Javanese Islamic works written before the 17th century have been preserved. They are learned and subtle speculations on the nature of God and the articles of faith. They include such works as the Malay translations of the *Aqa'id* of al-Nasafi, the *Burdah* of al-Busiri, and original Malay treatises by Hamzah Fansuri (Sharab al-Ashiqin, 'The Drink of the Lovers'), or the so-called 'Admonitions of Seh Bari' in Javanese. These works were clearly not intended for the layman.

The rural Qur'anic schools (*pesantren,* 'places of the pious Muslims') which are so important in Java and in other islands as centres of Islamic education, are not documented before the 18th century. However, they appear to be related to religious communities (mandalas and *dharmas*) of Hindu-Buddhist times.

It seems probable that in the earliest Islamic period, religious education was given in this type of school remote from political centres. It seems that some of the more important characteristics of Indonesian Islam have existed since the earliest times, such as opposition between mystics of the *wujudiyya* and the orthodox followers of the Islamic tradition, have been alive ever since, and continue to form the basis of political issues in contemporary Indonesia.

BATU ACEH
This form of tombstone was the first and most distinctive form of sculpture to develop in early Indonesian Islam. Arabic inscriptions, usually a Qur'anic quote, are often decoratively used, the characters being fashioned to form patterns. Floral or vegetal webs, geometric, mihrab (niche) and 'vase' shapes predominate among the motifs used.

Some part of the lotus is depicted on all Batu Aceh. The form the lotus often takes suggests that it had its origins in medieval Egypt, although the symbolism of the lotus was borrowed by the Buddhists from Brahmanism where it symbolised divine birth and mortality.

Intricately carved door to the tomb complex of Sunan Kudus, one of the wali songo or nine people credited in folkore with bringing Islam to Java.

Mystical Islam. Many early Muslims were attracted by Islamic mysticism. Today many adherents still follow mystical practices such as visiting the graves of Java's early Muslim proselytisers.

Megalithic monuments in west Sumatra in a form variously interpreted as birds' heads or kris hilts. The same form was used for early Muslim graves in Sumatra and elsewhere in Indonesia

The ruler of the kingdom of Buleleng, north Bali, and his scribe, mid–19th century. The king holds a palm–leaf document (lontara), while the scribe holds ready the instruments for writing.

An 838–page treatise on Javanese gamelan music in both the slendro (pentatonic) and pelog (diatonic) scales, composed by K.R.T. Krtanagara in 1889. It is written in New Javanese using both Javanese and Latin scripts.

«A Batak datu reads from a bark manuscript (pustaha) written in a local variant of a script originally derived from south India. Such manuscripts usually consist of magic spells and guides to divination.

HERITAGE OF INDONESIAN LITERATURE

Indonesia must have had a substantial body of oral and dramatic literature in the prehistoric period. Many Indonesian ethnic groups still retain a rich tradition of such literature. The recitation of one of these epics sometimes requires 30 or 40 hours. A performance may be spread over several days, usually conducted at night. People who specialise in memorising these literary cycles can still be found, but their inheritance is endangered; few people are willing to undergo the arduous training involved, and as the older generation dies, so does part of the Indonesian cultural heritage.

One of the most important factors which led Indonesians to become interested in South Asian culture was undoubtedly the Sanskrit literary heritage. The epics of the Ramayana and Mahabharata were introduced to many parts of Indonesia in the first millennium AD. Themes from these works found their way into all levels of Indonesian society, from the courts to the villages. Through the shadow play and related dramatic performances, many generations of Indonesians acquired role models.

Our knowledge of Indonesian literature only becomes relatively detailed during the Kadiri period, in the 11th and 12th centuries. The Kadiri court produced little in the form of sculpture or architecture, but more than compensated for this with an outpouring of literature which survives today. More great literary works were produced in the succeeding Majapahit period. Few nations in the world can boast of such an ancient continuous literary tradition as Indonesia.

Indonesian literature of the classic period consisted of numerous genres, some adopted from elsewhere, others developed according to local concepts of appropriate literary forms for various uses. Different genres influenced one another. Indonesian authors created new narratives incorporating characters from South Asian sources. What has been preserved is undoubtedly only the tip of the iceberg; only a small proportion of ancient works have been preserved, just enough to give us a general impression of the sophistication of classical literary culture. Poets were given the exalted title of Mpu; their names are preserved, but in the form of *noms de plume*, usually of a self–deprecatory nature. The ability to compose poetry was one of the qualities expected of sophisticated courtiers.

The introduction of Islam added new genres to the Indonesian repertoire, but did not immediately result in the loss of pre–existing literary forms.

Singing Literature

Much of Javanese literature is in verse form meant to be chanted aloud. Those forms used from the late 16th to the early 20th century were predominantly of a single kind known as tembang. *Given the rigidity of the metrical rules that govern tembang, it is remarkable how versatile and enduring it has proven to be in the literary history of Java and the neighbouring islands.*

» Court official at Yogyakarta chanting aloud from the text of Bharatayuddha, 'War of the Bharata'.

Formal Rigidity

To someone accustomed to Western poetry, its free verse and its metrics based on stress or syllable length, *tembang* appears strange and unusually rigid. It is well suited, however, to the structure of the languages in which it has been applied: primarily Javanese, but also Sundanese, Madurese, Balinese and Sasak.

A *tembang* stanza consists of a fixed number of syllables and a fixed vowel in the final syllable. Every verse form has its own distinctive configuration of number of lines, line lengths, and final vowels. In the course of time more than a hundred different forms have been developed, although only about a dozen have found widespread currency. *Pangkur* and *mijil* are among these forms. A stanza in *pangkur* is made up of seven lines. The first line has eight syllables, the last of which contains the vowel a, the second line has 11 syllables with a final i, and so on. The metrical structure of a full *pangkur* stanza can be represented as 8a–11i–8u–7a–12u–8a–8i. *Mijil* has the formula 10i–6o–10e–10i–6i–6u.

Literary works usually contain several cantos, series of stanzas in the same verse form or, in some older texts, in alternating pairs of stanzas in different verse forms (AA–BB–AA–BB, etc.) The number of stanzas in a canto varies; in 17th century texts it is often around 100 and later around 40, but cantos of as few as one and as many as 600 stanzas may occur too.

Tembang does not only have a metrical but also a melodic aspect. Each verse form has several mutually related tunes. *Tembang* texts tend to be sung aloud. They can also be read with the intonation of speech, but this is called 'reading as prose' and is done for analytical purposes. To bring out the poetic qualities of a *tembang* text it is necessary to apply a tune to it. This is why someone reading in private, for personal enjoyment, will also sing aloud.

Versatility

The rules of *tembang* are rigid indeed. But it is a mistake to think that this formal regulation correlates with strict rules for content. *Tembang* accommodates a wide range of genres. It has been the vehicle for myths and romances, historical narratives, stories of the prophets of Islam, moralistic treatises, mystical songs, prayers and magical formulas, social and cultural criticism, novels, letters, even calendars and lists of synonyms. Furthermore a large number of *tembang* stanzas, some originally quotations from literary works, circulate in oral tradition.

How can such a strictly regulated poetic form be so versatile where contents are concerned? First it must be noted that *tembang* is essentially a matter of sound shape: phonology and intonation contour. It leaves the choice of registers and topics largely free. Hence *tembang* verse can make use of vocabularies ranging from the archaic and arcane to the colloquial. According to Javanese court poetics of the 18th century and later, each verse form expresses a certain mood, and contents are supposed to be in accordance with these moods, but such rules do not seem to have applied in earlier periods and even in court works their application was flexible and subject to variation.

Tembang does not easily bore because it is sung and each verse form has several tunes. This allows readers to introduce melodic variation even where the metrical form remains the same for long stretches of text. Several verse forms are used in most works, leading to metrical variation as well.

Because *tembang* verse is typically audible to others, the reading of *tembang* easily becomes a social activity. *Tembang* literature was often recited at poetry gatherings where several participants sang from a

Two pages from the 547–page manuscript Serat Purwakandha written in the poetic tembang form. It tells stories of ancient kings, beginning with Adam and ending with a story from the Indian epics. It was written by a royal scribe at Yogyakarta on the order of Sultan Hamengkubuwono VIII, and took four years to complete, the last line being written on 28th July 1927.

THE ROMANCE OF DAMAR WULAN

Manuscript illustration from Damar Wulan, a manuscript containing 153 coloured drawings presented to the India Office Library in 1815 by Lt–Col. Raban, resident of Cirebon 1812–1814, during the British occupation of Java. It is an epic poem set in the time of Majapahit, written in a form designed for oral recitation. Damar Wulan is the protagonist, set against his uncle Logender, vizir of Majapahit, who is afraid Damar Wulan will rise higher than his own two sons; and against Menak Jingga, demonic king of Balambangan, who proposed marriage to the queen of Majaphit. She refuses and he declares war. Damar Wulan is ordered to kill Menak Jingga. He succeeds, marries the queen of Majapahit and obtains the title of Brawijaya.

The first illustration depicts a scene from a masked dance drama (*dhalang penopengan*). The main dancer has taken a mask from a chest. Behind him is a masked clown. Female musicians play a double hanging gong, a pair of *kethuk*, and a pair of drums. At the bottom, the *dalang*, narrator, is reading a text, and another man is smoking opium. The meaning of the picture is unclear, but it may be a representation of the reading aloud of the Damar Wulan legend.

The second illustration is taken from the same manuscript and depicts two men riding on horseback to fight a battle against the forces of the evil Menak Jingga. The figure riding in front is Watangan, the son of Rongga Lawe, an old noble who has been slain in battle. He is followed on the horse behind by Demang Gatul an old servant of Rongga Lawe. He wears a kris with an unusually shaped hilt on his back.

The manuscript is written in Javanese language and script, in ink, colours and gold on Dutch paper.

manuscript in turn.

Because they took place at night, such sessions would simultaneously serve as vigils. They were held when there was a religious need for a group of people, usually older men, to gather and bestow their good wishes on the host's family. This is one of the main objectives of all manner of life–cycle ceremonies in Java and the surrounding islands. Reading sessions could be organised for childbirth, circumcision, marriage, anniversaries, and the redemption of vows. Hence there was a demand for texts that could provide a virtuous focus of attention during such nocturnal celebrations.

Not all *tembang* texts were equally suitable for group reading. Another important factor is that linking words and melodies facilitates the memorisation of texts. *Tembang* was considered an effective instrument for the education of young people. But in all cases of the use of *tembang* the social aspect was important: *tembang* was the medium *par excellence* for texts that should be heard by others — human as well as supernatural.

Historical Endurance

It is not known when *tembang* was created. The oldest works that can be dated with certainty derive from around 1600, but it is likely that the use of *tembang* was already well established at that time. According to later tradition, *tembang* was developed by the *wali*, the legendary Muslim saints who spread Islam in Java in the 15th and 16th centuries. But *tembang* is also found in Bali, an island that was never Islamised, and in a number of literary works from Java that show no influence of Islam. This points to the possibilty that *tembang* already existed in Majapahit times.

From the 17th century onwards many works were composed in *tembang*. Poets were active in courts and villages, in secluded Hindu–Buddhist mountain hermitages and in the busy Muslim ports that dot Java's north coast. Alongside original works, they wrote *tembang* adaptations of Malay and later also European texts, and the major Old Javanese poems were recast in *tembang*.

Tembang used to be associated with Javanese literature, but was not limited to Javanese speaking areas, also being found in regions with other vernaculars — Palembang in Sumatra, West Java (where Sundanese is spoken), Madura, Bali, and Lombok. Beginning in the late 18th century, *tembang* works were composed in Balinese and Madurese. Sundanese and Sasak followed suit in the 19th century. Even Malay texts are known.

Tembang's endurance as a vehicle for creative writing was finally exhausted in the 20th century, as the printing press and Western schooling made their impact on cultural life by promoting other genres. Although a few poets still compose in *tembang*, Indonesian has taken over the role of literary medium from the 'regional languages', Javanese, Sundanese, Balinese, and Sasak included. This does not mean, that *tembang* is dead. It is rarely used for writing, but it is often heard, for *tembang* is common in lyrics sung in traditional music and drama, and these performing arts remain popular in traditional ceremonies still held in many areas.

Coin–like objects found in east Java are decorated with motifs taken from the Damar Wulan story. It has been suggested that these date from the Majapahit era, but some scholars believe that the Damar Wulan story was only written after the fall of Majapahit. This example shows the clown–like servants of the hero; they are similar to the figures of Semar and the other Panakawan in the shadow plays.

Interpretations of the Indian Epics

The two great Indian literary epics, 'Ramayana' (Rama's Journey) and 'Mahabharata' (Great Bharata) influenced many literary works in Indian local languages and throughout much of Southeast Asia. Outside India, the epics (viracarita) took on many local characteristics. Not only were the plots transformed, but the original forms of the viracarita *were forgotten. Indian names were retained for cities, districts, mountains, rivers and lakes. The main characters and episodes were nationalised.*

Ink drawings of the Ramayana were made in Bali in the early 19th century. This drawing depicts heavenly musicians. Just as in the reliefs on Borobudur and Prambanan in the 9th century, musicians continue to be seen in Bali as necessary attributes of the abode of the gods. This particular scene takes place in the mountains north of the palace of Rawana, where the gods are entertaining themselves with flutes and stringed instruments.

Golden bowl from the Wonoboyo hoard made in central Java around AD 900 and decorated with scenes from the Ramayana. This particular panel depicts Rama's wife, Sita during her abduction by the demon king, Rawana.

The Indonesian Ramayana

The oldest known Indonesian text of this story was composed in *kakawin* form in central Java in the 9th century. There is evidence that the sources of the Javanese version stem from a 5th century Kashmiri text. Like the Kashmiri version, the oldest Javanese text does not contain the Uttarakanda section found in the well-known version by Valmiki. Approximately a century later, the Uttarakanda appeared in Old Javanese, as a separate text.

In later times the two texts underwent parallel but separate revisions. Yasadipura I wrote an adaptation of the Ramayana under the title Serat Rama in 19th century Surakarta. The Uttarakanda was revised around 1367 in the kingdom of Majapahit by Mpu Tantular as the kakawin Arjunawijaya. Important changes include the insertion of Buddhist elements. This text was revised again by Yasadipura I and II and entitled Serat Arjunasasrabahu, in two forms: *macapat* and *kawi miring*.

Other variant texts inspired by the Ramayana include Serat Kanda, which contains Muslim elements. For example Adam replaces Visnu or Siva. Another text which belongs to the same tradition is the Serat Kandaning Ringgit Purwa which, according to Ras, is a Pasisir (north coast) text combining elements from the Ramayana and Mahabharata. Here Rama and Sita are ancestors of the Pandawa. The *dalang* of Java followed this tradition in such *wayang* stories as Semar Boyong, Rama Nitik, and Rama Nitis. All these Ramayana texts show that the stories were reinterpreted in each generation in accordance with contemporary culture.

Interpretations of the Ramayana were not only reflected in literature, but in archaeology. Ramayana reliefs are found at Prambanan and Panataran. The Dutch archaeologist, W.F. Stutterheim has shown that the Prambanan reliefs tend to be closer to folk traditions, while those at Panataran are closer to the Ramayana kakawin.

The Mahabharata

The oldest Mahabharata text found in Indonesia is an Old Javanese version partially composed during the reign of Dharmawangsa Teguh Anantawikrama in the 10th century, of a genre usually termed *parwa*. There are 18 *parwa* in the Indian Mahabharata, of which only nine are known in the Old Javanese literary tradition: Adi, Sabha, Virata, Udyoga, Bhisma, Mosala, Asramawasaparwa, Mahaprasthanika, and Swargarohana. The last four *parwa*, according to P. J. Zoetmulder, were composed much later than the other five, during the Majapahit era. Compared to the Sanskrit Mahabharata, the Old Javanese *parwa* are much shorter, but the narrative content is quite similar. Thus J. Gonda termed these *parwa* 'translational literature', which conforms to a statement found in the Adi and Virata *parwa*: *manjavaken byasamata* (Javanising the text). Local myths played no part in the translation process.

Such a translation process was apparently not conducted by only one person. The *parwa* reflect several different religious orientations. For example the Adi *parwa* lays more stress on the worship of Siva; the Virata *parwa* focuses on the worship of Krishna Dvaipayana, who according to research is the manifestation of Brahma. The Bhisma *parwa* centres on on the worship of Hari (Visnu). The adaptation of the Mahabharata to Old Javanese *parwa* was not conducted at the same time. Supomo shows that the Virata *parwa* was probably first; in fact in Java this *parwa* is called *manggala* Mahabharata.

This interpretation is also suggested by the fact that the Bharatayuddha is not found in *parwa* form. This does not mean that this story is not known in Java. The story of this war is found in kakawin form, composed by Mpu Sedah and Mpu Panuluh, in the 12th century reign of Jayabhaya in Kadiri. With the existence of the Bharatayuddha kakawin, the Javanese Mahabharata became complete. But is it true that the Bharatayuddha was never known in *parwa* form? In 1986 Supomo tried to locate such a text. He compared sections of the Drona, Karna, and the Salya *parwa* from the Bharatayuddha kakawin with the same sections of the Mahabharata. His conclusion was that the *parwa* form once existed, but was lost. Further research on this topic is required.

During the Majapahit period this *vira-carita* appeared in another genre, the *tutur*. Examples include the Korawasrama and Nawaruci. The former text relates the story of the resurrection of Korawa by Vyasa, after the Bharatayuddha. This episode may have been meant to demonstrate the philosophy of complimentary dualism which was enjoined by the religion which the patron of this text espoused. The latter text presents the story of Bima's search for the elixir of immortality at the instruction of Drona. The Mahabharata characters are modified to become means for the expression of esoteric beliefs. At the end of the classic period, Bima seems to have become a separate deity associated with a cult emphasising immortality.

During the Surakarta period of literature, the Bharatayuddha kakawin was readapted as the Serat Baratayuda, in both *macapat* and *kawi miring* form. Both the *parwa* and kakawin later became sources for shadow-play episodes, in large numbers with a wide variety of cultural backgrounds. These episodes or *lakon* include Bale Sigala-gala, Babad Alas Mrentani, Pendhawa Dhadhu, Arjunawiwaha, Baratayuda, and so forth. Of course the Mahabharata traits in the shadow play episodes were adapted to the puppet stage, which in ancient times was part of ritual performance.

In the Javanese *babad* genre, the Mahabharata was readapted, becoming a genealogical narrative. Its main characters, including Arjuna, became ancestors of the Javanese kings in a line termed Sejarah Pangiwa. The Ramayana and Mahabharata were then fused, legitimising the kingship of the Javanese rulers, for Rama and Arjuna, as descendants of Indra, were seen as ideal kings according to the Hinduised Javanese tradition. Thus the Mahabharata in Java, and in fact in all Indonesia, was interpreted in new form so as to relate to a variety of aspects of life.

Archaeological remains also illuminate the local interpretation of the Mahabharata. Bosch has shown that the reliefs at Jalatunda bathing place contain the story of the Adi Parwa. He concluded that two traditions were influential in the carving of the Adi Parwa. The first was the Old Javanese Adi Parwa tradition, especially the Draupadiharana section; the second was the folklore tradition. The two were packaged as a single narrative distinct from both the Old Javanese and Sanskrit traditions. This difference may have been linked to the function of the Jalatunda bathing place in its social setting. Jalatunda seems to have been the beginning of a pilgrimage route to the summit of Mount Penanggungan, east Java. Pilgrims of both higher and lower status may have bathed themselves in this place as part of the ritual before continuing their journey. The carvings may have been installed during two phases of construction. One phase could have reflected the taste of the upper class, the other being more attuned to the types of illustrations with which the common people were more familiar.

SHADOW PLAYS

One of the most popular media for depicting the story of the Mahabharata is the shadow play. Leather figures are manipulated on one side of a translucent screen with a lamp which projects shadows of the puppets so that the audience sees only the shadows when seated on the other side of the screen.

The craft of carving these leather puppets became a special art form in itself, particularly in Java. Elaborate conventions govern the forms of their bodies, postures, colours, clothing, weapons, head gear and movements giving each puppet a distinctive and readily identifiable character. Here, from left to right are figures from the Mahabharata: Pandu, father of the five Pandawa brothers; Drupadi, the wife of the Pandawa brothers, Srikandi, a female warrior and Sadewa, one of the five brothers.

Balinese lontar of the Adi Parwa, first book of the Mahabharata. (Top) A priest meets a magic cowherd who helps him to reach the palace quickly. (Below) The priest who has become ritually impure bathes to restore his holiness.

Bima was the biggest and strongest of the Pandawa brothers. In the late classic period, he became the object of a specific Javanese cult in which he was associated with immortality and virility. He was frequently depicted in Late Classic sculpture.

Wayang figures of Arjuna (left), one of the Pandawa brothers about whom many stories and legends are told in Indonesian literature, and his brother Bima (right).

Kakawin Literary Forms

One of the most outstanding cultural products of early Indonesia is to be found in the field of literature: the kakawin*. This genre was developed by the civilisation that flourished for many centuries on the island of Java, blending Indian with indigenous elements. The kakawin is sometimes said to be the equivalent of the Sanskrit* kavya*, but this may not do full justice to the contributions of the Javanese and Balinese authors who developed their own special conventions.*

»»A lontar copy of the Desawarnana kakawin (1365), now kept in the National Library, Jakarta.

Kakawin as Poetry

The term kakawin itself means 'product of the *kawi*', and *kawi* is the term for 'poet' in Old Javanese. But if we then call it 'poetry', we have to bear in mind that this is poetry in a particular form, namely long, narrative works composed of fixed metrical patterns. The form was indeed based on an Indian model, and the system of metres using the principle of quantity was adopted from the Sanskrit. Even so, the language is Old Javanese, and the idiom is highly sophisticated and poetic. This is perhaps why the major works of this genre have remained little known in the West, and why even in Indonesia few scholars have taken an interest in them.

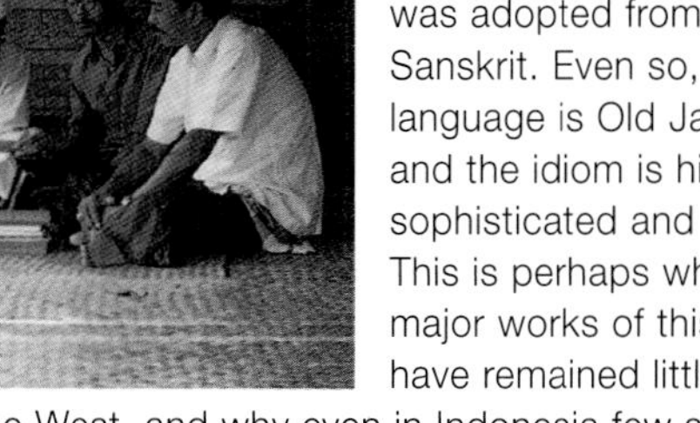

A group of Balinese singing from an Old Javanese text; one man has the manuscript in front of him on a tray, and the friend on his right is giving a commentary in Balinese. The text is the Kakawin Arjunawiwaha, a famous specimen dating from the 11th century.

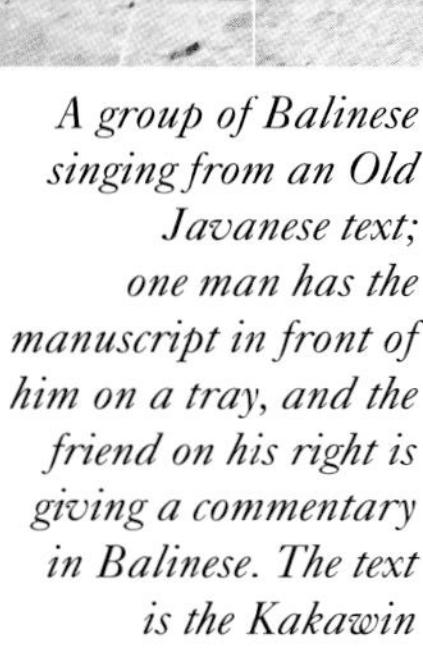

The context of kakawin is the courts which existed in Hindu Java, centred first in central and later east Java. Such literary works owe their survival to an unbroken tradition of textual activity, extending from early Java down to modern Bali.

Kakawin Sources

The earliest example of the genre and, some say, the finest, is the Old Javanese version of the famous Indian epic Ramayana. This was probably written in central Java as early as the mid-9th century. In language and style it stands apart from later works, and was so highly esteemed that it served as a model and source of inspiration for later authors. The next most famous work goes under the title of Arjuna-wiwaha, 'The Marriage of Arjuna'. The hero is Arjuna, one of five Pandawas in the epic Mahabharata, who engages in ascetic exercises in order to obtain supernatural weapons from the gods to help restore his family's fortunes. After successfully completing his meditation, he assists the gods in repelling a threat from the demon Niwatakawaca and is rewarded with marriage to seven delightful nymphs in heaven. This gives an impression of the theme of most kakawin: tales of gods and demons, kings and legendary heroes, and of course powerful holy men.

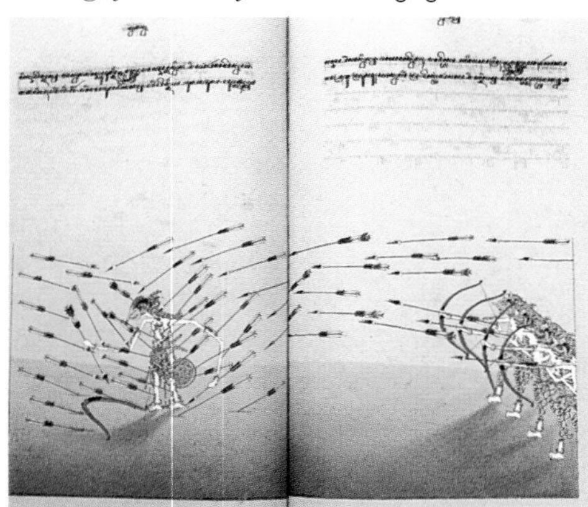

Pages from the Bharatayuddha, written in kakawin form, depicting the killing of Abhimanyu.

The greatest kakawin were written when the capital of Java's paramount kingdom was located at Kadiri, during the period from the mid-11th century up to 1222. Their titles are Bharatayuddha, Hariwangsa, Ghatotkacasraya, Smaradahana, Krsnayana and Bhomantaka. The courts of this period seem to have excelled in producing poetry, just as the following Singasari period specialised in creating sculpture. There was another productive period in the second half of the 14th century, when the poems Arjunawijaya, Sutasoma and Desawarnana (or Nagarakrtagama) were written.

The last mentioned is worth describing in more detail. In fact it is quite atypical, as it provides an eye-witness account of the kingdom of Majapahit in 1365, as seen by the Superintendent of Buddhist Affairs, Mpu Prapanca. This work includes concrete information on the royal family, the capital, the dependencies, court festivals and lists of religious domains and the author describes a 'royal tour' on which he accompanied his king, Hayam Wuruk, hence the name of the work which can be translated as 'Description of the Districts'.

Kakawin in Bali

Apparently there was another flowering of literature in the latter half of the 15th century, shortly before the end of the Hindu-Javanese period. During that century Islam began to expand in Java, but this did not mean the end of the literary tradition; it had become deeply rooted in Bali. Hindu-Buddhist civilisation has continued to evolve in Bali down to the present day, and an essential part of this civilisation is literature, including of course the kakawin. The texts were tirelessly recopied by Balinese scholars on palm-leaf manuscripts (called lontar), which represent the main sources for Western scholars wishing to gain access to the texts.

In this tradition, the act of writing itself belongs to the sphere of the sacred, and the same applies to the kakawin literature. The act of composition was a religious one, and according to the convention expressed by the poets themselves, the poem was a vehicle for mystical union with the deity of beauty. There is no doubt that the aims of the poet were on a higher plane than mere worldly amusement. The motifs and use of language are stereotyped, and appear to have conformed to rules passed down from teacher to pupil. The poets occupied a high rank at court, and were often commissioned by the ruler to create a poem, which may have contained allegories about himself and his exploits.

In contemporary Bali, kakawin texts are kept in private libraries and are also studied in 'reading clubs', the members of which learn how to recite the Old Javanese poetry and how to paraphrase it in Balinese. The technique of recitation is considered essential, as the text is intended to be heard (rather than read silently), and the melodic line is co-ordinated with the metrical pattern. The texts preferred for recitation are those which contain passages of teaching, as these are regarded valuable as a guide to ethics and spirituality appropriate to the Hindu society of Bali.

However, kakawin contain passages of various kinds, as required by the conventions of the genre. For example, the Western reader is struck by the very extensive descriptions of battles, and by the use of natural phenomena in elaborate metaphors and similes, linking the moods of the natural world with the emotional state of the human actors.

An example of this use of nature as a mirror of human emotions is found in the text Sumanasantaka. The kakawin describes the mood of the nymph, Harini, as follows:

'She walked wearily and her feet were heavy, as she had never before gone roaming among the woodland hermitages. The flowers of the *asana* trees formed parasols, as if to shade her when the sun shone hot; Deeply moved, the bamboo stems stood to attention, as if hoping to be taken as her staff, motionlessly awaiting her there, And the *gadung* vines seemed beside themselves with love, sprouting new tendrils as if wanting to lead her forward along the path'.

The following passage in the Arjunawiwaha is quoted in Bali:

'Om! May the reverence of one without protector be seen by Him who is the refuge of the three worlds!
My obeisance is both inward and outward, and is made at your feet only.
You are like the fire that appears from wood, and like the butter that appears from milk, the holy one who emerges whenever a man turns his mind to pure thoughts'.

Illustrated lontar of the Smaradahana, from the palace of Buleleng, north Bali. This text was written in about the 12th century by a poet who called himself Dharmaja. The script is Balinese, but the language is Old Javanese. (Courtesy of the National Gallery of Australia, Canberra).

SMARADAHANA

This Balinese painting from the collection of the Rijksmuseum of Leiden, Netherlands originally formed a partition in a Balinese sleeping pavilion. In upper left a group of gods, led by Indra, look on. The story centres around Indra's plan for Kama, god of love, to shoot Siva with his arrows, causing Siva and Uma to have a son, Ganesha, who would conquer demons. In the top centre beside a tree in which a bird perches is the sleeping pavilion of Ratih, divine wife of Kama. Next Ratih with loosened hair, a sign of mourning, is seen walking to the place where Kama, god of love, was burnt to death by the flame of Siva's third eye.

In the third scene, Ratih is digging up Kama's skull and bones, some still smouldering. In the fourth scene, lower left, Siva is seated beneath a tree with his guards Nandiswara and Mahakala. In the centre is a conflagration in which Ratih and her maids are being consumed. Their heads are still visible among the flames. After the death of Kama and Ratih, Siva finally was caused to fall in love with Uma.

Panji Tales

The Panji tales are of indigenous inspiration, rather than a reworking of themes borrowed from elsewhere. They originated in Java, but they became popular over a wider area including Malay–speaking areas of western Indonesia, Borneo, and as far as Thailand. There are many tales in the Panji cycle, and the genre's wide distribution and frequent appearance in old manuscripts provide strong evidence of their former popularity. Temple reliefs and statuary from ancient Java were also based on variants of the Panji stories.

Two figures from Candi Jago wearing headgear which are normally characteristic of Panji and Candra Kirana.

Mask of Klana, a king from overseas. The red face and bulging eyes in Javanese symbolism stand for the inability of an individual to master emotions.

The Plot

The stories that make up the Panji cycle are set in ancient Java, where the four kingdoms of Kuripan, Daha, Gegelang and Singasari, are each ruled by one of four brothers. Historically these kingdoms coexisted during the period from the mid–11th century until 1222. Daha (also known as Kadiri) was the foremost of these. The son of the eldest brother, the king of Kuripan, is Raden Inu. Raden Inu is betrothed to the daughter of the king of Daha. She bears the title of Raden Galuh. Just before they are due to marry, the princess disappears. So Raden Inu goes in search of her. He does this in disguise, his alias containing the title Panji, hence the name of the tales. The prince is always accompanied by a group of younger relatives and followers. In the course of his travels Panji has occasion to attack and conquer hostile kings, demonstrating his prowess as a warrior; he performs shadow–theatre at court, showing that he is a master of the arts; and avails himself of opportunities to charm the female courtiers. His journey takes him through the countryside as far as Gegelang and Singasari. During his adventures he occasionally meets his betrothed, but they do not recognise each other. After many twists and turns in the plot, the two are finally married and return home to general rejoicing. Raden Inu resumes his identity and succeeds his father as king of Kuripan.

The Form

Although the basic outline of the plot is fixed, there is ample scope for improvisation and expansion of its various themes. The story is found in both literary and dramatic forms, these being closely related in Indonesia. Panji stories exist in Middle Javanese in the form called *kidung* preserved in Bali; in classical Modern Javanese in the *macapat* verse form; and in Malay in the form of the prose *hikayat*. In Java there is a type of shadow theatre called *wayang gedhog*, now practically extinct, which takes its stories from the Panji repertoire, and there is also a masked dance–drama termed *topeng* which features characters from the tales. Furthermore, there are also little–told folktales about a son of Panji, once popular in east Java.

Historical Influences

Scholars have taken a special interest in the origins of the Panji tales. The setting of the four kingdoms is based on kingdoms existing in the second half of the 11th century. But it was probably not until the Majapahit period (14th–15th centuries) that the stories became popular, and were regarded as a recognised literary form. At this time the kingdom of

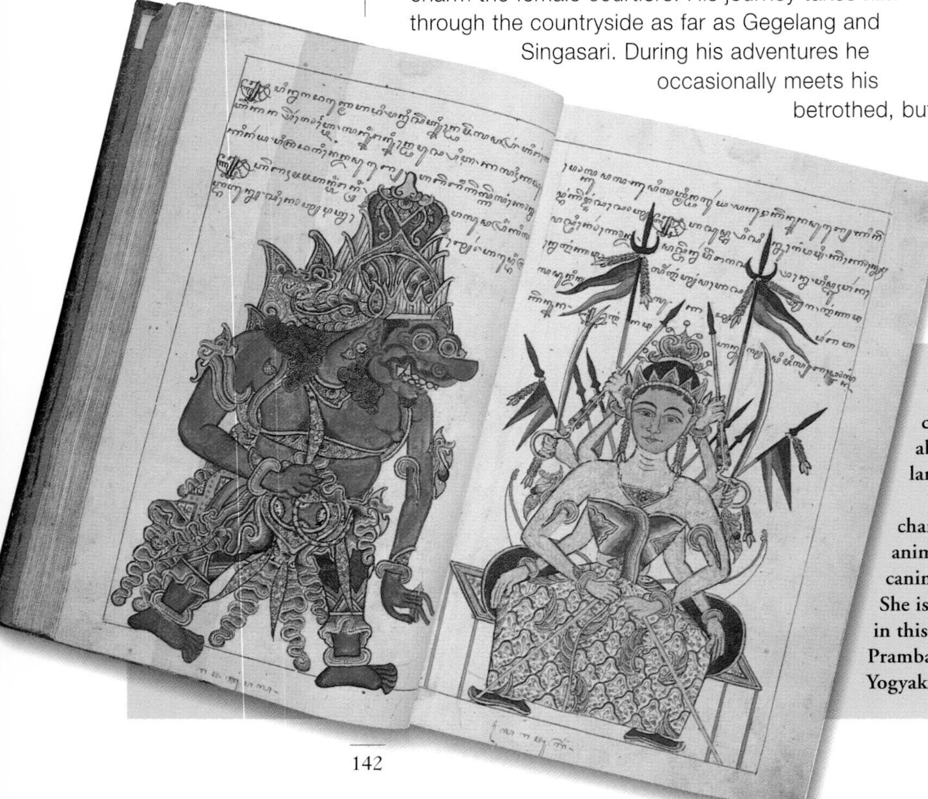

A PANJI TALE

This Javanese manuscript in the John Rylands University Library collection in Manchester, England, contains a narrative poem about the adventures of Prince Panji. It is written in the Javanese language and script, in ink, colours and gold on European paper. The main characters are depicted in *wayang* style. The character on the left of the page is the demon king, his demonic and animal–like nature evident from his bulging eyes and prominent canines. Seated on the right hand side is the princess Lara Jonggrang. She is depicted in the style of a Hindu–Javanese statue, and the figure in this painting was probably inspired by the famous Durga statue at Prambanan. In this manuscript, which was written in 19th century Yogyakarta, the Panji tale is preceded by the origin myth of Prambanan.

Majapahit in east Java was prosperous and powerful, and Javanese culture was carried to all the islands nearby. These included, in the first place Bali, where the story was developed and passed down in the form of palm leaf manuscripts (lontar). These faithfully record the influence of early Javanese culture. Over time the story expanded, until it reached its longest form as the poem *Malat* in the 18th century. Shorter versions from the same corpus are the *Waseng* and *Wangbang Wideya*. The classic drama of Bali, *gambuh*, takes episodes from *Malat*.

Under Javanese influence in the Majapahit and Demak periods, the Panji theme was also carried to

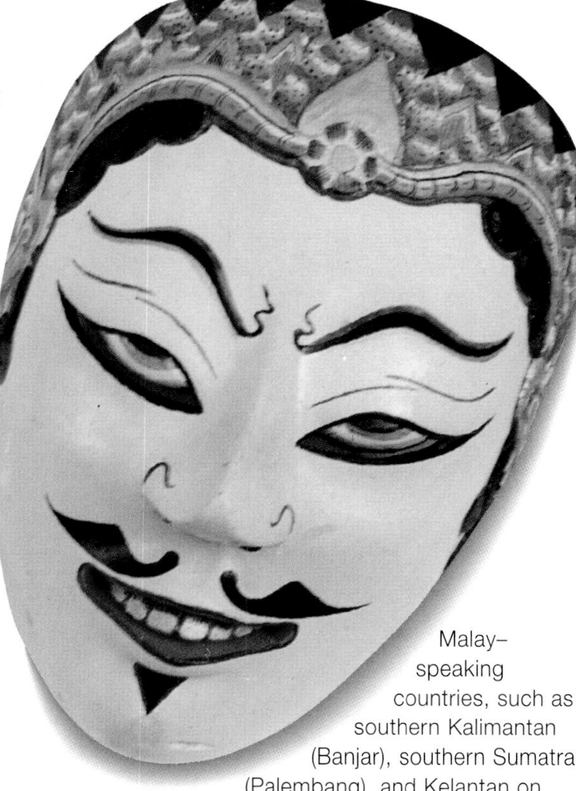

Malay-speaking countries, such as southern Kalimantan (Banjar), southern Sumatra (Palembang), and Kelantan on the east coast of the Malay Peninsula. These places were accessible by sea and artists sailed to Java to study. It is possible these performers became familiar with Panji dramas in Java and after returning home rendered them into Malay in the form of the *hikayat*, intended for recitation by storytellers before an audience. The Panji stories also found their way northward into Thailand via Kelantan and Patani. There they became transformed into one of the classics of Thai literature; the *Inao*, in particular the version composed by King Rama II, which was also translated into Cambodian. In Java itself the tales of Panji were incorporated into the great legendary histories, and rewritten as poetical works.

Learning from the Tales

The cultural background depicted in the Panji stories, which is both Javanese and Malay, is of special interest. They provide a picture of courtly life that existed in early Java before the arrival of Islam. This was a world where the nobles had the leisure to devote themselves to the arts. There are many descriptions of wayang performances, for example, which give the impression of their growing importance during this period. Detailed descriptions of clothing; including the type of cloth used, its colour and pattern, and of personal adornment, suggest a society rich in wealth and high ideals of beauty — a refined civilisation. These different themes of beauty and pleasure included an exploration of the erotic, an aesthetic sense that was cultivated in Java, derived ultimately from India. The stories are narrative, rather than lyric, with strong dramatic tension.

In the search for the origins of the Panji story, early Dutch scholars attempted to interpret the meaning of the Panji tales in terms of a mythology of a primeval Javanese society which has long since disappeared. The most prevalent of these theories sought to link the Panji themes to an assumed moiety system of social organisation in ancient Indonesia. The moiety pattern consists of a social structure in which all people are divided into two groups. These two groups perform distinct and complementary roles in ritual and ceremony and a person from one moiety must marry someone from the other. Each moiety is associated with a particular set of symbols. These symbols usually consist of a series of dualistic oppositions such as male/female, light/dark. Panji and Candra Kirana would have symbolised these two groups. In such societies, men are often required to undergo an initiation ceremony during which they ceremonially "die" and "return", just as Panji often dies in these stories, only to return to life later. The happy union of the couple depicted in the stories performed in the *wayang gedhog* versions are said to have made it a favoured entertainment at the celebration of royal marriages.

Panji and his princess, Candra Kirana.

«Panji and one of his servants.

««Mask of Gunungsari, younger brother of Princess Daha who married Panji's younger sister.

Painted Balinese cloth from the Tropenmuseum, Amsterdam, depicting Panji (upper right) engaged in writing a poem expressing his love for a princess. He is surrounded by a group of servants.

Early Islamic Literature of Indonesia

Written literature appeared in various Indonesian languages long before the coming of Islam. The spread of Islam provoked a major change in these writing traditions as a consequence of the veneration for the language and the script of the Qur'an.

Muslim scribe in Mecca, 19th century.

A syair written by Hamzah Fansuri, courtesy of the Bodleian Library, Oxford.

The use of Malay

The Malay language was the lingua franca of the archipelago for centuries, and became the language of the preaching of Islam. It was also the vehicle of a literature written in an Indian script that was forsaken and superseded by Arabic script, or rather, the Persian one, slightly adapted by the addition of a few letters. This new script was called Malay (Jawi) script or 'bald Arabic' (*Arab gundul*).

The Arabic alphabet was also used for writing Javanese (*pegon*) in a limited way, without supplanting the use of the Indian type script. Most of the Islamic literature in Javanese, as well as in other languages of the archipelago was to be adapted from Malay. The first specimens of this new Malay literature may have been religious texts translated from the Arabic. The oldest extant Malay manuscript is a copy of a short treatise on the articles of the Islamic creed, the *Aqa'id* of Umar al-Nasafi with an interlinear translation. This manuscript reflects the polemics at that time, opposing the theories of theologians to those of sophists or pseudo-Sufis about the existence of realities and objectivity of knowledge. A Javanese text of the same period, the Admonitions of seh Bari, expounds the basic principles of mysticism. This text shows the influence that al-Ghazali was to have on Malay scripture.

Literary Influences from West Asia

Arab, Persian and Indian scholars were influential in the western ports of the archipelago. Being endowed with high prestige due to their origin, which made them closer to the cradle of Islam, they may have been instrumental in the adaptation of foreign works and the creation of new indigenous genres. This was the case again at another stage of the development of Malay literature, in the 19th century.

The initiators of the new Malay literature were not only foreigners, nor were their texts limited to translations: some indigenous authors produced treatises on various aspects of the Islamic faith.

Text on criminal law, from the British Library, Sloane collection, based on Arabic sources. It lists the punishments for crimes such as homicide, fornication, slander, and highway robbery. This example dates from the late 17th or early 18th century.

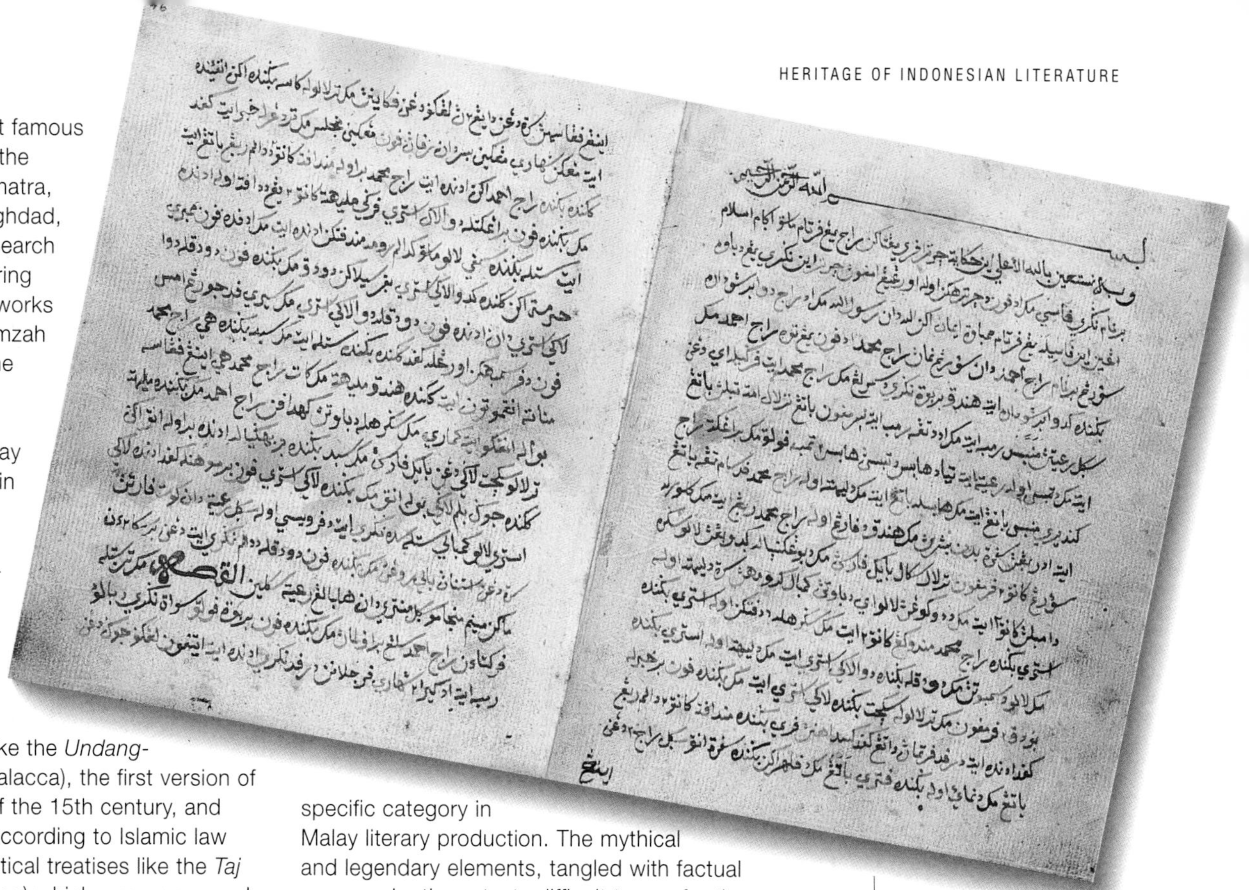

Hamzah Fansuri is the most famous of them. Born in Barus, on the western coast of North Sumatra, Hamzah visited Mecca, Baghdad, Jerusalem, and Ayuthia in search of the Lord, before discovering God in himself. Only a few works by his hand are known. Hamzah is of prime importance to the history of Malay literature, because he seems to have been the initiator of the Malay *syair* which became the main poetic genre during the following three centuries. Despite their esoteric inspi–ration and use of Arabic terminology, Hamzah's poems show a high degree of aesthetic refinement.

The influence of Islam was also felt in legal texts like the *Undang-Undang Melaka* (Laws of Malacca), the first version of which dates from the end of the 15th century, and which combines penalties according to Islamic law and Malay custom; and political treatises like the *Taj al–Salatin* (Crown of the Kings) which was composed in Aceh in 1603.

Tales of Heroic Warriors

The contacts with Muslim India were important during that period, and it is probably from there that the Malay world inherited Persian works about the early heroes of Islam. Those works were translated and became part of the classics of Malay literature. The so–called *Sejarah Melayu* (Malay Annals) relate how, on the eve of the Portuguese attack on Malacca in 1511, the young nobles of the town asked to read the *Hikayat Muhammad Hanafiyyah*, and the Sultan, regarding the bravery of that personnage to be too high, gave them the *Hikayat Amir Hamzah* instead. This shows that these literary texts were exemplary stories to be used as models of behaviour. The anecdote also informs us that the Sultan himself was the keeper of those precious manuscripts.

The *Hikayat Iskandar Zulkarnain* was probably translated during the same period from an Arabic or Persian source. This Islamic version of the legendary history of Alexander the Great tells how this emperor converted the world to Islam. The hero is an unrivalled warrior, and the tale is full of the richest literary inventions. As for the *Hikayat Amir Hamzah* which relates the deeds of the Prophet's uncle, it was adapted into Javanese, and became part of the repertoire of the *wayang golek* (puppet theatre).

Hence in the 15th century, the two main genres of Malay literature *(syair* and *hikayat)* were well represented under the influence of Persian models. Both genres were used for various types of narratives. Even the chronicles of several sultanates were named *hikayat*. The *Hikayat Raja–Raja Pasai* tells the history of the first Islamised realm in North Sumatra. This type of historical work constitutes a specific category in Malay literary production. The mythical and legendary elements, tangled with factual ones, make these texts difficult to use for the reconstruction of historical facts. However, they show a historical awareness.

Expansion into Eastern Indonesia

In the early phase of the Islamic period, the intellectual and literary activity in Malay was concentrated in the western part of the archipelago. In the 17th century new cultural centres emerged further east, and Malay works were produced in Borneo, Sulawesi and Maluku as well, and would circulate from one place to the other. Examples include the *Hikayat Banjar*, from south Kalimantan, and the *Hikayat Tanah Hitu*, from Ambon. In Makassar, an indigenous tradition of literature written in Indic script was augmented by a systematic compilation of court diaries. For centuries Malay had been a language of communication from Sumatra to the eastern islands, spread mainly as a medium of commerce. The expansion of Islam further solidified Malay's position as the cement of a cultural sphere throughout the entire archipelago.

Hikayat Raja–Raja Pasai, the oldest known history in the Malay language, believed to have been composed in the 15th century. It describes the coming of Islam to the now vanished kingdom of Pasai in Sumatra. Only two known manuscripts of this text exist. This one from the British Library collection, written in Malay in Jawi script, was obtained in Semarang and was probably copied in 1797.

CENTRES OF EARLY ISLAMIC LITERARY ACTIVITY

Glossary

A

amabak: extensive cultivation of agricultural crops.

astabrata: eight principles that a king has to fulfil.

B

babad: a Javanese traditional chronicle.

Bahal: a Nepalese term for a two-storied temple of the Vajrayana sect, which was extremely influential in Indonesian Buddhism.

Bhairawa: a being in Buddhism, who embodies negative impulses.

Bhatara Guru: the name used for **Siva** in ancient Indonesia.

Bhudhara: a mountain.

Bhurloka: the world of mortals.

Biaro Bahal: a site in Padang Lawas. Biaro is derived from Vihara. The word **Bahal** in the name indicates that it is derived from esoteric Buddhist shrines in Nepal and Sri Lanka.

Bodhisattva: beings who help others to gain enlightenment.

Brahma: a four-headed deity of Hinduism, associated with creation.

C

cakravartin: a universal ruler.

candi: architectural remains from the Classical Period.

candikagrha: the dwelling place of Candika, Goddess of Death and consort of **Siva**.

cella: an inner room containing the statue of a divinity.

chalcedony: siliceous rock used for ceremonial objects in the shape of stone tools.

Chola: a south Indian dynasty who conquered **Sriwijaya** in the early 11th century.

D/E/G

dukkha: the Buddhist notion of suffering.

Eight-fold Path: Buddhist teaching.

Gajah Mada: a Prime Minister of **Majapahit** in the 14th century.

gandharva: celestial beings.

Ganesha: the elephant-headed deity of the Hindu pantheon.

Gunung Kawi: a site of rock-cut shrines in Bali.

H

hadith: the sayings attributed to the prophet Muhammad.

hikayat: a Malay prose form, similar to a historical romance.

Homo erectus: 'man who walks erect'; a term given to fossils believed to be ancestral to modern humans.

Homo sapiens: anatomically modern man.

J

jawi: the Malay language written in Arabic script.

jina: the (conqueror) Buddhas.

juru kunci: custodians of historic sites.

K

Kadiri: the most important of several kingdoms which ruled east Java from the mid-11th century until 1222.

kakawin: an Old Javanese verse form.

kala: a legendary demon, also called Rahu, who stole the elixir of immortality. A motif found over temple doorways and niches for statuary in Java, Sumatra and Bali.

karma: the Buddhist doctrine of cause and effect.

kawi: an Old Javanese literary language and, by extension, authors who wrote in that language.

kendi: a water ewer, especially associated with religious ceremonies.

keramat: a place associated with a person who is believed to have particularly strong spiritual power.

kinnara: the half-human, half-bird musicians (male) living on the slopes of Mount Meru.

kinnari: the female ***kinnara***.

Kota Cina: 'Chinese Stockade', an early trading port in North Sumatra.

kraton: the residence of the ruler.

Krishna: an incarnation of Visnu as a young, handsome man; in the **Mahabharata**, an adviser to the **Pandawa**.

Kurawa: the family who constitute the adversaries of the **Pandawa** in the **Mahabharata**.

L

Lara Jonggrang: 'slender maiden' in Javanese, a legendary princess after whom the Sivaite temple complex at Prambanan is named.

lingga: a phallic symbol representing **Siva**, often found in Hindu temples together with its female counterpart, the **yoni**.

lokapala: guardian gods of cardinal directions.

M

Mahabharata: a Hindu epic about the conflict between the **Pandawa** and the **Kurawa**.

Mahayana: 'Greater Vehicle'; schools of Buddhism which espouse the belief in other enlightened beings besides Sakyamuni.

Majapahit: an east Javanese kingdom of the late 13th to early 16th century.

makara: a mythical beast with an elephant's trunk, a lion's mane, a parrot's beak and a fish's tail. It symbolised Kama, god of love; a sculptured form placed at the wings of stairways in Sumatran and Early

Classic Javanese temples, and at lower corners of niches for statues.

Manasara Silpasastra: an Indian text giving instructions on choosing temple sites.

mandala: mystic symbols in the form of concentric circles; used as aids to meditation; territory under a **cakravartin**.

mandibles: jawbones.

Mataram: the kingdom which ruled central Java during the Early Classic period; the name was revived by the early Islamic–period kingdom centred in the same area.

megalithic: pertaining to monuments constructed primarily of large stones; associated with Preclassic societies.

menhir: a type of megalithic creation: a tall monolith.

meru: a mountain abode of the gods at the centre of the universe.

mesjid: a mosque.

microliths: stone tools, typical of late Paleolithic technology.

N

Nagara or rajya: a capital city.

Nagarakrtagama: a 14th century poem detailing court life and the activities of the **Majapahit** kingdom; correctly known as Desawarnana.

Neolithic: 'new stone age'; the period during which farming began.

nusantara: a term referring to all the islands of Indonesia, the Philippines and the southern Malay Peninsula.

P

Padang Lawas: 'Broad Plain'; the site of numerous temple complexes in North Sumatra's hinterland.

paddle and anvil: a technique of decorating earthenware pottery by impressing wet clay with a carved piece of wood.

paduraksa: a gateway form which includes a lintel.

Palaeolithic: 'old stone age'; phase that produced the oldest tools.

palapa: word of unknown meaning, the subject of an oath taken by **Gajah Mada**, symbolic of his resolve to unify the region of **nusantara**.

Pallava (script): a monumental script (named after a South Indian dynasty which issued inscriptions in this type of script).

Pandawa: the five brothers in the **Mahabharata.**

Pararaton: a 16th century Javanese text, the 'Book of Kings'.

parwa: divisions of the Ramayana.

pedharman: 'place of the Doctrine'; a holy place.

pelinggih: a seat for invisible gods in Balinese shrines.

pendopo: from South Indian *mandapa*, a 'pillared hall-way'; in Indonesian, a term for an unwalled pavillon.

peripih: a container for ritual items, placed beneath the ***candi***.

pisis: a term in Javanese inscriptions for Chinese cash and for local copies.

Pithecanthropus: 'ape-man', an old term for premodern hominid fossils.

pkan: a periodic market.

Pradakshina: the clockwise circumambulation of a ***candi,*** performed as an act of worship.

pranapratistha: ceremonies to invoke the deities.

Prasawiaya: the counter-clockwise circumambulation of a ***candi***; a practice associated with Tantrism.

punden: locations on high places, generally associated with village founders.

pura: specifically a Balinese temple; in Java, a royal enclave.

R/S

rsi: a holy, wise man; a hermit or an ascetic.

San-fo-qi: a Chinese term designating a polity in Sumatra which sent embassies to China during the Song dynasty.

Sang Hyang Kamahayanikan: the oldest surviving Javanese text on Buddhism, written around 925–950 AD.

Sanskrit: the literary and sacral language of ancient India.

sembah: a gesture of respectful salutation, with the palms of the hands joined before the face.

Shi-li-fo-shih: the Chinese transliteration of **Sriwijaya** used during the Tang Dynasty; one of the major trading operators of Southeast Asia.

sima: special zones with certain rights and duties concerning religious establishments, to which nobles transferred some or all of their tax rights.

Singasari*:* a kingdom centred in east Java that lasted from 1222 to 1292.

Siva: a Hindu deity, one of the major trinity, the most widely revered god in ancient Java.

T

tambo: a traditional literary genre which focuses on genealogies.

Trimurti: the trinity composed of the principal deities of Hinduism: Brahma, the creator, Visnu, the preserver and **Siva**, the destroyer.

tutur: a literary genre.

tympanum: the flat surface of a drum which is struck.

V

vahana: the vehicles of the Hindu gods; Garuda for Visnu, Nandin for **Siva** and Hamsa for **Brahma**.

vidyadhara: celestial beings.

vihara: a monastery.

W

Wallace line: demarcation line proposed by Alfred Russel Wallace, between the western part of Indonesia with predominantly Asian wildlife, and the eastern part dominated by typical Australian species of plants and animals.

Wallacea: the transitional zone between the Asian and Australian faunal and floral complexes; roughly between Borneo and New Guinea.

wayang kulit: shadow puppets.

wono: a Sanskrit word for forest.

Y

yoni: the counterpart of the **lingga**; female principle.

yupa: stone pillars to which sacrificial animals were tethered.

Bibliography

GENERAL WORKS

Coedes, G. 1968. *The Indianized States of Southeast Asia.* Honolulu: University of Hawaii Press.

Fontein, J. (ed.) 1990. *Sculpture of Indonesia.* New York: Abrams.

Groeneveldt, W.P. 1960 [1880]. *Historical Notes on Indonesia and Malaya Compiled from Chinese Sources.* Jakarta: Bhratara.

Holt, C. 1967. *Art in Indonesia: Continuities and Change.* Ithaca: Cornell University.

Miksic, J.N. 1989. *Old Javanese Gold.* Singapore: Ideations.

Soekmono, R. 1965. 'Archaeology and Indonesian History'. In Soedjatmoko et al., (eds.) *An Introduction to Indonesian Historiography.* Ithaca: Cornell University, pp. 36–46.

Wheatley, P. 1983. *Negara and Commandery.* Chicago: University of Chicago, Department of Geography, Research Papers 207–08.

PREHISTORY

Bellwood, P. 1985. *Prehistory of the Indo-Malaysian Archipelago.* Sydney: Academic Press.

Bellwood, P. 1992. 'Southeast Asia Before History'. In Tarling, N. (ed.) *The Cambridge History of Southeast Asia. vol. I: Early Times to ca. 1800.* pp. 55–136. Cambridge: Cambridge University Press.

Casparis, J.G. de. 1956. *Prasasti Indonesia II. Selected inscriptions from the 7th to the 9th century AD.* Jakarta: Masa Baru.

Casparis, J.G. de. 1975. *Indonesian Palaeography.* Leiden: E.J. Brill.

Casparis, J.G. de and I. Mabbett. 1992. 'Religion and Popular Beliefs of Southeast Asia Before c. 1500'. In Tarling, N. (ed.), *The Cambridge History of Southeast Asia. vol. I: Early Times to ca. 1800.* pp. 276-340. Cambridge: Cambridge University Press.

Haris Sukendar. 1993. *Arca Menhir di Indonesia (Fungsinya dalam Peribadatan).* Ph.D. Dissertation. Jakarta: Universitas Indonesia.

Heekeren, H.R. van. 1972. *The Stone Age of Indonesia.* The Hague: M. Nijhoff.

Heekeren, H.R. van. 1958. *The Bronze–Iron Age of Indonesia.* Verhandelingen van het Koninklijke Instituut voor Taal, Land– en Volkenkunde vol XXII. The Hague: M. Nijhoff.

Hoop, A.N.J. Th. a Th. van der. 1932. *Megalithic Remains in South Sumatra.* Zutphen: W.J. Thieme.

Hutterer, K.L. 1977. 'Reinterpreting the Southeast Asian Palaeolithic'. In Allen et al., *Sunda and Sahul.* London: Academic Press, pp. 31–72.

Kaudern, W. 1938. *Megalithic Finds in Central Celebes.* Goteborg: Elanders.

Glover, I.C. 1977. 'The Late Stone Age in Eastern Indonesia', *World Archaeology* 9 (1): 42–61.

Glover, I.C. 1981.'Leang Burung 2: an Upper Palaeolithic Rock Shelter in South Sulawesi, Indonesia', *Modern Quaternary Research in Southeast Asia* 6: 1–38.

Glover, I.C. 1986. *Archaeology in Eastern Timor, 1966–67.* Canberra: Terra Australia 11.

Marschall, W. 1988. 'On some Basic Traditions in Nusantara Cultures'. In D.S. Moyer and H.J.M. Claessen (eds.), *Time Past, Time Present, Time Future.* Verhandelingen van het Koninklijk Instituut 131: 69–77.

Soejono, R.P. 1977. *Sistim–sistim Penguburan pada Akhir Masa Prasejarah di Bali.* Ph.D. Dissertation. Jakarta: Universitas Indonesia.

THE DAWN OF INDONESIAN HISTORY

Ardika, I Wayan and P. Bellwood. 1991. 'Sembiran: the Beginning of Indian Contact with Bali', *Antiquity* 65 (247): 221–32.

Sutayasa, I Made. 1972. 'Note on the Buni Pottery Complex, Northwest Java.' *Mankind* 182–84.

EARLY CLASSIC PERIOD

Bernet Kempers, A.J. 1959. *Ancient Indonesian Art.* Amsterdam: van der Peet.

Bernet Kempers, A.J. 1991. *Monumental*

Bali. Berkeley Singapore: Periplus.

Coedes, G. and L.C. Damais. 1992. *Sriwijaya: History, Religion and Language of an Early Malay Polity.* Kuala Lumpur: Malaysian Branch of the Royal Asiatic Society Monograph no. 20.

Dumarçay, J. 1991. *Borobudur.* Kuala Lumpur: Oxford University Press.

Dumarçay, J. 1986. *Temples of Java.* Kuala Lumpur: Oxford University Press.

Edwards McKinnon, E. 1985. 'Early Polities in Southern Sumatra'. *Indonesia* 40: 1–36.

Fontein, J. 1989. *The Law of Cause and Effect in Ancient Java.* Amsterdam: Koninklijke Nederlandse Akademie van Wetenschappen, Verhandelingen Afdeeling Letterkunde, n.s., vol. 140.

Glover, I.C. (ed). 1992. *Southeast Asian Archaeology 1990.* Hull: Centre for South-East Asian Studies.

Gomez, L.O. and H.W. Woodward. (eds). 1981. *Barabudur. History and Significance of a Buddhist Monument.* Berkeley: Asian Humanities Press.

Klokke, M. 1992. 'Iconographical Traditions in Late East Javanese Narrative Reliefs'. In I.C. Glover (ed.), *Southeast Asian Archaeology 1990.* Hull: Centre for South-East Asian Studies, pp. 75–84.

Kulke, H. 1993. '"Kadatuan Srivijaya" — Empire or Kraton of Srivijaya? A Reassessment of the Epigraphical Evidence', *Bulletin de l'Ecole Française d' Extrême-Orient* 80 (1): 159–180.

Lunsingh Scheurleer, P. and M.J. Klokke. 1988. *Ancient Indonesian Bronzes.* Leiden: E.J. Brill.

Miksic, J.N. 1990. *Borobudur: Golden Tales of the Buddhas.* Singapore: Periplus.

Naerssen, F.H. van and de longh. 1977. *The Economic and Administrative History of Early Indonesia.* Handbuch der Orientalistik. Leiden: E.J. Brill.

Sarkar, H.B. 1971. *Corpus of the Inscriptions of Java.* Calcutta: Mukhopadhyay.

Subhadradis Diskul, M.C. ed. 1980. *The Art of Srivijaya.* Kuala Lumpur: Oxford University Press.

Wisseman Christie, J. 1983. 'Raja and Rama: the Classical State in Early Java'. In L. Gesick (ed.) *Centers, Symbols, and Hierarchies: Essays on the Classical States of Southeast Asia.* New Haven: Yale University Press.

Wolters, O.W. 1967. *Early Indonesian Commerce.* Ithaca: Cornell University.

Wolters, O.W. 1979. 'Studying Srivijaya' , *Journal of the Malaysian Branch, Royal Asiatic Society* 52 (2): 1–32.

MIDDLE CLASSIC PERIOD

Boechari. 1979. 'Some Considerations of the Problem of the Shift of Mataram's Center of Government from Central to East Java in the 10th century A.D.' In R.B. Smith and W. Watson (eds.), *Early South East Asia.* London: Oxford University Press, pp. 473–92.

Edi Sedyawati. 1994. *Ganesa Statuary of the Kadiri and Singasari periods.* Leiden: Verhandelingen van het Koninklijk Instituut voor Taal-, Land- en Volkenkunde 160.

Rumbi Mulia. 1980. *The Ancient Kingdom of Panai and the Ruins of Padang Lawas (North Sumatra).* Jakarta: Berita Pusat Penelitian Arkeologi Nasional no. 14.

Sastri, K.A.N. 1932. *A Tamil Merchant Guild in Sumatra.* Bandung: Nix.

Satyawati Suleiman. 1977. *The Archaeology and History of West Sumatra.* Jakarta: Berita Pusat Penelitian Arkeologi Nasional no. 12.

Schnitger, F.M. 1964. *Forgotten Kingdoms in Sumatra.* Leiden: E.J. Brill.

LATE CLASSIC PERIOD

Klokke, M. 1993. *Tantri Reliefs on Javanese Candi.* Verhandelingen van het Koninklijke Instituut vol. 153.

Pigeaud, H.G. Th. 1960–63. *Java in the 14th Century,* (5 vols.) The Hague: M. Nijhoff.

Worsley, P. 1986. 'Narrative Bas-Reliefs at Candi Surawana'. In D.G. Marr and A.C. Milner, (eds.), *South East Asia in the 9th to 14th Centuries.* Singapore: ISEAS, pp. 335–68.

EARLY ISLAMIC PERIOD

Graaf, H.J. de and Th. G. Th. Pigeaud. 1984. *Chinese Muslims in Java in the 15th and 16th Centuries.*Monash Papers on Southeast Asia No. 12.

Moertono, S. *State and Statecraft in Old Java.* Ithaca: Cornell Modern Indonesia Project Data Paper 43.

Reid, A. 1988/1993 *Southeast Asia in the Age of Commerce, 1450–1680.* (2 vols.) New Haven: Yale University.

Ricklefs, M.C. 1993. *A History of Modern Indonesia Since c.1300.* Stanford: Stanford University Press

Uka Tjandrasasmita. 1975. *Islamic Antiquities of Sendang Duwur.* Jakarta: Archaeological Foundation.

Wolters, O.W. 1970. *The Fall of Srivijaya in Malay History.* Ithaca: Cornell University.

HERITAGE OF INDONESIAN LITERATURE

Bosch, F.D.K. 1961. *Selected Studies in Indonesian Archaeology.* The Hague: M. Nijhoff

Gallup, A.T. and B. Arps. 1991. *Golden Letters: Writing Traditions of Indonesia/Surat Mas Budaya Tulis di Indonesia.* London: British Library; Jakarta: Yayasan Lontar.

Guy, J. 1982. *Palm Leaf and Paper.* Melbourne: National Gallery of Victoria.

Rassers, W.H. 1959. *Panji, the Cultural Hero.* The Hague: M. Nijhoff.

Robson, S. 1988. *Principles of Indonesian Philology.* Dordrecht: Foris.

S. Supomo. 1993. *Bharatayuddha: An Old Javanese Poem and Its Indian Sources.* New Delhi: International Academy of Indian Culture and Aditya Prakashan.

Zoetmulder, P.J. 1974. *Kalangwan.* The Hague: M. Nijhoff.

Index

Photo Credits

The publishers have made every effort to ensure that all photographs and illustrations contained in this volume have been correctly credited, and apologise if any omissions or errors have occurred. These will be amended in the next printing.

Pictures not credited here were supplied by John Miksic.

The Publisher acknowledges the kind permission of the following for the reproduction of photographs.

Chapter openers: Land, People and History, Candi Lara Jonggrang by Leo Haks, and Sir Stamford Raffles by Antiques of the Orient. Prehistory, Hanuman 13's jaw by Francois Semah. Indonesia at the Dawn of History, John Miksic. Early Classic Period, Buddha by Leo Haks, and the Profile of the Hidden Foot by Tara Sosrowardoyo. Life in Early Classic Indonesia, Archer from Prambanan by Tara Sosrowardoyo. Middle Classic Period, John Miksic. Late Classic Period, Kala Head by Tantyo Bangun. Early Islamic Period: 1300–1600, Sendang Duwur gateway by Dirk Bakker, and Masjid Panjuran by Amir Sidharta. Heritage of Indonesian Literature, Treatise on Javanese Gamelan, by permission of the National Museum of Jakarta, and A Batak datu reading a pustaha. by kind permission of The British Library.

Reproduced by kind permission of the Australian National Gallery, Canberra. p. 138, the page from the Ramayana Kakawin, Accession no. 1990.1775; and p. 141, Smaradahana [The Burning of the God of Love], Accession no. 1994.1234.

Reproduced by kind permission of The Bodleian Library, University of Oxford. p. 20, Rasacarita or religious treatise, MS Jav. b. (1) R; p. 22 Pawukon or almanac, MS Jav. d.2 ff 49v–50r; and p. 144, a syair by Hamzah Fansuri, MS Malay e. 2 (R).

Reproduced by kind permission of The British Library. p. 137, Damar Wulan, IOL MSS. Jav. 89, f.192v, and IOL MSS. Jav. 89, f. 73r, Javanese; p. 144, Undang Undang, Sloane 2393, ff. 19v–20r, Malay; and p. 145, Hikayat Raja Pasai, Or. 14350, ff. 45V–46r, Malay.

Reproduced by kind permission of the National Museum of Jakarta. p. 10–11, Kuvera, flask, and Naga spout; p. 16, painting from slab grave; p. 17, projectile points, stone chopping tool, Neolithic chalcedony adze, chalcedony bracelets, Bronze Age axes, and drinking vessel from Melolo; p. 21, copper plate inscription of Krtawijaya (John McGlynn) and bronze mirror handle; p. 23, Batak divinatory calendar (John McGlynn) and zodiac beaker from Kadiri; p. 33, drinking vessel from Melolo; p. 38, frog on Dong Son drum and bronze ceremonial axe, Roti; p. 40, bronze grave goods and adze; p. 41, bronze axe and stone bracelets; p. 44, bronze figure, Bangkinang; p. 45, flask in Dong Son style; p. 52, Kutai inscription, (John McGlynn); p. 53, Telaga Batu inscription; p. 57, gold lingga; p. 82, Maitreya; p. 88, Siva, gold Buddha, bronze Padmapani and silver Siva; p. 89, Buddhist sculpture; p. 96, water dipper, golden box and Ramayana bowl; p. 97, gold ladle, covered bowl, makara spout and gold finial; pp. 102–103, Amoghapasa; p. 104, dancing figures and Adityavarman; p. 112, Kendis and coins; p. 114, bronze lamp; p. 136, Serat Purawkandha; p. 139, Ramayana bowl, wayang kulit figures, and Bima; p. 140, Nagarakrtagama kakawin (Photographer – Tara Sosrowardoyo).

Reproduced by courtesy of the Director and University Librarian, the John Rylands University Library of Manchester. p. 142, Javanese MS 16, fols 31v, 32r.

Reproduced by courtesy of Rijksmuseum voor Volkenkunde. p. 141, Smaradahana, RMV 1586–34.

Collection Royal Tropical Institute (R.T.I.), Tropenmuseum, Amsterdam, photo: L. Lange. p. 143, documents on Panji Tales and Balinese painting, coll. nr. 903–15 and 1882–1.

Reproduced by kind permission of the University of Hull museum. p. 16 , Moko drum (photograph by Lewis Hill).

Amir Sidharta, p. 122, Paduraksa gateway.
Ping Amranand, p. 72 Monk, and p. 77, Candi Bima.
Antiques of the Orient, p. 50, tortoises; p. 55 house on raft; p. 98, market scene; p.112, Candi Berahu; p. 126, Bandung mosque; p. 130, Banten market; and p. 131, pepper.
I. Wayan Ardika, p. 42, heart-shaped axe, and human burial.
Bruno Barbey, p. 91, ploughing.
Peter Bellwood, p. 32, maros points, and hand stencils.
Jan Christie, p. 98, ship relief, Borobudur; and p. 99, gold coins and silver alloy coins (extreme left).
Alain Compost, p. 15, Aru islanders.
Victor Esbensen, p. 15, Rambutans and Gunung Rinjani.
John Falconer, p. 51, clove.
Jill Gocher, p. 91, planting.
John Guy, p. 139, Balinese lontar of the Adi Parwa.
Leo Haks, p. 58, Balinese meru; p. 66, Dieng plateau; p. 79 Prambanan ruins; and p. 113, Bubat massacre.
Rio Helmi, p. 71, Sanur and Besakih; and p. 122, Kebo Edan.
Julia Howells, p. 133, mystical Islamic ritual.
Denys Lombard, p. 131, Aceh procession.
Pierre Yves Manguin, p. 54, Seguntang hill; p. 55, glass beads and short inscription; p. 82, Maitreya, excavation site and Siva temple; p. 83 ceramic wares and bronze Buddha; p. 102, Chinese porcelains; and p. 103 , Prajnaparamita.
Kal Muller, p. 16, bronze moko drum from Alor; and p. 86, Agastya.
Stuart Robson, p. 140, group of Balinese singing; p. 142, mask of Klana; and p.143, mask of Gunungsari.
Guido Rossi, p. 103, Muara Takus – 2 pictures.
François Sémah, p. 27, pollen grains; p. 28, Java man's skull; p. 29, Cemoro river; and p. 31, Ngebung excavation.
Tantyo Bangun, p. 21, bronze mirror handle; p. 49, Gunung Kawi; p. 63, Candi Bima; p. 67, Arjuna group; p. 86, deities of Lara Jonggrang; p. 91, harvesting and bunding; p.108–109, commemorative statues; p. 119, Candi Naga; and p. 120, Panataran roundels.
Tara Sosrowardoyo, p. 14, cinema posters; p. 57, lingga 3, lingga 5; p. 81 pools; p. 88, Queen Maya, and Gautama reliefs; p. 115, Candi Bajangratu; p.116, turtles; p.116–117 Candi Sukuh; p.117, Bima, and Jalatunda; p. 118, Candi Panataran; p. 127, Menara Kudus and ceramic plate; and p. 128, Taman Sari – 3 pictures.
TAP, p. 51, nutmeg.
Roxana Waterson, p. 16, Toraja tau-tau.
Alan Watson, p. 27, mangrove.
Mike Yamashita, p. 91, winnowing & pounding.

The following illustrators have also contributed:
François Brosse, p. 48, Gedong Songo; p. 65, edifice from Gedong Songo; p. 66, Candi Arjuna; p. 74–75, Stages of Borobudur.
Julian Davison, p. 19, stratigraphic diagram; p. 27, bone tools and megalithic figures; p. 30, animal horns; p. 31, stone artefacts; p. 64, wooden building; p. 115, dwelling plan; and p. 133, Batu Aceh.

The following illustrations are adapted from J. Dumarçay's drawings: p. 19, stratigraphic diagram; p. 48, Gedong Songo; p. 64, wooden building; p. 65, edifice; p. 66, Candi Arjuna; p. 76–77, plan of Candi Sewu and axonometric drawing of Candi Sewu, and, p. 79, Candi Apit.